CENTRAL LENDING
TEL 2478270

3/04

22 DEC 04

17 SEP 2004

24. SEP. 04.

21. OCT. 04.

CW00518989

LD 2143891 9

JERUSALEM

A.D. 33

JOSHUA,
THE MAN THEY CALLED

JESUS

BY

IAN JONES

Lothian
BOOKS

LEEDS LIBRARY AND INFORMATION SERVICES	
LD21438919	
H J	26/06/2000
232.9	£21.95
S004535	

Thomas C. Lothian Pty Ltd
11 Munro Street, Port Melbourne,
Victoria 3207

First published 1999

Copyright © Ian Jones 1999
The moral rights of the author are hereby asserted.

All rights reserved. No part of this publication may be reproduced,
stored in a retrieval system or transmitted in any form by any
means without the prior permission of the copyright owner.
Enquiries should be made to the publisher.

National Library of Australia
Cataloguing-in-Publication data:

Jones, Ian.
  Joshua: the man they called Jesus.

  Bibliography.
  Includes index.
  ISBN 0 85091 812 X.

  1. Jesus Christ – Biography. 2. Christian biography. I.
  Title.

232.901

Cover and text design by Dennis Ogden
Endpapers, map (page vii), Roman legion emblem and
  Capernaum illustrations by John Ward
Index by Russell Brooks
Printed in Australia by Griffin Press Pty Limited

Contents

Preface and Acknowledgements

This book is about two men — Jesus Christ and the man to whom Christians give that title, whose name was Joshua.

Christians are often surprised to learn that 'Jesus Christ' is an Anglo-Latin version of the Greek, Iesous Christos, from the Hebrew Yeshua Mashiah which means 'Joshua the Messiah'. The translators of the King James Bible underlined the fact by twice naming Jesus when the Old Testament's Joshua was intended — in Acts 7:45 and Hebrews 4:8. (Some manuscripts also confuse Jesus and Joshua in verse 5 of the Epistle of Jude.) An immediate question is posed: why use the Graeco-Roman 'Jesus' rather than the Jewish 'Joshua'? And for that matter, why call him 'Christ' rather than 'the Messiah'?

Asking these questions represents a first exploration of the process through which the life and teaching of Joshua were adopted and adapted to create the Jesus of the Gospels; and through which a Jewish Messianic figure became the Christ of Christianity. They should be the same man. Unfortunately they are not. Jesus Christ of the Gospels — as presented in writings of the Christian canon — is a theological-literary creation of remarkable power and, often, great beauty. However, it is my belief that he is also a vehicle for the developing beliefs, policies, problems, neuroses and mythology of 'Gentile Christianity'.

Initially, 'Joshua' might seem no more than a code name for 'the Jesus of History' so often quoted in contrast to 'the Christ of Faith' — a distinction that defines a problem while doing little to solve it. Behind both figures lies the human Jesus, whose bowels functioned, who experienced anger, doubt, despair and sexual desire; who knew intimately the cement-like dust of the Jordan Valley and the frosty limestone of the highlands; who enjoyed good food, good wine, good company and laughter; and who, above all, was a Jew. It is Joshua, the human Jesus, the Jewish Jesus, whose life I try to recover in this book.

Christianity evolved from Judaism *via* Joshua, but Joshua did not create Christianity. He lived and died a devout Jew and his disciples continued as devout Jews, 'continually in the Temple praising God' (*Luke* 24:53). They were described as 'all zealots of the Law [of Moses]' (*Acts* 21:20). The first congregations who followed Joshua's teaching and revered his memory worshipped in synagogues as a Jewish sect for more than fifty years after his death. The sequence of events that split Joshua's movement from Judaism — largely, I believe, through a fanatical campaign by the self-styled 'Apostle' Paul — is an extraordinary story. It is also a tragic story that culminated in the killing of six million Jews during the Second World War.

The ultimate irony of history is that Joshua had come to believe he was the God-sent redeemer of the Jewish people. Almost equally ironic is the fact that Joshua was killed by Romans, who eventually assimilated his movement, blamed the Jews for his death and made this the justification for a fifteen-hundred-year campaign of vilification and persecution that has endured into the present century.

My book does not tell this appalling story, merely how it began — with the life of a Jew called Joshua.

✝✝✝

My fascination with the life of Jesus started when I was five. For that birthday my grandparents gave me a copy of *The Children's Friend* by 'Mrs Adelaide Bee Evans', a charming, profusely illustrated retelling of the Gospel stories. Its page edges were marbled; proper names were spelt out in syllables; illustrations ranged from rather naïve studies to some of Hofmann's superb drawings. I was particularly taken with a painting by one 'A. Twidle' which shows Jesus at an open doorway, warm light streaming from behind him as he bends to welcome a group of very young children. A baby points, a toddler kneels to pick up a leaf from the doorstep, one little girl is about to take Jesus' offered hand. The caption told me that this was 'Jesus receiving the children into the home he has gone to prepare for them'. I knew that these children had died and I found the image very moving; I still do. You may ask how this relates to my quest for the human Jesus when we are here so clearly talking about the immortal and divine Christ. My answer is simple and to some, I'm sure, heretical.

Joshua, the man, loved children as deeply as Mrs Adelaide Bee Evans's Jesus; and his humanity was no bar to his immortality. When I was twenty-four I came close to death in St Mary Abbot's Hospital, London. One of the nurses who watched over me had been killed in an air raid eleven years before. My encounter with her was brief but unforgettable, the first of several experiences which have convinced me that human devotion does not necessarily end with death. I don't know how many patients between life and death have been watched over by that London nurse (or by the more famous Grey Lady of Charing Cross Hospital), any more than I know the number of children who have encountered Joshua. I *know* only what I have experienced.

✝✝✝

When I was eight or nine an unexpected light shone on the 'gentle Jesus meek and mild' of my childhood images and prayers. In a school textbook, called — I think — *The Story of Christ*, I found a startling little anecdote about Jesus and his disciples coming across a dead dog. The disciples commented on how badly it smelt. Jesus said, 'How white its teeth are!' The writer simply called it 'a story that was told about Jesus'. Who told it? When? Where? It was many, many years before I found that it came from an Islamic text of the Middle Ages. By then I had also learnt, to my surprise, that Jesus (*Isa ibn Maryam*) is an honoured figure in Moslem tradition — ranked as the fourth of the major prophets immediately preceding the fifth and last of the line, Mohammed himself.

When I was ten I came across two contradictory books about the outlaw Ned Kelly and almost immediately began a quest for the 'true' story of his extraordinary life. Some time later, a wonderful idea struck me. I could do the same with Jesus! So I trotted up to the chaplain of Carey Baptist Grammar School, the Reverend John Morley, and asked where I could find documents about the life of Jesus.

Mr Morley smiled and held up his Bible. 'They're all in here, Ian — *Matthew, Mark, Luke* and *John* — four books that tell you everything you need to know.' I still cringe when I recall my earnest reply.

'Mr Morley, imagine I told you about three books that said Ned Kelly was the finest man who ever lived, that he never did anything bad, that he wasn't *really* a criminal and that these books were written by Dan Kelly, Joe Byrne and Steve Hart. You'd say, "But these were the members of Ned Kelly's gang!

Of course they'd say that! Where are the police reports, the trial records, the newspaper accounts?"'

Mr Morley took it very well, but he couldn't help me with those records that told the other side of the Jesus story. They didn't exist. I believed in the books written by members of the Jesus Gang or there was nothing. Then I remembered my grandfather telling me how often he questioned his father about the Bible and how Great-grandfather — a fire-and-brimstone, Bible-thumping, Presbyterian Scot — would be pushed to the limits of knowledge and argument, usually fairly soon, and how he would then pick up the Bible and tap it as he glared at my grandfather with his one, piercing eye.

'It's in the Book,' he'd say. 'And you'll believe it! Or you'll have no peace in your nights!'

From being a lad who won scripture prizes at school and who briefly considered becoming a clergyman, I drifted away from the church. Blind faith was not for me. Then slowly I began to reach back past the Gospels. An encounter with Furneaux's *The Other Side of the Story* fascinated me. I later found that it was a reworked condensation of Robert Eisler's massive *Jesus the Messiah and John the Baptist* but it introduced me to the Slavonic texts of the Jewish historian Josephus. According to Furneaux here was a new Jesus, a dwarf Jesus, a Zealot Jesus. I quickly discarded most of it but my search for the 'real' Jesus was revitalised. It would take another forty years, woven through a couple of careers.

The first fragments of this book were written twelve years ago. Now, two books on Ned Kelly have preceded its completion and those earlier fragments have been discarded or completely rewritten as the trail has led into a paper chase of material pouring from the 'Jesus of History' industry. There has been plenty of loopy theorising (Jesus as a sacred mushroom, a woman, an ancestor of Charles de Gaulle, and so on), much intellectual arm-wrestling, some fine scholarly writing and some equally fine popular works. In them, Jesus is an eschatological (end times) prophet, a social prophet, a Zealot, a Mediterranean peasant, a Cynic philosopher, a Pharisee, a Jewish misfit, a well-to-do savant … the labels keep coming. The point is that, while he was some of these things, he was none of them in isolation. None of the labels is adequate.

My long search to understand the life of Joshua led me to a surprising con-clusion: that most of his forty-odd years on earth represented his own search to understand God's purpose for him. This is why attempts — both scholarly and popular — to fit him into an all-inclusive mould are never satisfactory.

The life is moulded to fit the interpretation instead of the interpretation evolving with the changing patterns of Joshua's life. It has been said that the picture presented in the Gospels is more like a landscape than a portrait. Put differently, the life of Joshua is a journey involving often-abrupt changes of direction through varying terrain in a progress which he sees as being dictated by one inescapable fact: that his destination is God-ordained. Given this faith, he is often guarded, ambiguous, even contradictory, in the course of a journey that can be defined only by its end.

In studying the New Testament I have compared the *King James Version*, the *New Revised Standard Version*, the *New International Version*, the *Revised English Bible*, the *Jerusalem Bible*, the literal translation by Jay P. Green in his *Interlinear Greek-English New Testament*, the *Unvarnished Gospels* translated by Andy Gaus, the *Scholars Version* translated by the Jesus Seminar and the *Jewish New Testament* translated by David H. Stern. Quotations have been prepared with reference to the original Greek, supported by scholarly arbitration on controversial words and passages. I hope that the absence of familiar cadences and phrasing will encourage more effective engagement with the content and flavour of quoted passages. Especially in the case of *John* and most notably in his account of the resurrection, the roughness of the prose has an immediacy which is lost in reverent and carefully polished translations.

Acknowledgements

It is impossible to acknowledge everyone who has contributed, directly or indirectly, to this book. I must thank my dear friend and onetime colleague, Johanna Parsons-Nicholls, whose search for Joshua paralleled mine over many years and who presented me with copies of several hard-to-find sources — as did Ron Shaw. He and his wife Nancy have shown unflagging interest and support. My son Darren accompanied me in my first exploration of the places Joshua knew, under the guidance of Jakov Heligman. My wife Bronwyn shared further travels in Israel and, by her loving support, made this book possible. My son Angus and daughter Elizabeth provided timely research back-up.

Dr Noel Bailey and Rod Sangwell have open-handedly shared their scholarship and I have greatly valued the perceptions of Pastor George Spence, Bishop Andrew Curnow, and Reverends Barry Smith, Joanne Hall and Sue McPhee-Wright. I greatly valued Eric Barto's help and know that he waits, red pencil in hand, for publication day.

I am indebted to my old comrade, Barry Jones, for help with sources, for constructive criticism of the MS and for the photos of the *titulus* in Santa Croce, Rome. The debt extends to Shayndel Samuel, Don Bennetts and Gary Presland for long-term loans from their personal libraries. The archaeological enthusiasm and travels of my cousin, June Anderson, have helped me keep in touch with the Bible lands, as has my friend, Sister Winifred McManus, recently returned from the Sisters of Zion Convent, Jerusalem.

Kim Rubenstein and Gary Sturgess have enriched my experience of Judaism and were instrumental in my meeting Rabbi Shimshon Yurkowicz, who gave me free access to the library of the Malvern Chabad Synagogue and discussed several issues. Folk at the Australian Institute of Archaeology were unfailingly helpful — especially former Administrator Alida Sewell, former director Piers Crocker and Education Officer Gary Stone. Tanya Hill, Astronomer at the Melbourne Planetarium, research assistant Richard Allen and former manager Zelko Karlovic have given ready assistance. For medical advice, I have been able to call on Doctors Keith Davis, Sybil Kellner, Bryan Barraclough and Chris Higgins. Geoff Shaw and my old friends, Andrew Swanson and Gil Brealey, have all provided pieces of the jigsaw; and Diana Denley gave me my title. I am specially grateful to Bernadette Brady and Darrelyn Gunsburg for introducing me to the work of Ralph Holden and Rudolf Smit on the Star of Bethlehem.

My thanks to Helen Chamberlin, Senior Editor at Lothian, who nurtured this project; my editor, Gwenda Smyth, who brought her scriptural knowledge, warm calm and keen mind to the book; artist John Ward for his continuing dedication to exacting historical work; to Russell Brooks for a characteristically thorough index; to Ailsa Richardson and Veda Currie who put my idiosyncratic typescript onto disc; and to designer Dennis Ogden, once again, for his talent and care.

Finally, a dedication — to my grandchildren. May they live to see a world where Christianity, Judaism and Islam can recognise the forest they share, rather than the trees that divide them.

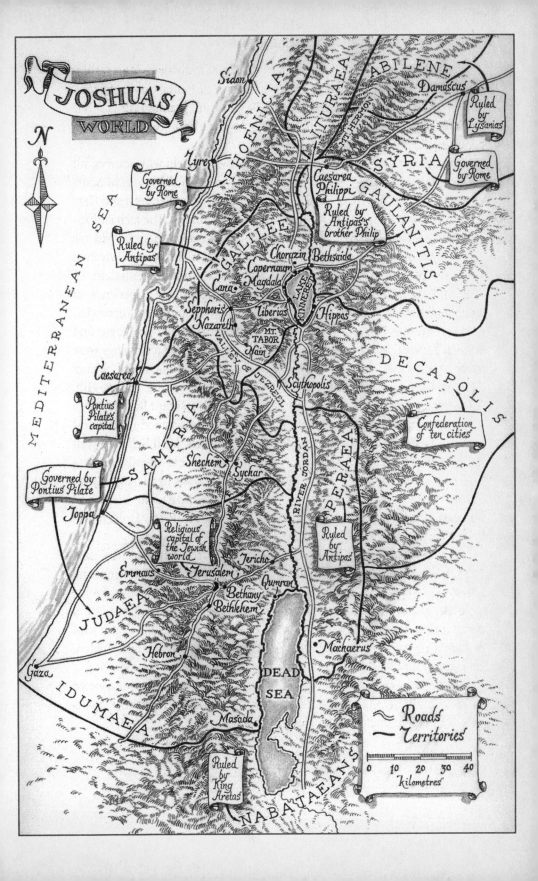

CHAPTER 1

The Search for an Eyewitness

Every biographer trying to recover a life from the past seeks the eyewitnesses through whose memories we can reach across the years, centuries or millennia, to see and hear, almost touch the living person.

Like many Christians, when I began my boyhood search for the story of Joshua's time on earth, I imagined that the Gospels provided this tactile link with his life; but by the time I saw *Jesus Christ Superstar* and heard the Apostles sing, 'When we retire we will write the Gospels', I knew that this was a piece of lyrical whimsy. By then — in fact many years earlier — I had learnt that the Gospels are four books written at unknown times in unknown places by unknown men.

Christian hackles rise. Of course the authors are known! They're Matthew, Mark, Luke and John. Matthew was a disciple of Jesus — a reformed tax collector. Mark was a young man called John Mark, a travelling companion of the disciple Peter. Luke was a doctor friend of the 'Apostle' Paul. John, a Galilean fisherman, was also a disciple — probably 'the beloved disciple'.

This is an impressive line-up — which is the very reason why these men's names were linked to the Gospels in the century after they were written. Unfortunately there is no hard evidence that they were the authors, and much to suggest that they weren't — with one exception. Luke, the only one of the four with no direct connection to the life of Jesus, probably wrote *Luke*. His association with Paul is not an impressive credential. Paul called himself an Apostle but had never seen the living Jesus and preached his own version of the Christian message for years before he met a genuine Apostle. Luke's prologue to his Gospel is illuminating.

> Since many have taken it upon themselves to set down an account of these events that have occurred among us, as passed on to us from the very beginning by eyewitnesses and servants of the Word, it seemed good to me, too, to set [them] down in order for you, most noble Theophilus, so that you may know the absolute truth about what you have been told. (*Luke* 1:1-4)

He is quite specific: the 'many' accounts of Jesus' life and ministry that have preceded his book recorded the transmitted oral traditions of eyewitnesses and 'servants of the Word' (perhaps Apostles). Luke is unaware of any prior Gospel actually written by an eyewitness (which of course would include an Apostle). He gives his book the same degree of authority as the earlier works and even suggests that it will be more reliable and appropriate to the needs of 'most noble Theophilus', a highly placed Roman, perhaps a governor.

Luke is a Gentile, crafting his Gospel in superb Greek for a Gentile reader. He is a consummate stylist, concerned to give his account the imprimatur of history in the Graeco–Roman manner while also aspiring to the benediction of Jewish scriptural style as reflected in the famous Greek translation, the Septuagint (in much the same way that many present-day Christians still use the 'thees' and 'thous' of the King James Bible when they pray). Luke gathered oral history in Caesarea and Jerusalem and drew on the work of the Jewish-Roman historian, Flavius Josephus (not without making a few errors which some Christian scholars have tried to justify by suggesting that Luke corrected Josephus!). Luke based his narrative on *Mark*, possibly an earlier Gospel and a hypothetical collection of Jesus' sayings (in scholarly circles codenamed 'Q', from the German *Quelle*, 'source').

Whether or not the author of *Luke* was Paul's physician friend, we certainly know *what* the man was — the *compiler* of a superior piece of missionary literature. With the other three Gospellers, too many questions remain unanswered.

If Matthew was the former tax gatherer (actually a *telones*, a customs duty collector) who became a disciple of Jesus, why did he need to borrow so much of his material, and even his wording, from the Gospel of Mark, who was not one of the Twelve? And if *that* highly influential book was written by John Mark, a young man from Jerusalem, why didn't he know more about the country, the people, the language? Certainly, the *Gospel of John* shows this sort of Jewish local knowledge, but if it was written by John the

Galilean fisherman, why don't we hear more of what happened in Galilee? And why is he the only Gospeller who leaves out Jesus' Transfiguration, when John was one of only three witnesses of that remarkable event? He also omits every other incident specifically involving John and his brother James as described by the other three Gospellers.

As for when the Gospels were written, at one time or another every one of them has been identified as the first. The early Church gave *Matthew* the number one place, the position it still occupies in the New Testament. Modern scholars believe that Mark's Gospel was the earliest (c 70 AD) and that Matthew (c 80–90 AD) and Luke (c 80 AD) drew from his work as well as from the lost 'Q' collection of Jesus' sayings. There has been a recent attempt to give *Matthew* an earlier date on the basis of ten partial verses of *Matthew* 26 on three scraps of papyrus controversially dated to 70 AD or earlier. Apparent paraphrases of the Gospel in the letters of Paul (who died about 64 AD) could also suggest an earlier date for *Matthew*, even that Matthew was the author of 'Q', which could have been written soon after Jesus' death. This possibility — like the very existence of 'Q' itself — remains a theory.

Some twelve years ago, a theological think-tank called the 'Jerusalem School for the Study of the Synoptic Gospels' decided that *Luke* was the first to be written because much of its material translated easily into Hebrew. This meant that, in their judgement, the 'many' earlier works cited in Luke's prologue did not include any of the accepted Gospels. If so, why would all those books vanish without a trace while *Luke* and the other Gospels survived?

About twenty other Gospels exist — in whole or in part — but most of them are embarrassingly florid elaborations of the standard four and clearly date from successive centuries. It is significant that, though frowned on by the Church, much of this dross has survived. More important documents, such as the *Gospel According to the Hebrews*, the *Gospel of the Ebionites* and the *Gospel of the Egyptians*, have vanished. The *Gospel According to the Hebrews* — which portrayed Joshua as being conceived and born of human parents — may have represented the original Hebrew or Aramaic version of *Matthew*. It was often quoted by early fathers of the Church, but, apart from these quotations, nothing remains.

Here, as in other cases, it seems likely that the Church simply destroyed material that did not follow the 'party line' as set out in the 'Canon' of the New Testament (an interesting term derived from the Greek word for a measuring stick). One set of early Christian documents escaped this conformist campaign — a collection of thirteen papyrus books discovered at Nag

Hammadi, Egypt, in 1945. Written by the Christian branch of a wide-ranging Gnostic (secret wisdom) sect, the 'library' includes Gospels of Thomas, Philip and Mary. The *Gospel of Thomas* is highly regarded by many modern scholars and by America's controversial 'Jesus Seminar' (an association of up to 200 scholars who have debated the authenticity of the Gospels twice a year since 1985). The Seminar ranks it with the four 'Canonical' Gospels (their 'Scholars' Version' is entitled *The Five Gospels*).

Church scholars accuse the seminarians of being too eager to treat such documents as more reliable than the standard Gospels. Nag Hammadi advocates concede that the texts are slanted to a Gnostic viewpoint but stress that the Gospels of Matthew, Mark, Luke and John are equally slanted to the viewpoint of Paulian Christianity and represent a tradition that had developed far beyond the original teaching of Joshua.

Just to cap the whole dilemma, while almost everyone from the earliest Church recordists down to avant-garde, present-day scholars agree that John's Gospel was the last to be written (c 90–100 AD), Dr J.A.T. Robinson argues that it was the first (and in fact that all the Gospels were written pre-70 AD). He is supported by two Australians — scholar-bishop, Dr Paul Barnett (who gives *John* at least a dead heat with *Mark)* and Dr Barbara Thiering — who agrees with Robinson on *John's* primacy but insists that the Gospel was dictated by Jesus soon after his crucifixion).

There is a far more basic problem. Which of the four Gospels do we believe? Christians who don't read the Gospels — a depressingly high proportion — imagine that they all tell the same story and that they represent 'Gospel truth'. It is true that *Matthew*, *Mark* and *Luke* often agree (the Australian Donovan Joyce dubs them 'the agreeable trio') which is why they are called the 'Synoptic' Gospels, a term from the Greek meaning that they can be viewed together, read side-by-side. Yet they also disagree on some crucial details of what happened, when and where it happened and what was said. The 'inerrancy' of the Gospels becomes a confusing position; they can't all be right.

As we will see, Matthew and Luke tell markedly different stories about the miraculous birth of Jesus (and his lineage, to a degree that shook the faith of St Augustine) while Mark has nothing to say on the subject. Matthew tells of the Sermon on the Mount; Luke writes of the Sermon on the Plain; Mark gives no hint of either event. Most surprisingly, the three Gospellers' accounts of the resurrection of Jesus vary widely. Despite this, their overall agreement is so close, sometimes almost word-for-word, that we are obviously not dealing with three independent accounts of the same events; we are dealing with three treatments of interrelated material, on occasions apparently altered at the whim of the author. Even the American scholar, Timothy Luke Johnson — a former Benedictine monk and spirited defender of the Gospels — concedes that they show 'authorial creativity'.

The modern approach to this problem is to admit that the Gospels are documents of faith, not history — which prompts an obvious response: how valid is that faith if based on questionable history? Timothy Luke Johnson is highly critical of attempts to reconstruct a historical narrative from the Gospels. He admits, 'the present shape of the canonical Gospels is not such as to encourage the historian.' In a recent book subtitled 'The Misguided Quest for the Historical Jesus and the Truth of the Traditional Gospels', Johnson launches a lofty attack on biographer A.N. Wilson and the radical American Bishop John Shelby Spong. He consigns them both to 'Amateur Night' and complains of their 'inventive speculation', which, he says,

> is not a reasonable alternative reading based on the available evidence, but *a complete reshuffling of the pieces, yielding a picture more satisfying to the aesthetic or religions sensibilities of the authors.* [my italics]

Ironically, this is the very process followed by the Gospellers. In theological jargon, they build up their narratives from 'pericopes' (Greek *perikope*, 'a piece cut out'), story fragments that are juggled or combined to produce a different sequence or emphasis — a 'cut-and-paste' exercise.

The Fourth Gospel, *John*, is very different from its fellows in both content and style. Some commentators explain this by claiming that it was intended to supplement the three earlier books. *John* supposedly assumes that the reader is already familiar with the 'synoptics' and provides fresh material they had omitted. This doesn't hold water. John seems to have read *Mark* and *Luke*, but more often than not he contradicts 'the agreeable trio'. They show Jesus' ministry lasting a single year — most of it set in Galilee, with a single, fateful visit to Jerusalem. John portrays a ministry of at least three years with Jerusalem playing a far more central role. The first three Gospels contain between twenty-seven and fifty of Jesus' parables (depending on how a parable is defined); *John* — again depending on definition — contains none or one. Jesus of the synoptics speaks in a direct, pithy style, characterised by 'aphorisms' — what we today call 'one-liners'; John's Jesus delivers rambling discourses which often sound like dialogue from a religious pageant scripted by a worthy and wordy cleric — precisely the way John writes his Epistles, especially *1 John*.

John's narrative sequence clashes with the other Gospels — and sometimes with the internal logic of his own account. Some rearrangement is clearly deliberate but much seems accidental. It is as though some chapters and pages have become mixed up — which may be precisely what happened. *John* may have been written as a *codex*, a book, a huge advance on the old scriptural style of texts written on lengthy and unwieldy scrolls. Like all new technology, the codex had its problems. A scroll remained in order; a separated codex with unnumbered pages could easily become a shambles. Attempts to reassemble it would produce a result very much like the Fourth Gospel.

John is a baffling book. In some ways it is the most Jewish of all the Gospels. It contains thirteen references to places in the land of Israel not mentioned in the others; and the Christian Jewish scholar Edersheim is struck by 'the peculiarly Judaic character' of its Old Testament quotations. Yet the book is also strongly *anti*-Jewish. It mentions 'the Jews' some seventy times (compared with five or six references in the other three Gospels), usually as the stereotypical enemies of John's Jesus. Like the endlessly reworked speeches — and their heavy theological content — this argues for a composition date late in the first century when Jews had become enemies of 'Christians' and John had been plaiting words and ideas in perhaps sixty years of preaching (Eusebius, *History*, 3, 24, 1–13).

Jesus' teaching had inspired John's sermons; so by now these sermons had come to replace that teaching. Jesus had brought John closer to an understanding of God; John had recognised God *through* Jesus. So John's Jesus can make Godlike statements that go further than any other Gospel in deifying him.

From John saying, 'Jesus is the way, and the truth and the light' to John's Jesus saying, '*I* am the way, and the truth and the light' (*John* 14:6) is a small step for a preacher, but it prepares the ground for a quantum leap in theology. That leap travels from recognising God *through* Jesus to recognising Jesus *as* God.

America's Jesus Seminar declared in 1993 that only 18 per cent of the words attributed to Jesus in the Gospels were actually spoken by him *and not a single verse of John qualified* (though one was voted 'probable' and another was rated as expressing ideas similar to those of Jesus). The work of the Jesus Seminar is highly controversial (their 'Scholars' Version' of the Gospels sometimes sounds like dialogue from a gangster movie) and their 'committee' approach produces some aberrant results — especially when the views of respected scholars like Crossan, Funk and Borg are given the same weight as those of other less distinguished seminarians. Nevertheless, the Seminar points *towards* valid conclusions: that 'Gospel truth' is a far more elastic term than many Christians are prepared to admit; and that *John*, especially, is not a reliable guide to what Jesus said.

The Jewish scholar Schonfield considers John's Jesus 'a posturing polemical figure with a streak of antisemitism' and suggests that:

> it is not to the credit of the Church that it has taken this presentation of a pathological egoist to its bosom as the veritable Jesus.

Yet Schonfield acknowledges that John 'had access to some genuine unpublished reminiscences of the unnamed "beloved disciple" … which makes us thankful for the book's preservation.' Later he concedes: 'Through the Fourth Gospel we can still have access to the last-surviving direct disciple of Jesus'. Given Schonfield's rejection of John's dialogue, this is an impressive endorsement of the book's *factual* authenticity, echoed by other Jewish scholars. Even Jacobs, who considers *John* 'practically a work of religious imagination', is prepared to admit that 'he apparently had access to some trustworthy traditions about the last days'.

At last, in the person of this 'unnamed … direct disciple', we may have an eyewitness. But who was he? As we've seen, internal evidence makes it highly unlikely that the author was the Galilean fisherman, John, son of Zebedee, a conclusion supported by a body of evidence that John died either with or soon after his brother James, whose death can be fixed at 44 AD — at least forty-six years before the Fourth Gospel was written (according to the most credible datings).

Mark 10:39 shows Jesus predicting the martyrdom of the two brothers, a detail that would not have been included unless their deaths had occurred before this earliest Gospel was written. Papias, second-generation father of the Church, is twice quoted as saying that, 'John the Divine and his brother James were killed by the Jews,' and two early Church calendars record their joint martyrdom on 27 December. Yet there is also evidence that John the fisherman *was* the Gospel's author. At first it seems persuasive.

Irenaus, Bishop of Lyons, recorded in about 180 AD that the Gospel was the work of 'John the disciple of the Lord'. The Muratorian Fragment (part of a treatise believed to have been written by the Roman Presbyter Hippolytus about 170 AD) is equally specific that 'the Fourth Gospel is that of John, one of His disciples.' Immediately afterwards the treatise tells how 'Andrew, one of the Apostles' urged John to set down 'in his own name' his reminiscences and those of 'his fellow disciples'. While it is usually assumed that the passage refers to John as one of the inner circle of twelve disciples, sometimes called Apostles ('messengers' or 'envoys'), note that it differentiates between John as a *disciple* and Andrew as an *Apostle*. It seems to say that John was not one of The Twelve but rather one of the broader group of Jesus' students. The text of the Fourth Gospel has more to tell us about the identity of its author.

Most accept that *John* was written by 'the beloved disciple', who is mentioned five times in the Gospel and can be identified in two other passages. This pointedly unnamed character is placed next to Jesus at The Last Supper and leans against his chest during a confidential exchange (*John* 13:23–5). He is 'known to', or according to one manuscript 'related to' Caiaphas, the high priest, and can have Peter admitted to Caiaphas's Jerusalem home immediately after Jesus' arrest (18:15–16). He is the only male disciple who is present at the crucifixion (19:25–7) and is clearly the eyewitness who insists on the reliability of his testimony (19:35). He outruns Peter when Mary Magdalene reports that Jesus' tomb is empty (20:1–10). He witnesses a lakeside resurrection appearance by Jesus (21:7–23) and at the end of the Gospel is specifically identified as the author (21:24). On every occasion but one, he is linked with Peter in some way.

Two of these references are surprising. How could this disciple of Jesus be such a familiar figure at the home of the high priest, an arch-enemy of his Master? And why was he the only male disciple at the crucifixion? Both questions are easily answered if 'the beloved disciple' was a Jerusalem resident, as borne out by numerous details of the Gospel. Galileans had highly recognisable accents, a fact that is stressed when the unnamed disciple gains Peter's entry to the high priest's home and Peter is immediately suspected as a disciple of Jesus because his speech identifies him as a Galilean. Obviously 'the beloved disciple' did not have a Galilean accent and could therefore also attend the crucifixion without being identified as a follower of the condemned man.

There is one other fragment of evidence that helps complete the 'John' jigsaw. Polycrates, second–century Bishop of Ephesus, wrote to Victor, Bishop of Rome, 'John is buried at Ephesus, he who leaned on the breast of the Lord, *who carried the insignia of a priest*' [my italics] (Eusebius, *Ecclesiastical History*, 3, 31, 3).

The phrase, 'insignia of a priest', is variously interpreted but inescapably refers to the Jewish priesthood (which seems surprising until we recall *Acts* 6:7, where 'a great many' Jewish priests became early-day 'Christians'). This would mean that 'John' was of Levitical descent, an essential qualification for priesthood.

Our profile of 'the beloved disciple' is almost complete: a resident of Jerusalem known to the high priest and who seems to have been a friend of Peter. He attended The Last Supper in a position of honour next to Jesus (even though he was probably not one of the Twelve!) and may have been of Levitical descent. In the whole New Testament, only one man fits the description: John Mark, sometime travelling companion of Peter and supposed author of *Mark*. Less than six weeks after the crucifixion, the disciples were living in an 'upper room' of his mother's home in Jerusalem (*Acts* 12:12). It seems more than likely that this was the same 'upper room' where The Last Supper had been held. Since John Mark's mother was clearly a widow, he would have occupied an honoured place as host at this all-male function. The traditional (and probable) site of The Last Supper was only 70 metres from the supposed site of the high priest's home. More than this, John Mark's cousin Joseph (nicknamed 'Barnabas' in the early Church) was a Levite (*Colossians* 4:10; *Acts* 4:36), suggesting that John Mark, too, could have been of Levitical descent, a possibility that links not only to the mention of him as a priestly figure and to his relationship with the high priest, but that also explains a familiarity with Temple ritual and the festal calendar shown in the *Gospel of John*.

John's Levitical associations could also explain how a young man living in an affluent area of Jerusalem and mixing in Sadducean (aristocratic) circles could still write what has been described as 'barbarous' Greek — largely through his attempts to render Aramaic grammar with a rather limited Greek vocabulary. Classical Hebrew of synagogue and Temple and the Aramaic of the ordinary Jewish people were his preferred languages. Like many devout Jews, he could have seen the pervasive Graeco–Roman culture posing a threat to the Jewish religion — a first wedge between his piety and the Temple–Jerusalem establishment.

Identifying John Mark as the author of the Fourth Gospel has a profound impact on the search for Joshua. His special and personal knowledge will illuminate several incidents; on occasions his very identity will point to unusual discrepancies in his account and provide the key to unlocking their mysteries. It is ironic that a text which goes further than any other Gospel in isolating Jesus from his Jewish context will often prove the most effective instrument to recover the reality of *Joshua's* life and death.

CHAPTER 2

The Birth of Joshua

It is appropriate — even inevitable—that in the Nativity stories, the Gospel accounts of the birth of Jesus Christ, we will meet many of the processes and problems that complicate our search for the life of Joshua.

Every Christian, and countless millions of people who aren't Christians, know the Nativity story and are reminded of it every Christmas. Even to unbelievers, it is a magical tale which sits happily with the other firelit and star-dusted images of the season.

In the reign of Herod the Great, the Virgin Mary, betrothed to the carpenter Joseph of the House of David, is visited by the angel Gabriel who tells her that she is to bear a child to God (the Annunciation). When Mary becomes pregnant, Joseph is told in a dream that the baby has been divinely conceived and that he will name it Jesus.

As Mary approaches full term, Augustus Caesar proclaims a worldwide census which demands that Joseph and Mary journey from their home town of Nazareth in Galilee to Joseph's ancestral home of Bethlehem in Judaea. When there is no room for them in the inn at Bethlehem, Mary must have her baby in a stable; a manger becomes the cradle of the holy child. As a moving star comes to a halt over Bethlehem, angels announce the birth to shepherds guarding their flocks at night and they come to the stable to pay homage. Three kings or wise men, who have followed the moving star to Bethlehem, also arrive to lavish presents of gold, frankincense and myrrh on the Christ child. Soon afterwards, King Herod, who has been told of the Messiah's birth, orders his soldiers to kill every child in Bethlehem under the age of two (the Massacre of the Innocents). Joseph is warned in a dream and escapes with Mary and the baby Jesus to Egypt (the Flight to Egypt). After Herod's death the family returns to live in Nazareth.

This story is adapted from two almost totally different versions supplied by the Gospels of *Matthew* (1:18-2:23) and *Luke* (2:1-39). *Mark* and *John* make no mention of the Nativity. The merging and embellishment of the two stories is accepted so uncritically that most Christians are surprised to learn that Luke does not mention the star, the wise men, the Massacre of the Innocents or the Flight to Egypt; Matthew omits any reference to the Annunciation, the census, the inn, the manger, the angels or the shepherds, does not mention a star over Bethlehem at the Nativity and does not specify *three* wise men.

Neither Gospel describes Jesus being born in a stable (though Luke uses a word that can mean 'manger') and, while Luke has Joseph and Mary travelling to Bethlehem from Nazareth, Matthew has them living in Bethlehem until the Flight to Egypt, which is ignored in Luke's account. Apart from the names of Jesus' parents, the only points common to *Matthew* and *Luke* are Mary's pregnancy to God (which is not mentioned again by either writer and is totally ignored by Mark and John) and the fact that Jesus was born in Bethlehem. The first became essential to Gentile Christianity's concept of Jesus, the second was supposedly seen as essential to his Jewish Messiahship.

Given this meagre factual harmony between the two Gospels, it seems unlikely that a miraculous element which appears in only one of them could throw any historical light on the birth of Joshua. Yet one such detail from Matthew's Nativity — the Star of Bethlehem guiding the wise men to the birthplace of Jesus — not only supplies one of the Christmas story's most vivid symbols, but also provides an instrument which seems to confirm several events of that story and locates them in both place and time with impressive precision.

✝✝✝

Bethlehem's miraculous star has been variously identified as Halley's Comet, a super nova — even a UFO — without a satisfactory explanation of why the 'wise men' or 'kings' should imagine that this sky sign was leading them to a new-born Messiah. The answer lies in their identity and the nature of the 'star'.

First, Matthew tells us that they were Magi (Greek *Magoi*), a priestly caste originating in Persia who practised astronomy and astrology. In the last twenty-five years, representatives of these disciplines have done intensive and — significantly — independent work on both the Star phenomenon and the reason for the Magi to recognise it as a Messianic portent. The Australian, Ralph Holden, an unusual combination of clergyman and astrologer, took his research a vital step further and asked why, having recognised the sign, these supposedly Gentile Magi would then make a journey of hundreds of miles to see the infant Messiah and present him with expensive gifts. Even more, why would they tell King Herod that they wished to 'worship' or 'pay homage to' the baby (*Matthew* 2:2)?

Holden argues persuasively that these Magi were Jews, descended from the thousands of deported inhabitants of Judah who elected to remain in Babylon after their liberation by Cyrus in 538 BC. This would explain both their interest in the Messiah and their veneration of him. Holden's argument is strengthened by a piece of evidence he apparently missed. During the Jewish captivity in Babylon, the prophet Daniel won the favour of King Nebuchadnezzar by interpreting royal dreams and was appointed 'chief of the wise men' or 'master of the Magi' (*Daniel* 2:48) — thus establishing a Jewish influence and, credibly, an ongoing Jewish presence among the Magi of the city.

The Gospels make it clear that Joshua was born in the last few years of the reign of Herod. In trying to identify the Star of Bethlehem, the date of Herod's death (4 BC) rules out Halley's Comet (12 BC) and a conjunction of Jupiter and Venus (3 BC). A comet recorded by Chinese astronomers in 5 BC fits the time frame but has nothing to mark it as a Messianic sign. It was Johannes Kepler, the great German astronomer of the seventeenth century, who first linked the Star with a conjunction of Jupiter and Saturn in the constellation of Pisces — a phenomenon that occurred in 7 BC. To Jewish astrologers, Pisces was the sign of Israel and the Messiah; Jupiter was the planet of kingship; Saturn was associated with Israel and its God. Not surprisingly, Kepler found a reference in Jewish literature to a conjunction of these planets in Pisces as a sign of the Messiah's coming.

The Kepler conjunction identifies a phenomenon clearly recognisable to Babylonian Jewish astronomer/astrologers as a Messianic portent yet not spectacular enough to attract the attention of Jewish laymen. It fell within the period when Joshua's birth must have occurred — in the very year favoured by many scholars — and we know that the sky sign was observed in Babylon. Three Jupiter/Saturn conjunctions of 7 BC were meticulously recorded on clay tablets, recovered during excavation of the Babylonian Astronomical College at Sippar and translated in 1923. There is, however, a major problem.

The Nativity story does not describe the Magi making an observation of the conjunction, nor does it describe their journey as an investigation of it. Matthew tells us that they followed a moving star that led them to the Land of Israel. Or does he?

> When Jesus was born in Bethlehem of Judaea in the days of Herod the King, wise men from the east arrived in Jerusalem, asking: 'Where is he [who has been] born king of the Jews? *We saw his star when it rose* and have come to pay homage to him.' [my italics]   (*Matthew* 2:1–2)

Once again, Christian tradition has shown appallingly careless use of sources. Matthew is quite specific: the Magi have observed an astronomical phenomenon and are investigating it. He also tells us much more about this occurrence than is conveyed by most English translations.

'When it rose' renders the Greek *en te anatole* often translated simply as 'in the east', which would have been *en tai anatolai*, a form found elsewhere in the New Testament. Matthew's phrase, unique to this passage, represents a technical description of the phenomenon — perhaps best translated as 'we saw his star rising with the sun' — what astronomers and astrologers call 'heliacal rising'.

Jupiter and Saturn rose with the sun on 12 April in 7 BC. They were almost ten degrees apart but heralded a conjunction that was already predictable on the sophisticated star charts used by Babylonian astronomers. On 27 May, Jupiter and Saturn rose, 'fully visible in the morning sky for two hours before dawn', less than one degree apart. Watching in wonderment from the roof of the great astronomical college at Sippar, the Jewish Magi stared at the double star in the brightening sky until the sun rose in what they believed to be the dawn of the Messianic age. The Messiah had been born.

Ralph Holden theorises that they waited to observe a second conjunction in October; then, with the brutal midsummer of Mesopotamia giving way to autumn, they made their six-week journey to Jerusalem. Why Jerusalem? They would believe, reasonably enough, that the King of Kings had been born to the royal family — or that this seat of Jewish learning would have shared the revelation. Matthew describes Herod's reaction to the announcement of their pilgrimage:

> When Herod the King heard this, he was troubled, and all Jerusalem with him. And gathering all the priests and scribes of the people, he enquired of them when the Messiah would be born. And they told him, 'In Bethlehem of Judaea, for so it was written by the prophet...' [*Micah* 5:2]. Then, secretly summoning the Magi, *Herod learnt from them the exact time of the star's appearance.* And he

sent them to Bethlehem, saying, 'Go and search thoroughly for the child; and when you find him, report back to me so that I too can go and pay homage to him.' [my italics] (*Matthew* 2:3–8)

Up to this point, Matthew has provided a surprisingly precise description of the heliacal rising and the Magi's investigation of it. But now he seems to launch out on a flight of pure fancy.

When they had heard the king, they set off; and there! the star they had seen at its rising went ahead of them until it came and stood over [the place] where the child was. (*Matthew* 2:10)

At last we seem to have the moving star of Christian tradition, leading the Magi from Jerusalem to Bethlehem and magically coming to a halt over the very house where the Messiah is to be found.

In fact, if the Magi's journey followed Holden's highly plausible itinerary, they had reached Jerusalem by the beginning of December when Jupiter and Saturn appeared in a third and final conjunction. The Magi's 8-kilometre journey to Bethlehem took them due south from Jerusalem. Directly ahead, the twin star shone in the evening sky, *seeming* to lead them on, until, as Bethlehem came in sight, it poised above the hilltop village. Matthew can be forgiven his single embellishment — implying that the star marked where the child was to be found. In fact, he has already described, in precise terms, the mechanics of locating the Messiah — and will later reiterate the method when Herod kills …

all the male children in Bethlehem and surroundings, of two years old and younger, *in accordance with the time established by the Magi*. [my italics]
(*Matthew* 2:16)

The Messiah had been born when the twin star rose on 27 May (see note pp. 26–7). A few enquiries by the Magi in Bethlehem would establish the male child born at, or close to, that time. In such a small population — a few hundred at most — the search would not be difficult. And the quest was over. The Babylonian Jewish Magi's confrontation with Joseph, Mary and the six-month-old Joshua becomes highly credible.

Saying that this was possible is not to say that it happened, though the symmetry between Matthew's story and the Jupiter–Saturn conjunction of 7 BC seems to stretch coincidence. Yet is it also coincidence that, in 66 AD, a year when Halley's Comet reappeared, three princely Magi made a much-publicised journey to Rome — alarmingly, to confirm Nero's divinity? On the one hand the event is perfectly timed to inspire the writing of Matthew's story; on the other hand it confirms that such expeditions were made by Magi and, incidentally, as recorded by classical historians Cassius Dio and Pliny, it could have inspired the identification of Matthew's Magi as the 'three kings' of Christian tradition.

The Star of Bethlehem remains a beacon of *possibility* to illuminate the charming hologram formed by the interface of Matthew's and Luke's Nativities. In its light, their few points of congruence seem almost enough to unite the other varied elements. But a basic flaw cuts away half their common ground.

For Jesus to qualify as the Messiah, he had to be in the line of descent from King David. To demonstrate this, both Matthew and Luke publish genealogies which trace Joseph's ancestry from Abraham via David (*Matthew*) and back to Adam via David (*Luke*). But if Joseph is not the biological father of Mary's son, how can that son belong to the House of David? Unblushingly, some commentators point to *Matthew's* genealogy and say that, though it purports to be of Joseph, it actually traces *Mary's* descent from David. This seeks to explain why even the name of Joseph's father differs from that given in *Luke* and how the divinely conceived Jesus can still belong to the Jewish royal line.

Re-allocation of the *Matthew* genealogy is unconvincing and now generally rejected by Christian commentators, who admit that the genealogies were created to serve theological rather than historical ends. Clearly then, when they were composed, the divine conception of Jesus was not the theological issue. The entire exercise was intended to prove Jesus' Jewish Messiahship by showing that he belonged to the royal line of David; but both genealogies miss that mark.

In designing his genealogy to fit into an esoteric pattern (three groups, each of fourteen generations), *Matthew* simply drops four generations from the genealogy of Solomon, son of David, as set out in *1 Chronicles* 3:10–16. Jehoiakim is among the deleted descendants of Solomon; yet Jehoiakim's son, Jeconiah, is named as an ancestor of Jesus. This is doubly unfortunate because, after damning Jeconiah as 'a discarded vessel', the prophet Jeremiah declares that 'none of his descendants will have the good fortune to sit on the throne of David and rule again in Judah (*Jeremiah* 22:24–30).

Luke's list of Jesus' ancestors is similarly flawed. It traces the lineage of Jesus via David's son, Nathan, yet only descendants of Nathan's brother, Solomon, were to inherit kingship (*1 Chronicles* 22: 8–10; 28: 6).

This does not disprove that Joshua belonged to the house of David — nor does it say that he was not of the royal line more narrowly defined within that house (not too narrowly when one considers that Solomon had 500 wives!). In their eagerness to establish Jesus' Davidic lineage, Matthew and Luke were simply careless in putting together their evidence.

Jewish sources do not deny that Joshua was of royal descent. Even the *Toledoth Yeshu* (a bitterly anti-Christian work of the Middle Ages, which embodies early tradition) accepts that Joseph was a member of the house of David; and the Talmud concedes that Joshua was 'connected with royalty' (*Sanhedrin* 43a). The 'Apostle' Paul showed little interest in biographical details of his Gentile-orientated Jesus but recorded: 'he [Jesus] came from the seed of David according to the flesh' (*Romans* 1:3).

Paul's mentions of 'seed of David' and 'flesh' do not sit easily with the idea of a virgin birth (or, more accurately, virgin conception) and in his very next words, while acknowledging Jesus as son of God, he clearly shows he is unaware of a miraculous birth story that established this sonship: '... and through the spirit of holiness [he] was powerfully shown to be the Son of God *by his resurrection from the dead*' [my italics] (*Romans* 1:4).

'Son of God' is a Jewish title usually applied to a man who has achieved a special relationship with God, like the Galilean *hasid*, Hanina ben Dosa. The example with greatest relevance to the life of Joshua is that of King David, the most human of men, yet a 'son of God'. His coronation psalm has God proclaim:

'You are my son;
Today I have begotten you.'

(*Psalm* 2:1)

David's son, Solomon, is also identified as a son of God, with God saying to the prophet Nathan: 'I will be a father to him and he will be a son to me' (*2 Samuel* 7:14; *1 Chronicles* 22:9–10; 28:6). The theme recurs in the Dead Sea Scrolls which speak of the sect's Messiah being 'begotten' or 'fathered' (*yolid*) by God (1QSa 2, 12).

We will see Joshua reach towards sonship with God and experience his acceptance. Joshua's disciple John Mark goes further than any other Gospeller in portraying his Jesus as divine, yet he declares: 'To those believing in his name he gave authority for them to become children of God' (*John* 1:12). John is saying, here as elsewhere, that others can achieve Joshua's filial relationship with his heavenly Father. It is a question of obedience and total commitment *to* God and acceptance *by* God — the re-creation of an adult life; a re-birth rather than conception.

From such a thoroughly Jewish concept came the totally *un*-Jewish idea of God making a virgin pregnant. However, while this idea was completely unacceptable to Jews, it was commonplace to Graeco–Romans whose mythology and cosmology featured many liaisons between gods and mortal women. So the Nativity story became a metaphor — a Jewish 'son of God' presented in missionary literature designed for a Gentile readership in terms that would give Jesus appropriate man–god stature beside the deities of the pagan pantheon. Matthew tries to place the divine conception of Jesus in the Jewish Messianic tradition by quoting *Isaiah* 7:14:

> The virgin will conceive in her womb and she will give birth to a son and they will call him 'Immanuel', which means, 'God is with us'.   (*Matthew* 1:23)

It is often pointed out that in the original Old Testament passage from Isaiah, the Hebrew word used is *ha'almah*, meaning 'young woman', and that Matthew's 'virgin' derives from *parthenos*, a mistranslation of *ha'almah* found in the Septuagint, the famous Greek version of the Old Testament. (This error points to a later Greek interpolation in the translation from the Aramaic or Hebrew of *Matthew*.) Quite apart from this, the passage from *Isaiah* is not a Messianic prophecy; Isaiah's intention is to provide the evil King Ahaz with a 'sign' from God.

This is the first of five Old Testament 'prophecies' quoted in Matthew's birth and infancy narrative, each of them concerned with unrelated events in long-lost ages. In the most flagrant example, the family's settling in Nazareth supposedly fulfils the prophecy, 'He shall be called a *Nazarene*' [meaning a person from Nazareth] (*Matthew* 2:23). No such prophecy is known: but in *Judges* 13:5, when the birth of Samson is announced to the barren wife of Manoah, 'the angel of the Lord' tells her, 'The boy will be a *Nazirite* [a man dedicated to God, who, as one of the signs of his devotion, never cuts his hair]'. There is no connection between the two words — or the two prophecies. Matthew has introduced us to a disturbing Gospel pattern — contorting prophecies to fit details of Jesus' life; or even contorting details of his life to fit prophecy.

✝✝✝

Luke's Nativity story is very elaborate, intriguingly intertwined with the miraculous conception and birth of John the Baptist. John's mother, the elderly Elizabeth, wife of the priest, Zechariah, is supposedly Mary's 'kinswoman'. As we will see, the Gospels were keen to establish links between their Jesus and the far more famous Baptist. The supposed family tie therefore warrants scrutiny, especially as it clashes with Gospel evidence that John did not know Jesus (*John* 1:31).

Luke's story, told in a clever imitation of Greek Old Testament style, is characterised by a series of songs which give the narrative a charming theatricality. The songs have a strongly Jewish character and it has been theorised that Luke adopted them from the liturgy of the early Jerusalem 'Church'. The most famous is Mary's *Magnificat* ('My soul magnifies the Lord ...') (*Luke* 1:46–55), an extraordinary psalm to the God of Israel which is closely based on the song of Hannah celebrating the miraculous conception of the prophet Samuel (*1 Samuel* 2:1–10). Tellingly, in the earliest texts of *Luke* (now lost but attested by early scholars Irenaeus and Nicetas of Remisiana), the *Magnificat* was declaimed by Elizabeth, not Mary. From the mouth of either woman, it sounds a revolutionary and militant note strangely at odds with the candle-lit, incense-wreathed air of its use in Christian liturgy.

> Showing the mighty power of His arm,
> He scattered the proud in their self-esteem,
> He toppled rulers from their thrones
> And raised up the lowly.
> The hungry He filled with good things,
> The rich He sent away empty.
> He has helped His servant Israel.
> Remembering his mercy,
> Just as he promised to our fathers,
> To Abraham,
> And to his seed forever. (*Luke* 1:51–5)

Here, and in another song supplied by Luke for the Baptist's father (the *Benedictus*), the underscore of social and political upheaval is easily missed in the setting of the two miraculous pregnancies. Yet in all of Luke's Christmas-pageant prologue, it is only these unlikely songs that have any relationship to what lies ahead.

By Chapter 2 of Luke's Gospel, Joseph and Mary know nothing of the extraordinary events surrounding Mary's pregnancy in Chapter 1. And while there are indications that the author of *John* had read *Luke*, he seems unaware of a miraculous conception or even that Jesus had been born in Bethlehem (*John* 7:40–2). Everything suggests that Luke's original Gospel started at Chapter 3 with his historical scene setting and the genealogy which now begins with Jesus, 'being *as was supposed* the son of Joseph ...' [my italics]

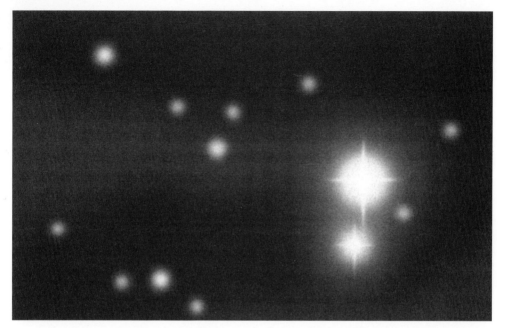

The Star of Bethlehem? The conjunction of Jupiter and Saturn in the constellation of Pisces, as it would have appeared to the Magi, in the southern sky above Bethlehem on the evening of 4 December 7 BC. In the 'birth' constellation of 27 May, the two planets were closer together. (Digital image by Dennis Ogden, after Keller)

The traditional site of Christ's birth is marked in Bethlehem's Church of the Nativity by a fourteen-pointed silver star, each point marking a generation in Matthew's three numerology-driven lists of ancestors. The star dates from 1717 and only 133 years later was made one of the pretexts for a dispute between Russia and Turkey that led to the Crimean War. Far from believing in this precise site, many present-day scholars even doubt that the birth occurred in Bethlehem.

Ignoring the Moslem mosque and the large Christian buildings, this 1839 view of Nazareth by David Roberts gives some idea of what the obscure little village could have looked like in Joshua's time. Today it is a city of 60 000.

A nineteenth-century lithograph underlines two themes of the Nativity stories. Joseph is portrayed as elderly (to make Mary's ongoing virginity more credible) and John the Baptist, precociously wearing his prophet's costume, is shown as a member of the family. Evidence suggests that Joshua had not met John before his baptism and that stories of the family's links to the Baptist represented a Gospel campaign to exploit the ongoing reputation of this charismatic figure.

(*Luke* 3:23), an amendment by Luke or his editor that makes nonsense of an exercise to trace Jesus' descent from David.

The whole problem of the virgin birth is summed up nicely by Beth Moshe:

> We do not doubt that the miraculous birth could have occurred, for surely God can do anything. Nevertheless we are stating that we do not have New Testament corroboration.

The development of the Virgin Mary cult is outside this work. In the Prologue to her superb study of Mariology, *Alone of All Her Sex*, Marina Warner comments:

> I have not pursued the historical Mary, the woman of Nazareth, because theology and belief have rarely focussed on her.

Similarly, the Church's Virgin Mary (an extraordinary elaboration of the Gospel figure) has no role in the story of Joshua. Let it only be said that what began as an attempt to convey the divinity of Jesus ended in the creation of a figure with particular appeal to sections of the early Church — a mother goddess who did not also enshrine female sexuality. While Matthew is quite specific that Mary had normal marital relations with Joseph after her son's birth (*Matthew* 1:25; cf. 1:13), the Church decreed that she remained a perpetual virgin — in spite of four other sons and at least two daughters attested by the Gospels. As Bishop Spong observes:

> Few people stopped to realize that the woman who was being hailed as the ideal model was a woman who had been totally defined by men. That a permanent virgin can be an ideal woman only to a celibate male did not appear to be obvious as the values of the church were presented as objective revealed truths.

This veneration of asexuality has blighted Christianity for almost 2000 years. True, it has nurtured lives of wonderful dedication; it has produced saints. It has also wrought cruel havoc both inside and outside the Church to a degree that is only beginning to emerge.

The appearance of the Virgin Birth stories among Gentile Christians led to an inevitable backlash from Judaism. Given the claim that the Christians' Jesus was not fathered by Mary's espoused husband, stories inevitably circulated to explain the phenomenon (as well as the ugly epithet, 'son of a harlot', used in rabbinical literature: *Pesiqta Rabbah* 21, 100b).

In the most popular version, Jesus became *Yeshua ben Pandera* — Joshua the son of Pandera — Pandera being a Roman soldier (Talmudic texts *Sanhedrin* 67a; *Shabbath* 104b; Origen, Christian scholar of the second to third century, *Against Celsus* 1, 28). Bishop Spong does not address this specific possibility but advances the suggestion that Mary was raped while Joseph was tied up in their home — an action that would remain unpunished only if the attacker were such a man. The fact that *Panthera* (Latin for 'panther' or 'leopard') seems to have been a comparatively common name or nickname in the Roman army, hardly proves the hypothesis. There could have been a *Yeshua ben Pandera* in first-century Israel (perhaps several) and the emergence of the 'miraculous birth' stories could have encouraged the name being attached to *Yeshua ha-Notzri* (Jesus the Nazarene) — as a coarse joke, maliciously or in a genuine attempt to explain the alleged mystery of his conception. The *Toledoth Yeshu* has a variant. Mary's husband is 'Joseph Pandareus' and while he is away from home, a neighbour, 'Johanan the Wicked, a transgressor and adulterer', comes to her at night. Believing her husband has returned, Mary is made pregnant.

These stories are the other side of the Virgin Birth medal and equally unsupported by evidence. There is no good reason to doubt that Joshua was the son of Joseph, conceived in a natural and beautiful way in obedience to God's very first commandment to man and woman: 'Be fruitful and multiply' (*Genesis* 1:28).

Mary (*Miryam* or *Maryam*) would have been no more than fourteen or fifteen years old; Joseph (*Yosef*) perhaps twenty — normal marriage ages for the place and time. Consistent portrayals of Joseph as elderly (ninety in one piece of Apocrypha!) were clearly supposed to make Mary's perpetual virginity more credible. While scholarly fashion now leans to Nazareth as Jesus' birthplace, there is much to support Matthew's ignored picture of Joseph and Mary living in Bethlehem before the birth and moving to Nazareth later. In defiance of Christian orthodoxy, Mary's traditional birthplace is beside the Pool of Bethesda in Jerusalem, only 8 kilometres from Bethlehem.

Bethlehem (*Beit Lechem*, 'House of Bread') was an already-ancient village on a limestone ridge overlooking the bare, folded hills of the Wilderness of Judaea. Its cluster of white houses by the high road from Jerusalem to Hebron would have held no more than a few hundred people. Olives, figs and grapes grew on small crescents of field scooped from the steep hillside and terraced with white stones, like a rambling stairway to the crop fields and pastures below.

Here, a thousand years before, David had tended his father's sheep; and, according to the prophet Micah (5:2), from here the Messiah would come. Modern scholars — Jewish and Christian — relate this prophecy to Bethlehem as springhead of the Davidic line rather than as birthplace of the Messiah. Not so the *meturgeman* of Joshua's day — the officer of the synagogue who recited the *Targum* ('Translation'), an Aramaic paraphrase of the scriptures, for the benefit of the many Jews who could not speak Hebrew in the post-Exile centuries. The *Targum of Jonathan*, commenting on *Genesis* 35:21, describes *Migdal Eder* ('Tower of the Flock'), a site near Bethlehem, as 'the place from which the Messiah is to be revealed in the last days'.

Luke provides a precise historical frame for the event which, he claims, drew Joseph and Mary from Nazareth to Bethlehem.

> And in those days, a decree went out from Caesar Augustus for all the inhabited world to be registered ('taxed', King James Version). This registration first took place when Cyrenius was governing Syria and all went to be registered to his own city.　　　　　　　　　　　　　　　　　　　　(*Luke* 2:1–2)

Luke seems to confirm Matthew's dating of the Nativity to the reign of Herod. Certainly, some fifteen months before the birth of Jesus, when the angel Gabriel tells Zechariah that he and his wife will have a son, Luke specifies that Herod is King of Judaea (*Luke* 1:5). The problems of this chronology are well-worn; perhaps too well-worn. It is easy to follow the wheel-ruts of successive scholars and miss possible turn-offs.

Put briefly, Luke seems to be speaking of the first Judaean census conducted by Quirinus (Cyrenius), Governor of Syria, in 6 AD — ten years too late for any connection with Herod, who died in 4 BC. The argument goes even further than this. The census of 6 AD was demanded by Roman annexation of Judaea when the disastrous reign of Herod's son, Archelaus, was abruptly terminated. Augustus Caesar banished him and appointed a prefect to govern Judaea as a Roman province. This required the census as a prelude to Roman rule and Roman taxation.

Obviously, no such situation existed during the reign of King Herod. He was a *rex socius*, a client king under Rome, and taxation was a matter between him and his subjects. The historian Robin Lane Fox says bluntly: 'If Herod was king, there was no census according to Caesar Augustus.' Pointing out that *apographe*, Luke's word for 'registration', was *usually* related to taxation in ancient sources, Fox comments: 'An emperor would not be imagined to have registered his Jewish subjects for any other purpose.' Yet there is evidence of a

Roman registration of Judaea in the reign of Herod; and it was not related to tax.

The Roman historians Suetonius and Tacitus record that, late in his reign, Augustus commissioned a survey of the Roman world which eventually made up a book, *Statistics of the Empire*. This ambitious work has not survived but Tacitus sketches its contents:

> It gave the number of regular and auxiliary troops serving in the army; the strength of the navy; statistics concerning the provinces *and independent kingdoms*; direct and indirect taxation; recurrent expenditure and gifts. [my italics]
>
> (Tacitus, *Annals*, 1, 11)

The registration of Judaea demanded by this ambitious undertaking would have been carried out after Herod's death. However, about 207 AD, Tertullian, who worked as a jurist in distinguished Roman circles, recorded that a similar exercise had been initiated during the Syrian governorship of Sentius Saturninus, 9 BC to 7 BC (*Against Marcion*, 4, 19). Egyptian papyri record a registration of 20 AD and establish that such exercises were generally carried out at fourteen-year intervals, giving a possible date of 8 BC for a registration coinciding with Saturninus's time in Syria. Suetonius confirms that there was also a Roman census that year (*Augustus*, 97). This was four years before Herod's death, when Judaea was one of Rome's 'independent kingdoms'.

Herod, always eager to please his Roman patron, would have organised the required registration himself. If Augustus issued his decree in 8 BC, Herod could have had the process underway by the last year of Saturninus's governorship, 7 BC. This offers a solution to one of our problems with Luke — an Augustan registration of Judaea during the reign of Herod the Great. The problem remains of Luke dating it to the Syrian governorship of Quirinius — ten to thirteen years after Herod's death.

It is clear that Luke was wrong about Quirinius — he simply confused Saturninus's registration with the high-profile (and deeply resented) Judaean census of 6 AD about which he had read in Josephus. The more important issue is that a registration of Judaea seems to have been made during the reign of Herod. It did not involve taxation and need not have followed Roman procedures. Consequently, rather smug arguments against Mary and Joseph trekking to Bethlehem do not apply; all such arguments are based on Roman precedents. It is *possible* that Herod conducted his registration on the Jewish basis of tribes and/or clans, as dictated to Moses by God in *Numbers* 1:2, thus encouraging more willing cooperation from his subjects and avoiding the explosion of resentment which made the Roman tax census of 6 AD such a landmark. It is also *possible* that Luke is describing a registration carried out in 7 BC. This whole exercise establishes only possibility. The point is that current wisdom rejects the *Luke* story as being impossible. In history — particularly in ancient history — this is a dangerous position.

Ironically, having established that Luke's story of Joseph and Mary's journey to Bethlehem is feasible, it must be said that it is less likely than Matthew's widely ignored version — that the couple live in Bethlehem and continue to live in Bethlehem *in a house* for some time after the birth.

This touches another point. If Mary and Joseph travelled to Bethlehem for registration, then by definition of the exercise, they almost certainly had relatives there and would have stayed with them, especially in view of Mary's advanced pregnancy. Why then does Luke say that they tried to lodge at an inn? He doesn't. As Jerome Murphy-O'Connor points out:

> The Greek underlying the phrase, 'she laid him in a manger because there was no room for them in the inn' (*Luke* 2:7) can also be rendered, 'she laid him in a manger because they had no space in the room.'

It emerges that Joseph and Mary were quite poor at this stage, possibly still living with Joseph's parents. A room dug from the hillside at the back of the house, where animals sheltered in winter, could have provided a more suitable birthing space than the crowded living area — complete with a rock-cut manger. And of course, if Herod's tribal or clan registration was possible, it is equally possible that Joseph and his parents were accommodating relatives who had turned the occasion into a family reunion. Even less space in the room.

Again as with the story of the star, we are tempted by the possible. The great problem with both Nativities is that they have no impact on what follows. Mary, of all people, is later shown as being reluctant to accept her son as a wonder-working Messianic figure. Except in *John*. Yet John, as we've already noted, who seems to have read Luke, knows nothing of 'signs' associated with the birth of his Jesus, even seeming to be unaware that it took place in Bethlehem (*John* 7:42).

Luke, like Matthew, seems to have originally written a Gospel that lacked the Nativity. Perhaps his later encounter with stories of the Baptist's miraculous conception inspired his birth and infancy prologue. It is beyond belief that these two chapters were added by a second writer of Luke's talent. He has a story of Joseph and Mary attending the Temple forty-one days after the birth to tender the five-shekel 'redemption' for a firstborn male and offer a sacrifice to secure Mary's purification after childbirth. It is a nice detail that the young couple cannot afford the prescribed sacrifice of a year-old lamb and a young pigeon or dove; they offer the concessional sacrifice of two pigeons or doves (*Leviticus* 12:2–8).

At the Temple, Joseph and Mary encounter the aged Simeon (Simon), who is 'righteous and devout, eagerly awaiting the consolation of Israel'. He takes the baby Jesus in his arms and offers another of Luke's songs (the *Nunc Dimittis*):

Master, let your slave depart in peace,
According to your promise,
Because my eyes have seen your salvation
Which you have prepared before the faces of every people;
A light of revelation to the [Gentile] Nations
And a glory to Your people, Israel …

A little later, Simeon tells Mary:

This [child] is destined to cause
The fall and rise of many in Israel
And to be a sign that is spoken against.
A sword will pierce your own soul
So that the thoughts of many hearts
May be revealed.   (*Luke* 2:29–32; 34–5)

On this same visit to the Temple, Luke tells how an old prophetess called Anna ('the daughter of Phanuel of the tribe of Asher') approaches Joseph and Mary and, after thanking God, 'spoke of him [Jesus] to all those looking to the redemption of Jerusalem' (*Luke* 2:36–8).

A Jewish scholar unhesitatingly describes Simeon and Anna as 'the two Essene saints' and Josephus records an incident only ten years after the Nativity when 'Simon, a man of the sect of the Essenes', accurately predicts the banishment of Herod's son, Archelaus (Josephus, *Antiquities of the Jews*, Book 7, Chapter 13, Section 3). Following so closely on Luke's miraculous Nativity, in these resoundingly Jewish passages Joseph and Mary are promised a momentous Messianic destiny for their son. Yet only ten verses later, when Luke's Jesus is twelve and shows precocious religious learning after being accidentally left behind at Jerusalem's Temple, his worried parents are mystified when he asks them: 'Why did you look for me? Didn't you know that I must be involved in my Father's concerns?' (*Luke* 2:49).

Luke tells us, 'they did not understand the words he spoke to them', and that 'his mother carefully kept all these sayings in her heart' (*Luke* 2:50–51), reactions that sit very strangely with what has supposedly preceded this incident. It is *just* credible that the encounters with Simeon and Anna had so little impact; but it is utterly inconceivable that the angel Gabriel's announcement of Mary's divine pregnancy could have left her so unprepared for what she now hears. Luke has further discredited his own narrative.

✝✝✝

In *Matthew*, after the Nativity, Joseph is warned in a miraculous dream (a favourite device of this Gospeller) and escapes the Massacre of the Innocents by taking Mary and their infant son to Egypt. Portrayed in Apocrypha and religious art as an epic Nileside journey among pyramids, it took only three days' southward travel from Bethlehem to reach Egypt's border at the broad valley of the Wadi El Arish, which offered refuge for Jewish fugitives. The chaos in Judah surrounding the dying days of Herod's reign would have been enough to prompt such a journey, though, perhaps surprisingly, the fourth-century pagan writer, Macrobius, refers to 'the two-year-old children butchered by Herod in Syria' (*Saturnalia*, 2,4,11), Judah then being part of Roman Syria. Unfortunately, one must suspect that the Flight to Egypt simply enables the infant Jesus to emulate Moses in the return journey to the Promised Land (a suspicion underlined by one of Matthew's 'prophecies'). The reign of Herod's son Archelaus in Judah impels Joseph to trek far north and settle in Nazareth under the more benevolent rule of another son, Herod Antipas. For Luke, there are no such complications. In his Gospel, after the registration in Bethlehem and the birth of Jesus, the family simply return to their home in Nazareth.

What can we make of it all? Stripped of the unsupported (and self-contradicted) miraculous elements, the registration is possible, the birth in Bethlehem and the Journey of the Magi are possible, the Flight to Egypt is possible. Yet many scholars believe that Mary and Joseph lived in Nazareth, that Jesus was born in Nazareth and that the family simply continued to live there. It seems that on this question at least, the jury will be out for eternity.

There is one near-certainty — that from early childhood, at least, Joshua lived in Nazareth, a small and obscure village in Lower Galilee, built across a southern slope in a semi-circle of fourteen stony hills opening onto a valley that wound down to the valley-plain of Jezreel. Houses of white stone, some of them two-storeyed, were dug into the hillside, with cooking alcoves, silos, olive presses, mangers, cisterns, and storerooms cut from the limestone. A haphazard mesh of stone fences, terraces and laneways strung the little settlement together and a bountiful spring in a western gully provided water — the one feature of present-day Nazareth that can be confidently dated to Joshua's time.

Joshua was, as Luke says, the 'firstborn' (*Luke* 2:7); and, as Paul tells us, 'firstborn among many brothers' (*Romans* 8:29). The Gospels record that Joseph and Mary had four other sons: James (Jacob), Joses (Joseph), Simon (Simeon) and Jude (Judah or Judas); and there were also at least two daughters (*Matthew* 13:55; *Mark* 6:3). Joshua was the eldest in a family of seven children, possibly more. Attempts to 'prove' that the brothers and sisters were in fact cousins (an inspiration of St Jerome) are sad products of the Perpetual Virgin cult.

Joshua was probably a teenager when the last of his brothers and sisters were born, a fact that illuminates his demonstrated love of children and his ability as a storyteller. The small stone house in Nazareth was a warm crucible in which a remarkable life was nurtured; the house no different from those around it, the life apparently with nothing yet to mark it as exceptional. Yet forces within that house and from far beyond it were already at work to shape an extraordinary destiny.

✝✝✝

Note

Holden was apparently unaware that, about 200 AD, the Church father, Clement of Alexandria, recorded a tradition that Jesus was born 'on the 25th of the month of Panchon' — about 20 May — one week from the date calculated by Holden in 1975. Regarding this date, the English astronomer David Hughes and the Australian astrologer Rudolf Smit both opt for a mid-conjunction rising of Jupiter and Saturn on September 15 as marking the birth of Jesus. Smith rejects Holden's conjunction of 27 May because the planets rose two hours before the sun and therefore the phenomenon was not a true 'heliacal rising'. Yet Smit's and Hughes's preferred date marked an evening event. The planets rose in the east while the sun was setting on the opposite horizon — an 'acronychal rising' — the direct antithesis of the phenomenon described by Matthew.

December 25 did not emerge as the birthdate of Jesus until Rome became Christian in the fourth century. The midwinter festival of the god Mithras on 25 December was a popular Roman feast, a highlight of the Saturnalia. It was shamelessly adopted as Christ's birthday. As we will see, this was not Christianity's only borrowing from Mithraism.

The broader issue of Christian dating was hopelessly confused in 525 AD when a monk called Dyonyius Exiguus (Denis the Little) was given the job of rearranging the Church calendar. He calculated that Christ had been born in the Roman year 754, which became Year One of the new era. Yet Herod had died in 750 and, as we have seen, Joshua was probably born some three years before this. Little Denis had blundered by at least four years and probably by seven years in fixing the start of our era. As a result, we entered the new millennium, without fanfare, in the early 1990s.

CHAPTER 3

Joshua's World

Joshua was born into a world dominated by two opposing imperatives — the rule of God and the rule of Rome. Supposedly in the last week of his life, he acknowledged these rival claims to his allegiance in words that have been widely interpreted through the millennia:

> 'Give back to Caesar the things that are Caesar's, and the things that are God's to God.'
> (*Luke* 20:25)

At that time he is also said to have predicted that Jerusalem and its magnificent temple — the shrine of Israel's God — would be destroyed, as indeed they were, only thirty-seven years later. Most scholars accept the account of Joshua's prediction as authentic, albeit because Jewish religious nationalism made conflict with Rome both inevitable and imminent; and even the prophet Zechariah's vision of eventual Jewish triumph had accepted that it would follow the sack of Jerusalem. Joshua, like many men of his time, believed that the Jewish world was on the brink of a final conflict in which the Jews would be the allies of God in subjection of his enemies and establishment of his rule over all the earth.

Ever since the golden days of King David and his son, King Solomon, Israel had looked to a leader who would pave the way for God's kingdom on earth — a descendant of David who came to be called 'the Anointed', in Hebrew *Mashiach* — 'Messiah'. Prophets like Jeremiah, Ezekiel and Daniel spoke of him (Daniel being first to use the title 'Messiah'), and, as the centuries passed, Jewish scholars searched the scriptures for further clues to the time and circumstances of his coming. The Talmud, a vast treasury of Judaic oral law, records many heated debates among the sages and Rabbis (one exchange condemns attempts to foretell the Messiah's arrival then proceeds to do just that). As the subjection of the Jewish people to a series of conquerors continued, the role of a Messiah became more compelling, more complex; the looked-to Messianic age became more perfect, even though it might follow cosmic warfare. Yet always, the Messiah was a man, divinely sanctioned to fulfill a divine purpose — the redemption and final triumph of Israel in a world ruled by God. Now, under the rule of Rome, the Messiah must confront this ultimate barrier to God's universal kingship, this ultimate challenge to belief in Israel's God-ordained destiny and the fulfilment of 2000 years of Jewish history.

The remarkable saga that shaped Joshua's world, his life and his death, had begun with a covenant between the nomadic patriarch Abraham and God — a promise of God's support for Abraham and his descendants in return for their obedience to the divine will, symbolised by males being circumcised. The Covenant was renewed while Moses led the Children of Israel from Egypt in a mysterious forty-year Exodus to the Promised Land. During that journey Moses gave them the Law, built on the Ten Commandments delivered to him by God on Mount Sinai, and developed in an extraordinarily detailed code of 613 laws which governed every aspect of life: religious, moral, social, financial — even medical. Contrary to the repeated claims of the 'Apostle' Paul, this was the Law Joshua would uphold all his life, the Law he regarded as inviolate. He would argue over its interpretation but never question its central role in human obedience to God.

The Mosaic code was embodied in five books of *Torah* (Learning) that provided the core of the Bible. Two other sections would be added, *nebiim* (prophets) and *ketubim* (writings), initial letters of the three sections, T, N and K, providing the acronym *Tanakh* for the Hebrew scriptures.

Moses' successor, the first Joshua (so named by Moses), led the Twelve Tribes of Israel across the Jordan River in their conquest of the land of Canaan. By the eleventh century BC, a loose confederacy of the tribes spread over much of what is now Israel and part of Jordan. Under the first kings, Saul (who suffered a very bad press), David and Solomon, they won further territory.

King David established his capital in a captured highland stronghold between the fertile coastal land and the broad, deep valley of the Jordan River. Here, a mysterious priest king called Melchizedek, who ruled over the miniature city state of Salem, had been hospitable to the patriarch Abraham when he went there in pursuit of cattle thieves. The name of Melchizedek will have meaning in the story of Joshua/Jesus — quite apart from the fact that the priest king's ancient hill city became David's Jerusalem.

King Solomon, son of David, built a magnificent temple there to replace the nomadic tabernacle that had accompanied the Israelites on their journey to nationhood. To the Jews, Jerusalem became the centre of their land, its magnificent temple the heart of Judaism, the place where God's presence (the *Shekinah*) sanctified an inner chamber called the Holy of Holies. On a huge altar in the temple court, priests sacrificed cattle, sheep, goats and pigeons in daily worship of God and in a cycle of festivals that observed the agricultural seasons and commemorated milestones of Jewish faith and history. Most important of these were the three pilgrim festivals that summoned all adult male Jews to Jerusalem.

The Passover (*Pesach*), inaugurating the Feast of Unleavened Bread, was in early spring, celebrating the liberation from Egypt and the start of planting. Summer's Feast of Weeks (*Shavuoth*) marked the wheat harvest and the giving of the Law on Mount Sinai. The Feast of Tabernacles or Booths (*Sukkoth*), inaugurated by the Day of Atonement (*Yom Kippur*), was an autumn vintage festival, also honouring the wilderness encampment of the Israelites during the Exodus.

✝✝✝

After the death of Solomon, his realm was divided into a southern kingdom of Judah, based on Jerusalem, and a northern kingdom, Israel, with its capital at Shechem (Samaria).

Ever since Abraham and Moses, Judaism had been marked by men and women who communicated with God. Such a person was usually given the generic name *nabi* (perhaps 'spokesman'), translated as 'prophet', even though a Hebrew prophet's activities went far beyond mere prediction of the future. 'Prophet' is the only title that Joshua readily applied to himself, in full knowledge that a false claim to this role was punishable by death; and that even true prophets followed a dangerous path. Joshua spoke of Jerusalem, 'killing the prophets and stoning those who are sent to her' (*Matthew* 23:37).

Prophets made many enemies. They were often radical critics of Jewish rulers, like Nathan, at the elbow of King David, and Elijah, who dogged King Ahab. Some, such as Isaiah and Micah, stressed that observing the ritual of sacrifice did not compensate for a lack of genuine piety and sense of social justice; others, like Jeremiah, railed against Jewish society at large when it fell short of its obligations to the Covenant. The prophets showed concern for the poor and harshly criticised the rich, often equating poverty with virtue, wealth with greed. They became the conscience of Judah and Israel, predicting dire punishment for their people's rebelliousness against God.

That punishment fell on the northern kingdom in the seventh century BC, when it was conquered by Assyria and its population deported — the ten Lost Tribes. Judah narrowly escaped conquest by Assyria but was overrun by Babylon in the fifth century. Its people too were marched off to exile in Babylon; Jerusalem and the Temple were destroyed.

In an extraordinary display of resilience, Jewish religion and culture flourished in Babylon. When the great city and its empire fell to Cyrus of Persia sixty years later, most Jews elected to remain there and made it a stronghold of Judaism, while some 40 000 of the tribes of Benjamin and Judah began a new exodus back to Jerusalem. Speaking the Aramaic language they had learnt in Babylon, they accepted the exile as punishment for their rebellion against God, renewed their Covenant with him and worshipped with fresh zeal in the rebuilt Temple under the kingly high priest Joshua, second great figure of that name in Jewish history.

Prominent in the rebirth of Temple Judaism was the prophet Zechariah — almost the last of the line — whose book incorporated some of the most remarkable visions of Messianic triumph and the forging of God's rule on earth. These visions powerfully influenced Joshua in the last week of his life and, perhaps more than any other factor, impelled him on the course of action that led to his death.

† † †

In the third century BC, Alexander the Great advanced through Judah on his conquest of the known world. He and his army were met outside Jerusalem by the people of the city, led by the Temple priesthood and the high priest in full regalia. Impressed, Alexander left Jerusalem untouched; yet his worldwide legacy of Greek language and culture came to represent almost as great a threat to the Jewish nation as did the dynasties created by his generals after his death in 323 BC — the Ptolemies in Egypt (who claimed Judah) and the Seleucids in Syria. The Syrian Greek Seleucids defeated the reigning Ptolemy and won Judah in 198 BC.

Some thirty years later, the Seleucid king Antiochus Epiphanes set out to destroy the religion that made the Jews troublesome subjects. Antiochus desecrated the Temple by setting up an image of the Olympian Zeus and by sacrificing pigs — animals that were ritually 'unclean' to Jews. All over the country, Syrian Greek officers forced Jews to take part in similar sacrifices and eat pig flesh on the threat of being tortured to death. They had become victims of 'the first religious persecution known in history'. A priestly family, the Hasmoneans (nicknamed 'Maccabee', probably from the Aramaic for 'hammer'), rebelled and launched a guerrilla war against the Syrians. After three years of bitter campaigning, the desecrated Temple was won back by Judas Maccabee and cleansed in a triumphant ceremony still honoured by Jews as the Feast of *Hanukkah*.

In thirty years of conflict, the Maccabees gained total victory and reigned over Judah as high priests. After four generations they assumed kingship as the Hasmonean dynasty, even though they were not of the house of David, the true royal lineage.

The dynasty flourished, suppressed a rival form of Judaism in Samaria, then conquered Edom (Idumaea) to the south and Galilee to the north, forcing all non-Jewish males there to be circumcised. All three conquests reverberated in the life of Joshua. Samaritans remained hostile to Temple Judaism and at least once provided shelter for Joshua when he was in conflict with Jerusalem's religious authorities. An Edomite royal family scarred his life from birth to death, and from Galilee he gained his own rebellious spirit as well as his staunchest followers. There were other echoes. The huge death toll from the Maccabees' rebellion and subsequent conflict encouraged belief in resurrection. And the religious differences that emerged in the ranks of the Maccabees' most zealous supporters created three of the major Jewish sects — the Pharisees, Sadducees and Essenes — all devout Jews, yet each group clinging to its own distinct views of what constituted the best way to fulfill Israel's Covenant with God.

The Pharisees, from whom the Rabbis later emerged, and the Essenes, a more ascetic and fanatical sect, looked to a Messiah. Sadducees professed to find little sanction for this idea in scripture and became wary of such a cosmic death blow to the prevailing order. Increasingly, as the group most closely aligned with the Temple authorities and the Jerusalem aristocracy, they had too much to lose. More of these sects later, as their beliefs and interests strike resonance or discord with those of Joshua.

Eventually, with the country torn apart by a Hasmonean squabble over the throne, the two claimants, and the people they sought to rule, all petitioned Rome to intervene. It was a fateful move.

A thousand years earlier when King David was leading Israel to its age of glory, the Romans were obscure barbarian invaders of the Italian peninsula. Now they ruled the world, exporting a vulgarised form of Greek culture that often thinly veiled the barbarism of Rome's origins. Yet to tractable peoples they could be benevolent rulers. In return for substantial taxes collected under a corrupt, privatised system, they allowed political and sometimes religious autonomy under the protection of Rome's awesome military machine.

In response to the initial Jewish overtures, the Roman general Pompey, later rival of Julius Caesar for leadership of Rome, took Judah by force in 63 BC. From that time, it was known by its Roman name, Judaea. Pompey appointed a puppet ruler, with a brilliant Edomite called Antipas (or Antipater) as his right-hand man. As Antipas rose to power, he advanced his son, Herod, as governor of Galilee.

The twenty-five-year-old quickly made his name in the Roman world by moving against 'a large band of men' identified by Josephus as 'robbers' who were making cross-border raids from Galilee into Roman Syria. Although their leader, Hezekiah, was described by Josephus simply as 'captain of a band of robbers', rabbinical sources give a very different picture: 'a righteous man' fighting in a cause 'which the elders of Israel approved of' (*Antiquities*, 14,9,2; *Wars* 1,10,5; *Koheleth Rabbah* 1, 11). Hezekiah's incursions into Syria were not mere banditry; he was reclaiming lost lands of the Davidic kingdom. Herod defeated these Galilean patriots and executed 'a great number' of them without trial, including Hezekiah, but not before Hezekiah had fathered a son called Judas who would impact on the life of Joshua and his family.

Herod was called to trial for murder before Jerusalem's Sanhedrin, the seventy-man council of elders. Instead of following the usual custom of accused men and appearing dressed in black, Herod defied this supreme court of Israel, 'clothed in purple' and accompanied by fully armed soldiers, before escaping to Roman Syria where he was feted as a hero (*Antiquities*, 14, 9, 3).

When Pompey was defeated by Julius Caesar, Herod threw in his lot with Caesar, killed the Hasmonean heirs to the Jewish throne and made a Hasmonean princess one of his ten wives. Out of the shambles that followed the assassination of Julius Caesar, Herod first courted the favour of Marc Antony, then switched allegiance to Antony's victorious opponent Octavian. Herod was crowned as *rex socius* ('associate king') in 37 BC with the blessing of Octavian, who had become Augustus Caesar, Rome's first emperor (a title Julius Caesar had declined, though ironically his name became attached to the office).

Herod was called Herod the Great — largely because he was the first, the oldest of a line of pseudo-kings to bear that name. His reign was marked by crippling taxes, lavish building programs, rampant paranoia and extreme brutality. Herod set the tone for his governance by killing forty-five members of Jerusalem's seventy-man Sanhedrin — the men who had arraigned him for murdering the Galilean patriots. It was more than revenge. He disposed of his harshest critics and created a model that prevailed in Joshua's time — a Sanhedrin allowed considerable independence so long as it did not challenge the ruling power. The conservative Sadducees accepted this as a means to maintain their status and wealth; the liberal Pharisees conformed more reluctantly, as a means to further their religious agenda for Israel.

Under Herod, Graeco–Roman culture thrived, culmination of an age in which Jews embraced the Greek way, some even undergoing operations to reverse circumcision. There had been a high priest called Jason (like 'Jesus', a Greek translation of Joshua), and even the names of such paradigmatic Jewish institutions as the Sanhedrin and the synagogue were derived from Greek. Transformed by Herod's building boom, Jerusalem soon had an open-air, Greek-style theatre and a Roman-style circus where twelve-horse chariots raced and condemned criminals fought wild beasts. These pagan innovations were only partly offset by Herod's vast programme to rebuild and enlarge the Temple — a project that continued for more than sixty years. In a symbol of Jewish loathing for Herod, this superb structure was not recognised as the Third Temple. It continued to be described as the Second Temple, modestly rebuilt five hundred years before under Joshua, the kingly high priest. When conspirators planned to murder Herod, the man who betrayed the plotters and saved the tyrant's life was torn to pieces by an enraged citizenry and fed to dogs.

It was in the last, tortuous years of Herod's thirty-three-year reign that Joshua was born. Whether or not it is factual, the Gospel story of Herod's role in the Nativity is completely true to character. He would fear the house of David as neurotically as he feared the Hasmonean line — a neurosis that led him to murder his Hasmonean queen, Mariamne, and the two sons born to her. It is a measure of his ruthlessness that he had truly loved Mariamne; a measure of his near-insanity that, after her death, he had servants call her name along the echoing halls of his Jerusalem palace.

In 4 BC, when Joshua was only three, Herod's poetically just and lingering death from natural causes signalled anarchy in Judaea. The people of Israel did not want a Herodian dynasty; the name of Herod was so despised that no Jew would be permitted to mourn or fast, for any reason, on the anniversary of his death.

Herod's will divided his realm between three of his sons — Archelaus, Herod Antipas and Philip. Archelaus, who was allotted the major share — Judaea, Samaria and Edom (Idumaea) — quickly showed himself a true son of his father by slaughtering 3000 protesters at Jerusalem's Passover festival.

When Archelaus went to Rome in a bid to gain his father's entire kingdom, Herod Antipas, who had been willed Galilee and Peraea (Transjordan), sailed in pursuit with a rival claim, while 'a great and wild fury spread itself over the nation, because they had no king to keep the multitude in good order' (Josephus, *Antiquities*, 17, 10, 6).

Herod's winter palace at Jericho was destroyed and part of Jerusalem's Temple burnt in full-scale warfare between rebels and a Roman legion sent from Syria. Only five kilometres from Nazareth, Judas of Galilee, son of the executed rebel patriot Hezekiah, seized the armoury and treasury at Herod's palace in the capital city of Sepphoris. With money, arms and popular support, Judas and his followers made the city theirs, a first step in his bid to reclaim the Jewish crown from Roman puppets.

Rome moved quickly. Two more legions were hurried into Judaea, the rebellion was crushed and 2000 rebels were crucified. Sepphoris was burnt, its population sold into slavery. One of Joshua's earliest memories would have been the smoke of burning Sepphoris; the flames of the dying capital were visible from the crest of the hill above Nazareth. And Joseph might have taken Joshua to see some of the bodies of Judas's men nailed to crosses along the roads to the devastated city, honouring their deaths as Jewish patriots and confronting the ugly face of Roman domination. It seems more than coincidence that three of Joseph's sons carried the names of Judas and his rebel sons, Simon and Jacob (James), particularly since two of these brothers of Joshua grew to manhood as Zealots, members of the fanatical religio-patriotic sect spawned by Judas in his Galilean uprising.

The historian Josephus, who was to command the men of Galilee in a later revolt against Rome, spoke highly of their fighting mettle and commented, 'the Galileans are inured to war from their infancy' (Josephus, *Wars of the Jews*, 3,3,2). Coupled with their unorthodox and often charismatic religious zeal, it is not surprising that Galileans were regarded with wariness by Judaeans, especially at festival time in Jerusalem where their notorious 'north country' accents identified them as potential troublemakers. It was in this breeding ground of saintly rebels and rebellious saints, in a village which seems to have gained special notoriety, that Joseph and Mary had set about raising their growing family.

✝✝✝

With rebellion crushed, Augustus Caesar confirmed Herod's sons in their princedoms. Herod Antipas, tetrarch (ruler) of Galilee, almost immediately set about rebuilding Sepphoris as his capital, a godsend for a tradesman like Joseph with a growing family of sons in a village only an hour's journey from a vast construction project that would create a walled city of 30 000 people. It was very much a Graeco-Roman metropolis and, in his most impressionable years, young Joshua would have spent much of his time there, possibly learning to speak Greek.

While working on Sepphoris's 4000-seat theatre, perhaps while helping to build the wooden, 52-metre-wide stage, he could have learnt the Greek word *hypokrites* — a stage actor, masked or made up to seem someone he was not. It was an image Joshua would apply with poetic venom to some of his enemies; the Gospels quote him using the word seventeen times. (There is no equivalent in Hebrew or Aramaic.) Archaeologist James Strange, a key figure in the excavation of the city, was particularly struck by *Matthew 6:5*.

> 'And when you pray, you will not be like the hypocrites, for they love to pray standing in the synagogues and at the corners of the streets, so that they can display themselves before men ...'

The Greek word used here for 'streets', *plateion*, means specifically 'colonnaded streets', such as Joshua would have seen in Sepphoris. Linked with the image of the hypocrite, it places the speaker squarely in the setting of this luxurious, hilltop city, with its markets, shops, fountains, public baths, central bank and royal palace.

More than fifty years after Madeleine and Lane Miller linked this Nazareth family of tradesmen with the rebirth of Sepphoris, modern scholars rightly reject the image of Joseph and his sons as 'humble carpenters' and accept that they were probably also builders.

The Greek word used in the Gospels to describe Joseph and Joshua, *tekton*, means a worker in wood or stone, possibly translated from the Aramaic *naggar*, whose meaning could be broadened to a master of any craft or even a branch of learning. There have been attempts to leap from this fact to a complete rejection of the 'tradesman' image. Jesus becomes the scholarly son of a well-to-do family, a member of the burgher class. There seems only a germ of truth here. True, an Apocryphal text gives Joseph a vineyard, which *could* explain the amount of viticultural detail in Joshua's teaching; and Joshua's brother James wrote of riding a horse as a ready-to-hand image. Yet Justin Martyr, a native of neighbouring Samaria, later recorded that, about 120 AD, ploughs and oxen yolks made by Joshua were still in existence (*Dialogue with Trypho*, 88). It was the worker of stone and wood who found God's blessing in hard physical labour: 'Split a piece of wood, I am there. Lift a stone and you will find me there.' According to the *Gospel of Thomas* (sayings 77 and 58), he declared, 'Blessed is the toiler' (in Australia, a truer translation would be 'Blessed is the battler').

Long before he started to learn his father's trades, Joshua's Hebrew education had begun. As the Talmud has it, 'As soon as the child can speak, his father teaches him the Torah' (*Tosefta Sukkah* 42a). Probably the first text he ever learnt was the *Shema*, the Mosaic statement of faith that opened every Sabbath service in the synagogue, 'Hear, O Israel, the Lord our God, the Lord is one' (*Deuteronomy* 6:4). Typically, a child would start to study the Torah in Hebrew at five or six years of age. Within a year formal schooling would begin under a system of universal and compulsory education that had been developing for some seventy years — almost certainly the first programme of its kind in history.

Nazareth's synagogue, at the highest point of the village, probably facing a small marketplace, was simply a house where the people met on the Sabbath to pray and participate in readings from the Torah and the Prophets — an institution that had developed during exile in Babylon. Services were led by the 'president' or 'ruler' (*archon*), an unpaid layman who followed his trade during the week. He was assisted by a full-time *chazzan*, a sort of curate, who took part in the Sabbath services and conducted a school in the building. The *beth ha-keneset*, House of Meeting, was also a *beth ha-sefer*, House of the Book, where boys studied first the Torah, then the Prophets and Writings.

For some seven years, young Joshua studied the Hebrew scriptures and began to form a relationship with the God of Israel. Then the last pieces of his world mosaic fitted into their destined places.

In a rare display of unanimity that illuminates the scale of the problem, Judaea and Samaria petitioned Augustus Caesar for removal of Herod's son Archelaus as their ruler. Augustus banished him to Gaul, but instead of granting his domain to his brothers, Antipas or Philip, he made Judaea and Samaria part of Syria and appointed a prefect to govern these new subjects of Rome. The first prefect, Coponius, established his capital at Caesarea on the

Samaritan coast, only 50 kilometres from Nazareth, and was allocated some 3000 troops — about half a legion — to establish his authority. They were soon needed.

As an essential prelude to Roman taxation, the Syrian legate, Quirinius, conducted his famous census of the new provinces. Declaring that, 'this taxation was no better than an introduction to slavery' (*Antiquities*, 18, 1, 1), Judas of Galilee and his Zealots again rose in short-lived rebellion. He was killed, his men scattered. This was 6 AD; Joshua was thirteen. He left boyhood with the Jewish heartland of Judaea under Roman rule.

True, Galilee was still ruled by Herod Antipas; but wealthy, conservative and cosmopolitan Sepphoris — sited as it was in the very heart of rebel country — had a semi-permanent Roman military presence (even little Capernaum on the shores of Galilee's Lake Kinneret had eighty men under a centurion) and no part of Israel reacted more strongly to displays of Roman authority. Judas of Galilee was dead; more of his men were nailed to crosses. But the spirit of Judas was kept alive there by his Zealot movement and by his three sons. Simon and Jacob would be crucified by a Roman prefect before the great revolt of 66 AD, but that year a third son, Menahem, was to capture the Roman fortress of Masada, besiege Jerusalem and take the Temple before being defeated and executed. Even then, the line of Judas was not extinguished. A nephew, Eleazar, would lead the Zealots' defence of Masada against a Roman siege — to this day a supreme symbol of Jewish defiance.

While the story of this Galilean rebel dynasty is well known, a key detail escapes attention. Judas had shown, according to Josephus, 'an ambitious desire of the royal dignity' (*Antiquities*, 17, 10, 5). This seems to contradict the Zealot philosophy, 'that God is to be their only ruler and lord' (*Antiquities* 18, 1, 6). Yet Judas's son, Menahem, advanced on Jerusalem 'in the state of a king' and, after capturing the Temple, went to worship there, 'adorned with royal garments, and had his followers with him in their armour' (*Wars*, 2, 17, 8 and 9). Judas was a sage and teacher; in the next century he would have been called a Rabbi. It seems that the claims to 'royal dignity' made by him and by his son could only have been based on the fact that they belonged to the House of David; and that their aim was to establish God's rule, to bring about the day when 'the Lord shall be King over all the earth; in that day the Lord shall be one and his name one' (*Zechariah* 14:9). They saw themselves as Messiahs, establishing the kingdom over which God would reign, just as Simon bar Kochbar of the House of David would lead the last great Jewish war against Rome, hailed as a Messiah and ruling as 'prince'.

The chain of coincidence stretches further. Joseph also belonged to the House of David, lived at the epicentre of Judas's rebellion, named three of his sons after this Messianic rebel dynasty and two of them emerged as followers of Judas's Zealot movement. Joshua grew to manhood in a household linked geographically, philosophically and by blood to the mainstream of Galilean rebellion against Rome.

At thirteen, Joshua would have started to attend classes at the synagogue's *beth ha-midrash*, usually translated, rather inadequately, as 'house of learning'. *Midrash* is the Jewish process of investigating the meaning of scripture and searching out interpretations which underlie a literal meaning. A rabbinical explanation of *Midrash* likens it to a hammer, 'which splits the rock of Torah into many pieces'. In this phase of his education, Joshua learnt the oral Torah, the vast body of law and tradition, preserved by the Pharisees, which amplified and extended the Tanakh and was set down in coming centuries as the Mishnah and the Talmud. As we will see, Joshua was a diligent student and obviously gained valuable experience in the spirited debates that characterised Pharisaic study in both *haggadah* (Law) and *halakkah* Tradition).

The Gospels present a confused and confusing picture of their Jesus as a bitter opponent of the Pharisees, yet he honours their wisdom in his teaching, time and time again. He is treated with respect by many Pharisees, who entertain him as a dinner guest, warn him of danger, honour him in death and form a significant group among the earliest Christians. Joshua was taught *by* Pharisees and he taught *as* a Pharisee. Of all the labels that might be applied to him, identification of him as a Pharisee is probably the most all-embracing and yet the hardest for Christians to accept, conditioned as they are by the Gospel portrait of the Pharisees as vindictive, hidebound hypocrites — a serious distortion of the truth. There is a good reason for this. Sadducees — the more wealthy and aristocratic class closely aligned with Jerusalem's priesthood — were desperate to avoid conflict with Rome. The Pharisees were less prone to compromise with any ruler, be it a fanatical Hasmonean, Herod the Great or the Romans. Significantly, the co-founder of the Zealot movement was a Pharisee called Zadok and the Zealots remained a militant wing of Pharisaism. So when Christianity was gaining strength in the Graeco-Roman world and the Jewish revolt of 66–73 AD made the Jews arch-enemies of Rome, Pharisees, the great popular leaders of

Israel, were also portrayed as enemies of the Gospels' Jesus. His arguments with more extreme representatives of the movement were exaggerated; other disputes were invented. Jesus was shown adopting essentially Pharisaic positions against attacks on him which no Pharisee could have made.

Three Gospels show Jesus making only one visit to Jerusalem during his ministry. Some scholars accept this as accurate — in spite of the fact that observant homeland Jews visited Jerusalem for three pilgrim festivals each year and even Jews of the dispersion voyaged or travelled to Jerusalem for Passover. I see no reason to doubt that, from childhood, Joshua and his family regularly visited the sacred capital of Israel, travelling in family and parochial caravans down the Jordan Valley to Jericho, then making the 40-kilometre, 1000-metre climb up through the *Midbar Yehudah*, the Wilderness of Judaea, across the Mount of Olives and the Kidron Valley to the spine of the range where Jerusalem crowned its ridge, walled and magnificent, dominated by the Temple.

The historian, Josephus, born only seven years after Joshua's death, gives a vivid picture of the Temple as he knew it. He tells us how it seemed, at a distance, 'like a mountain covered with snow; those parts of it that were not gilt, were exceeding white'. The square facade of the building was 50 metres high, 'covered all over with plates of gold of great weight, and at the first rising of the sun, reflected back a very fiery splendour, and made those who forced themselves to look upon it to turn their eyes away, just as they would have done at the sun's own rays' (*Wars* 5, 5, 6).

In front of this magnificent centrepiece stood the altar, 7 metres high, with a ramp for priests carrying up the sacrifices which were offered on its constantly burning fires. Four towering golden candlesticks, each with four lamps, were set around this inner Court of the Priests. Separated by a balustrade was the Court of Israel, where Jewish men could attend. Past a gate in a row of columns, and fifteen steps lower, was the Court of Women. Then beyond another colonnade and a bank of fourteen steps was the Court of Gentiles that surrounded the whole Temple complex. This was a vast, paved area, the size of several city blocks, built on a terrace that extended from the level of the Temple Mount out over the valleys to each side, and towered over surrounding streets and buildings. This huge court, in turn, was bordered by roofed colonnades of marble columns more than 12 metres high.

One of the wonders of the Temple was the southern colonnade — the Royal Stoa — 162 pillars in four lines, creating a broad, 200-metre nave with aisles to either side and an intricately carved and gabled cedar ceiling

30 metres above the paved floor. The western end of the stoa, reached by a monumental staircase, looked out on the Upper City which rose from the Valley of Cheesemongers and up the slope of Mount Zion, in Josephus's words, 'in the manner of a theatre'. The far, eastern end of the stoa was at the corner of the Temple terrace above the Kidron Valley. Here, like Josephus, young Joshua would have been fascinated by the sense of altitude, commonplace to modern city dwellers, but a rare experience in the first century.

> While the valley was very deep, and its bottom could not be seen, if you looked from above into the depth, this further vastly high elevation of the cloister stood upon that height, insomuch that if anyone looked down from the top of the battlements, or down both these altitudes, he would be giddy, while his sight could not reach to such an immense depth.   (*Antiquities*, 15,11,5)

Only one thing marred the glory of the Temple. Built onto the colonnade at its north-west corner was the Antonia — a onetime palace redeveloped by Herod the Great as a palatial fortress — a classic, square castle with four battlemented towers. Now that a Roman prefect governed Judaea, the Antonia housed a Roman garrison — 1000 troops including Samaritan cavalry. This permanent force was reinforced by an extra cohort of 500 to 1000 soldiers for the pilgrim festivals when Jerusalem could hold up to 300 000 people; a time when Jewish religious nationalism was at its most volatile, especially at Passover and the Feast of Unleavened Bread, celebrating the Israelites' liberation from Egypt. For this feast the prefect made it his custom to travel up from Caesarea and occupy Herod the Great's Palace at the highpoint of the Upper City. Roman–Jewish tension at festival time was heightened by the unpalatable fact that the high priest's garments were held under guard in the Antonia and had to be retrieved for seven days' purification before they could be worn (*Antiquities*, 18, 4, 3). Perhaps the practice also served as a reminder that the high priest himself was appointed (and subject to dismissal) by the Roman prefect.

From the time when Joshua could first join his father in the Court of Israel he would have been aware of the overshadowing presence of the Antonia; the strident notes of the *cornu*, the Roman military trumpet, constantly sounding its defiance of the Jewish ram's horn and the priests' silver trumpets; and the movement of troops up and down twin staircases between the fortress and the Court of Gentiles.

These were not Roman legionaries; they were auxiliaries, men recruited from conquered countries — Samaritans, Syrians and Syro-Phoenecians —

commanded by Roman centurions and senior officers. They did not wear the banded armour and red-plumed helmet so familiar from hundreds of paintings, plays and films. Theirs was the uniform of an earlier age — wool tunic with a short-sleeved shirt of chain mail and 'sporran' of metal-studded leather straps to protect the genitals. They wore the auxiliary's unplumed helmet of bronze or iron, had shortsword and dagger slung on a belt, carried a javelin, a huge, semi-cylindrical shield, and clashed across the paved courts in hobnailed sandal boots. In the cooler months of the year they added tight, calf-length breeches. Like the tunic, these were red, to help hide blood that might encourage an enemy. Such were the soldiers young Joshua would come to accept as part of Jerusalem's festival scene; such soldiers would initiate his execution and stand by him as he died.

✝✝✝

Another twenty-three years passed in the cycles of seasons and festivals. The Gospels are silent on them, apart from the closing verse of Luke's prologue:

And Jesus developed in wisdom and stature and favour with God and men.

(Luke 2:52)

Luke has directly quoted the description of the prophet Samuel's boyhood (1 Samuel 2:26); he has already echoed the prayer of Samuel's mother, Hannah, in Mary's *Magnificat*. Yet, as Luke himself will demonstrate, through these twenty-three years Joshua showed no signs of being a prophet; he gave no reason for people to see him as anything but a deeply religious young tradesman, son of a tradesman, brother of tradesmen.

Theories rush in to fill the vacuum of these years — perhaps most notably that Joshua travelled to Tibet and studied the teaching of Buddha, to be revered in Tibetan writings as Saint Issa; but no extant Tibetan texts support such a notion.

We can say with confidence that Joshua spent most of his time among the people of Galilee, observing their foibles, sharing their pleasures in simple food and wine and storytelling, travelling the roads of this bountiful province, among the orchards, groves and vineyards of the hills and the hesperidean richness of the sub-tropical lands by Lake Kinneret, where, according to Josephus, grapes and figs hung on the trees ten months of the year. Called in the Gospels the Sea of Galilee, Kinneret was a harp-shaped body of water, whose name echoed *Kinnor*, Hebrew for 'harp'. The lake was 21 kilometres long by 12 kilometres at its broadest point, fed by the Jordan, tempered by hot springs and teeming with fish. Near some of these springs, Herod Antipas created a luxurious resort city, Tiberias, dominated by his golden-roofed palace. No matter that he had sited his city on an ancient burial ground and that one of Jewry's great dreads was contact with corpses, graves or tombs that could incur 'corpse impurity'. Settlers were bribed or forced to inhabit the place and it thrived, though Joshua — like other devout Jews — probably avoided the city.

On the far, eastern shore of Kinneret was the Decapolis, a confederation of ten Gentile cities. To the north, snow-crowned Mount Hermon reigned over the source of the Jordan; to the south, at the pointed end of Kinneret's harp, the Jordan River escaped on its journey to extinction in the Dead Sea.

Lake Kinneret, which would become the heart of Joshua's teaching ministry, also defined his world. Hundreds of thousands — Jews to the west, Gentiles to the east — lived around its shores. Industries thrived — glass making, pottery, fish farming, ship building, silk spinning, weaving, dyeing. Fleets of fishing boats plied Kinneret's waters to supply the district's tables and meet the huge demands of a fish-preserving industry that served all of Israel and most of the Roman world. And a remarkable range of produce poured from the lake's hinterland: beans, rice, millet, meadow berries, melons, shallots, crab apples, cucumbers, onions, white figs, Persian figs, endives, leeks, carob, cauliflower, chick peas — and, of course, a cornucopian flow of wheat, olives and grapes. It was said: 'It is easier for a man to feed a legion on the olives of Galilee than one infant in the rest of Israel' (*Genesis Rabbah* 20:6). The bounties of Galilee led to overpopulation. In the words of Josephus:

> The cities lie here very thick; and the very many villages there are here [else-where he speaks of 240 towns and villages] are everywhere so full of people by the richness of their soil, that *the very least of them contains above fifteen thousand inhabitants*. [my italics]　　　　　　　　　　　　　　　　　　　(*Wars*, 3,3,2)

This is probably one of Josephus's characteristic mega number errors and he means fifteen *hundred*, but the fact of overpopulation remains. Antipas's development of Tiberias as a new capital near the already-prosperous lake-side centre of Magdala — while Sepphoris still thrived in the hills — meant that no town or village in Galilee was now more than 24 kilometres from a city of some 30 000 people. A Roman pattern of regional urban development was being repeated. To feed these growing populations, subsistence farming gave way to cash crops and many small holdings were consolidated in large estates often owned by Sadducees and priests, though some Pharisees also appeared as 'landed gentry'. Even though a typical Galilean estate remained 'a field, a vineyard and an olive grove', the Mishnah would speak of a Rabbi owning 'one hundred vineyards, one hundred fields' (*Leviticus Rabbah*, 30, 1; *Shabbath* 25b). Often, absentee landlords operated through tenant farmers.

Extremes of wealth and poverty were less marked than in Judaea, but the pattern was the same: the big man thrived, the little man was pushed to the wall, all under a big-spending, increasingly centralised regime that could take half a family's annual income in taxation — poll tax, property tax, taxes on meat, bread, roads, houses. Debt became endemic, loan sharks thrived. Farmers borrowed impossibly on their property and lost it to creditors, with their debts still not covered. At best, they would battle to survive as labourers or tenant farmers; at worst, they and their families would be sold into slavery, a cruel cycle with which Joshua proved to be familiar.

On top of it all, the distant Temple required its regular contributions of sacrificial birds and animals, payment of tithes on produce and an annual temple tax. And everywhere Galileans could see the steady erosion of Jewish culture, with Romanised architecture, dress, decoration and lifestyle as constant reminders that, while nominally subjects of a Jewish princeling, they were under the ultimate rule of an indomitable foreign power whose emperor had taken on the status of a God.

These were the dark undercurrents of the world in which Joshua passed his twenties and early thirties, far removed from the world Israel's God intended for his people, the world his prophets had envisaged — a world of justice and peace where God ruled with infinite power and infinite love. Small wonder that Israel looked to a Messiah more keenly with every year; and on every Sabbath in every synagogue in the Jewish world, they offered the prayer:

> Speedily cause the offspring of David, thy servant, to flourish,
> And let his horn be exalted by thy salvation,
> Because we wait for thy salvation all the day.
> Blessed art thou, O Lord, who causest the horn of salvation to flourish.
>
> (*Benediction* 15)

For some, these words were simply part of the Sabbath liturgy. But for most, they burned in the soul. According to some sages, the Messiah had been born, and was living his life, unrecognised, unaware of his destiny until the prophet Elijah returned to the earth and anointed him. It was a beautiful thought; like an extra cup of wine and an open door at the Passover meal always awaiting Elijah's return, always offering the promise, the possibility. Perhaps not this year, but now, perhaps within a lifetime.

CHAPTER 4

Private and Public Lives

Given Nazareth's obscurity, it seems almost fanciful to recover details of Joshua's life there during the years of Gospel silence. Yet it was in this village that the very core of his teaching, the driving force of his ministry, was shaped. It was here, through the written and oral Torah, that he absorbed the wisdom of the prophets and sages to illuminate and be illuminated by his experience of the world beyond the fourteen stony hills and the green valley that pointed the way south to Jerusalem. Above all, it was in the obscurity of Nazareth that he developed an extraordinary intimacy with his God.

Joshua came to think of God — and to address him — as 'Abba', an Aramaic word that falls almost indefinably between 'Daddy' and 'Father', neither as childish as the one nor as formal as the other. It is a word that slips easily from a baby's lips and carries into adult life the earliest associations of warmth, protection, belonging and an implicit depth of love and respect. 'My beloved father' is too stiff, but touches the meaning.

This level of intimacy with God was almost unique in Judaism. Of course, God the Father is a definitive Jewish image and the Jewish scholar Vermes suggests that a similar intimacy was characteristic of Galilean *hasidim* (charismatic holy men) like Hanina ben Dosa and Honi ha-meaggel (the *Circle Drawer*). Yet there is no evidence that either man called God 'Abba'. Honi's grandson, Hanan ha-Nehba, certainly *referred to* God as 'Abba'. When some children pleaded with him, 'Abba, give us rain!', Hanan said, 'Lord of the Universe, render a service to those who cannot distinguish between the Abba who gives rain and the Abba who does not' (*Ta'anith* 23b). This is charming — and intriguing, because there have been attempts to identify Hanan as John the Baptist; but there is a universe of difference between a devout Jew using 'Abba' in this whimsical way in front of children and making it his personal form of address to God.

Joshua's use of 'Abba' may link with a key mystery of his life — the disappearance of his father, Joseph. After describing the family's trip to Jerusalem when Jesus was twelve years old, Luke does not mention Joseph again. Two references in other Gospels cloud the issue.

Early in Joshua's ministry, the people of Nazareth were asking: 'Isn't this the carpenter, the son of Mary ?' (*Mark* 6:3). Some point to this as confirmation that Joshua was a *mamzer*, a bastard, while others see it as saying that Mary was a widow, supposedly confirmed when the dying Joshua appoints 'the beloved disciple' as a son to take Mary into his home (*John* 19:26) — as we will see, an incident open to very different interpretation. However, *John* also supplies what some see as evidence that Joseph was still alive late in Joshua's ministry. Some of his listeners ask: 'Isn't this Jesus, the son of Joseph, whose father and mother we know?' (*John* 6:42). Because 'the Jews' who say this are not from Nazareth, it seems more likely that the passage simply means that Joshua is still called Yeshua bar Yosef (Joshua son of Joseph), that these men from Tiberias and Capernaum know *the identities* of his parents (they could have met Mary) and find it hard to reconcile such a normal Galilean background with John's Jesus making some of his most unlikely and outrageous statements of divinity.

It has been suggested that Joseph divorced Mary after enduring doubts about the conception of his son; but this presupposes either a divine conception or infidelity — with no evidence to support either possibility. It is dangerous to assume that Joshua's unusually strong statements against divorce confirm the theory; we will identify clear 'political' motives for these attacks.

Most commentators consider it likely that Joseph died between Joshua's twelfth year and the beginning of his ministry. My own father lost his father in childhood and told my mother after their wedding, 'It's wonderful to be able to call someone "father" again.' Such a simple, human need could have been the key to Joshua's developing a new intimacy with his God, discovering a new dimension of God the Father; transferring to him all the warmth and love and trust he had shown Joseph; turning to him as a confidant, a guide, a protector. Again, he could call someone 'Abba'.

The relationship could heal the emotional wound of his father's death and create in Joshua an almost physical sense of the *Shekinah*, a loving presence to accompany him in every facet of his life. This would explain how Joshua came to speak of his God in a way that conveyed to listeners like John Mark an overwhelming sense of closeness and inseparability. A sense of oneness. In every Jewish story, God is a central theme. In the story of Joshua he becomes a character.

In assuming that Joseph died, it is rarely considered that Mary could have remarried. Yet, if we are not bound by the idea of Mary-ever-Virgin (or the 'Apostle' Paul's perverse views on widows marrying again), this is a reasonable assumption. More than that, it may be possible to identify Mary's second husband. A number of unrelated pointers to his identity are scattered through the Gospels; an early and respected fragment of Apocrypha contains a vital clue; and second-generation Church fathers supply useful evidence.

The Gospels reveal remarkably little about Mary. One of the few personal details is supplied in *John* 19:25, when we are told:

> Standing by the cross of Jesus were his mother, and his mother's sister, Mary [the wife] of Cleopas, and Mary Magdalene.

Apart from its potential ambiguity, there is something very odd about this passage. Why would John leave Jesus' mother unnamed yet name the wife of Cleopas, especially when the man rates no other mention in John's narrative?

Eusebius, Christianity's first great historian, identifies Cleopas (or Cleophas or Clopas) as a brother of Joseph. He also says that Simon, who succeeded Joshua's brother James the Just as leader of the Jerusalem 'Church', was the son of Cleopas and, we assume, 'the other Mary'. Gospels identify this Mary as being the mother of Joshua's disciple James the Younger, who, according to some translations, has a disciple brother called Judas. They also tell us that she has a son called Joses (*Mark* 15:40, 47; 16:1; *Luke* 6:15–16, 24:10; *John* 19:25; *Acts* 1:13). It seems very odd that Mary the mother of Jesus should have a sister also called Mary and that they should have three or four sons with the same names — James, Joses, Simon and Jude (or Judas). Could Mary the wife of Cleopas and Mary the mother of Jesus be the same person — Cleopas becoming her second husband after the death of Joseph?

First, we would have to assume that Eusebius was wrong in naming Cleopas as Joseph's brother. Under Jewish law, a man was obliged to marry a brother's widow if she was childless; but if she had children, the marriage was forbidden. We would also have to assume an error in the Gospel text that speaks of Mary the wife of Cleopas as the sister of Jesus' mother. An error seems possible, until we recall that the author was John Mark — as we will see, an eyewitness of the crucifixion. How could he, of all writers, make such a blunder? He probably didn't. Before 'publication' of the Gospel, which almost certainly occurred after his death, another hand could have made a simple alteration during the editing process indicated in *John* 21:24.

Suppose that the original, unpunctuated passage, written or dictated by the aged John Mark was along these lines:

> Standing by the cross of Jesus were his mother Mary the wife of Cleopas her sister and Mary Magdalene.

John Mark could have intended to list the three women as Mary — who was the mother of Jesus *and* wife to Cleopas — her unnamed sister and Mary Magdalene. Without any intention to distort, an editor or amanuensis could have tried to clarify John's apparent meaning by making Mary the wife of Cleopas the sister of Jesus' unnamed mother. Or, much later, the alteration could have been made deliberately to obscure Mary's second marriage.

If this seems fanciful, consider the ramifications of Joshua's mother being Mary the wife of Cleopas. This would identify Joshua's brother James the Just and the disciple James the Younger as the same man. Immediately it would be clear why James the Just — not previously regarded as a disciple — should take precedence over Joshua's closest associates and assume leadership after his brother's crucifixion (*Acts* 15 ff.). It would explain why the *Gospel According to the Hebrews* states that James the Just was present at The Last Supper, which was attended only by Joshua and the Twelve Disciples (and their host, John Mark). It would also become clear why Clement of Alexandria could write in the second century, 'There were two men called James', and proceed to describe the deaths of James the Older and James the Just (Eusebius, *History*, 2, 1, 4). James the Younger has vanished without a trace. To Clement — as to the writer of the *Gospel According to the Hebrews* — James the Younger was the man later called James the Just; the son of Mary the wife of Cleopas was Joshua's brother.

If Joshua's mother was Mary the wife of Cleopas, then Simon, who succeeded James as leader, would have been not a cousin but a brother of Joshua and James. Again, the succession becomes far more logical and in fact follows a dynastic line appropriate to Messiahship. According to Luke (24:13–32), one of Jesus' first appearances after his resurrection was to Cleopas and an unnamed companion (who was not one of the Twelve

Disciples) travelling to Emmaus. This has always given the obscure Cleopas an unusual significance — a significance which Joshua's stepfather would deserve and which Eusebius may have tried to justify by identifying Cleopas as Joseph's brother.

When Cleopas and his companion return to Jerusalem, they discover that Jesus has appeared to 'Simon'. Which Simon? Some assume Simon Peter; yet Luke usually calls him Peter at this late stage of the narrative. It seems more likely that Jesus has appeared to Simon the Zealot, who was one of the Twelve; or could it be Simon, the brother of Jesus, perhaps one and the same? Again, the reason for Simon's subsequent leadership role would be clear — not only a brother of Jesus but one of the Twelve Disciples.

As a final piece of the jigsaw, we should note that the *Gospel According to the Hebrews* has Jesus appear to his brother James, immediately after the crucifixion (cf. *1 Corinthians* 15:7). Thus, the first to see the resurrected Jesus would have been Mary Magdalene, James, Cleopas and Simon, who seem to share a familial significance. Yet Jesus' mother has been denied any role in the events of the resurrection — unless she was indeed Mary the wife of Cleopas, who is named by Matthew, Mark and Luke as one of Magdalene's companions when she discovers the empty tomb.

Because Luke's Gospel provides our sole glimpse of Cleopas as he is journeying to Emmaus, the Church assumed that this was his home and further assumed that el-Qubeiba, a village on the slopes west of Jerusalem, was Emmaus. A wall preserved in a church there as the remains of Cleopas's house, is probably from an Arab building of the eighth or ninth centuries AD. It seems most likely that Cleopas was a Galilean — a man who was warmly accepted by the adult Joshua as a stepfather, and who became a devoted disciple.

While Joshua's first thirty-five-or-six years slipped by in almost total obscurity, men who would help shape his destiny made their entrances and exits in the public life of Jerusalem and Rome.

In Joshua's twenty-first year, 14 AD, Augustus Caesar died (an event commemorated to this day by the month of his death being called August). Tiberius, stepson of Augustus, became emperor. He was already fifty-six, a military veteran with ruthless political skills and a dislike for the personal and public relationships demanded by court life. Increasingly reclusive, he entered his sixties painfully sensitive about his appearance. Tacitus recorded:

'Tall and abnormally thin, bent and bald, he had a face covered with sores and often with plaster' (*Annals*, 4, 56). Yet, however much Tiberius hated playing the public games of the palace, Senate and theatre, there was no escape — until Aelius Sejanus came to his rescue.

Sejanus was the son of a Tuscan knight, adopted by a wealthy debauchee and groomed for great things. He grew to be energetic, immoral and ruthlessly ambitious — one of the men who inspired Niccolo Machiavelli's philosophy of princely amorality. The year Tiberius became emperor, Sejanus was made prefect of the Praetorian Guard — an elite imperial military force with some of the qualities of Hitler's SS and SA. From this power base Sejanus launched a campaign to ingratiate himself with the emperor, playing the role of dedicated subordinate to perfection. Tiberius gave him greater responsibility, greater power, until Sejanus could see himself as the next Caesar. But the emperor's son, Drusus, was heir apparent; so, of course, he had to be removed.

Sejanus seduced Drusus's wife and, on the promise of making her his empress, arranged for Drusus to be slowly poisoned. Drusus died in 23 AD, the year when Sejanus consolidated the scattered cohorts of the Praetorian Guard into a single encampment of 9000 troops — the equivalent of one-and-a-half legions under his direct command. Within three years he had encouraged Tiberius to transfer the Roman court to some idyllic retreat — eventually the Isle of Capri — while he relieved the emperor of the routine burdens of governance.

That very year, 26 AD, the prefect of Judaea had to be replaced, according to the Slavonic Josephus, because he had accepted a bribe to appoint one Ishmael ben Pharbi as high priest. Normally, the appointment of a prefect to such an obscure province of the empire would not engage Sejanus's interest. He was, however, notoriously anti-Semitic and, in the words of Eusebius, 'worked eagerly in the city of Rome for the destruction of the whole Jewish race' (*History*, 2, 5, 7). This minor provincial posting was guaranteed to receive his special attention; and Tacitus pointed to 'the offices and governorships that were available for his [Sejanus's] dependants' (*Annals* 4, 1).

It needs little imagination to realise that the new prefect of Judaea would be one of these 'dependants'. His name was Pontius Pilate. Pilate, so prominent in the Gospels and Apocrypha, is an obscure figure in Roman history. He was born in France, apparently to a military family from the *Gens Pontia* of Central Italy, the area of the Pontine Marshes. He was probably one of Sejanus's former subordinates in the Guard, now an *equites*, a knight of the

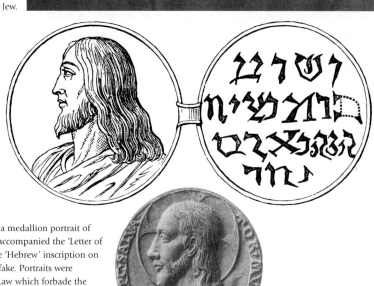

Rembrandt's 'Head of Christ' is a rare portrayal of him as a Jew. An Apocryphal 'Letter of Lentulus', from a Roman official to Tiberius Caesar, contains a preposterous but often-quoted description of Jesus, with grey eyes and 'hair of the hue of an unripe hazelnut'. Less often quoted is an even more preposterous interpolation in the Romanian text of the historian Josephus in which Jesus is seven feet tall with blonde hair and reddish beard. We can be confident that Joshua had olive skin, black hair and brown eyes, looking more like an Arab than the modern (or even Rembrandt's) image of a Jew.

A Victorian engraving of a medallion portrait of Jesus which supposedly accompanied the 'Letter of Lentulus' to Tiberius. The 'Hebrew' inscription on its reverse brands it as a fake. Portraits were against Jewish religious Law which forbade the depiction of any living thing. The profile itself is a romanticised nineteenth-century version of a medieval medal like the one (at right) in the British Museum.

Mary, the wife of Cleopas (envisaged here by the nineteenth-century artist, Loffz) is a mysterious figure. When a Gospel calls her 'the other Mary', to distinguish her from Mary Magdalene, she seems to be given greater prominence than Mary the mother of Joshua.

The sole artifact of Pontius Pilate's life — a partial inscription found at Caesarea in 1961 which commemorates his prefecture and a building, the 'Tiberieum', dedicated to the emperor. It reads:

TIBERIEVM	('Tiberieum
[PON] TIVS PILATVS	Pontius Pilate
[PRAEF] ECTVS IVDA [EAE]	Prefect of Judaea')

This Judaean *lepton*, a small bronze coin issued by Pontius Pilate in 29 AD, typifies his confrontational approach. With the inscription KAICAPOC (*Kaisaros*, 'of Caesar'), it carries a crook-like *lituus*, a Roman augurer's wand, a pagan symbol guaranteed to provoke the Jews. Earlier Roman prefects of Judaea had carefully avoided potentially offensive motifs on their coinage.

(Actual size)

Equestrian Order — a title which gave status to a broad class including former centurions, men who had earned imperial or political favour or who had simply won a respectable degree of wealth.

According to the Gospels, Pilate's wife (named in New Testament Apocrypha as Claudia Procula or Procla) either accompanied him to Judaea or joined him later in his term. This was unusual but feasible. Only five years before, Caecina, a former Provincial governor, had proposed to the Roman Senate that 'no-one appointed to a governorship should be allowed to take his wife'. Some of his reasons are fascinating, particularly in view of the role to be claimed for Pilate's wife in the events leading up to the death of Jesus.

> The wives attract every rascal in a province. It is they who initiate and transact business … and the women give the more wilful and despotic orders. They have burst through the old legal restrictions of the Oppian and other laws ['to curtail the expenses and luxuries of Roman women'], and are rulers everywhere — at home, in the courts, and now in the army.   (Tacitus, *Annals*, 3, 31–2)

After a spirited debate, Caecina's proposal was 'evaded'. The way was clear for the new prefect's wife to accompany him when he sailed for Judaea, probably in the early spring of 26 AD.

From the Gospels, Christians know Pontius Pilate as a well-intentioned though rather weak man who wants to save Jesus' life but is manoeuvred into complicity with 'the Jews' in having him executed. A famous Gospel scene has Pilate wash his hands in a gesture of dissociation from the sentence. In the light of this picture, it is perhaps surprising to find the first century Jewish philosopher, Philo of Alexandria, quoting a letter from King Agrippa to the emperor Caligula in which he speaks of 'the briberies, the insults, the robberies, the outrages and wanton injuries, the executions without trial constantly repeated, the senseless and supremely grievous cruelty', which, to him, characterised Pilate's regime in Judaea (*Embassy to Gaius* 38, 302). This is what we would expect from a protégé of Aelius Sejanus. We will see Pilate confirm these expectations.

Compared with the legates — men of senatorial and consular rank who governed provinces such as Syria and Egypt — Pilate was a minor Roman official. Yet he held the power of life and death over every man and woman in Judaea; he personally commanded half a legion seconded from Syria; and in any emergency he could call on some 48 000 troops stationed in Africa, Syria and Egypt. The people of Judaea were about to confront a formidable enemy.

Such was the man who would eventually weigh Joshua's life in a balance of political and personal survival. That balance would be influenced by forces from distant Rome as well as from Judaea, with the Judaean influence channelled through one man — the high priest, Joseph Caiaphas.

If Pilate emerges in the Gospels as a flawed but quasi-sympathetic character (in some Apocrypha he achieves a near-saintly quality) then uncritical reading of these same texts by Christians-at-large produces an image of Caiaphas as a clear-cut villain, a cruel and vindictive man determined to see Jesus nailed on a cross. A more measured and less tunnel-visioned assessment of the material in its historical context produces a different picture.

Coincidentally, Pilate was the fifth prefect since the Roman annexation of Judaea and Caiaphas was the fifth high priest. Pilate's predecessor, Valerius Gratus, marched into the Jewish homeland in 15 AD and immediately sacked the high priest Annas (also called Ananus and, in Jewish sources, Hanan) who had been appointed nine years earlier by the first prefect of Judaea. Gratus proceeded to appoint four high priests in three years, including Ishmael ben Pharbi, who had provided the alleged bribe that supposedly led to his removal.

This revolving-door high-priestly succession could only further damage an office that had slipped into disrepute under the later Hasmoneans and Herod, to decline progressively under Roman rule. The Temple had become a vast corporate headquarters handling an enormous volume of money and goods; a financial institution that housed staggering wealth. (When the Temple was sacked in 70 AD, the sale of its gold produced a 50 per cent drop in the commodity's price throughout Syria, even after much of the treasure had been taken by Zealots and the most spectacular items carried off to Rome.) It all provided a situation ripe for corruption.

Josephus recorded that in his time,

> such was the impudence and boldness that had seized on the high priests, that they had the hardness to send their servants into the thrashing-floors, to take away those tithes [of grain] that were due to the priests, insomuch that it so fell out that the poorer ... priests died for want. To this degree did the violence of the seditious prevail over all right and justice. (*Antiquities*, 20,8,8)

Perhaps the most damning indictment of the high-priestly caste in the first century is provided by the Talmud, quoting two revered Rabbis of the late first century.

> Abba Saul ben Bithnith and Abba Jose ben Johanan used to say:
> 'Woe is me because of the house of Boethus;
> woe is me because of their staves!

woe is me because of the House of Kadros;
woe is me because of their pens!
woe is me because of the House of Hanan;
woe is me because of their whisperings!
woe is me because of the house of Ishmael ben Phabi;
woe is me because of their fists!
For the high priests and their sons are Temple treasurers,
and their sons-in-law are trustees;
and their servants beat the people with staves.'   (*Pesahim* 57a)

This extraordinary lament embraces virtually all the high priestly families of the first century. While it can be read as accusing the House of Annas (Hanan) of nothing more serious than 'whisperings', Josephus describes Annas himself as 'a great hoarder-up of money' (the Talmud mentions his 'bazaars' on the Mount of Olives), and links him with the practice of taking by force the grain tithes due to lesser priests (*Antiquities* 20, 9, 2).

Joseph Caiaphas was the fourth high priest appointed by Gratus in three years. He took office in 18 AD, probably as a man in his late thirties, and, against all odds, held the position for eighteen years, ten of them under Pontius Pilate, a man hell-bent on confrontation with the Jews. Caiaphas played his impossible role with distinction, maintaining his position not only against the threat of removal by Gratus or Pilate, but also living in the shadow of his father-in-law, Annas, the deposed high priest. In the eyes of the Jewish people Annas retained his primacy in an emeritus role. As Josephus records: 'he increased in glory every day, and this to a great degree, and had obtained the favour and esteem of the citizens in a signal manner' (*ibid*). In the coming war with Rome, 8500 temple guards and volunteers were to die protecting him. Annas lived to see five of his sons and a grandson — as well as Caiaphas — hold high-priestly office.

Both Annas and his son-in-law were to play key roles in Joshua's story. Annas may have tried to save Joshua's life; the relationship — or lack of relationship — between Caiaphas and Pilate brought about Joshua's death. All three men saw the fate of this troublesome Galilean as a minor incident in a far greater drama. For Pilate it was a question of retaining his prefecture; and that, in turn, could be a matter of life or death. For Annas and Caiaphas, preservation of wealth and position may have played a role; but their dominant concerns were the survival of the Jewish people and their religion, centred on Jerusalem's Temple. If Joshua's life is seen as a sacrifice, it is offered by these three men on these altars.

CHAPTER 5

Pilate and 'the Abomination'

Archaeologist John Romer, a man used to the touchable reality of the ancient past and the texts that bring it alive, offers an interesting perception of first-century Palestine as it is portrayed in Christian writings:

> The Gospels' portrait of Jesus seems to be separated from real time. The central character is set in a series of rambling incidents and sermons, engaged in a mysterious progress revolving around an unstated drama that finally ensures his capture and death. Perhaps in response, modern histories, too, often lose all sense of reality as they approach the Holy Land. Neighbouring countries have economic histories and bloody political wars. All too often, however, the Holy Land is portrayed as a fairyland of country folk, wicked kings, corrupt priests, tax collectors and stock revolutionaries. But did these ancient Galileans really live with eyes fixed only upon the infinite? How, for example, did Jesus see his career on earth? Just as a healer and preacher? Did he consider the political or social consequences of his teaching?

Luke seems to have had a similar reaction to the material he found. Of all the Gospellers, he is the one who tries hardest to set his story in 'real time' with the result that his picture is more strongly political — as we have seen, even in the lyricism of his nativity story — so when he introduces us to the adult Jesus it is at a specific time within a framework of Roman and Jewish authority.

> In the fifteenth year of the reign of Tiberius Caesar, with Pontius Pilate governing Judaea, Herod ruling as tetrarch of Galilee, his brother Philip prince of Iturea and Trachonitis, with Lysanius as tetrarch of Abilene, in the high-priesthood of Annas and Caiaphas ...   (Luke 3:1–2)

Apart from the wild card Lysanius (who is often confused with a ruler who had been killed some sixty-five years earlier) this gallery of notables all play roles in the story — the first four, according to Luke, in its opening phase. Tiberius, who was now settled in his life of remote luxury on Capri, had taken the purple in 14 AD, setting Luke's time index, the fifteenth year of the reign, at 29 AD. Scholars who find this date inconvenient for their chronologies argue that Tiberius was joint ruler with Augustus for two years before his accession, and they therefore move Luke's marker back to 27 AD. This technicality is more than dubious. He means his story to start in 29 AD, some three years after Pontius Pilate's arrival in Palestine. Luke ignores those three years; we cannot.

Pilate probably arrived in Caesarea during the spring of 26 AD, when the Mediterranean sea lanes were reopened after the stormy winter months. This lavish, Samarian city with its handsome harbour, palaces, hippodrome and theatre, would be his base of operations. We know nothing of his movements during the early months of his prefecture. Then, with curious abruptness, Josephus provides a first vivid glimpse of the man in action:

> But now Pilate, the procurator of Judaea, removed the army from Caesarea to Jerusalem, to take their winter quarters there, *in order to abolish the Jewish laws*. So he introduced Caesar's effigies, which were upon the ensigns, and brought them into the city; whereas our law forbids us the very making of images; on which account the former procurators were wont to make their entry into the city with such ensigns as had not those ornaments. Pilate was the first who brought these images to Jerusalem, and set them up there; which was done without the knowledge of the people, because it was done in the night time.
> [my italics]   (*Antiquities* 18,3,1)

Pontius Pilate makes his entrance on the stage of history as Sejanus's man, implementing his patron's policy to achieve 'the destruction of the whole Jewish race' (Eusebius, *Proof* 11,5). His 'army' was about 3000 men drawn from the legions stationed in Syria. Of these about 1000 provided the permanent garrison in Jerusalem. Elsewhere, Josephus tells us that the Jerusalem garrison was reinforced by a second cohort to guard against trouble during the pilgrim festivals, when every male Jew in Palestine was obliged to attend ceremonies at the Temple. This meant that the extra troops were needed in Jerusalem through winter — from autumn (Tabernacles) until early summer (Pentecost). It was clearly this reinforcing cohort that carried the offensive 'ensigns' — Roman military standards — Pilate's first ploy in his campaign 'to abolish the Jewish laws'.

'Caesar's effigies' were bas-relief, medallion-like profiles of Tiberius mounted on the standards. Any human likeness would offend the Jews; this man was a demi-god. And, as well as portraits of Caesar, standards displayed Roman eagles — offensive in themselves to Jews as 'graven images' of living creatures, but also flaunting resonances of a golden eagle Herod had placed on the Temple facade in one of his Graeco–Roman excesses. Perhaps worst of all, the Tenth Legion was permanently stationed in Syria and frequently saw service in Israel. Its insignia, carried on their own special standards, were a bull and a boar. To Jews, the pig was an 'unclean' animal, whose flesh they were forbidden to eat and whose dead carcass they could not even touch.

Josephus tells us that the 'images' were 'set up' in Jerusalem after dark. He does not say where they were placed in the city, but obviously the precious standards remained with the troops as they took up their quarters in the Antonia Fortress. At daylight the people of the city discovered the display of pagan symbols on the battlemented walls of the Antonia, directly overlooking the Temple courts — an outrage to every pilgrim attending the Feast of Tabernacles, which was probably due to start within a matter of days. Pilate's calculated affront to Jewish belief would have produced a vigorous reaction at any time. But this Tabernacles Festival of 26 AD marked the start of *Shemittha*, a sabbatical year, the end of a seven-year cycle, 'a week of years', when farmers would let their fields lie fallow. The pilgrim crowds in Jerusalem this year would be bigger than usual and potentially more volatile.

Reaction was swift. If a delegation of Jews protested to the tribune in charge of the reinforcing cohort, they would get no satisfaction; he was acting under the prefect's orders. So they set off to Caesarea in their thousands and asked for the standards to be removed. Pilate refused, 'because it would tend to the injury of Caesar'. They persisted; he would not budge. And so it went on for five days. Josephus continues the story:

> On the sixth day he ordered his soldiers to have their weapons privately, while he came and sat upon his judgement-seat, which was so prepared in the open place of the city, that it concealed the army that lay ready to oppress them; and when the Jews petitioned him again, he gave a signal to the soldiers to encompass them around, and threatened that their punishment should be no less than immediate death, unless they would leave off disturbing him, and go their ways home. But they threw themselves upon the ground, and lay their necks bare, and said they would take their deaths very willingly, rather than the wisdom of their laws should be transgressed. (*ibid.*)

It was an extraordinary moment; thousands of men ready to have their throats cut for the sake of their religious beliefs, while a thousand or more Roman soldiers, with swords drawn, looked to the prefect for his signal to strike. According to Josephus, 'Pilate was deeply affected by their firm resolution to keep their laws inviolable.' It seems just as likely that he weighed the possible repercussions of a massacre on this scale and simply lost his nerve. He gave in and ordered the standards removed from Jerusalem.

The Jews had won their first round of the fight; but the new prefect's attempt 'to abolish the Jewish laws' had achieved greater significance than he could have imagined. The third-century Christian scholar, Origen, and Jerome of the fourth century both saw Pilate's act of desecration as a fulfilment of *The Book of Daniel*'s prophecy concerning 'the abomination of desolation'. Chapter 11 of *Daniel* predicts that a brutal ruler will 'vent his fury on the Holy Covenant':

> His soldiers in his command will desecrate the sanctuary and citadel [or fortress]; they will abolish the regular offering, and will set up 'the abomination that causes desolation'. *(Daniel 11:31)*

The 'abomination' prophecy and the passages preceding it match the events involving the Syrian Greek King Antiochus Epiphanes (175 to 163 BC), who set out, like Pilate, to destroy Judaism, profaning the Temple with an idol of Zeus and sacrifices of swine's flesh. Daniel was told that the end times, the coming of the apocalypse, would begin 'a time and times and half a time' after 'the abomination of desolation', a period later confirmed as three and a half years. This closely matches the time between the desecration of the Temple in 167 BC and Mattathias's launching of the Maccabean revolt in 164 BC.

Some scholars take these historical parallels as proof that the 'prophecy' was written during the Maccabean revolt, with the wisdom of hindsight, automatically rejecting any idea that the future can be predicted — even by divine inspiration. The historian Robin Lane Fox calls *Daniel* 'the first known book of resistance literature, a fiction and a fake in one'. Other scholars, a valiant minority, point to textual evidence that even the latest material in Daniel predates the Maccabean revolt and that some of the passages refer to Roman rule and were genuinely prophetic even if they *were* written in the second century BC.

Both viewpoints support one conclusion. The 'abomination' prophecy concerned events that took place 140 years before Pilate's arrival. Yet as the Qumran texts show, time after time, in the Second Temple period prophecy clearly intended for one age was applied to another. Its message remained significant to the people of the Covenant when they found themselves in a similar situation. In a spectacular example, *Isaiah* 10:28–32, which describes the Assyrian advance on Jerusalem, is seen as prophesying the Messiah's vengeful approach to liberate his people. Historian Fox accused the sectarians of 'torturing sense and meaning'. The Dead Sea Scrolls scholar John Allegro sees it differently:

> The Qumran commentator is not at all interested in the historical and social context of the biblical prophecy. For him, every word of scripture was pregnant with meaning for his own day ... In the process of arriving at its import for his time, nothing is barred to the commentator: any twisting of the meaning of words ... even rewriting the passage to suit his interpretation, all is legitimate to the Qumran writer who is himself fired with the spirit of prophecy.

The Gospels make it clear that this *pesher* approach to Jewish scripture was not confined to the men of Qumran in the apocalypse-haunted first centuries of our era. So it was that Origen could recognise the 'abomination' as Pilate's sacrilegious attack *and* as Caligula's attempt in 40 AD to have a statue of himself erected in the Temple. In this, Origen was probably inspired by Joshua. Matthew and Mark have him speaking of the 'abomination' as a future event, though in a strangely oblique way that could suggest some real and present danger — more appropriate to something that is current or from the immediate past:

> 'So when you see "the abomination of desolation" spoken of by the prophet Daniel, standing in the holy place (let the reader understand), everyone in Judaea must flee into the mountains ...'   (*Matthew* 24:15–16)

One thing is made very clear. To Joshua the 'abomination' foreshadows fearful things: war, earthquakes, 'the first birth-pangs of the new age' (*Matthew* 24:15–21; *Mark* 13:14–19). When these portents failed to appear, the early Christians (and probably the Gospellers) postponed the 'abomination' and the apocalypse from one generation to the next — a process which some Christians have maintained right up to the present. But to Joshua and the people of his day, the end times were near. This belief shaped their actions and reactions.

If Pilate's desecration of the Temple with pagan symbols was seen as fulfilment of the *Daniel* prophecy, then the beginning of the end times would be expected three and a half years later — halfway through the current 'week of years'. Those who looked to the end times with hope and those who looked to them with fear would be equally ready to anticipate the first signs of the apocalypse in 29–30 AD. And in 29 AD, according to Luke, a man emerged from the wilderness, calling for repentance, warning of the coming of God's kingdom and denouncing the 'generation of vipers' fleeing from 'the wrath to come'. The Slavonic text of Josephus describes him as 'a savage' and a 'wild man'. We know him as John the Baptist.

CHAPTER 6

Holy Warriors

John the Baptist is a fascinating and mysterious figure. Luke's Gospel devotes more space to John's portentous conception and birth than to the conception and birth of Jesus. Across the four Gospels, John is mentioned some ninety times — more often than any other person except Jesus himself — and the scholars of the Jesus Seminar believe that some views attributed to Jesus are in fact John's. Yet all the Gospels insist that John's mission had one purpose — to proclaim the coming of Jesus and offer a baptism by water which foreshadowed a baptism by Jesus with the Holy Spirit. It is surprising to find that the Gospeller Luke later contradicts this picture. In the book of *Acts*, Luke reports that on a visit to Ephesus, in what is today Turkey, Paul finds 'about a dozen men' who had been baptised by John perhaps twenty years earlier. They know nothing of Jesus and declare, 'we were not even told that there *is* a Holy Spirit.' (*Acts* 19:1–7).

If we treat Luke's and Matthew's nativity stories as more concerned with theological scene-setting than with biographical material, all four Gospels use John the Baptist to begin their narratives. Mark's Gospel, probably the earliest, introduces the Baptist in its opening verses:

> It is written in the book of Isaiah the prophet:
> 'I will send my messenger ahead of you,
> who will prepare your way …'

It's a wobbly start. The verse is from *Malachi*, not *Isaiah*; but Mark continues his quote with a genuine *Isaiah* passage:

'... a voice of one calling in the wilderness,
"Prepare the way of the Lord,
Make his paths straight."'
And John came, baptising in the wilderness and proclaiming a baptism of
repentance for the forgiveness of sins ...
John wore clothing of camel's hair, with a leather belt around his waist ...

(Mark 1:26)

Mark's description of John duplicates a description of the prophet Elijah:
'A man with a garment of hair and a leather belt around his waist' (*2 Kings*
1:8). The too-close match seems to have worried the historically-minded
Luke and he does not mention John's unusual clothing in his account.
Perhaps, too, he was wary of the prophet Zechariah's words:

> On that day every prophet will be ashamed of his prophetic vision. He will not
> put on his garment of hair in order to deceive.   (*Zechariah* 13:4)

The 'garment of hair' was made of the biblical 'sackcloth' which we tend
to think of as hessian but which was really a coarse, cheap cloth made from
the long, dark hair of a camel's hump. For any but the poorest Jews, to wear it
was a sign of mourning — as in 'sackcloth and ashes' — worn by the
prophets who mourned for the state of their country and, usually, for its
rulers. It also symbolised humility before God, as when Rabbi Jonah donned
sackcloth and stood in 'a hidden spot' before praying for the breaking of a
drought (*Ta'anith* 23b). It is believable that John wore 'a garment of hair',
but it is also clear that Mark was eager to highlight the Elijah image, because
God had promised: 'I will send you the prophet Elijah before the great and
terrible day of the Lord comes' (*Malachi* 4:6). Elijah, who did not die, but
was carried up into the sky from the banks of the Jordan by a whirlwind,
would return as 'messenger of the Covenant' to usher in the Messianic age.
For Mark, portraying John as Elijah was an essential first step in identifying
Jesus as the Messiah.

Surprisingly, the four Gospels show a less-than-united front on this
apparently seminal issue. Mark and Matthew both have Jesus saying that
John the Baptist *was* Elijah (*Matthew* 11:14 and 17, 17:10–13; *Mark* 9:11–13),
while Luke again hangs back and says that he was *like* Elijah (*Luke* 1:17) and
the Fourth Gospel makes the Baptist himself insist that he is *not* Elijah, nor
'the Christ' nor 'the Prophet' (*John* 1:19–21).

To understand Joshua we must first try to understand John the Baptist. Who
was he? And why should he cause such disagreement among the Gospellers?

The most obvious answer is only a restatement of the questions. He was a controversial figure — and has remained so, throughout the millennia.

In the century in which John lived, Josephus supposedly wrote of him (though probably not by name) as 'a good man' who urged Jews to live 'righteous lives' and 'to practise justice towards their fellows and piety towards God'. For reasons which are unclear (at least in the standard form of his text), Josephus says that this teaching made Herod Antipas fear that John's eloquence 'might lead to some form of sedition' and so decided to silence him 'before his work led to an uprising'.

In 1910, the German scholar Kaufmann Kohler advanced a theory (picked up in 1997 by the American Eisenman) that John was a wonder-worker called Hanan han-nehba — (Jo)hanan the Hidden or the Hiding One — who is mentioned in the Talmud as a rainmaker. The Talmud identifies Hanan as the son-in-law of a famous Galilean charismatic called Honi the Circle Drawer (*Ta'anith* 23b). If the Baptist's mother, Elizabeth, was related to Mary, then Mary's son would be related to Honi. This is intriguing but unlikely. Equally unlikely is an earlier Eisenman theory that John was the mysterious priest Zadok, co-founder of the Zealot movement in 4 BC (which would make the Baptist a man in his sixties by 29–30 AD.

Perhaps the most revolutionary modern interpretation of John comes from Australian Barbara Thiering, who identifies him as the Teacher of Righteousness, the otherwise unnamed but revered central figure (and probable founder) of the Qumran sect. The German scholar Robert Eisler reached the same conclusion in the 1920s (some thirty years before the discovery of the Dead Sea Scrolls) from his study of a single Qumran scroll, *The Damascus Document* (Geniza A and B), found in the storage room of a Cairo synagogue in 1896. However, Dr Thiering doesn't stop there. The Scrolls tell how the Teacher of Righteousness is opposed by a man known as the 'Wicked Priest'. According to Thiering, the Wicked Priest is Jesus, who survived the crucifixion, was twice married, had children and died in Rome at an advanced age. Dr Thiering's views have not been widely accepted (American scholar Luke Timothy Johnson calls them 'the purest poppycock, the product of fevered imagination') but they highlight a persistent strand of interpretation that links the Baptist (and Jesus) to the Qumran community.

Within ten years of the discovery of the Dead Sea Scrolls, a member of the original translation team, John Allegro, was saying: 'It does appear … that John belonged to the Essene movement', and 'much of John's message finds its parallels in Qumran teaching'. Allegro thought it possible that the celibate

Essenes had taken John in as a young child (a practice of the sect) and raised him as one of them (though it is surprising that Zechariah would surrender a cherished and divinely sanctioned son to men who were bitter enemies of the Jerusalem priesthood to which he belonged).

Links are obvious. John operated in the Jordan Valley within a few miles of Qumran, supposed headquarters of the Essenes, 'preaching a baptism for the remission of sins'. As in the Qumran sect, John's true repentants were 'purified in the flesh with water'. John supposedly believed that this baptism was a mere preparation for the approaching time when the Messiah would baptise 'with the Holy Spirit' just as the Qumran supplicant looked to a coming purification by God 'through the Holy Spirit ... sprinkling upon him a spirit of truth as purifying water' (1Q5).

Mark tells us that John ate 'locusts and wild honey' and Qumran's *Damascus Document* (Geniza A) specifies locusts as the only land creature that sect members could eat ('put alive into fire or water for this is what their nature requires').

There are striking echoes from the Dead Sea Scrolls in John's mission, most immediately the image of a man in the wilderness preparing 'the way'. Qumran's variously titled *Manual of Discipline* (1QS) urges its elect to 'separate from the sessions of perverse men to go to the wilderness, there to prepare the way of truth', quoting the same text from *Isaiah* used by the Gospels (and, like the Gospels, bending it to their own purpose).

The parallels go much further than this, though not in Mark, who offers only one more fragment of what John supposedly taught (really, a preview of coming attractions and suspect because it seems both a testimonial for Jesus and a first step in relegating John to a subordinate role):

> 'The one coming after me is more powerful than I; the thongs of his sandals I
> am not worthy to kneel down and untie. I baptised you with water but he will
> baptise you in the Holy Spirit.'   (*Mark* 1:7–8)

It is intriguing that the very first passages quoted by Matthew and Luke from their shared 'sayings of Jesus' document (the mysterious 'Q') are in fact sayings of John. They show him preaching powerfully in his own right:

> Then he said to the crowds coming out to be baptised by him [according to
> Matthew, to 'many of the Pharisees and Sadducees'], 'You brood [or genera-
> tion] of vipers! Who warned you to flee from the coming wrath? Bear fruit in
> keeping with repentance. And do not start saying to yourselves, "We have
> Abraham as our father" [i.e. "We are Jews"] because I tell you that out of these

stones God can raise up children of Abraham. The axe is already at the root of the trees, so every tree that does not produce good fruit is cut down and thrown into the fire.'

As in Mark, both Matthew and Luke have John speak of 'one more powerful than I' who will baptise 'with the Holy Spirit *and with fire*'. They go on to tell how he will gather up the wheat from the threshing floor and 'burn up the chaff with unquenchable fire' (*Luke* 3:17; *Matthew* 3:12), just as Qumran apocalyptic writings speak of destroying ungodliness with 'a flaming torch in the straw' (1QM XI).

John's vivid attack, 'You brood of vipers!', may represent much more than mere colourful invective. It seems to echo a passage from *Deuteronomy* also fastened on by the men of Qumran: 'Their wine is venom of snakes, the cruel poison of vipers' (*Deuteronomy* 32:33). Qumran's *Damascus Document* explains:

'The snakes' are the kings of the Gentiles and 'their wine' is their customs, and 'the poison of vipers' is the chief of the kings of Greece [who, in a later *pesher*, would have been seen as the king of the Kittim — Caesar].   (Geniza A)

If John, too, is attacking the corruption of Jewish life and faith by seductive Graeco-Roman culture, this would explain why he stresses that being Jewish is no guarantee of redemption, and why he asks Jews to undergo the same rite required for Gentiles seeking to join Judaism — the so-called 'proselyte [convert] baptism' — ritual cleansing of the impurity ingrained by pagan lifestyle and religious practices.

John's chill warning, 'the axe is already at the root of the trees ...' echoes a text from Isaiah again quoted in the Scrolls: '... and the tallest trees will be cut down and the lofty will be felled with the axe ... ' (*Isaiah* 10:33–4). The Qumran commentary explains:

This refers to the Kittim [the Romans] who will fall at the hands of Israel ... 'the tallest trees will be cut down' refers to the warriors [or 'the valiant'] of the Kittim ...   (4Q161)

Even in code, this is dangerously rebellious talk from the supposedly pacifist Essenes. And one of their documents, *The War Scroll*, (1QM) provides a remarkably detailed scenario of an apocalyptic war with the Romans, specifying the sect's weapons — swords 'of refined iron purified in the furnace' and javelins whose blades are engraved with texts like 'Missiles of blood to fell the slain by the wrath of God'. Banners, of specified sizes, emblazoned with invocations, are to be carried 'at the head of all the people' and before each tribe, each ten thousand, thousand, hundred, fifty and ten. Specially named trumpets signal each phase of the action. Battle formations are described in detail: 'The battle line shall be formed of one thousand men. There shall be seven forward rows to each battle line, arranged in order: the station of each man behind his fellow.'

As the battle approaches a bloody climax to signals from the Trumpets of Massacre blown by the priests, the Archangel Michael, warrior guardian angel of Israel, leads an 'angelic host' to join the Sons of Light in crushing the Roman cohorts and all the rest of the Sons of Darkness.

Professor Robert Grant calls the Qumran scenario, 'the *Mein Kampf* of the Dead Sea generalissimo', looking to a future when a victorious Davidic king is on his throne and all Israel follows the way of the New Qumran Covenant. Grant comments, 'No Gentile mission is contemplated. The Gentiles will be dead', concluding:

> The religion of the Qumran people was characterized by some of the most exclusive sectarianism the world has ever seen, an apocalyptic-eschatological sectarianism *which looked for triumph in this world, and soon.* [my italics]

It is not surprising that many scholars have challenged theories that the men of Qumran were Essenes and that Qumran was a sort of 'monastery'. 'Monastic' Essenes would have been celibate. Yet among the forty-one graves opened at random in the community's cemetery (which seems far too close to buildings for priestly purity) the skeletons of seven women and two children were found. These discoveries tally with sections of the community's *Manual of Discipline* (1QS) which detail the recruitment and training of young men on almost military lines. They are taken in as ten-year-olds and after ten years of service, they are permitted to marry, their wives becoming members of the community.

Some Israeli archaeologists believe that the Qumran complex was built as a Hasmonean fortress, pointing to its massive, square central tower with *glacis* of sloping stonework to deflect battering rams, and its elaborate provisions for water supply and storage — more like major public works than the communal effort of a monastic sect. The famous *scriptorium*, where the Dead Sea Scrolls were supposedly written by a team of diligent 'monks' could have been a mess room — a theory supported by the fact that the scrolls were written by hundreds of different hands, the same scribe rarely producing more than one scroll. And what of the thousands of cheap eating bowls stored in a 'pantry', when the complex probably accommodated only about fifty people at a time? Was this fortress also a mother house, where the members of the sect could eat in community during some annual muster — perhaps a ceremonial meal foreshadowing the Messianic banquet described in their writings? Recent translators of the Scrolls, Wise, Abegg and Cook, comment:

> The group thought of itself as warriors awaiting God's signal to begin the final war against the [Gentile] nations and the wicked among the Jews. Meanwhile they sought to live in a heightened state of purity, as the Bible required for Holy Warriors.

More and more, the 'Essenes' of Qumran sound like Zealots and it comes as no great surprise that a copy of one of the Dead Sea Scrolls was found among the seventeen sets of writings recovered from the ruins of Masada — the spectacular plateau-fortress where a force of *sicarii*, 'dagger men', the most extreme branch of the Zealots, held out against a Roman siege in 73–74 AD and killed themselves and their families when defeat was inevitable. Their 960 corpses gave the Roman commander a hollow victory.

Intriguingly, the Qumran scroll found at Masada, *The Songs of Sabbath Sacrifice* (4Q400 etc.) — worthy of nine copies in the Qumran library — is based on the 364-day solar calendar which governed the sect's liturgical year. From a single Qumran cave, over a dozen scrolls contained this unique calendar. Yet, as Wise, Abegg and Cook comment:

> For all the importance of the calendar to the scrolls, the only group of ancient Jews following it to whom the ancient sources give a name is the *sicarii*, the last defenders of Masada.

There is one more extraordinary link between the Dead Sea sect and the Zealots. The famous *Copper Scroll* (3Q15), found in Cave 3 at Qumran, lists and describes sixty-four sites where treasure and religious articles were hidden — amounting to 65 tons of silver and 26 tons of gold. Many believe that this secret hoard had come from the Temple in Jerusalem. The Temple was occupied by the Zealots in 66 AD and held by them against rival Jewish groups until the fall of Jerusalem and the destruction of the Temple in 70 AD. The list of Temple treasure in their hands and the directions to find each of the sixty-four caches were hammered into long strips of flexible copper and hidden with other leather and papyrus scrolls of the Qumran sect.

Mainstream scholarship doesn't accept that the men of Qumran were Zealots, arguing that there was no such sect when Qumran was founded in the second century BC. Yet the Zealots were certainly in existence when the

War Scroll was written, probably in the first century *AD*, and it is playing with labels to say that Zealots did not exist until 4 BC, when Josephus says that Judas of Galilee and the mysterious Pharisee priest Zadok founded the movement. Some 140 years earlier, the sons of the priest Mattathias, the rebel Maccabees, were true, 'small z' zealots. The *Book of Maccabees* tells how:

> Judas also called Maccabaeus escaped with about nine others into the desert, where he and his companions lived in the mountains, fending for themselves like wild animals, and all the while feeding on what vegetation they found there, *so as to have no share in the pollution.* [my italics]   (*2 Maccabees* 5:27)

In a way of life that sounds very much like that of the Baptist, they were purifying themselves for the Holy War to come. The Maccabees/Hasmoneans were a fanatical warrior priesthood who, like the Zealots, disdained kingship. When they won their victory over the Syrian Greeks, they ruled as high priests for four generations before taking the crown. Their first followers in the rebellion were *hasidim* ('Pious' or 'Holy Ones'), 'stalwarts of Israel, every one of them a volunteer in the cause of the Law' (*1 Maccabees* 2:42) — holy men who became warriors when Israel and its Holy Law were in jeopardy. They were zealous for the law and became zealots.

What does it all mean? If we reject simplistic and mutually exclusive labels like 'Essenes' and 'Zealots' to identify the men of Qumran, we're probably close to the truth. If fortress Qumran was in fact a 'monastery', we are looking at a sect of warrior 'monks' who accepted married 'holy warriors' in their ranks and were prepared to *live* their apocalyptic dream of battle with the Romans. Whatever we call these men, their citadel was destroyed, probably in 68 AD when Roman cohorts, massed behind the standards of the bull and the boar, besieged the 'holy warriors'. The Archangel Michael and the 'angelic host' did not come to their aid. Their fate is a mystery; only the burnt ruins of Qumran, some arrowheads, and the scrolls remain.

✝✝✝

In the nature of John's mission and in his preaching we have found many echoes of Qumran. So was he too a 'holy warrior'? His father, the Jerusalem priest Zechariah, seems to speak of him as one. In Luke's Gospel, the birth of John is hailed by Zechariah with a song known as the *Benedictus* or 'Blessed', the first word of its Latin version. Sung reverently in the language of the King James Bible, it tends to lose the powerful, radical underscore that emerges more clearly in modern translations.

Blessed is the Lord, the God of Israel!
For he has come to his people and *liberated them*,
He has raised for us *a powerful rescuer*
from the house of his servant David.
Just as he promised; age after age he proclaimed
by the lips of his holy prophets,
that he would *save us from our enemies*,
from the hands of all who hate us.
He would be merciful with our fathers
and remember his solemn covenant,
the oath he swore to our father Abraham,
to free us of fear,
so that we may serve him
in holiness and righteousness
all our livelong days. [my italics]   (*Luke* 1:68–74)

It is hardly surprising that the *Benedictus* was seen by the eminent New Testament scholar, Paul Winter, as a Maccabean battle song, popular among the Baptist's followers and recorded by Luke forty or fifty years later. If this is true, the second part of Zechariah's song certainly came from a very different source.

And you, my child, will be called a Prophet of the Most High,
for you will go before the Lord to prepare his way;
and give his people a knowledge of salvation
by the forgiveness of their sins;
through the tender mercies of our God.
His heavenly dawn will look down on us,
giving light to those who sit in darkness,
and in the shadow of death,
and to guide our feet into the way of peace.   (*Luke* 1:76–9)

Here is the problem of John the Savage become John the Baptist. The first is a man who sounds like one of the Maccabees, a 'holy warrior' concerned with freedom, deliverance from enemies and maintenance of Torah and Covenant; the second is concerned with 'knowledge of salvation' through forgiveness of sins. Yet it is the second man who takes on the shaggy mantle of Elijah as prophet and herald of the Messiah, God's chosen liberator and leader of the Jewish people.

If Luke correctly recorded the 'Maccabean battle song', John is being hailed as 'a powerful rescuer from the House of ... David'. And according to Clement, a Jewish sect of the second century regarded John as the Messiah

(*Recognitions* 1, 60). Because this evidence strongly clashes with the Christian portrayal of him as 'forerunner' of the Messiah, as 'one who goes before' Jesus, it is clearly not a product of the early Church. In fact, the Gospels are at pains to insist that John was *not* the Messiah (*Luke* 3:15–16; *John* 1:20 and 3:28) while anxious to establish links between him and Jesus.

It is obvious that John's status lent imprimatur to Jesus' career. Less obvious, but inescapable, to my mind — though to many unacceptable — is the fact that John's brief but explosive crusade both inspired and launched Jesus' ministry.

CHAPTER 7

'My Beloved Son'

In Christian imagination Jesus has been consciously preparing himself throughout thirty-six years for his divine mission as Messiah. The Gospels lend no support to this notion. If we trust their accounts, none of those who knew him best — family or neighbours — had any inkling of his plans or of his possessing the qualities demanded for this role. With the family, it was as though the miraculous events and portents of the Nativity had been forgotten. Or, more to the point, as though they had never happened. As for all the years passed in the tiny hillside community of Nazareth, it is very clear that study of the scriptures played an important part in Jesus' life and he was no stranger to religious discussion and debate. The Gospels demonstrate that he absorbed an enormous amount of the treasured oral law and lore of the Pharisees, the inspired traditions of *Midrash* and *Mishnah*, which preserved, defined, questioned and amplified every aspect of scripture, Law and Judaic wisdom. Yet, according to Mark, nothing had singled him out as anything more than a devout young tradesman. In John Romer's terms, it doesn't seem that his eyes were 'fixed only upon the infinite'. He had shown no great gift for preaching nor displayed unusual powers as a healer; he had done nothing that the people of his home town could look back on in a new light when he returned to speak in the synagogue early in his public life.

> … and many who heard him were amazed. They said, 'Where did this man get all this? What wisdom is given to him that such deeds of power are being done by his hands! Isn't this the carpenter, the son of Mary and brother of James and Joses and Judas and Simon, and aren't his sisters here with us?'   (*Mark* 6:2–3)

The Gospellers quite logically treat the appearance of the Baptist as the true start of their story. We need have no doubt that Joshua's baptism by John is an unassailable fact of his life if only because it was such a major embarrassment for the Gospel writers to admit that Jesus accepted baptism from another man for the forgiveness of his sins. Why did he seek baptism?

Jesus was, of course, sinless. Joshua, on the other hand, was human and, as such, liable to fall short of perfection, 'to miss the mark', which is what *hamartia*, the Gospel word for 'sin', really means.

Joshua was a man who often demanded extremely high standards of behaviour. He was no hypocrite, no masked Gentile actor playing a part on life's stage. He would not ask of others what he did not ask of himself. Inevitably then, if the standards were so high, there would be disappointment in himself, a sense of failure, of missing the mark; a sense of sin.

We can understand Joshua's willingness to accept baptism. But without a powerful sense of religious vocation, without some awareness of a world-shaping destiny, why did this Galilean carpenter abandon his work and make a three-day journey down to the Jordan near Jericho for his encounter with John?

The Fourth Gospel, always the maverick, manages to avoid actually saying that Jesus was baptised by John, but places their encounter near Bethabara where the Valley of Jezreel meets the Jordan, a comfortable day's journey from home. This enables Jesus to perform his first miracle at Cana, near Nazareth, scarcely two days later. It is altogether too neat. Too convenient. For John the Gospeller, the events surrounding the baptism could not be totally ignored but had to play a less significant role in his theological scenario.

Joshua the carpenter's long journey to a baptism site is easily explained. The presence there of other hard-working Galileans — fishermen from Lake Kinneret — provides the clue. Like Joshua they had been on their way to or from Jerusalem, before or after one of the pilgrim festivals, when they encountered John at a major crossing place on the Jordan.

For much of its length between Lake Kinneret and the Dead Sea, the river twists tortuously, falling more than two metres per kilometre (its name is from a Hebrew root meaning 'descend') and running so fast that pilgrims re-enacting John's baptising were often protected by ropes to save them from being swept away. Broad, shallow crossing places provided John with a ready-made stream of pilgrims and safer conditions for the immersion of repentants.

It is easy to imagine Joshua, perhaps at the end of his first day's journey from Jerusalem back to Nazareth, catching a first distant glimpse by dying sunlight of swarming pilgrims and caravans of animals at the river's edge, a colourful crowd constantly growing with new arrivals; closer — the first resonance of a raised voice, the first snatches of words, then the first, clear glimpse of the striking figure at the heart of the crowd and the first impact of his message: 'Repent, for the kingdom of God is at hand!'

We know how those words imprinted themselves in Joshua's mind. This would become his first 'gospel', his first proclamation, undoubtedly relayed by him with the rest of John's 'good news', though the Gospellers hesitated to show him following too faithfully in the footsteps of one they were anxious to portray as a mere forerunner, a herald, a preparer of the way.

The Jesus Seminar's theory that a major strand of Jesus' teaching was lifted by the Gospellers from John demonstrates the degree to which the messages of the two men could blur together. According to *Luke* 11:1, the Lord's Prayer was in fact a prayer that had previously been taught by John to his disciples. It seems equally possible that what Matthew and Luke present as John's Judgement Day preaching had been included in their 'sayings of Jesus' document because it was John's view of the end times as presented by Jesus.

Josephus testifies to John's extraordinary power as a preacher, how the crowds who gathered to hear him were 'greatly moved'; he speaks of 'the great influence John had over the people' and reports that 'they seemed ready to do anything he should advise' (*Antiquities* 18,5,2).

However, it is Joshua who provides our only first-hand account of John's impact. Perhaps a year later, he spoke of John to other men who had heard the Baptist preach:

> 'What did you go into the wilderness to see? A reed shaken by the wind? ... A man dressed in fine clothes? People in fine clothes are found in kings' palaces. So what did you go out to see? A prophet? Yes, I tell you, and more than a prophet ... Truly I tell you: among all those born of woman, no-one has risen greater than John the Baptist ... '   (*Matthew* 11:7-11)

Never before had Joshua heard a man speak as John did. A man who could address a crowd, yet in some mystical way make every word strike home to *him*, make every word seem meant for *him*; a man separated from him by tens of metres of river flat, by scores, even hundreds of people, yet able to make him see only that animated face lit by the fire he so often spoke of, as he drove home word after word, image after image, like the blows of the axe at the roots of the tree.

Suddenly, all the years of studying the *tanakh*, all the years of religious discussion and debate, of self-searching, reaching into himself and reaching up towards his Father in the Skies, his beloved *Abba* — suddenly it was all drawn together, focused, given new meaning.

The journey now had a destination. Until now it was as though he had been carving a piece of wood with care and skill, watching it take shape in his hands, yet without understanding its purpose. Now that shape and purpose were clear. It was like a yoke to settle across his own shoulders, giving him the ability to bear a far greater load, fully using all the spiritual and mental strength he had developed through the years.

Joshua may have been baptised that very night. We always imagine the baptism as a daytime event yet, surprisingly, a passage in the Romanian Josephus says that it took place at 'the seventh hour of night' — about an hour after midnight — harmonising with repeated statements in the Mandaean *Book of John* that the Baptist always preached at dusk and during the night. It also conforms to the earliest Christian practice of baptising candidates before dawn.

Joshua was almost certainly naked — as he is shown in the most ancient portrayals of his baptism — again establishing the practice followed by first-century Christians. He probably knelt in the waters of the Jordan by the light of the festival moon, as John's hand firmly guided his head down into the water, into the cold, swirling darkness.

We have no way of knowing what had been said and done in preparation for the rite. Early Christians prepared for three years, fasted for two days, performed a night-long vigil, were exorcised of demons and anointed from head to foot before entering 'cold, running water'. The rite was a 'mystery'. Its impact on the candidate was described as 'awe-inspiring'.

For Joshua the preparation had lasted much longer than three years and, without the elaborate rituals of early Christian baptism, his immersion in the icy waters of the Jordan produced an impact on him that was far beyond 'awe-inspiring':

The Baptist's hand released his head …

… and coming straight out of the water he saw the heavens torn apart and the Spirit came down on him like a dove. And a voice came out of the heavens: 'You are my beloved son, in whom I am delighted.' (*Mark* 1:10–11)

This is what Joshua *experienced*. Later Gospels would portray the moment as though John and those around Joshua saw and heard it all:

shafts of Cecil B. de Mille sunlight, a fog-filtered white dove fluttering down, a carefully modulated masculine voice speaking the adapted dialogue, '*This is my beloved son ...*'

Jewish religious tradition widely accepts the notion of the voice from the skies, the *bath kol*, literally 'daughter voice'. It has been described to me as 'a luminous thought, so bright that it becomes a voice'. It could be said that Joshua was conditioned to experience such a thing. The dove is another Jewish scriptural symbol, one that has exercised scholars as they pore over the baptism account. Does it refer to the spirit of God 'hovering' over the waters at the creation? To Noah's dove heralding the new world? Or does it meld both in Qumran's dove image — creation of a new world in the Messianic age? Might it echo Elijah telling Rabbi Jose, 'I have heard the *Bath Kol* which cooed like a dove' (*Berakoth* 3a)?

Such speculation misses the point. Joshua was describing a profound spiritual experience, a life-transforming moment, in the only spiritual language available to him. He embraced God as *Abba*. In this moment he felt the overwhelming conviction that God embraced him as a son. In the fullest sense of the word, this was a confirmation.

CHAPTER 8

The Voice of Satan?

The first three Gospels agree that immediately after his baptism by John, Jesus went off into the wilderness for forty days. The length of this interlude is 'Bible time'. It lends the weight of a holy number to something no more precise than 'two or three weeks' or even 'a week or two'. The event itself, however, is very much in character. Joshua often showed a need to get away from people so that he could become more sharply attuned to himself and to his God. The cathartic experience of his baptism would demand a time of self-searching and even redefinition before he could think of returning to Nazareth — or to the Baptist and his followers.

Traditionally he walked up into the naked, rain-shadow steppes of the Judaean wilderness and climbed to a cave in a spectacular peak overlooking Jericho, the Jordan Valley and the Dead Sea. It made a wonderful site for a nineteenth-century monastery, but the cave tradition was probably unknown before the twelfth century.

Mark claims Jesus was 'waited on by angels'. Luke says he was among 'wild animals'. A Jewish scholar suggests that this is a mistranslation of *halyuot*, 'holy men'. Could this mean that he sought out or stumbled on the 'monks' of Qumran? Probably not. Matthew and Luke say he fasted throughout the forty days. Joshua was a practical countryman. There was water to find and, near water, a few edible plants, herbs and berries. There was also whatever food he carried for his journey — scraps of bread, a few figs, perhaps some pickled fish. If Joshua wanted to fast — a common Jewish religious practice — he could. If he needed to eat, there was enough to keep him alive without the help of angels, or of holy warriors.

According to Matthew, Mark and Luke, it was during this time in the wilderness that Jesus was tempted by 'Satan', an event usually classified nowadays as either symbolic or mythological. Given Joshua's frame of mind in these watershed days, it would be unwise to reject the story too hastily. If it is not a total fiction, it could only have come from Joshua himself. Certainly, as the Jesus Seminar says, 'the dialogue is not subject to verification'. Perhaps more to the point, is it believable as a story told by Joshua? If so, why did he tell it?

Mark offers the bald statement that 'Jesus was being tested by Satan' for forty days (*Mark* 1:13). It is Matthew and Luke's 'sayings of Jesus' source that supplies the detail.

First, Satan says, 'If you are the Son of God, tell these stones to become bread.' Jesus answers, 'Man shall not live on bread only but by every word that comes from the mouth of God.'

Next, Satan takes Jesus to Jerusalem, sets him on the Temple's 'pinnacle' and says, 'If you are the Son of God, throw yourself down, for it is written, "He will command his angels concerning you, and they will lift you up in their hands, so that you will not strike your foot against a stone"'. Jesus counters, 'It is also written, "You must not tempt the Lord your God"'.

Finally, Satan takes him to a high mountain, shows him all the kingdoms of the world and says, 'I will give you all this, if you bow down and worship me.' Jesus, of course, has a ready answer: 'It is written, "You will worship the Lord your God and serve only him"'. (*Matthew* 4:1–11; *Luke* 4:1–13)

All Jesus' replies are from the book of *Deuteronomy* (8:3, 6:16 and 6:13), orations delivered by Moses on the Plateau of Moab across the Jordan. The sources and significance of Satan's enticements are less clear-cut.

The first temptation, to make bread from stones, has been related to everything from Christian Communion to the feeding of a Messianic army. If Joshua is hungry the resemblance of wilderness rocks to bread loaves seems inspiration enough for a very human temptation which is easily (and glibly) resisted.

The temptation to leap from the 'pinnacle' of the Temple and challenge God to send an angelic rescue team has been ingeniously linked to the death of Joshua's brother James (who was flung from the Temple wall and beaten to death), and to an execution for blasphemy (being hurled from a tower and stoned). Again, Joshua's inspiration may have been far more prosaic. Any visitor to the Temple who, like the historian Josephus, looked straight down the architectural perspective of Temple, terrace and city wall into the Kidron ravine would feel an almost hypnotic sense of peril and the possibility of deciding one's destiny with a single step. Many ordinary, sane people are fascinated by such immediate contact with the fine line they can tread between life and death. Sir Laurence Olivier used just such a situation — the view from Elsinore's parapet to rocks and breaking waves far below — as the filmic motivation for Hamlet's famous suicide soliloquy.

This is what the temptation story has been called — a soliloquy, Jesus debating these issues with himself, in much the same way that Jacob's night-long struggle with an angel (*Exodus* 35) can be recognised as a battle between the two aspects of Jacob.

Joshua, as he visualises this view from the Temple, which has probably attracted him since childhood, is struck by the thought that a single step could prove his affinity with God, here at the very heart of Israel; prove it to all people. And another temptation lurks here. This ultimate publicity stunt would also prove it to *him* in an ultimate test of faith.

Yet of all the temptations, the view of the world's kingdoms from the impossibly high mountain is the most challenging. Ignoring for the moment the price of earthly power as being worship of Satan, the third temptation strikes to the very heart of Joshua's story. It is the temptation to see himself as the Messiah, the human being who would rule the world as God's regent.

In the baptismal vision, God had confirmed Joshua's sonship just as he had confirmed King David's sonship. In fact, the New Testament's *Epistle to the Hebrews* and the Apocryphal *Gospel According to the Hebrews* both have the baptismal *Bath Kol* address Jesus in the precise words used by God in his coronation decree to David: 'You are my son, today I have begotten you' (*Psalm* 2:7 cf. *Hebrews* 5:5). Tellingly — in the light of the third temptation — the Davidic coronation decree continues:

'Ask of me
And I will make the nations your inheritance,
The ends of the earth your possession.'   (Psalm 2:8)

Could Joshua dare consider that he was intended as the heir of David, the Anointed One, the Messiah? That this was God's plan for him? If he did entertain the thought, even for a moment, he must have weighed God's words to David immediately after offering him the nations of the earth:

'You will rule them with an iron sceptre,
you will dash them to pieces like pottery.'   (Psalm 2:9)

This was a vision of earthly power such as the world had never seen. The Messiah would be 'the ultimate Jewish monarch'. Greater than all the previous kings of Egypt and Greece and Persia and Babylon. Greater even than Caesar. Ruling in God's name with God's omnipotence. Surely, to Joshua the Galilean carpenter, the idea that he could be the King Messiah was too fantastic to consider. Yet it had to be considered. It is hardly surprising that he needed to spend a biblical forty days away from the distractions of the everyday world.

The story of the temptations, so readily discarded as myth or symbol, is completely believable as Joshua's self-searching, described in terms that the people of his time and place could understand — even as *he* tried to understand it. The sense of 'specialness' he had experienced, all his knowledge, belief and faith, were focused, clarified and concentrated in an overpowering conviction of newly-gained power and authority.

This is what 'Satan' challenged him to confront. But who was Satan? The Gospel story suggests a dual identity. Matthew calls Satan the 'Tempter' or 'Examiner' or 'Tester', which carries the flavour of 'adversary', the Hebrew meaning of the name based on Satan's original Old Testament role as an accuser, a sort of prosecutor *for* God. Yet in challenging Joshua to worship him, Satan takes on his later post-Babylon biblical persona as an adversary of God — a personification of evil. So did Joshua actually claim to experience a vision of Satan and hear his voice, or was he again using biblical images to describe a more complex process?

The Gospel According to the Hebrews offers a startling interpretation. A fragment reads:

> 'Even now did my mother, the Holy Spirit, take me by one of my hairs and carried me away to the great Mount Tabor ...'

Immediately one is struck by the mention of Tabor — a spectacular peak rising abruptly to 562 metres above sea level, only 8 kilometres east of Nazareth. The mountain — and probably the sublime view from its summit — would have been known to Joshua since childhood.

Apart from this, Jerome, the great Christian Hebraist of the fourth century, who lived in Bethlehem for the last thirty-five years of his life, and the twentieth-century Jewish scholar, Jacobs, agree that the fragment is strongly Aramaic in its form, probably an accurately recorded saying. Here, we seem to have a pre-Gospel contact with some of Joshua's actual words — obviously referring to the temptation. Yet it is the Holy Spirit — surprisingly to Gentiles, in the female, compassionate aspect of the *Shekinah* — whom Joshua describes as carrying him to the mountain top. The 'Tempter', the 'Examiner', the 'Tester' is God.

The idea should not be totally unexpected. If the story of Job and his torments means anything, it represents a man's faith being tested to breaking point by God — or at least with God's complicity.

To Joshua God holds before him the *possibility* of worldwide kingship as God had held it before David: 'Ask of me ...', he had said. As Joshua showed later when he was again confronted by this temptation, it was a disturbing inner voice that tempted him to accept. And again he called that inner voice 'Satan'. To Joshua, in spite of the demands of Messiahship, there was something darkly disturbing in the concept of boundless power being placed in the hands of a man. Must its price be submission to Satan? In the words of Malcolm Muggeridge:

> Many have thought otherwise, and sought power in the belief that by its exercise they could lead men to brotherhood and happiness and peace; invariably with disastrous consequences. Always in the end the bargain with the devil has to be fulfilled — as any Stalin or Napoleon or Cromwell must verify.

If Joshua thought along such lines, he would consider David's abuse of power, Solomon's transgression of the Law, the atrocities of the more fanatical Hasmonean kings and, above them all, the countless crimes committed by King Herod of such recent memory. Of course, the Messiah would be untouched by the threat of corruption through power; even the absolute corruption of absolute power. He would achieve this by transcending ordinary humanity; he would remain a man, but a man reborn with holiness to match the limitless power at his disposal. Joshua had felt himself sanctioned as a Son of God, the baptism almost like an anointing. Yet the views from the Temple and Mount Tabor would continue to haunt him.

Joshua resisted 'Satan' — though only in this first encounter. In Luke's words: 'The devil departed from him *awaiting a better time*' (*Luke* 4:13). Joshua was to hear that voice again. According to the Gospels he eventually succumbed to all three temptations. Meanwhile he began to gather disciples. The Gospels don't agree as to how he did this or why those men were chosen. Both questions must be addressed.

CHAPTER 9

'Ruffians of the Deepest Dye'

Most Christians struggle to name the Twelve Disciples. It isn't surprising; even the Gospels don't agree as to who they were.

Matthew and Mark list them as: Simon, nicknamed by Jesus as 'Peter' (meaning 'Rock' — *Kepha* in Aramaic and *Petra* in Greek); Simon's brother, Andrew; another pair of brothers, James the Older and John, nicknamed by Jesus as *Boanerges*, 'Sons of Thunder'; Philip; Bartholomew; Thomas; Matthew, a customs duty collector; James the Younger, son of Alphaeus; Thaddeus, sometimes called Lebbaeus and in some Old Latin manuscripts, replaced by 'Judas the Zealot'; Simon the Canaanite; and Judas Iscariot (*Matthew* 10:24; *Mark* 3:16–19).

Luke has two lists which agree with these, except that he substitutes 'Judas [son or brother] of James' for 'Thaddeus' and 'Simon the Zealot' for 'Simon the Canaanite' ('Canaanite' probably sprang from confusion between the Hebrew words, *kanai*, 'Zealot' and *kena'ani*, 'Canaanite') (*Luke* 6:13–16; *Acts* 1:13).

John provides no list of disciples but immediately confuses the issue by making 'Nathanael of Cana in Galilee' the fourth or fifth man to follow Jesus (*John* 2:2–3). Nathanael is still there for Jesus' resurrection appearance in Galilee (*John* 21:2), yet no other Gospel mentions him. Since John ignores Bartholomew (along with five other disciples) and since the other Gospels don't mention Bartholomew outside their lists, some authorities opt for Bartholomew and Nathanael being the same man (with the ingenious explanation that 'Bartholomew' is *bar Talmai*, 'son of Talmai' and therefore the disciple's actual name is 'Nathanael son of Talmai').

The exercise probably illustrates what have been called 'harmonising tendencies' — overzealous attempts to avoid contradictions in the Gospels — as demonstrated by the King James Version when it combines two variant names as 'Lebbaeus whose surname was Thaddeus', thus disposing of one manuscript inconsistency. The problem of 'Judas the Zealot' is ignored.

This touches one of the less obvious mysteries. 'Thomas' is not a name but an identification or a nickname — Aramaic for 'the twin' (John calls him *Didymos*, Greek for 'the twin'). Clearly, 'the twin' also had a name. An early Syriac Gospel manuscript, the Church's first great historian, Eusebius, and the Gnostic *Gospel of Thomas* all call him 'Judas Thomas', which works perfectly well until we look at Luke's lists and find that we now have 'Judas (son or brother) of James' and 'Judas Iscariot' as well as '(Judas) Thomas' — *three* Judases.

Matthew and Mark create a similar problem. It is just possible to see their *Thaddeus* ('he that praises') as a confusion with Luke's *Judas* ('praise of the Lord'), but they both also list Judas Iscariot and Thomas — again giving us three Judases.

It is certainly possible that three disciples should have the same name. Half of the group have shared names anyway, and 'Judas' was specially popular in this place and time. However, it is equally easy to understand the early oral tradition becoming confused, especially when one of the Judases filled the role of traitor and blighted anyone else of the same name. It may well be that one of the Judases has been doubled up — two different ways of differentiating him from Judas Iscariot have become two different disciples, one of them filling a place among the Twelve actually occupied by one of the more obscure figures such as Thaddeus, Lebbaeus or Bartholomew.

Let's pursue 'Judas Thomas' a little further. If he was 'the twin', whose twin was he? The Gnostic *Book of Thomas the Contender* supposedly records 'the secret words that the Saviour spoke to Judas Thomas'. Startlingly, the second sentence spoken by Jesus begins, 'Now since it has been said that you are my twin and true companion ...' (Codex 11 Treatise 7).

If this were true — that Jesus had a twin brother — it would create gigantic problems, and not only with the Nativity.

If the resurrected Jesus was encountered in a situation where Judas Thomas was absent, how could anyone be sure that they were seeing Jesus rather than his twin? Ingeniously, it has been suggested that this was the inspiration for the story of 'Doubting Thomas' — the understandable doubts of the disciples being transferred to Thomas and expressed by him, then laid to rest when the twin brother meets the resurrected Jesus face-to-face and is invited to touch his wounds.

In a darker sidelight, an Apocryphal *Gospel According to Barnabas* tells how Judas Iscariot is miraculously transformed into Jesus's double and crucified in his place. Could this story spring from a tradition of Judas Thomas playing a similar role in the crucifixion narrative?

Both these works had very specific agendas. Making 'the twin' a twin of Jesus gave a Gnostic writer of the late second century an intimate setting (in 'knowing himself' he would also know 'the depth of the all') for a highly ascetic treatise which has little to do with Jesus and even less with Joshua. *The Gospel According to Barnabas* is dismissed by Apocrypha authority M.R. James as 'a forgery of the late fifteenth or sixteenth century, by a renegade from Christianity to Islam'. It seems highly unlikely that Jesus and Judas were twins.

There is a less startling but more likely solution to the 'twin' mystery. All four lists of the disciples place Judas ('not Iscariot') and Simon the Zealot together, suggesting some relationship. Apocryphal accounts have them preaching together in Mesopotamia and sharing martyrdom in Persia. As St Jude and St Simon, they have the same feast day, 28 October. If we recall the 'Old Latin' manuscript that spoke of 'Judas the Zealot' and then set him beside 'Simon the Zealot', we seem to have completed a picture of parallel lives. 'Thomas' has been lost — supposedly in India, but his bones mysteriously turned up in Mesopotamia.

It seems highly credible that Judas and Simon were the twins. If this is correct, a chain of relationship develops. Judas, according to Luke, is the son or brother of James the Younger, son of Alphaeus. Assuming for the moment that Judas is a brother, *his* father, too, would be Alphaeus. As we have seen, James the Younger was the brother of Jesus and they had a brother called Judas. Their father, however, was not Alphaeus but Joseph, though their stepfather was Cleopas. Now ... and we have to be careful that this is not another 'harmonising tendency' ... *John* 19:25 suggests that Cleopas and Alphaeus are the same man. 'Cleopas' and its variants, 'Clopas' and 'Cleophas', probably represent the Aramaic *Chalphai*. It is often pointed out that John's 'Clopas' is almost a Greek transliteration of *Chalphai* (via 'Colpa') while 'Alphaeus' is the name in a more obviously Greek form with the 'Ch' of 'Chalphai' becoming 'H', then disappearing.

Because James, who was younger than Jesus, could hardly have a son old enough to be a disciple, we have further confirmation that our assumption

A nineteenth-century engraving vividly portrays the south-east corner of the Temple terrace set above the steep flank of the Kidron Valley. In Joshua's day, the eastern end of the magnificent Royal Stoa towered 30 metres higher. This was the traditional 'Pinnacle of the Temple' where Joshua was tempted to literally throw himself on God's mercy. (Left), in one of James Tissot's illustrations to his *Life of Christ*, Satan carries Jesus, in a dream or trance-like state, above the Temple façade.

The nineteenth-century Danish artist Carl Bloch shows Joshua protesting to his disciples: 'Let the children come to me; don't stop them … Believe me, unless you can approach the kingdom of God like a small child, you will never enter it' (*Mark* 10:13–14). The interior is too lavish for a house of the place and time but Bloch's disciple figure is unique in religious art, highly believable as a tough young Galilean 'minder'. Such men probably protected Joshua from violence on more than one occasion.

As a five-year-old the author first saw this illustration by A. Twidle in Adelaide Bee Evans's, *The Children s Friend*. It shows 'Jesus receiving the children into the home He has gone to prepare for them'. More than sixty years later, the author comments: 'I knew these children had died and I found the image very moving; I still do.'

JOHN, THE BROTHER OF JAMES.

This extraordinary portrayal of the Apostle John (based on a Murillo painting of the Virgin Mary!) follows the traditional image of him as a rather effeminate-looking youth, which in turn springs from the belief that he was 'the beloved disciple' — a telling comment on the homosexual undertones that developed in Paulian Christianity. The real John was a tough, Galilean fisherman whose fiery temperament probably brought an early end to his life.

HCENCHMEION ^{Δε}
ΓΟΝ·ΟΥΤΟCECTΙΝ
ΑΛΗΘ ωCOΠΡΟΦΗ
ΤΗCΟEICΤΟΝΚ°^{εμ}°
ΕΡΧΟΜΕΝΟC·
ΙCΟΥΝΓΝΟΥCΟΤΙ
ΜΕΛΛΟΥCΙΝΕΡΧ^ε
CΘΑΙΚΑΙΑΡΠΑΖΕΙΝ
ΑΥΤΟΝΚΑΙΑΝΑ^{ΔΙΝ}ΑΠΟΙ^Ι ωCΙΝ
ΚΝΥΝΑΙΒΑCΙΛΕΑ
ΝΑ^{ΑΝΕΧ ωΡΙCCΕΝ}
ΑΦΕΥΓΕΙΠΑΛΙΝΕΙC^{ΤΟ}

Codex Sinaiticus of the fourth century, the earliest complete manuscript of the New Testament, shows characteristic lack of word separation and punctuation (and division into verses, which didn't happen until the mid-sixteenth century). This important passage from *John* (6:14-15) contains words and ideas central to Joshua's ministry: in the first line, *semeion* ('sign' or 'miracle'); at the end of the third line and the start of the next, *prophetes* ('prophet'); and at the end of the second last line, *basilea* ('king'). After the miraculous feeding of the 5000, the 'sign' prompts the crowd to hail him as 'the prophet', the one coming into the world. Joshua retreats, fearing that they are about to make him 'king'. At the start of the sixth line is *Isou* — 'Jesus'.

The climax of the Salome fantasy — based on a dubious Gospel story embellished by equally dubious use of historical sources. In Beardsley's illustration to Oscar Wilde's play, the evil and sensuous princess has won the head of John the Baptist by performing the Dance of the Seven Veils for her stepfather, Herod Antipas. All evidence suggests that John was killed by Antipas because he was seen as a political threat.

was right and Judas *was* the brother of James (as he identifies himself in *The Epistle of Jude*). This would mean then that the three disciples — the twins, Judas and Simon, and James the Younger — were brothers of Jesus, or, less provocatively and more accurately, all three were brothers of Joshua.

This goes against the normal Gospel image of Jesus being isolated from his family during his ministry. There is no indication — certainly not in Matthew, Mark or Luke — that anyone from his earlier life joined him. They portray every disciple as a new friend, someone encountered along the way, a surprising situation for a man of his obvious charm and sociability; also, one would feel, a challenging foundation for his ministry.

John contradicts this picture early in his Gospel when, less than a week after the baptism, Jesus' mother and brothers accompanied him and the disciples to Capernaum (*John* 2:12). Later, Jesus and his brothers prepared for a trip to Jerusalem to celebrate the Feast of Tabernacles (*John* 7:2–10).

John helps to confirm that from the beginning, at least one and possibly three of Joshua's brothers were followers, leaving only Joseph — probably the youngest — in Nazareth with Mary and the girls.

What of the other disciples? The one immutable fact is that there were twelve of them — one representing each tribe of pre-Exile Israel. The significance of this is driven home after the supposed suicide of Judas Iscariot. A man must be chosen to replace him; there *must* be a disciple for each tribe. Luke records Joshua telling them:

'You are the ones who have stood by me through my trials; and I bestow on you, as my Father has bestowed on me, a kingdom, so that you may eat and drink at my table in my kingdom, and you will sit on thrones judging the twelve tribes of Israel.' (*Luke* 22:28–30 cf. *Matthew* 19:28)

It is claimed, of course, that Joshua was speaking metaphorically, or symbolically, but this is not the way his disciples understood him. Shortly before this, James and John, the 'Sons of Thunder' had made a characteristically impulsive appeal, 'Grant us to sit, one at your right hand and one at your left, in your glory' (*Mark* 10:37). And, according to Luke, the last thing the disciples ever said to Jesus was the unequivocal question, 'Lord, is this the time when you are going to restore the kingdom to Israel?' (*Acts* 1:6).

Always the cry comes up that they misunderstood; that this was never the intention of his ministry. In Matthew Henry's commentary on this speech: 'Christ came to set up his own kingdom, and that a kingdom of heaven, not to restore the kingdom of Israel, an earthly kingdom.'

It is Joshua's stepfather, Cleopas, who laments after his death, 'We were hoping that he was the one who would redeem Israel' (*Luke* 24:21), prompting John Howard Yoder's comment that this 'is not just one more testimony to the disciples' obtuse failure to get Jesus' real point; *it is an eyewitness report of the way Jesus had been heard.*' [my italics]

Perhaps the clearest indication of 'the way Jesus had been heard' is to be found among the identities of the Twelve. Simon is named directly as a Zealot. Judas, brother of James, has been called a Zealot. Simon called Peter is identified as *Barjona* — usually read as 'son of John' or 'son of Jona'. *Barjona* or *Baryona* is Aramaic for 'one outside the law' — an outlaw, a Zealot. If this seems far-fetched, we will see Simon Peter urging Joshua to assume the role of a physical Messiah and he will emerge as the only one of the disciples to engage in armed violence. The Zealot label seems well applied to him.

If Peter was a Zealot and apparently a follower of the Baptist, was his brother Andrew, who was definitely one of John's disciples, also a Zealot? Like their friend Philip, they were fishermen, originally from Bethsaida, a fishing town on the shores of Galilee — men physically hardened by an outdoor life of rowing, hauling nets and manhandling their big boats.

James the Older and John were also fishermen. John usually figures in Christian art as a rather pretty teenager with long fair hair, presumably because he is imagined to be 'the beloved disciple' (hardly a testimony to Jesus' masculinity). There is no reason to see the two brothers as other than tough young fishermen; remember that Joshua calls them 'Sons of Thunder'. James was the first of the disciples to die — beheaded in Jerusalem in about 44 AD. In spite of traditions that John lived to a great age (perhaps a confusion with John Mark) we have noted the evidence that he died with his brother — a pair of hotheads who saw Joshua's mission as something to live and die for. It comes as no surprise that they, too, are sometimes seen as Zealots. With Simon Peter *Barjona* they formed the inner circle of the Twelve.

Judas Iscariot, that brooding figure among the disciples, held a position of trust as treasurer of the group, and, among men with a clear and probably aggressive sense of hierarchy, he occupied an honoured position at their meals.

The odd name 'Iscariot' has usually been interpreted as *ish Kerioth*, 'a man of Kerioth' but it is now widely accepted as *Sikarios*. Judas emerges as one of the *Sicarii*, 'dagger men', the Zealot extremists. Three times in *John*, Judas Iscariot is identified as 'Judas of Simon Iscariot' (*John* 6:71, 13:2 and 13:26). Quite arbitrarily, this is usually translated as 'Judas *son* of Simon Iscariot'. By using the equally legitimate reading, 'Judas *brother* of Simon Iscariot', we find that Judas *Sikarios* ('the Zealot') is a brother of Simon *Sikarios* ('the Zealot'). We seem to have rediscovered Joshua's Zealot twin brothers, Judas and Simon, with one of them in a most unlikely guise — as the 'traitor' Judas. In other words, St Jude the Obscure and Judas Iscariot appear to be the same man, a fusion that explains both the 'obscurity' of St Jude and the contradictory Gospel accounts of Judas Iscariot's death. For the moment, however, it is enough to understand that he is one of the *Sicarii*.

Of the Twelve, six or more were believably Zealots. It becomes clearer how a second-century Christian who wrote in the name of Barnabas could say of Jesus, 'It was in His choice of the Apostles, who were to preach His Gospel, that He truly showed Himself the Son of God: *for those men were ruffians of the deepest dye*, which proved that He came not to call saints, but sinners.' [my italics] (*Epistle of Barnabas* — very nearly included in the New Testament)

It is perhaps more understandable that they are 'ruffians' if we accept the traditional picture of Jesus wandering through Galilee and gathering his followers in a series of chance meetings; but this isn't the way it happened. These men were handpicked from a much larger group which gathered around Joshua in his early days as a preacher of the Baptist's Gospel. Luke describes this widely ignored process:

> It was during this time that he went up onto the mountain to pray; and he spent the night in prayer to God. And when day broke, *he called his disciples, choosing twelve of them, whom he also named apostles.* [my italics] (*Luke* 6:12–13)

Joshua selected his 'sinners' only after a nightlong prayer vigil. Among the 'saints' — or other 'sinners' — he rejected as Apostles were Nathanael, 'Joseph called Barsabbas, who was also known as Justus', and Matthias, all of whom had joined him immediately after his baptism (*Acts* 1:21–6). All remained with him until his death and then continued to follow the eleven surviving Apostles. (Matthias was chosen by lot to replace Judas and reconstitute the Twelve.) All these men were probably included in the outer circle of seventy disciples who were appointed by Joshua as evangelists (*Luke* 10:1).

It is often pointed out that this group replicates the seventy 'elders of Israel' of Exodus 24:1. It is worth noting that when the Zealots captured the Jerusalem Temple in 66 AD and began to take charge of the city, 'they called together, by a public proclamation, seventy of the principal men of the populace for a show, as if they were real judges ...' (Josephus *Wars* 4, 5, 4). The

Zealots were setting up their own Sanhedrin. It is likely that Joshua's seventy at least symbolised a senate of the coming kingdom — a symbol which would be seen by the 'Jerusalemites' as a threat to their power base and, if no such symbol were intended, the mere selection of seventy men was enough to alarm them.

To Matthew Henry and generations of Christian commentators, such alarm was misplaced. The Sanhedrin had nothing to fear from Jesus. His kingdom was not of the earth. This is our great problem as we confront his ministry.

If Joshua was concerned with some heavenly kingdom where all earthly concerns were irrelevant — or a spiritual kingdom in people's hearts — why would Zealots follow him in preference to the Baptist? Why would any first-century Jew follow him? The Kingdom of God and the Kingdom of Heaven were the same thing: the rule of God on earth administered by God's people with God's power. And that rule was incompatible with Roman domination of Israel.

It is argued by respected scholars that Rome's occupation of Israel was comparatively benevolent, low-profile, virtually non-existent in areas like Galilee. Ignoring the green memories of the hundreds of roadside crosses in the Galilean hills around Sepphoris, ignoring the funeral pyre of that city, ignoring the calculatedly obvious Roman military presence in Jerusalem at the very time when Galileans visited the city for pilgrim festivals — even ignoring all this, the prefecture of Pontius Pilate could not be ignored. Here was a man carrying out a policy of confrontation, of provocation; a man trying to pick a fight. The affair of the standards with Caesar's effigies was nearly four years earlier, and the Jews had won the fight; but what of Pilate's next move?

In an extraordinary replay of his gesture with the standards — an unspec-ified time later — Pilate had gilt 'votive shields' displayed around the huge Herodian palace he occupied while in Jerusalem. These were semi-religious plaques revering Tiberius as 'son of the divine Augustus'. Philo of Alexandria had no doubt that Pilate had placed them across this busy highpoint of the city 'more with the object of vexing the multitude than of doing honour to Tiberius'.

Pilate succeeded in his aim and held his ground so arrogantly against the outraged people of Jerusalem that they enlisted Herod's four surviving sons — Herod Antipas, Herod Philip, Herod Boethus and the obscure Phaesalus — to negotiate with the Prefect for removal of the offensive shields.

The four brothers put their case strongly, warning that these flaunted imperial icons could provoke 'a sedition', and politely asking if the emperor had authorised the display, 'so that we ... may cease to trouble you and may address our supplication to your master.'

Philo tells us that Pilate was shaken by this clever threat, but also 'exasperated ... to the greatest possible degree', and his rage would not allow retreat. He refused the request, probably confident that his Jew-hating patron, Sejanus, would support his action.

The four brothers sent their petition to Tiberius, a dangerous gamble for the two tetrarchs. Guy Schofield argues shrewdly that the ambitious Herodias probably urged her husband to take this action — as she would urge him to petition another Caesar in years to come. Antipas clearly knew of Sejanus's power, but was encouraged to count on his own Roman background and his friendship with the royal family to tip the scales against Pilate. There was another key factor. Undoubtedly, the brothers' petition again mentioned fear of 'a sedition'. However much Sejanus wanted to break the stiff-necked Jews, the threat of full-blown rebellion in this sensitive buffer-zone between Syria and Egypt might be enough to curb even him. The gamble worked. The petition was allowed to reach Tiberius and he immediately sent off a strongly worded dispatch ordering Pilate to take down the shields (Philo, *Embassy to Gaius* 38, 299–305).

Pilate was, says Philo, 'a man of most ferocious passions'. His anger at this second defeat is unimaginable. We are told that he regarded Antipas as an enemy (*Luke* 23:12) — if not before, certainly now. It was in this climate that Antipas saw John the Baptist's mission as threatening the stability of his tetrarchy of Galilee and Peraea, perhaps even touching Pilate's Judaea. Any show of weakness by Antipas would give Pilate the ammunition to take revenge and destroy him. No threat of 'a sedition' could be tolerated.

It might have taken months for Antipas to make his decision. Which would be the greater threat to the peace of his realm — making an unpopular move against an enormously popular figure, or letting the Baptist continue his destabilising mission?

Until the decision was made, Joshua and his first followers posed no great problem. If Antipas knew anything of the group, it would seem a mere sideshow of the Baptist's campaign — doing what the Baptist did, saying what the Baptist said. For the moment, the religious authorities of Jerusalem could keep a wary eye on this scruffy little band of wanderers. Antipas would be in excellent standing with the 'Jerusalemites' after the affair of the imperial shields, and they didn't want trouble with Rome any more than he did.

They would offer no protest at the arrest of the Baptist, and they could be counted on to harass the remnants of his movement in Judaea and throughout the provinces.

Antipas made his decision. John the Baptist was arrested.

CHAPTER 10

Salome Unveiled

Mystery shrouds the murder of John the Baptist — a very unlikely mystery when everything connected with the event is supposedly so well known. But when we ask the questions that are fundamental to any murder investigation, there are no unequivocal answers. Who was responsible for his death? Why was he killed? Where did he die? How was the murder carried out?

John died as he lived, a mysterious and controversial figure. His mission was supposedly 'to prepare the way' for Jesus. This was almost certainly untrue, yet, in a curious way, this is precisely what happened. John's 'way' led to his own imprisonment and murder, and, in following the same path, Joshua began his journey towards death on a Roman cross. At least that much is clear.

The Gospels provide most of the evidence for this conclusion while generally trying to obscure a direct relationship between the beginning of Jesus' ministry and the imprisonment of John. Immediately after the temptation, Matthew and Mark say that John the Baptist is arrested — without explaining why, at this point — and that Jesus goes back to Galilee, preaching John's message and starting to pick up disciples along the way. No connection is made; the events are simply described in sequence. Luke ignores the arrest of the Baptist until much later, and has Jesus return to Galilee, 'filled with the power of the Spirit'.

There is an uneasy sense of something missing from these accounts. Matthew and Mark write as though we already know of John's arrest, or as though it was in some way anticipated or expected ('Now after John was arrested ...'). We have encountered the beginning of what John Romer calls 'the unstated drama'.

It is the Gospel of John which, after glossing over the baptism and ignoring the temptation, points to some missing pieces of the story. And vital pieces they are.

At the outset, the Gospel claims that Jesus' first two disciples — Andrew and an unnamed companion — have been disciples of the Baptist, who supposedly points out Jesus to them and says, 'Look, here is the Lamb of God!' After talking with Jesus for several hours, Andrew tells his brother, Simon, 'We have found the Messiah' (*John* 1:35–41). It appears that Simon, too, has been a disciple of the Baptist.

John the Baptist's description of Jesus as 'the Lamb of God' is a symbol of sacrificial death, utterly meaningless some four years before the crucifixion and embarrassingly obvious as part of the Fourth Gospel's theological agenda. Not so its claim that Jesus began his ministry with disciples of the Baptist as his first followers — especially when this author has so carefully avoided the actual *fact* of Jesus' baptism by John. Later, the Gospel reveals that Jesus and his disciples conduct a baptism ministry in parallel with, or even in subtle competition with, John's (*John* 3:22–4:2). The Fourth Gospel also makes it clear that this ministry has made enemies for Jesus in Judaea, prompting him to make an apparently hurried departure (*John* 4:1–5) for Galilee via hostile Samaria. This is intriguing, especially as his stopping place, Sychar (the Old Testament city of Shechem), is recorded by Josephus as providing sanctuary for Jewish fugitives in dispute with the religious authorities of Jerusalem (*Antiquities* 11, 8, 7).

John's baptism ministry has led to his arrest. A similar ministry, conducted by Jesus and his disciples, makes him a fugitive. We have seen that Herod Antipas feared John's mission 'might lead to some form of sedition' and that John's imprisonment and execution was aimed at forestalling 'an uprising'. The Gospels tell us that Herod believes Jesus to be the Baptist returned from the dead, and that he wants him killed. This suggests that, in Herod's eyes, Jesus posed a similar threat of rebellion.

Josephus is no further help here. His account records Herod's fears of John but offers nothing to explain them. He does not even hint at John's fire-and-brimstone preaching, but simply has him urging virtue, righteousness and piety (*Antiquities* 18, 5, 1). Again, something is missing.

To Christians, there is no mystery about reasons for John the Baptist's imprisonment and death, because eventually the Gospels give their version of the story (*Matthew* 14:1–12; *Mark* 6:14–29). Herod Antipas has married Herodias, the wife of his brother Philip. The Baptist denounces the marriage as unlawful; an enraged Herodias wants him killed. Herod imprisons John but is reluctant to kill him because of the man's great popularity and/or righteousness. Then, at a banquet to celebrate Herod's birthday, Herodias's daughter dances for her stepfather. Traditionally, she performs the Dance of the Seven Veils, the archetypal striptease. Even the editors of the sober New International Version of the Bible comment in a text note: 'The dance was unquestionably lascivious.' Herod is delighted and rashly swears to give the girl anything she wants, 'even half my kingdom'. Herodias tells her daughter to ask for the Baptist's head. It is delivered to her on a platter. According to early traditions recorded by Jerome and Nicephorus, Herodias sticks needles through John's tongue and has his body thrown into a chasm beside the palace .

Not surprisingly, this is one of the great set pieces of the New Testament — a perennial delight for poets, playwrights, librettists, artists, composers, choreographers and film-makers. Even writers of history nail their colours to the mast with a biblical footnote or two and summon images of the nubile temptress, the drunken, lecherous stepfather and the malignant woman manipulating them both.

Other details are drawn — rather carelessly — from Josephus's account; that the married Herod fell in love with Herodias while staying with her and her husband on a visit to Rome; that the girl who danced for Herod was called Salome; that John was imprisoned and executed in the palace fortress of Machaerus beyond the Dead Sea.

An extraordinary amount of bad history has been built on the blending of these sources. The evidence needs to be examined very carefully. What happened to John is intriguing. To know *why* it happened is vital to an understanding of Joshua's ministry.

✝✝✝

As soon as we look at Josephus's account of the romance between Herod and Herodias, the Gospel story has to be modified. Matthew and Mark say that Herodias was the wife of Herod's brother, Philip. They are wrong.

Herod Philip, the Tetrarch of Israel's north-eastern province, was Herod Antipas's half-brother, a son of Herod the Great. When Philip died childless in 33–34 AD he was married to Salome, daughter of Herodias (*Antiquities* 18,4,6; 18,5,4). The Herods were noted for inbreeding, but marriage between father and daughter was beyond the pale, even for them. The problem of Philip being childless seems a minor complication.

Faced with this genealogical dead-end, generations of Christian scholars have invented a second Herod Philip to justify the Gospellers' error, creating a forest of Herodian family trees to perpetuate this fiction.

Herodias's husband, the father of Salome, was not Philip but another half-brother of Herod Antipas, another son of Herod the Great. He was called Herod (*Antiquities* 18, 5, 4), one of only two of the old despot's sons actually named after him (the others had 'Herod' added to their given names as a dynastic title). Sometimes called Herod Boethus after a famous great-grandfather on his mother's side, he had been seen as Herod's heir until his mother was accused of complicity in a plan to murder her husband. She was divorced and her son, Herod, disinherited. There is no evidence that this man, Herodias's husband and Salome's father, carried the name of his brother Philip, whether as 'Herod Philip' or 'Philip Boethus'. It all seems a trivial matter but it encourages wariness of equally self-deceptive scholarship being brought to bear on weightier issues.

(In defence of Luke's historical ability, it must be pointed out that, having read Josephus, he does not follow Mark and, like some later manuscripts of Matthew, says that Herod Antipas married Herodias, who is described simply as 'his brother's wife'.)

Some historians, clinging to Mark's error, note that Philip the Tetrarch died in 33–34 AD, assume that this left Herodias as a widow and therefore have her marry Herod Antipas after this date, helping to calculate a date of 36 AD for the death of Jesus. Others, while avoiding the trap of having Philip married to Herodias, still argue, from flawed reading of Josephus, that Philip's death preceded the marriage of Herod and Herodias and they therefore arrive at the same 36 AD date for Jesus' execution.

The facts are straightforward. Josephus records Philip's death in 33–34 AD. He then says that 'about this time' Herod and Aretas IV, King of the Nabatean Arabs, had a 'quarrel'. He traces this back to Aretas's daughter, Herod's wife, fleeing to her father when she got wind of Herod's plans to divorce her and marry Herodias. This, says Josephus, was 'the first occasion' of bad blood between the two rulers, which was later aggravated by a border dispute — the actual 'quarrel' — and eventually degenerated to the point of warfare, a chain of events stretching across some six years.

Josephus tells the story of Herod's and Herodias's romance as a flash-back, setting the scene for the escalating feud between Herod and his former father-in-law. More importantly, according to the Gospels he is setting the scene for John the Baptist's fatal conflict with Herod. Josephus records Philip's death and continues:

> About this time Aretas (the King of Arabia Petrea) and Herod had a quarrel, on the account following: Herod the Tetrarch had married the daughter of Aretas and had lived with her a great while; *but when he was once at Rome*, he lodged with Herod [Boethus], who was his brother indeed, but not by the same mother ... However, he fell in love with Herodias, this last Herod's wife, who was the daughter of Aristobulus their brother ... [Antipas] ventured to talk to her about a marriage between them; which address when she admitted, an agreement was made for her to change her habitation, and come to him *as soon as he should return from Rome*: one article of this marriage was also this, that he should divorce Aretas's daughter. *So Antipas, when he had made this agreement, sailed to Rome*; but when he had done there the business he went about, and was returned again, his wife having discovered the agreement he had made with Herodias ... desired him to send her to Machaerus, which is a place on the borders of the dominions of Aretas and Herod, without informing him of any of her intentions ... and she soon came to her father, and told him of Herod's intentions. So Aretas made this the first occasion of his enmity between him and Herod who had also some quarrel with him about their limits at the country of Gamalitis.
>
> [my italics] (*Antiquities* 18,5,1)

You don't have to read the original Greek to realise that Josephus's best-known translator, Whiston, has made a simple mistake, indicated by the three emphasised passages. Antipas did not stay with Herod Boethus and Herodias while *at* Rome but while he was *on his way to* Rome and obviously while still in Israel. As a member of the royal family barred from succession, Herod Boethus — and Herodias — could have lived in one of the 'several' palaces at Caesarea, Antipas's port of embarkation, though it seems more likely that the Tetrarch broke his journey at Sepphoris, a comfortable day's travel from Tiberias and a logical, attractive place for wealthy royals to establish their home.

At first glance Whiston's error, which has been followed by innumerable historians, seems unimportant. Surely, *what* happened is more important than *where* it happened. On the contrary, the relocation means that this royal scandal did not take place in the capital of debauchery, faraway Rome, but in the Jewish homeland less than 100 kilometres from Jerusalem and probably only a few kilometres from Nazareth. More than ever, this meant that the next phase of the story played a crucial role in the lives of John and Joshua.

Again from Josephus:

Herodias ... had a daughter Salome; after whose birth Herodias took upon her to confound the laws of our country, and divorce herself from her husband while he was alive, and was married to Herod Antipas, her husband's brother.

(Antiquities 18,5,4)

Under Roman law (possibly invoked by Antipas on his visit to Rome) it was permissible, even commonplace for a woman to divorce her husband; yet as Josephus makes clear, this was against the Jewish Law, which permitted only divorce of a wife by her husband. To observant Jews, Herod Antipas and his new wife were guilty of adultery. Further, under Jewish Law it was forbidden to marry a brother's former wife — even after his death — if she had borne him a child. In yet another blight on the union, Herod had married his niece, a relationship not forbidden under the Mosaic code, but regarded by the Qumran sect as 'abominable'. Whether or not they shared this last view, John and Joshua would have seen the marriage as another assault on Jewish belief, as another display of Gentile contempt for the rule of God, and as further confirmation that the end times were beginning.

It is undoubtedly true that John criticised Herod's marriage with Herodias. After John's death, this line of attack lay behind some of Joshua's teaching. He adopted an extreme position in opposing divorce, declaring: 'Whoever divorces his wife and marries another, commits adultery against her; *and if she divorces her husband and marries another she commits adultery*' [my italics] (*Mark* 10:10–12). As we've noted, divorce of a husband was a situation completely outside Jewish Law, but a burning issue in Galilee after Herodias divorced Herod Boethus to marry Antipas. This explains why the normally liberal Joshua took a harsher approach to divorce than any Pharisees of his day. In Israel, politics and religion were always two sides of the one medal, or — more accurately perhaps — two angles on the one hologram. Joshua tilts the hologram, the politics of the divorce question shine out from his teaching in a clear accusation that Herod and Herodias are living in adultery.

The American scholar E.P. Sanders argues strongly that John's attack on the marriage and his fiery end-times preaching — as described in the Gospels — were enough to trigger Antipas's fear of rebellion, which was stated by Josephus as the reason for John's arrest and execution. This is certainly true. The problem is that Josephus does not mention John's denunciation of Herod's marriage, yet he records that the Tetrarch's defeat in a border battle with his former father-in-law was seen by his subjects as divine retribution for killing the Baptist. Surely, if Josephus had known of John's attack on Herod's marriage — an attack on the primary cause of this enmity — he would have included it as a key element of his story. Divine punishment for sinful behaviour was one of his favourite themes. In the same way, Josephus offers no hint of John's apocalyptic message, but merely shows him extolling the classic virtues of Judaism. It is generally agreed that early Christian editors have tampered with Josephus's text. However, it is inconceivable that they would have removed material which supported the Gospel accounts.

The conclusion seems inescapable: Josephus's original account included other reasons for Herod to see John as a threat — reasons which may have outweighed the marriage issue and the warnings of 'the wrath to come'. For the moment let us assume that, according to Josephus, Herod decided to move against the Baptist for these unstated reasons. Josephus tells us:

> Herod thought it best, by putting him to death, to prevent any mischief he might cause, and not to bring himself into difficulties, by sparing a man who might make him repent of it when it should be too late. Accordingly he was sent a prisoner, out of Herod's suspicious temper, to Machaerus, the castle I before mentioned, and was there put to death.   (*Antiquities* 18,5,2)

In whatever way John was 'put to death' (the form of execution is never specified), Josephus leaves no doubt that, to him, the guilt is entirely Herod's. Yet the Gospels lift most of the guilt from his shoulders and dump it squarely on Herodias. Immediately, this poses a problem.

Matthew and Luke are concerned to show that John the Baptist *was* the prophet Elijah, and in their treatment of John's arrest and death they have created a situation which closely parallels the story of Elijah and his stormy dealings with King Ahab, who was married to the pagan Jezebel — her name to this day a synonym for an evil, designing woman. When Ahab wants a neighbour's vineyard as a palace garden and the neighbour refuses to sell, Jezebel contrives a charge of blasphemy against the man (supposedly by forging documents from Ahab) and he is stoned to death. Ahab gets his vineyard — and the condemnation of Elijah. Yet it is Jezebel who is blamed for the King's meanest crime (*1 Kings* 21).

After describing John exactly as Elijah was described, and after having John play a similar role to Elijah in challenging a ruler, Matthew and Mark complete their picture by portraying Herodias as a Jezebel who contrives a man's death, supposedly against the wishes of her husband. Matthew and Mark say that Herod is 'grieved' at having to kill John; in the Septuagint version of the Book of Kings, Ahab weeps at the death of his neighbour.

Josephus sets the scene for the death of John. He tells us that the Baptist was imprisoned in Machaerus, a sumptuous but gloomy palace fortress built on the edge of a sheer plateau, looking out to the Dead Sea about 5 kilometres to the west. The palace was flanked by plunging chasms where strange plants grew that were said to kill at a touch, and sulphurous springs rose steaming from the ground near other springs whose waters were ice-cold (*Wars* 7, 6, 13). Machaerus was a magnificently atmospheric setting for the dark deed to come but, in every other respect, the very last place Herod would choose to imprison John. The castle was in the farthest corner of Peraea, 96 kilometres south of Tiberias and on the border of Nabatea, the domain of Aretas, Herod's hostile father-in-law. In fact, when Herod's Arabian wife fled to her father, a year or so earlier, Josephus noted that Machaerus was 'subject to' King Aretas (*Antiquities* 18, 5, 1).

This made Machaerus a particularly unlikely place for John's imprisonment and death, more unlikely with every year as the quarrel developed between the two rulers.

According to a Christian tradition, John died at Sebaste in Samaria, and an early church marked the tomb where his head was supposedly interred. This site, too, is unlikely. Samaria was hostile to Jews, subject directly to Rome and outside Herod's jurisdiction.

The Gospels and logic both suggest that John was imprisoned in Galilee. When Herod held the infamous banquet to celebrate his birthday (or, more likely, his 'anniversary', the date of his accession), Mark says that it was attended by 'his courtiers, officers and the leading men of Galilee' — obviously not at Machaerus or Sebaste. Herod's palace was at Tiberias and for centuries its ruins were pointed out on Mount Berenice, which rises abruptly behind the lakeside city. Recent excavation there found only the remains of a Christian church dedicated to an ancient and mysterious anchor stone.

On some as yet undiscovered site, Herod's spectacular, golden-roofed palace dominated the glittering, brand-new city-state. In a dungeon below the palace, or in accommodation more suited to a visiting minor dignitary, John spent the last days, months, perhaps even the last year of his life. The Gospels describe his disciples as having free access to him and speak of his discussions with Herod.

So what of the anniversary banquet and Salome's Dance of the Seven Veils?

The banquet would have been a segregated affair — as acknowledged in the Gospel account. When Herodias's daughter has performed her 'unquestionably lascivious' dance and Herod has made his impulsive offer, Mark tells us 'she went out' to ask her mother's advice, then 'rushed back' (*Mark* 6:24–5). When men and women are dining apart, the idea of a girl of princessly rank — a princess of Hasmonean descent at that — performing *any* sort of dance for her stepfather and his well-primed male guests is beyond belief. The Dance of the Seven Veils is nothing but a raunchy fantasy built on this unlikely foundation.

It is a minor detail that the girl could not have been Salome who, by 33–34 AD, was married to the Tetrarch Philip and was probably betrothed to him at the time of the Baptist's death, perhaps two or three years earlier. Josephus is usually credited with naming Salome as the daughter who danced for Herod. He names her as *a* daughter of Herodias — the last child born before her divorce; nothing more. According to the Slavonic Josephus, there were three other children. And some of the most reliable manuscripts of Mark identify the dancing daughter as Herodias, named after her mother. The admirable Andy Gaus and the *New Revised Standard Version* so name her in their translations. Other readings avoid this identification as being obviously wrong — everyone knows it was Salome who danced for Herod.

† † †

We must treat the Gospel versions of John's death with great wariness. Apart from cloaking the political shadows of Herod's fear of rebellion, and casting John in the mould of Elijah against a Jezebel, the story could have sprung from palace scuttlebutt. Loyal courtiers may have tried to blame Herodias for Antipas's troubles and unpopular actions. There were two possible Gospel sources of such pro-Herod, anti-Herodias tales — Joanna, wife of Herod's household manager, soon to become a disciple of Joshua (*Luke* 8:3), and Menahem (Manaen) who had grown up with Herod and is sometimes described as his foster-brother. He, too became a Christian (*Acts* 13:1).

Our wariness of the banquet tale shouldn't extend to John's attack on the marriage. As we've noted, Joshua was to continue that strain of the Baptist's campaign, just as he continued to issue John's messages of the wrath to come. But what of Josephus's unstated reasons for Herod's wish to have John killed? They have vanished from our text of his history, probably through the work of Christian editors. Fortunately, there was no centralised policy of censorship and amendment — especially between the Eastern and Western Churches. Some passages deleted from Western versions have been retained in the East. Some passages completely rewritten in the East have been altered less radically in the West.

The Slavonic versions of Josephus — among some bizarre and often baffling interpolations — offer us what some leading scholars of the texts believe to be passages from the historian's original Greek or Aramaic. After introducing John as an unnamed 'wild man' ('in countenance he was like a savage'), these versions record:

> He came to the Jews and summoned [or 'lured'] them to freedom, saying: 'God hath sent me to show you the way of the Law, whereby ye may free yourselves from many masters; and *there shall be no mortal ruling over you*, but only the Highest (or 'Most High') who hath sent me ...' and he did nothing else to them, save that he dipped them into the stream of the Jordan and let (them) go admonishing them to desist from evil works; (for) *so would he give them a king who would set them free* and subject all (the) insubordinate, but he himself would be subject to no one. [my italics]

It would be easy to dismiss this passage — as easily as other passages in the Slavonic Josephus can be dismissed — as 'Byzantine interpolations'. It would be equally easy to embrace it as confirmation of a thesis that John's mission was far more 'political' than the Gospels wish us to know. This, of course, is the whole point. The passage does not serve Christian interests, yet it matches the black star around which the story revolves. This is the line that connects the dots to give them shape and meaning. Without this account of John's message, the great gap in Josephus's account must be synthesised. The respected New Testament scholar, C.K. Barrett does so when he says of the standard text, 'references to Herod's fear of a revolutionary movement show that the Baptist was concerned in Messianic activity which either was, or showed the possibility of becoming, political and military'.

Against this view, John's scholarly biographer, Dr Scobie of the Church of Scotland, can declare, 'It is not at all clear that even the Slavonic version regards John as a political figure'. Herod would not agree.

John is preaching the physical redemption of Israel and, inevitably, the overthrow of 'many masters' — the puppet rulers and their Roman overlords. Here are drumbeat echoes of Luke's 'Maccabean battle song', but even more striking resonance of the Zealots' philosophy as described in Josephus's standard text:

> They have an inviolable attachment to liberty; and they say that God is to be their only ruler and Lord. They also do not value dying any kind of death, nor indeed do they heed the deaths of their relatives and friends, nor can any such fear make them call any man Lord ... (*Antiquities* 18,1,6)

Now it becomes clear why John should have been arrested as a fomenter of rebellion and why, when this happened, Joshua should promptly return to Galilee. It is also clearer why the first two Gospels *imply* that Jesus began his ministry after John's imprisonment. They are happy to have Jesus illuminated by the Baptist's fiery fame, while reluctant to show him playing any role in this anarchic mission. Yet they cannot avoid Jesus' proclamation of John's message in the heart of Herod's domain immediately after the arrest: 'Repent, for the kingdom of God is at hand!'

In the compulsion to provide a label for Jesus, a steady stream of scholars and popular writers have portrayed him as a Zealot. Joshua certainly wasn't that; in fact it may have been reluctance to embrace the more aggressively political aspects of John's mission that encouraged him to form a splinter group among the Baptist's followers — a group that inevitably included Zealots, whose hopes for Joshua would not always match his intentions. The end times had begun; he accepted that. But was the next move to liberate Judaea from the rule of the impious Pilate and the Romans? To free Galileans from their nominally Jewish ruler? To challenge the Temple faction's policy of compromise with the Roman regime? There is no indication that Joshua had any such plans. On the contrary, everything suggests that he was working his way towards a partly comprehended goal by a route which opened in front of him as he moved forward. On that way forward was he to see himself as a prophet? As a charismatic in the tradition of Honi, Hanan and the others? Could he possibly think of himself as the Messiah?

Time and time again, Joshua answered questions in an oblique, almost evasive way. And this approach was reflected in several aspects of his ministry, even in his matchless parables. In their original form, these seem to have been unexplained and tended to be misinterpreted by the Gospellers. It was an approach that emerged most clearly in Joshua's reluctance to accept titles that demanded a definition of his role.

Joshua's hesitation to present himself openly as the Messiah is vividly symbolised in his frequent identification of himself as 'the Son of Man' (*huyos tu anthropu*). While, in Aramaic usage, this could mean simply 'myself', in the sense of 'this mother's son', it could also be a title with apocalyptic and Messianic associations (as in *The Book of Daniel*). The ambiguity of the phrase perfectly suited Joshua's hesitation to be identified as the Messiah *and* the subsequent need for secrecy when he reluctantly accepted the role.

Even though much recent scholarship denies that he spoke of himself as 'Son of Man' in a Messianic or apocalyptic sense (partly the result of a thirty-year campaign by the Jewish scholar Vermes), it is significant that the Talmud ranks Joshua's self-identification as 'Son of Man' with his supposedly saying 'I am God' and 'I will go up to heaven' (j. Ta'anith 65b). To the Talmudist, Joshua was using the title in its most exalted, Messianic sense — described by David Flusser as 'the sublime eschatological judge ... the highest conception of the Redeemer ever developed by ancient Judaism'.

Joshua, in Luke's phrase, was 'filled with the power of the Spirit'. Since his baptism by John, he had experienced an empowering sense of destiny and authority, awareness of a role to play in the realisation of God's kingdom. How was that to happen? By showing that it *was* happening. Acceptance of that as reality would *make* it reality. God would reveal his plan in its execution.

With total faith in his God and with his new conviction of power and authority, Joshua began to preach, to proclaim the kingdom so effectively that Herod saw him as a resurrected Baptist. Some of his disciples saw him as the Messiah. Joshua saw himself as a man selected by God for some purpose, required by God to play a central role in establishing the kingdom; but he hesitated to define that Divine purpose, the role he was to play. God would reveal it to him, to all men, in the appropriate season.

One thing was certain; the end times were advancing, the arrest of the Baptist was one more proof of this. Joshua turned his face to Galilee; his first disciples followed him; *he* followed the Will of God.

CHAPTER 11

The Politics of Miracles

The Gospels disagree over Joshua's first mission. Matthew, Mark and Luke place it in Galilee, and show its fame spreading from there, while John says it was in Jerusalem and Judaea, with news of 'the signs that he was doing' being carried back to Galilee by festival pilgrims. John also has Jesus' disciples performing baptisms, which are ignored by the other Gospellers. The four Gospels agree on only one thing: miracles were performed. Perhaps surprisingly, they are supported in this by non-Christian sources — Jewish, Roman and Islamic — which confirm that miraculous events were associated with Joshua's ministry.

The Talmud says that Jesus 'practised sorcery' (*Sanhedrin* 43a) and, as *Yeshua Ben Stada*, he is accused of smuggling witchcraft out of Egypt with spells or charms scratched into his flesh (*Shabbath* 104b). Egypt's ancient magical tradition is recorded in the Torah when Moses has his remarkable contest with Pharaoh's sorcerers (*Exodus* 7:9–12), while the Talmud acknowledges the unusual power of the country's magic in the dictum: 'Ten measures of sorcery descended into the world; Egypt received nine, the rest of the world one' (*Kiddushin* 49b). Clearly, in linking the Ben Stada story to Jesus, the Talmudists recognised that his 'sorcery' was so remarkable that it could only have come from Egypt.

Josephus speaks of Jesus performing 'wonderful works' (*paradoxa erga*) — one of the few aspects of the *Testimonium* which most authorities accept as original, though some dispute it (in spite of this detail being available to Josephus in the Jewish oral tradition just noted).

The Koran quotes Jesus as healing lepers, giving sight to the blind and raising the dead — 'by Allah's leave' (the *Imrans* 3, 49ff). This touches the heart of the matter. Most Christians imagine that Jesus proved his divinity by performing miracles. They are wrong on both scores. The miracles were not performed *by* Jesus; they did not prove and were not *intended* to prove his divinity.

Simon Peter Barjona was one of Joshua's closest companions throughout his ministry. Less than two months after the crucifixion, he spoke of 'Jesus the Nazarene, a man attested to you by God with deeds of power, wonders and signs that God did through him among you' (*Acts* 2:22). Every word of this description drives to the core of what Joshua was about: a *man* singled out by God; miracles accomplished by God *through* him, as a demonstration of *God's* power and the authority a man could attain from his own belief in that power and others' recognition of it.

Even John, who goes further than any other Gospeller in claiming divinity for Jesus, also stresses that God 'has given him authority' (*John* 5:27). He follows this with Jesus saying, 'I can do nothing on my own (literally, "from myself"); I seek to do not my own will but the will of him who sent me' (*John* 5:30).

Luke and Matthew attribute to him the clearest statement of how the miracles were performed and also what they meant. 'If it is by the finger of God that I cast out demons, then the kingdom of God has come to you' (*Luke* 11:20; *Matthew* 12:28).

All this demands a first-century view of the miracles. Some canon lawyers and conservative theologians of Joshua's time were certainly wary of the phenomenon; but they did not question the fact that Joshua performed miracles; they questioned only the *source* of the power he displayed. Their attitude is mirrored by the third-century Christian theologian, Origen, who came from Alexandria and was familiar with Egyptian sorcery. Origen wrote:

> The magicians of Egypt cast out evil spirits, cure diseases by a breath, call up the spirits of the dead, make inanimate things move as if they were alive ... But because they do such things shall we consider them the sons of God? Or shall we call such things the tricks of pitiable and wicked men? (*Against Celsus* 1,68)

In relation to miracles, as to everything else, Joshua functioned within the belief system of a place and time. A world that believed in healing miracles was a world in which healing miracles could be performed. In the same way, because the world of Judaism believed that the prophets had been able to control forces of nature, then a display of this power would proclaim that the age of prophecy had returned to Israel in a shining promise of the coming kingdom. Conversely, with belief in the rebirth of prophecy and the dawning of the kingdom would come readiness to believe in nature miracles and, perhaps, the power to perform them. Cause and effect are delicately balanced. Miracles nurture faith, faith nurtures miracles.

Some Christians are uncomfortable with the idea of Jesus' miracles being related to 'faith healing'. Alan Richardson flatly rejects such a suggestion:

> The faith which Jesus demands of those who come to him to be cured is not, of course, faith in the modern sense of 'faith healing' — such a notion is utterly foreign to the Gospel atmosphere — but a believing relation and attitude to his own person as Messiah and Son of God, *even though those who came to him to be healed could not have articulated their belief in so precise a formula as this*. [my italics]

No first-century Jew could have thought of Joshua as 'Messiah' or 'Son of God' in Christian terms. Furthermore, neither a Jewish Messiah nor a Jewish Son of God would be automatically considered a healer or a miracle worker. There could be 'a believing relation and attitude' to Joshua only as a man capable of healing and performing miracles — a man who rejected titles and definitions, a man who commanded faith through his actions and words. We cannot ignore what the people of his time believed; nor can we ignore what *he* believed.

Almost at the end of his ministry, after some four years of healing and preaching, Joshua restored sight to a blind man and told him, 'Your faith has healed you' (*Luke* 18:42). This perfectly balances a phenomenon from the ministry's early days. Joshua preached at Nazareth and was disillusioned by the attitude of people who had known him for most of his life and simply could not accept his new status. Mark tells us:

> And he was unable to do any miracles there except that he healed a few sick people by laying his hands on them; and he was amazed at their unbelief [or 'lack of faith'].   (*Mark* 6:5–6)

However much the subject of miracles is smothered in theology or superstition, the Gospels demonstrate that we are observing an interaction between human beings of the first century with God as the catalyst. And if we are tempted to doubt this, the Gospels and *Acts* show us Joshua's disciples also achieving miraculous cures (*Matthew* 10:1; *Mark* 6:13; *Acts* 2:43; 5:12–16) while the Talmud records healing and 'nature' miracles by Christians more than a century later (*j. Sanhedrin* 25d; *j. Shabbath* 14d).

Frustratingly, neither Matthew, Mark nor Luke tells of the first miracle, that first occasion when Joshua felt empowered or even impelled to become an instrument of God's might, a burning glass to focus divine energy, a matrix of God-given belief in himself and the interface of that belief with the readiness of others to believe.

Only John shows Jesus performing a first miracle — and a rather embarrassing miracle it is; embarrassing because it is a trivial exercise, because it involves Jesus producing an extraordinary quantity of alcoholic beverage for a function and because it has uncomfortable links with a pagan bacchanalia.

According to *John*, three days after his baptism, Jesus with Mary 'and his disciples', attends a wedding at Cana in the hills near Nazareth. When Mary tells Jesus that the wine has run out, Jesus answers, 'Woman, what is that to me and to you? My hour has not yet come.' Mary ignores this and tells the servants, 'Do whatever he tells you.' Nearby are six stone water pots used for purification rites, each holding 'two or three measures'. Jesus instructs the servants to fill the pots with water.

He then asks them to pour some out and take it to the master of ceremonies, who tastes it and tells the bridegroom, 'Every man first puts out the good wine; then, when everyone is tipsy, he puts out the poorer stuff. But you have kept the best wine until now' (*John* 2:1–11).

The Christian interpretation of this strange story is deftly summarised by Marina Warner:

> The sequence of thought skips like a dusty gramophone needle. Mary, apparently rebuffed quite brutally by her son, understands that he will nevertheless perform a miracle. In Mariological teaching, her intervention illustrates her pity, compassion and thoughtfulness; but more importantly, its prompt effect — the inauguration of Christ's mission by a spectacular miracle — radiantly reveals the efficiency of her intercession with Christ, *while the actual prodigy itself, the transformation of Jewish purificatory water into wine, prefigures the passing of the Old Covenant before the New, with a miracle that symbolizes the central mystery of eucharistic wine.* [my italics]

Alfred Edersheim recognises in the Jewish water/Christian wine symbol, the Gnostic message that the God of Jesus was 'another and higher than the God of the Old Testament' — a concept that would have appalled Joshua. His God *was* the God of the 'Old Testament' in all his baffling complexity.

It is very unlikely that John intended such interpretations. He certainly says that the water pots were 'according to the purification of the Jews', yet he is the one Gospel writer who makes no mention of wine at The Last Supper and offers no link with Christian communion. It seems most likely that, for John, these six stone pots, each holding the equivalent of 90 to 135 litres, simply provided appropriate and available containers for 'a spectacular miracle' — producing between 540 and 810 litres of quality wine.

Turning water into wine was a popular pagan miracle. Each year on the *nones* of January at the Dionysian festival on the sacred Aegean island of Andros, a water fountain ran with wine (a phenomenon regarded with some cynicism by several ancient writers). The early Church chose to celebrate the Cana miracle on 6 January, the day after the Roman *nones*, combining this observation with the anniversary of Jesus' baptism, even though John says that the two events were three days apart. Later, 6 January was also nominated as the date when the 'wise men' brought their gifts to the infant Jesus, still celebrated as Epiphany. It is hardly surprising that the Church's barefaced appropriation of a famous pagan festival should lead to suspicions that, in the Cana story, 'John has Christianised a popular tale'.

There have been innumerable attempts to rationalise the Cana miracle — that everyone was too drunk to tell wine from water, that Jesus hypnotised the guests, and so on. The most popular Christian explanation points to rain falling on a vineyard, nurturing the vines to produce grapes that become wine in an annual miracle as old as time. Inevitably one must suggest that, wondrous as it is, this 'miracle' — like the pagan and later Christian efforts to reproduce it on cue — requires a lot of human participation.

What is to be made of it all? The devout scholar, A.T. Olmstead, finds John's story, 'a charming idyll, no doubt improved by memory'. Reaching back to that 'idyll' before its improvement, it seems likely that Joshua, his brothers, Mary and some of his disciples did attend a wedding at Cana (a town mentioned by John and the historian Josephus but ignored in the other Gospels). It has become popular to suggest that it was really Joshua's wedding, otherwise why would Mary be so worried about the wine, and how else would she be in a position to give orders to the servants? The only early tradition, preserved in the Romanian Josephus, is that it was the marriage of Simon the Zealot. Mary's involvement could certainly be seen as a confirmation that Simon was one of her sons. In a curiously persuasive detail it is recorded that the bride lived only two years after the marriage. We know that Simon's twin brother Judas also married (his grandsons make a fascinating appearance in the reign of Domitian when they are questioned about their Davidic descent) (Eusebius, *History*, 3, 19–20). Perhaps Judas, too, lost his wife and the twins were reunited in their shadowy mission to Mesopotamia before sharing martyrdom.

Only *possibilities* are there: the possibility that it was Simon's wedding; the possibility that there *was* a Cana wedding on a Wednesday evening (the traditional time for a marriage ceremony) in the home of a family wealthy enough to use expensive stone water pots of the kind and size found in Jerusalem's most luxurious, priestly homes. Those who wish to or need to, can believe the rest of John's story, while others disbelieve, or seek symbols that were never intended, or look for some 'rational' explanation. To this extent, Cana is an appropriate first miracle.

✝✝✝

Allowing some leeway for differing versions of the same event, the Gospels record some thirty-seven miracles by Joshua. Of these, eighteen are healings and seven are exorcisms of demons. Here, definition becomes a problem because the two categories overlap and, in doing so, they highlight a key facet of the miracle phenomenon.

Sometimes the demons 'cast out' by Joshua seem to match what we would today regard as manifestations of mental illness — perhaps schizophrenia presenting as a conviction that an evil spirit is inhabiting the victim; perhaps something akin to the popular modern myth of alien possession. Sometimes the demon-possession seems to represent a sort of fit — a boy frothing at the mouth, collapsing and becoming rigid or going into convulsions (*Luke* 9:38–42). Again, we have 'a demon-possessed man who was blind and dumb' (*Matthew* 12:22) and on another occasion we find Joshua 'casting out a demon that was mute' (*Luke* 11:14). Sometimes the demon speaks to Joshua, often Joshua speaks to the demon; he 'rebukes' it or, more literally, 'yells' at it.

One day at Capernaum, he yells at a demon possessing a man and, soon afterwards, in precisely the same way (with precisely the same word) yells at a fever which grips Simon Peter's mother-in-law, then goes on to yell at 'many' demons that evening (*Luke* 4:33–41).

Among the Dead Sea Scrolls is an exorcism formula which addresses the male-wasting demon, the female-wasting demon, the fever demon, the chills demon and the chest-pain demon (4Q560). This resonates with many of Joshua's healings. The people of his time believed that demons were a cause of illness. Joshua also believed this. *Jesus*, of course, would have *known* that this was not so — being all-seeing and all-knowing. Why then did he bother with demons? Presumably, because this is what the victim believed: but that would take us back to faith healing, pure and simple. So perhaps we were right the first time. Whatever Jesus *should* have known and believed, Joshua knew and believed only what he had been taught. As a healer, as a miracle worker, he operated within the belief system of Israel in the first century. This suggests that God's power, too, operated within a frame of time, place, belief and faith. It could be argued that it always has and always will.

Does this mean that Joshua's power was bounded only by the limits of his faith, his belief? After all, he said:

> 'I tell you truly, if you have faith as [big as] a mustard seed, you will tell this mountain, "Move from here to there!" and it will move. And nothing will be impossible for you.'　　　　　　　　　　　　　　　　(*Matthew* 17:20)

This is certainly what he believed; and eventually this belief was to bring about his death. But, for the moment, does it explain the other healings, the raisings from the dead and the miracles in which he controls the powers of nature, like the prophets of the past ages?

Joshua cured several lepers. It is often argued that 'leprosy' was a loosely used term in New Testament times. This hardly matters. The power of the human mind — expressed in hypnotism, self-hypnotism and faith healing — has certainly cured similar diseases. It has even cured cancer ('spontaneous remission' remains a fall-back position for modern medicine when a patient's recovery defies explanation in any other terms).

Can it cure blindness? At some levels it can. Traumatic blindness is an acknowledged phenomenon, demonstrated by the 'Apostle' Paul. Adolf Hitler was another famous example. Near the end of World War I he was blinded by mustard gas. He regained his sight but lost it again, temporarily, when he learnt that Germany was negotiating an armistice.

What then are the limits of such mental powers in their impact on the physical? The Gospels tell of Jesus healing a man who had been blind from birth. Even though his powers were clearly exceptional, has the story gained something in its retelling? Like many of the miracle stories, it probably has. When we come to Jesus raising three people from death, the rationalists have a field day. Even today, medical professionals can be tricked by a cataleptic or catatonic, death-like state; how much easier for first-century peasants or townsfolk to mistake such a condition for death. With vital signs operative but virtually undetectable, the brain does not deteriorate and awaits that all-but-indefinable signal to resume its normal functions. We can imagine a man with Joshua's extraordinary power being able to provide that signal. But without such a signal the cataleptic would be considered dead, and entombed.

Joshua's contemporaries were well aware of this danger. The *Mishnah* directs:

> One should go to the cemetery to check the dead within three days and not
> fear that such smacks of pagan practices; it once happened that a [buried] man
> was visited and went on to live another twenty-five years.   (*Semachoth* 8)

It is often pointed out that when Jesus raised the twelve-year-old daughter of Jairus, Capernaum's synagogue leader (the only raising from the dead
attested by more than one Gospel), he told her mourning family, 'Why are
you making a commotion and weeping? *The child has not died; she is sleeping*'
[my italics] (*Mark* 5:39). In a charming scene, he takes the girl by the hand
and says '*Talitha cum*' — Aramaic for 'Little lamb, get up'. The child wakes and
Jesus orders 'that no-one should know of this' and asks for her to be given
something to eat (*Mark* 5:43).

The Gospels report that the death had occurred immediately before Jesus
reached Jairus's home. The story is totally credible as a resuscitation —
remarkable, miraculous, but, in the late twentieth century, explicable — perhaps fitting St Augustine's fifth-century view that miracles were not contrary
to nature, but 'contrary to what is [now] known of nature' (*De Civitate Dei*,
21, 8). God does not break his own laws, though he can certainly use them to
stretch the bounds of the possible *towards* the impossible. Rationalists may
well try to confine Jesus' miracles too tightly within those bounds; but it
seems that the Gospellers often felt a need to extend them.

This tendency seems to be shown in the story told only by Luke
(7:11–17) in which Jesus is entering the town of Nain, at the head of his disciples and a large crowd, when they meet the funeral procession of a widow's
only son. Deeply moved by the mother's grief, Jesus touches the 'coffin' (it
would have been a bier — more like a stretcher) and says, 'Young man, I say
to you, get up.' The widow's son sits up, starts to speak and is reunited with
his mother.

Secrecy surrounds the raising of Jairus's daughter, which is reported by
three Gospels. Luke's miracle is in front of a crowd and supposedly its fame
spreads throughout Galilee and Judaea. Yet only Luke's source has heard of it.

Furthermore, Luke's account closely resembles the story of a pagan mystic,
Appolonius of Tyana, who raised a bride during her funeral procession
(Philostratus, *Life of Appolonius*, 4, 45). It also parallels (and verbally echoes) the
raising of a widow's son by the prophet Elijah (*1 Kings* 17:17–24). One must
suspect that Luke (or his source) has combined both elements — interrupted

funeral procession and widow's son — into a miracle that is, quite literally, more of a crowd-pleaser than the well-attested raising of Jairus's daughter.

Despite Luke's creativity, most Christians forget both these examples of the dead being brought back to life. Both are outshone by the raising of Lazarus — a man given prominence in John's Gospel as someone Jesus loved, an apparently well-to-do supporter who lived in Bethany, just outside Jerusalem, with his sisters, Martha and Mary.

The early part of John's story is awkward and alienating. Told that his dear friend Lazarus is ill, Jesus deliberately waits for two days before he leaves for Judaea, announcing: 'Our friend Lazarus has fallen asleep; but I am going there so I can waken him.'

He has already said that Lazarus's fatal illness was for the glorification of the Son of God. Now he tells his disciples, 'For your sakes I am glad I was not there, so you may believe.'

When Martha and Mary meet Jesus at Bethany, both tell him, separately, that if he had been there, their brother would not be dead. There is some dialogue in John's most florid 'religious pageant' mode, then comes a well-crafted climax — a superb build-up to the moment when Jesus has the stone rolled away from the entrance to Lazarus's tomb, despite Martha's warning that, after four days, her brother's body will be putrescent. Jesus prays for a time then calls, 'Lazarus, come out!' And Lazarus struggles into the light, his hands, feet and face still bound with burial wrappings (*John* 11:1–44).

The raising of Lazarus assumes great significance in John's Gospel. Here, it is one of the key factors in the Temple faction's decision that Jesus must die. John also suggests that it helps to attract the crowds who greet Jesus on his Palm Sunday entry to Jerusalem. Yet no other Gospel knows of it — unless we accept as genuine a strange fragment of a 'secret Gospel' by Mark. (This is suspect as a creation by one of the homosexual groups that were drawn to Christianity in its earliest days.) In this fragment, an unnamed youth of Bethany who is raised from his tomb declares his love for Jesus and pleads 'that he might be with him'. Subsequently, the youth, 'wearing a linen cloth over [his] naked [body]', passes a night with Jesus while he is taught 'the mystery of the kingdom of God'.

Supposedly, this passage fits into *Mark* Chapter 10, between verses 34 and 35. There is a problem here. Jesus has been on his way to Jerusalem, but the 'secret Gospel' fragment ends with Jesus returning 'to the other side of the Jordan'. Mark's narrative then continues with Jesus arriving in Jericho on his way to Jerusalem. In other words, after this odd incident at Bethany, Jesus doubles back to Jericho, then immediately doubles back *again* along the road to Bethany and Jerusalem.

Only one detail of the story really fits with *Mark*. When Jesus is arrested and the disciples flee:

> ... a certain young man was following him, having thrown a linen cloth upon [his] naked [body] and the young men seized him; but leaving the linen cloth, he fled from them naked.
>
> (*Mark* 14:51–2)

Far from corroborating the 'secret Gospel' fragment, this odd incident could have inspired it, as it inspired General Lew Wallace, who made this 'young man' his hero, Ben-Hur.

The raising of Lazarus remains an enigma — heightened by the only other mention of a Lazarus in the Gospels. *Luke* has a parable of a rich man and a beggar called Lazarus who sits by the rich man's gate as dogs lick the sores covering his body. Both men die and Lazarus goes to 'Abraham's bosom' while the rich man goes to Hades. The rich man pleads with Abraham to let Lazarus return and warn his five brothers of the fate that awaits them unless they repent of their indulgent ways. Abraham replies, 'If they will not hear Moses and the prophets, they will not be persuaded, *even if one of the dead should rise.*' [my italics] (*Luke* 16:31)

As a mere sidelight: the story of a woman anointing Jesus, which *John* places in the home of Lazarus, appears in *Luke* at the home of Simon the Pharisee and in *Matthew* at the home of Simon the Leper. The name 'Lazarus' is from 'Lazar', a shortening of 'Eleazar'. It is just possible that there was a wealthy young man called Simon Eleazar who was a Pharisee cured of leprosy by Jesus. Unfortunately, it seems more likely that the three Gospellers have simply cut-and-pasted the one incident in three different places.

✝✝✝

The so-called 'nature' miracles are the most challenging of all. There are nine of them. Jesus changes water into wine; gives his first disciples a miraculous haul of fish; calms a storm on Lake Kinneret; walks on water; feeds two huge crowds — one of 5000, the other of 4000; instructs Simon Peter to catch a fish which has in its mouth a coin to pay the Temple tax; kills a barren fig tree with a curse; and, after his resurrection, produces another remarkable catch of fish for disciples.

At the start, we must accept that the only miracle recorded by all four Gospellers is a nature miracle — the miraculous feeding of the 5000. It will be given special attention later.

The nature miracles have to be looked at quite apart from the healings and exorcisms. There were other healers in Joshua's time, other exorcists; but apart from rainmaking, which was performed by some of the *hasidim* and charismatics, there was no-one performing nature miracles — certainly not of the type and scale attributed to Jesus. Nothing of the kind had been seen since the days of Moses and the prophets. And this was the whole point.

A passage from *Isaiah* 61, which Joshua reads in the synagogue at Nazareth, relates healing miracles to the redemption of Israel. In similar vein, Isaiah proclaims the wonders to be seen when the land is freed from its enemies:

> Then the eyes of the blind will be opened,
> and the ears of the deaf unstopped.
> Then the lame will leap like a deer,
> and the speechless sing aloud.   (*Isaiah* 35:5–6)

Even further, it was believed that all the miracles of the past would be repeated in the Messianic age with the reappearance of Elijah (*Midrash*, *Ecclesiastes* 1:9 and *Lamentations* 4:22).

We've seen that Jesus' raising of the widow's son echoes the raising of a widow's son by Elijah. Similarly, the feeding of the 5000, described by all four Gospels, seeks to outdo a similar miracle by this prophet (*2 Kings* 4:42–4).

Early in the ministry Mark reports that people were saying of Joshua, 'It is Elijah!', while others saw him as 'a prophet, like one of the prophets of old' (*Mark* 6:15). Joshua was wary of accepting any title. Yet we will see clear evidence that he saw himself as a prophet, and further, as a prophet to lead the people of Israel into a New Covenant with God, the *berith hadashan* as looked to by the prophet Jeremiah and the Qumran sect. The shaggy mantle of the Baptist had settled on Joshua's shoulders and he was impelled, or even compelled, to meet the expectations of his disciples and all those who had looked to John as the 'Messenger of the Covenant'.

There is a passage in the Gospels which clashes sharply with their attempts to show John as a self-proclaimed forerunner of Jesus. It has the ring of truth about it.

> John, hearing in prison of the works of Christ, sent two of his disciples to ask, 'Are you the Coming One or should we look for another?' Jesus said to them, 'Go and tell John what you hear and see: the blind receive their sight and the lame walk, lepers are cleansed and the deaf can hear; the dead are raised and the poor are given the good news.'   (*Matthew* 11:2–4; *Luke* 7:18–22)

Joshua's reply to John represents a collection of Messianic prophecies gleaned from *Isaiah* chapters 26, 39, 35, 42, 61 and from Psalm 146; but there is also a startling echo here of the Dead Sea Scrolls which seems to foreshadow the prophet of the end times and speaks of God ...

> ... setting prisoners free, opening the eyes of the blind, raising up those who are bowed down ... He shall heal those badly wounded, he shall resurrect the dead, he shall send good news to the poor [or 'afflicted'].
>
> (*Messianic Apocalypse*, 4Q521)

Characteristically, in his reply to John, Joshua avoids accepting the title the 'Coming One' — just as he avoids other titles. Instead, he answers with an apocalyptic image which will be familiar to John. The 'footfalls of the Messiah' are there to be recognised. Let John say who Joshua is; let John define his role.

Touching that role, the Slavonic Josephus has an extraordinary passage about the unnamed 'wonder-worker' clearly identifiable as Jesus: 'Some said of him, "Our first law-giver is risen from the dead and hath performed many healings and arts". The translator, Thackeray, comments, 'the identification with Moses in this passage is unparalleled.' Yet according to John, Jesus comes very close to identifying himself with the 'first law-giver' when he says, 'If you believed Moses, you would have believed me, for he wrote about me' (*John* 5:46) — a clear reference to the words of Moses in *Deuteronomy* 18:15: 'The Lord your God will raise up for you a prophet like me from among your own people.'

'The Prophet' — whether Moses, a prophet *like* Moses or Elijah — would be associated with 'nature' miracles signalling the Messianic age. So did Joshua perform such miracles or did his followers *believe* that he had performed 'wonders and signs' of this scale?

Each miracle presents its own problems. The miraculous haul of fish from Lake Kinneret is described by Luke (5:4–11) and by John in a strange post-resurrection replay of the incident (*John* 21:1–11). Veteran Kinneret fisherman Mendel Nun finds Luke's description of season, time, place, fishing method and even the quantity of fish, all totally convincing — pointing out that it occurred in winter when 'musht' (*Tilapia galilea*) form large shoals, attracted to the northern section of the lake by the warm springs of the Capernaum area. Luke speaks of the disciples washing their nets in the morning. This shows Nun that they were using a 'trammel' net, a vertically hung, three-layered net that must be cleaned of silt after a night's work in the musht season — even, as in this case, an unsuccessful one. Nun continues his expert assessment of Luke's story:

> While Jesus is preaching from the boat, he sees a school of musht nearing the shore, as often happens during the morning hours of winter. Following Jesus' instructions, Simon's boat immediately takes off. The trammel nets, having been already washed, are lowered at the spot indicated by Jesus. The catch is enormously successful ...

Nun records, 'Veteran fishermen speak of memorable single hauls of as much as half a ton.' Interestingly, in John's post-resurrection version of the miracle, he specifies 153 fish. Taking four and a half pounds (seven kilograms) as the average weight for musht, this would bring John's 'miraculous draught' well within the half-ton.

Matthew and Mark have the story of a fig tree that bears no out-of-season fruit for Jesus and is killed by his curse in what looks like a fit of pique (*Matthew* 21:18–22; *Mark* 11:12–14). It is a silly tale. As E. P. Sanders comments, 'Sometimes Christian authors wished so strongly to present Jesus as being able to employ supernatural powers that they depicted him as being no better than a god of Greek mythology in a bad mood.'

Seeking some meaning in the story, scholars have pointed out that fig trees are used in the Bible as a symbol of Judaism, so the story is another prediction by Jesus that the Temple will be destroyed. The explanation doesn't work. There is a world of difference between cursing the Temple and predicting its destruction, and only a particularly rabid Gentile could imagine Jesus cursing Judaism itself.

Using a hook and line, Simon Peter may have caught a fish (according to Mendel Nun, a barbel) with a coin in its mouth, just when it was needed to pay the temple tax. Peter may have been following Joshua's directions. It was perhaps a miracle, though more likely a tall story or a coincidence. It is exclusive to Matthew (17:24–7). Intriguingly, musht (the fish involved in the miraculous haul) have a coin-like mark on their heads which probably earned them the nickname 'St Peter's Fish', even though they can't be caught with hook and line like Matthew's Temple-tax-coin specimen.

The famous story of Jesus walking on the waters of Kinneret while his disciples are fighting a headwind (*Matthew* 14:25; *Mark* 6:48–51; *John* 6:19–21) has been seen as a post-resurrection appearance transferred to Jesus' lifetime; as an illusion (Jesus walking on a submerged rock or sand bar); or as a straight-out symbol of Jesus' transcendence of the physical. It is significant that the Greek word *epi*, used in all three accounts, can mean that Jesus was walking 'on' the water or 'by' the water (similar ambiguity exists in Hebrew) and while Matthew and Luke play the scene in the middle of Kinneret, John has the disciples' boat very close to shore. As we will see, he provides a cohesive account of the disciples being unable to land because of a violent headwind, when Jesus appears on the shore, calls out to them not to be afraid and the wind drops.

Of all the Gospellers, only Luke ignores the 'walking on water' story. Perhaps his local research identified its philological source. He accepts from Mark, however, a closely related Kinneret story of Jesus calming a storm, and includes details that impress Shelley Wachsmann, a present-day Israeli marine archaeologist.

One evening, after a day's preaching during the Galilee mission, Jesus asks to be taken across the lake and his disciples set off in one of their boats — a typical Kinneret fishing boat with a mast, square sail, perhaps four oarsmen and a helmsman in the stern with a steering oar.

> And a great windstorm rose and the waves drove into the ship so it was soon being swamped. And he was in the stern asleep on the pillow. And they woke him and said to him, 'Teacher, don't you care that we are perishing?' And, now awake, he yelled at the wind and told the sea, 'Quiet! Be still!' And the wind dropped and there was a great calm. And he said to them, 'Why are you so afraid? How can you have no faith?' And in great fear they said to each other, 'Who is this, that even the wind and the sea obey him?'   (*Mark* 4:37–41)

The thing that struck Wachsmann was the way Jesus slept, 'in the stern … on the pillow'. Boats or small ships like this one had a 'table' across the stern, a small deck to carry big seine nets and provide a working platform for the steersman. The space below this stern deck was 'the most protected area of the boat … which was out of the way of the other people on board'.

'The pillow' (*to proskephalaoin*) on which Jesus slept was almost certainly a 'ballast pillow' — a sandbag used to trim the boat when sailing. 'When not in use they were stored beneath the stern deck, where they could be used as pillows by crews resting there'. The setting seems accurate; but what of the miracle? A vivid and revealing description of a Kinneret storm is provided by John Macgregor, a Scots adventurer who navigated the lake in 1868:

> Just as [we] passed below Wady Fik, a strange distant hissing sounded ahead, where we could see that a violent storm was raging. Instantly all hands were on the alert to meet it. The waves had not time to rise. The gusts had come down upon calm water, and they whisked up long wreaths of it into the sky. The sea birds sailed with the roaring blast, which rushed on with foam and fury …

Doré's engraving of Joshua casting out a demon from a young man, one of seven exorcisms described in the Gospels. This case (*Luke* 9:38-42) sounds like epilepsy; others relate to blindness and dumbness; even a case of fever seems treated as demon possession, all suggesting that Joshua, like the people of his time, believed that illness was caused by demons.

The miracle of turning water into wine at the Cana wedding is a rare example of straight-out magic being performed by the Gospels' Jesus. This nineteenth-century German engraving downplays the amount of quality wine produced. According to *John*, each of the six stone pots held between 90 and 135 litres.

A haloed Jesus sleeps in the stern of a Galilean fishing boat caught in a sudden storm on Lake Kinneret (*Mark* 4:35–9). An Israeli expert points out that such boats usually had a small rear deck as a platform for the steering oarsman and for the deployment of fishing nets. It provided a convenient sleeping shelter with the bonus of a sand-filled ballast 'pillow' as a headrest — a detail referred to in the Gospels.

Joshua with the dead daughter of Capernaum's synagogue leader, just before Joshua brings her back to life. In Gabriel Max's portrayal, an unromanticised Joshua and the poignant little corpse insist that this is no grand set-piece. In spite of being the best attested and most believable of the three raisings from the dead described in the Gospels, it is often forgotten by Christians.

In this fifth-century Italian diptych carved from ivory, a beardless Joshua performs six miracles. Clockwise, from top left, he feeds thousands with five loaves and two fish; raises Lazarus from death; turns water into wine; cures a leper; enables a paralysed man to walk away carrying his bed; and heals a blind man. Intriguingly, on the two occasions when he uses a 'wand', he lacks a halo.

A reconstruction by John Ward of the Roman Tenth Legion's boar emblem. This symbol of Roman occupation is clearly involved in the curious miracle story of Joshua healing a demon-possessed man (below). One of the demons declares, 'Our name is *Legion*' and Joshua expels them into a herd of 2000 *pigs* which stampede over a cliff into Lake Kinneret, leaving the former prisoner free to follow his liberator.

This torrent of heavy cold air was pouring over the mountain crests into the deep cauldron of the lake below, a headlong flood of wind, like a waterfall into the hollow; just as is said in Luke (VIII.23) — 'there came down a storm of wind upon the lake'.

The peculiar effects of squalls among mountains are known to all who have boated much on lakes, but on the Sea of Galilee the wind has a singular force and suddenness; and this is, no doubt, because the sea is so deep in the world that the sun rarefies the air in it enormously, and the wind, speeding swift above a long and level plateau, gathers much force as it sweeps through the deserts, until suddenly it meets this huge gap in the way, and it tumbles down here irresistible ...

By pressing onwards ... with more exertion than at any time during the cruise, we gained at last the windward shore, and here we could look with safe amazement at the scud of the gale, careering across the lake, and twisting the foam in the air as if tied in knots of spray, which sparkled in the sun like 10 000 diamonds, while the sea-birds still flew helplessly down-wind ...

Swift as the tempest had come down, it vanished away as swiftly, and when we turned our bow to sea again, there was only a fine fresh breeze and common waves to meet.

The suddenness of the windstorm, its extraordinary violence and its equally sudden calming are all replicated in the Gospel story. At first, the panic of the disciples seems unlikely. Surely professional fishermen would be familiar with the vagaries of the lake's weather; but there is no indication that Simon Peter, Andrew, John or James are aboard. They could have entrusted one of their boats to the party for a simple, 7-kilometre trip on a calm evening. Did Joshua genuinely believe that he could hush the storm with a command? Perhaps. Or did he yell, 'Quiet! Be still!' *at his disciples*, annoyed at being woken from a badly-needed sleep by their panicking? Either way it is more than possible that the windstorm abated soon after he spoke.

Among the 'nature' miracles, the calming of the storm is both credible and spectacular. Its effect on the disciples is easily imaginable. On their return to Capernaum, the story would lose nothing in its telling. And if Peter, Andrew, John and James had previously experienced equally sudden delivery from Kinneret storms or for that matter, equally large hauls of fish they would look at these events as first-century Galileans prepared to believe in the limitless power of their God, given a new immediacy and accessibility through the faith of Joshua and through their faith in him.

Fisherman Nun, archaeologist Wachsmann and adventurer Macgregor help us recognise a strong, factual core in Gospel accounts of the Kinneret miracles; the phenomena become highly credible, almost mundane. It is only their *timing* that elevates them to the miraculous; and to the modern mind this can be dismissed as coincidence. The disciples saw it differently.

Even if natural laws had operated to produce desired results at appropriate times, it *was* a miracle. Joshua *was* a prophet. And perhaps more. The footfalls of the Messiah were being heard across Galilee, in Judaea, and even in Jerusalem. John had spoken of the coming Kingdom. Joshua's miracles were beginning to prove that it was here. This was dangerous. Joshua, like the imprisoned Baptist, was becoming a political threat.

✝✝✝

In the strangest of all the miracle stories — part exorcism, part nature miracle — a political agenda is most clearly visible. Jesus expels a demon from a man near Gadara or Gerasa — Gentile cities of the Decapolis, south-east of Kinneret — or near the uncertain 'Gergesa'. (In the third century the Church nominated a site near Kursi, which lies in coastal hills directly opposite Capernaum. It suits the Gospel accounts — apparently the only reason for its choice.)

Naked and violent, the possessed man lives in tombs, howls by night and day, gashes himself with rocks and breaks chains used to restrain him. When Jesus speaks with one of the man's demons and demands its name, it replies, 'My name is Legion, for we are many,' and pleads with Jesus to be sent into a herd of 2000 swine grazing nearby. Jesus complies and the animals stampede over a cliff into the lake — a lengthy stampede on any of the sites! (*Matthew* 8:28–34; *Mark* 5:1–15; *Luke* 8:27–35).

Most commentaries recognise symbolism. The name 'Legion' is the key — a clear reference to the Roman army (Aramaic uses the same word for 'legion' and 'soldier' which means that the number of pigs need not match the 6000 men of a legion). When the Gospels were written, the Tenth Legion permanently occupied Israel and as we've noted before, its emblem was a boar. Even without being aware of this connection, the American scholar John Dominic Crossan says bluntly that the story 'openly characterises Roman imperialism as demonic possession'.

It is possible that this interpretation was overlaid on the story of a noisy exorcism which caused suicidal panic among some pigs, but the variations in location and other details (Matthew has *two* demoniacs) suggest shaky factual foundations. We are left with a revolutionary fable. If it was told in

Joshua's lifetime, it would have delighted the ordinary folk of Israel with its image of the Roman invaders — as despised pigs — disappearing into the lake, like Pharaoh's army engulfed by the Red Sea. Their former victim, free of his tormentors, wants to follow Jesus.

In all three Gospel accounts, the destruction of the Roman-legion swine immediately follows the calming of the storm. This was no coincidence. In the *Tanakh*, storms and raging seas occur as symbols of the chaos wrought by evil forces and the enemies of Israel. The common theme of the two miracle stories is seen in Psalm 65:

> Through fearsome deeds you answer us with victory,
> God our saviour ...
> *You quell the roaring of the seas,*
> *the roaring of their waves,*
> *and the tumult of the [Gentile] nations.*
> Those who live at the ends of the earth
> are awestruck by your signs. [my italics]   (Psalm 65:5, 7–8)

To the first hearers of these stories — even without later embroideries — the resonances would be clear; as clear in the villas of Tiberias and the mansions of Jerusalem as they were in the humble homes of Galilee. Then, as now, the accuracy of the miracle stories was less important than the reason for their being told; and repeated; and recognised — as promises or warnings.

CHAPTER 12

'Nowhere to lay his head'

The earliest reports of Joshua's healings and exorcisms seem to have generated suspicion and even hostility in the Sanhedrin. This was demonstrated when Nicodemus, an elderly Pharisee member of the council, 'came to Jesus by night' while he was in Jerusalem for a Passover festival (*John* 3:1–2). There have been various attempts to explain why John specifies 'at night'. Inescapably, the words give Nicodemus's visit a secretive quality which is borne out by subsequent events.

Nicodemus tells Jesus, 'No-one can do the signs which you do, unless God is with them' — an opinion which is obviously not shared by his fellow councillors. Because the ensuing dialogue between the two men consists of Johannine sermonising by Jesus and a display of dull-wittedness by Nicodemus, it is tempting to see the encounter as one of John's theological vignettes — in fact, to see Nicodemus not as a historical figure but as a 'type', a character created to typify the devout and well-intentioned Jew who was incapable of recognising Jesus' divinity (which, after all, was not there to be recognised) or who hesitated to declare himself a believer because of his position in Jerusalem society. At the end of the story he emerges as something of a secret disciple and helps a fellow Sanhedrin member, Joseph of Arimathea, with the burial of Jesus, providing a princely quantity of expensive perfume and embalming material.

The Talmud mentions a wealthy Jerusalemite called Naqdimon ben Gorion who seems to provide a coincidental match for Nicodemus — two well-to-do men of Jerusalem with the same name (*Ta'anith* 19b, 20a). But in a fascinating detail the Talmud points out that ben Gorion's real name is not Naqdimon but Buni; and another Talmudic passage names a Buni (an uncommon name) as one of Jesus' disciples (*Sanhedrin* 43a). Coincidence may still be at work, but John will prove deceptively reliable with other Jerusalem links to Joshua's story.

While still wary of the Gospel's chaotic chronology, we should note John's report that on this visit to Jerusalem by Jesus, 'many believed in his name because they saw the signs that he was doing'. John goes on to make the intriguing comment, 'But Jesus for his part would not entrust himself to them … because he knew what was in all men' (*John* 2:23–5). John's man-God again reveals a very human dilemma facing Joshua. What did the people in Jerusalem believe of him that made his trust in them an issue? The implication is that in acknowledging their belief he would make himself vulnerable; but to what?

The most likely explanation of this oblique passage is that some Passover pilgrims were seeing Joshua as a Messiah — inevitably, in relation to the redemption of Israel, the great central theme of the Passover which commemorated the deliverance of the Hebrews from their bondage in Egypt. Yet this was the very time when the Romans were poised to crush any hint of a threat to their authority, with the garrison's festival reinforcements patrolling the northern colonnade of the Court of the Gentiles as a constant reminder of that readiness. Even as Joshua spoke with his fellow pilgrims in the sunny court, his eye would have been drawn to the warning glint of bronze helmets and the lizard sheen of chain mail in the shadows among the columns.

If Joshua did anything to encourage his would-be followers in their talk of Messiahship, he would be placing his life in their hands. Any outburst on their part would make him a target for Pilate's Roman auxiliaries or the paramilitary temple guard who were at the bidding of the Temple Captain, Jonathan, brother-in-law of the high priest Caiaphas. Pilate, after two defeats by the Jews of Jerusalem, was spoiling for another fight; Caiaphas was just as eager to *avoid* trouble and preserve the current order of coexistence with the Romans. Both men's interests would be best served by prompt action against any Messianic disturbance.

For Joshua, beyond the risk of personal danger — even beyond jeopardising his mission — there was a more profound issue. It was not a question of what these Passover pilgrims wanted of him, however desperately. It was a question of what God wanted.

Some time later, in John's account, when Jesus learns that Jerusalem religious authorities are aware that his mission is proving more successful than the Baptist's, he leaves the city in apparent haste. He and some disciples travel back to Galilee via hostile Samaria and rest in Sychar, a city of refuge for Jewish religious fugitives. Here, in an extraordinary conversation with a local woman at the Well of Jacob, he admits that he is the Messiah and spends two days successfully preaching in the city (*John* 4:1–43). It seems that in anti-Jerusalem Sychar, Jesus can admit to a role he is reluctant to accept in the Holy City.

Several details suggest that this story, like so much of *John*, is based firmly on fact. But when did it happen? The Gospel provides no unambiguous clues. However the Gospeller Luke has another story of Joshua accepting a title perhaps earlier in his career — a pivotal episode that may help to explain other occasions when he shows great reticence, even secrecy, in such matters.

Luke tells how, at the height of his fame in Galilee, Joshua returned to his home town, Nazareth. We have already noted Mark's account of the strange reception he received — the inability of the townsfolk to accept him as anything but the carpenter, the son of widowed Mary and brother of the girls who still lived in the town. (A remark Mark attributes to the townspeople, 'Aren't his sisters here [or 'still'] with us?' [*Mark* 6:3], effectively confirms that the brothers had left with Joshua.)

On the Sabbath, the good, pious folk of Nazareth hurried up to the synagogue, not only because it was the custom to hurry there, but because this was an unusual occasion — to see Joshua bar Joseph and his brothers and unlikely disciples in the comfortable, familiar, religious context of the undoubtedly humble building where this district celebrity had studied and worshipped among them.

The hubbub of comment and gossip hushed for the *Shema*, the Benedictions and the reading from the Torah. Then came the awaited moment. The leader of the synagogue invited Joshua to give the second reading for the service. Luke quotes part of it, the first two verses of *Isaiah* 61. In a three-year cycle of readings, generally used at this time, *Isaiah* 60:17 to 61:6 was the text from the prophets prescribed for the sixty-second Sabbath. We can place it on the third Sabbath in December, 31 AD — according to the Julian calendar, 15 December.

The *chazzan* handed Joshua the scroll and he went to the reading desk on the *bema*, facing the Ark and the row of elders, with the congregation seated to either side of him. He spread the scroll on the lectern and began to read the last verses of Chapter 60. Here, in resounding poetry, Isaiah gives his vision of Jerusalem's rebirth in the Messianic age. How Joshua must have savoured those sonorous words and images:

> 'Instead of bronze I shall bring you gold,
> and in place of iron, silver,
> copper for wood and iron for stone;
> I shall appoint peace to govern you
> and make righteousness your ruler.'

Joshua paused after each three verses to let the *meturgeman* deliver the Targum, the Aramaic paraphrase for those members of the congregation who did not understand Hebrew. After the second Targum recitation, Joshua resumed his reading at the start of Chapter 61:

> 'The Spirit of the Lord is upon me,
> because he has anointed me to bring good news to the poor.
> He has sent me to heal the broken-hearted,
> to proclaim deliverance to the captives
> and for the blind to see again,
> to let the oppressed go free,
> to proclaim the year of the Lord's favour ...'

Luke quotes the reading up to this point but then cuts off the end of the sentence and the verse: '... and the day of vengeance of our God'.

Joshua knew that 'the year of the Lord's favour' referred to *Yovel*, the Jubilee, the end of seven 'weeks of years', a time of liberation and the redemption of ancestral land. He understood why this should be linked symbolically with God's vengeance. He also knew that a few turns of the ornate roller in his left hand, a few passes of his right hand to draw out another few columns of the scroll, and he would be looking at *Isaiah* 63 with its terrible image of the Lord in garments splattered with red, 'like theirs who tread the winepress', announcing:

> 'I trampled the [Gentile] nations in my anger,
> I crushed them in my wrath,
> and I poured out their lifeblood
> on the earth.'

Such was Isaiah's picture of 'the day of vengeance of our God', Israel's triumph over her enemies, the Jubilee's ultimate liberation and redemption of the land. Joshua may well have been glad that this later passage did not fall to him, that he had been required to read only of triumph and re-birth, deliverance and healing; but it is ludicrous to suggest that he, not Luke, deliberately omitted the line which referred to the day of vengeance and foreshadowed the fearful, bloodstained figure.

Luke the historian does not usually shrink from the political shadings of his story, yet it seems that on this occasion he has rather clumsily and pointedly avoided the implications of a redeemed Jerusalem — the overthrow and, at least to Isaiah, the destruction of Gentile oppressors. Proclaiming such ideas would not endear Luke's Jesus to the 'most noble Theophilus'. So Luke continues his narrative with Joshua giving a most unlikely commentary on the reading.

It starts credibly. Joshua perhaps rereads that central passage — the start of Chapter 61 with its talk of anointing and liberation and healing — then rolls up the scroll, hands it back to the *chazzan*, sits, and tells the hushed congregation:

'Today this scripture has been fulfilled in your hearing.'   (*Luke* 4:21)

It is a powerful and provocative statement, usually seen as a claim to Messiahship. Yet when Isaiah says, 'The spirit of the Lord is upon me because he has anointed me,' he is speaking as an anointed *prophet*, not literally consecrated with oil but 'authorised' by God.

This was serious. In applying these words to himself, Joshua was claiming to be a prophet; and for any man falsely claiming such a role, the penalty was death. In the words of God to Moses:

'A prophet who presumes to speak in my name anything
I have not commanded him to say, or a prophet who speaks
in the name of other Gods, must be put to death.'   (*Deuteronomy* 18:20)

Incredibly, in spite of their inability to see Joshua as anything but an ordinary local, Luke's synagogue congregation is not offended but 'amazed at the gracious words'. Joshua continues:

'Doubtless you will quote to me this proverb,
"Physician, heal yourself!" And you will say, "Do
here in your home town the things we have heard
you did in Capernaum." ... Truly I tell you, no
prophet is accepted in his home town.'

No margin for error here. No chance to misunderstand. This is Joshua, the carpenter of Nazareth, telling his former neighbours and friends, with more than a touch of defiance, that he is a prophet. But when Luke continues, it is Luke's *Jesus* speaking, with a warning that prophets spurned by the people of Israel and their rulers will turn to the Gentiles. He tells how 'there were many widows in Israel' during a three-and-a-half-year drought yet Elijah was 'sent' only to a widow in Gentile Sidon; and how in spite of all the lepers in Israel at the time of Elisha, only one man was cured — a Syrian nobleman called Naaman.

There are clear echoes here of the speech Luke attributes to Stephen, the first Christian martyr, a self-destructive, anti-Judaic tirade delivered by Stephen to the Sanhedrin before he is stoned to death by an understandably enraged mob (*Acts* 7:1–60). The unlikely outburst Luke provides for Jesus has a similar effect.

> Everyone was filled with rage, hearing this in the synagogue. They got up, drove him out of the town, and led him to the brow of the hill on which their town was built, so they could throw him down. But he passed through the midst of them and went on his way. (*Luke* 4:28–30)

As written, the story is nonsense. Joshua showed, time after time, that he was not interested in taking the 'good news' to Gentiles. And a congregation concerned with the Mosaic Law would not leap up from Sabbath worship and try to throw someone over a cliff. The people of Galilee in general, and Nazareth in particular, were a volatile lot. But if they had been moved to such an improbable outburst of violence, the priests and Pharisees among them would have curbed the hotheads. Whatever *they* thought of Joshua's claim to be a prophet, this was the Sabbath.

If there is a germ of truth in Luke's story of Jesus handing plaudits to Gentiles, it can only represent a skewed version of the Baptist's warning that being Jewish does not in itself guarantee a place in the kingdom. Some ruthless landlord scribes are Jewish, the Sadducees are Jewish, the 'foolish pietists' among the Pharisees are Jewish; but this does not mean that in attacking them, Joshua turns away from his people. He later declared that weeds are left to grow with the wheat until God's harvest, then separated, gathered and burned (*Matthew* 13:24–30). Above all, he proclaimed: 'I am sent only to the lost sheep of Israel' (*Matthew* 15:24).

It has been suggested that Luke not only distorted the commentary on the reading, but even supplied the text itself as a vehicle for Jesus to declare his Messiahsip. If this was true, Luke would have selected a less controversial passage — one that did not involve his Jesus with the proclamation of a bloody apocalypse and so demand such obvious editing. It seems far more likely that Joshua himself had 'selected' the Isaiah text by choosing to be at Nazareth on the appropriate Sabbath. The reading seemed to offer the perfect vehicle to proclaim his mission in his home town.

But the people of Nazareth could not accept him as the people of Capernaum had done. Mark tells us, 'he was amazed at their unbelief' and that 'they took offence at him', while giving no hint of the violence described by Luke (*Mark* 6:1–6). Yet when Joshua demanded, above all, that he should be accepted as a prophet, the townsfolk's 'unbelief' branded him a false prophet and their 'offence at him' made violence all but inevitable. So in spite of Luke's pro-Gentile warp and dramatic license, there is a credible core to his account.

That evening when the Sabbath sun had set and the first three stars had appeared, perhaps the next morning, a hostile mob drove Joshua from the town or snapped at his heels as he headed up across the hills to more receptive congregations. Perhaps he was tempted to give one last blistering condemnation of their disbelief — and they attacked him, tried to hustle him to a bluff and 'throw him down'. We imagine this as a simple attempt to hurl him over a cliff. Actually it was the first step in execution by stoning — to push the victim face downwards from an elevation twice his own height from the ground. If he survived the fall, a large rock was smashed onto his body. If he still lived, 'all of Israel' battered him with rocks and stones until he died (*Sanhedrin* 45a).

Luke offers no explanation of how Joshua 'passed through the midst of them'. Some clutch at divine intervention, suggesting that some supernatural force protected him or even that he disappeared; but Luke would not have ignored such a 'sign'. Joshua's own physical power and charismatic bearing could have held the mob back. Someone had to lay the first hand on him, someone had to be ready to cast the first stone. You? Or you? He could challenge them by name.

Or perhaps it was his Zealot twin brothers and James and a group of tough Galilean fishermen who gained him a safe departure from Nazareth, leaving a frustrated mob on the roadway to yell their parting abuse.

As they crossed the ridge did Joshua look back at the gaggle of white buildings and laneways and stone fences that had once been such a comfortable place to return to? It seems he never went back to Nazareth, the first of many towns to reject him. This was perhaps the first time he found himself a fugitive; almost certainly it was the first time his life was threatened. Over the next two years he was a fugitive for much of the time and there were other threats of violence and death some, like this one, the spontaneous reactions of a mob, and some made by men of power who feared any man daring to claim a power greater than theirs.

For a time, lakeside Capernaum was Jesus' home, a place where people believed in him. Yet while he still lived there, he told a would-be disciple: 'The foxes have holes, and the birds of the air have nests; but the Son of Man has nowhere to lay his head' (*Matthew* 8:20), seemingly a measure of how deeply he had been wounded by his rejection at Nazareth.

It might have been on this journey back to Capernaum, with Nazareth still an open wound, striding briskly with his brothers and friends across the chill highlands, that Joshua felt a new sense of direction opening before him like the changing panorama of winter fields, fruitless trees and naked vines.

Faced with the threat of opposition and hostility, he will choose the Twelve from the group of disciples who have been following him. This is a symbolic first step in the creation of God's kingdom on earth: two men for the remaining two tribes of Israel, ten for those that had been lost — a promise of restoration and the glory to come. Before Nazareth he had continued the work of the imprisoned Baptist; he had relayed John's Gospel of repentance and the day of wrath; he had challenged the people of Galilee with healings and exorcisms. Now he will start preaching his own Gospel, his own proclamation of the coming kingdom.

As they walked through the hills of Zebulun, the great blunt cone of Mount Tabor loomed out to their right; Tabor with its troubling vistas of cities and principalities, images of earthly power. If that nagging inner voice was there it had to be drowned out, if not by the voice of Abba then by the voices of others who had spoken for him through the years, helping to shape Joshua's view of the perfect world and the perfect life to be lived there, in the way that would please God and bring every man, woman and child to a new understanding of their duty to him and to each other.

As the waters of Kinneret came into view, the harp symbol of its shape and name could have drifted the mind to Joshua's ancestor David and his Psalms. Kinneret could seem, like the Psalms, a great reservoir fed by the stream that defined Israel. The waters of that stream had consecrated Joshua, just as King David had been anointed. David, though a flawed human being, had come to speak with divine inspiration and his voice was one of those Joshua would have heard, like a tributary of the stream that flowed out into the harp lake and mirrored the heavens.

All the ideas, all the voices blended and that dark, inner voice could not make itself heard, even when he and his companions looked down on gleaming white Tiberias at the lakeside and the golden roofs of Herod's palace where John the Baptist was still held prisoner. Joshua's narrow escape from death may have illuminated for him the jeopardy of following the Baptist's way too closely. Perhaps it seemed a symbol of this realisation when he and his followers turned from the main road that led down into Gentile, corpse-impure Tiberias and took the bypass created by observant Jews; a rougher road, a slower road, a muddy road in winter, but a better way.

CHAPTER 13

A Sermon Somewhere

Many years ago I was surprised when a Jewish friend heard part of the Sermon on the Mount for the first time and described it as 'a wonderful expression of Jewish philosophy'.

He was, of course, right. This best known, most often quoted and most comprehensive body of Joshua's teaching represents a distillation — almost a crystallisation — of biblical and rabbinical wisdom. Virtually every verse, every statement, echoes passages from the *Tanakh* or parallels the oral tradition as set down through the following centuries in the Mishnah and Talmud. It is profoundly ironic that the Gospels — which so often portray Joshua as the enemy of the Pharisees — should give us the earliest written record of many pharisaic concepts and precepts. To suggest that Joshua stole this teaching from the Rabbis would be as wrong as claiming that the Mishnah and Talmud stole material from the Gospels. All three sources record a common tradition of religious and social philosophy.

Only Matthew and Luke record this important sermon — though with major differences. Matthew portrays it as a briefing session for the disciples — at this stage, according to him, only Simon Peter, Andrew, John and James the Older. Luke, on the other hand, places it immediately after the selection of the Twelve and has Joshua also addressing a large crowd. Matthew presents this heart of Joshua's teaching in a single three-chapter block (*Matthew* 5, 6 and 7). Luke includes part of it as a sermon (*Luke* 6:20–49) and spreads other passages through later chapters. Matthew makes the sermon more determinedly 'theological' while Luke gives his version a harder social edge.

127

In the most obvious and intriguing contrast, Matthew has Joshua deliver the sermon on a mountain and Luke sets it on a plain. To some scholars this suggests that the Gospellers have simply cut-and-pasted material from their 'Q' source and then invented a location; but there is a deeper significance in the two settings. In Aramaic, *tura* means 'mountain' but also 'open country' in the sense of 'not settled', and is easily translated as 'plain'. This points to independent translations from a shared Aramaic source. Clearly, this source linked the location to the material, suggesting that there *was* a sermon and that it is not entirely a collection of Joshua's more characteristic aphorisms.

Aspects of Joshua's teaching seem contradictory. On the one hand there is no room for compromise — he seems to set impossibly high standards; yet he chooses to surround himself with flawed human beings who continue to display human failings and weaknesses — as he does himself. He shows anger, doubt, despair and — surprisingly — lack of compassion. He betrays uncertainty, he can be unforgiving.

Words are part of the problem. Even in the rare cases where we can have some confidence that his actual words have been recorded, we are insulated from their meaning by two layers of translation — from his original Aramaic to Greek and from Greek to English. These two critical and often-flawed processes have generated dangerous misconceptions about his teaching.

For centuries Christians believed that Jesus commanded them, 'Be ye therefore perfect, even as your father which is in heaven is perfect' (*Matthew* 5:48 KJV). This was seen as 'the key to the whole Sermon on the Mount ... to prepare men for grace by crushing them under the demands of an unattainable Godlikeness'.

While modern translations lean to 'good' rather than 'perfect' (though sometimes the 'goodness' is 'limitless'), clearly Joshua meant that human goodness must be unconditional, like God's. This is what he conveyed when he spoke of love in this same passage. This was the real key to his message of people's relationship with God and with each other — giving open-handedly, without expecting a reward.

Implicit in Joshua's teaching about love was his insistence on the importance and dignity of every individual. While other teachers of his day — and even his disciples — could address their messages exclusively to men, Joshua included women and children. His insistence that children possessed admirable qualities which were lacking in adults was as remarkable as his acceptance of women among his disciples — and the special status he accorded to Mary Magdalene. More of this later.

128

In teaching that every human being had an equal and unconditional right to dignity, Joshua insisted that the use of a demeaning word like 'idiot!' would not be forgiven by God (*Matthew* 5:22). It is the only sin which he judged worthy of hellfire. There was no point in a man performing a sacrifice at the Temple if he had any lurking ill-feeling against a brother; in Joshua's eyes all men and women were to regard each other as brothers and sisters (*Matthew* 5:23–4, 43–8).

Joshua drew a careful line between self-esteem and self-importance. To see oneself as being loved by God as His child was the ultimate in self-esteem. To see oneself as superior to any other human being was mere self-importance. Denying the importance of self was essential to anyone hoping for a place in the kingdom.

And here was the core of Joshua's teaching: the kingdom. For his disciples and Israel at large, this was his message. Not pie in the sky. Not somewhere over the rainbow. Here and now. The Baptist had said the kingdom was near. Joshua said it was *here*. It was not a matter of preparing for what was to come. It was a matter of living the kingdom to make it a reality — in the timeless Jewish concept of 'creating the fact'.

To Joshua there was no basic distinction between the setting of the coming kingdom and the world around him. Again, words have wrought havoc with his ideas. Since the seventeenth century, Christians have clung to the mistranslation, 'The kingdom of God is within you' (*Luke* 17:21), seeing the kingdom as internal, almost subjective, matching other misconceptions of it as an ethereal, otherworldly realm. Joshua actually told his listeners, 'The kingdom of God is *in your midst*' — they were already part of it.

Matthew is partly to blame for the notion of the kingdom as a realm of the spirit. As a devout Jew he hesitated to repeat the name of God and, instead of 'the kingdom of God', he wrote 'the kingdom of Heaven'. Heaven, the sky, was 'the throne of God'. Joshua and the people of his time had no concept of human beings living there, or even going there after death.

John also shares blame for the idea of a cloud-castle kingdom when he has his Jesus say, 'My kingdom is not of this world' (*John* 18:36). While John is rarely a reliable source of what Jesus *said*, the words here are snatched from their context — the Roman interrogation of Jesus on a capital charge. To say that he spoke of a worldly kingdom would have made a death sentence inevitable. Yet even here, the passage carries a shade of meaning that some translators miss or avoid. Jesus is suggesting a change of concept. He has believed that the kingdom will be an earthly monarchy. Now, in a moment of revelation — and perhaps numbing disillusionment — he realises that he has been wrong. Even John, with his reinterpreted, theologically reinvented image of Jesus' mission, has him say, 'My kingdom is not of this world. If my kingdom were of this world, my followers would have fought to save me from being handed over to the Jews. *But now* my kingdom is not from here' [my italics] (*John* 18:36). The subtext is there of a recognition he struggles to understand. This brutal realisation lies slightly more than a year ahead.

✝✝✝

On the mount or plain near Lake Kinneret, in the optimism of this spring-time of 32 AD, Joshua tells his disciples about the kingdom in what are called the 'beatitudes' (from the Latin for 'blessed'), a catalogue of people who are disadvantaged in various ways but whose fortunes are changing with the coming of the kingdom. Luke's version is probably closest to what Joshua said.

(Many translators point out that 'blessed' is not really what Joshua calls his disadvantaged ones. Some versions 'congratulate' them or hail them as 'fortunate'. In the end, 'blessed' seems the best translation, if we ignore its stricter religious meaning, just as 'woe to' seems closer to what he said than the various modern alternatives.)

> Blessed are you the poor, because the kingdom of God is yours.
> Blessed are you who are hungry now, because you will be filled.
> Blessed are you who are weeping now, because you will laugh.
> Blessed are you when men hate you and shun you and blame you and call you evil for the sake of the Son of Man ...
> But woe to you who are rich, because you have had your time of comfort.
> Woe to you who are full, for you will go hungry.
> Woe to you who laugh now, because you will mourn and weep.
> Woe to you when all men speak well of you, because their fathers did the same to the false prophets. (*Luke* 6:17–22; 24–6)

Matthew dilutes the strong socio-political tone of Luke's beatitudes. He blesses 'the poor *in spirit*' and 'those who hunger and thirst *for righteousness*' and omits the 'woes', while adding blessings to the peacemakers, the meek, the merciful and the persecuted.

(*The Gospel of Thomas*, sayings 54, 58, 68 and 69, has Jesus blessing 'the man who has toiled' and 'you who are hated and persecuted' as well as confirming blessings on the poor and hungry without Matthew's 'theological' qualifications.)

In the great prophetic tradition of Israel, Joshua saw no distinction between the religious and social obligations of man. Within a year he expressed more aggressively radical concepts which spoke of a total change in the structure of Jewish society. Some scholars protest that these views were not to be taken literally. Yet it is all here in the inaugural sermon. The poor are the blessed ones, the fortunate ones; the kingdom of God will belong to them. The rich are condemned to misery; their good fortune has run out, their time is past. Nothing could be clearer.

One of Joshua's listeners is his brother James. Some twenty years on, James spoke of the poor as 'heirs of the kingdom' (*James* 2:5) and launched an extraordinary attack on the wealthy.

> Now, you who are rich, weep and howl over your coming misery. Your riches have rotted and your clothes are moth-eaten. Your gold and silver are corroded and their corrosion will condemn you and eat your flesh like fire. You have hoarded treasure in the last days. You have held back wages of the labourers harvesting your fields; they cry out, and the cries of those harvesters have reached the ears of the Lord of Hosts. You have lived on this earth in luxury and indulgence; you gorged yourselves on a day of slaughter. You condemned, you murdered the righteous one; he does not resist you. (*James* 5:1–6)

Here is all the passion of the Sermon on Mount or Plain with the added bitterness of Joshua's death to darken the message. Yet in the heart of that bitterness, Joshua's commandment of love still shines as James quotes what he calls 'the royal law of scripture': 'You must love your neighbour as yourself' (*James* 2:8).

Joshua spoke in the passionate belief that he understood God's intentions for his people. In echoing the teaching of sages like the Pharisee, Hillel (who had died during Joshua's boyhood), he acknowledged their divine inspiration. He understood and believed in that inspiration because he, too, had experienced it. As a Jew, he did not and could not claim divinity (*Mark* 10:18). But as a Jew he could and did see himself as a vehicle to express God's will, in terms which seemed to him simple, straightforward, achievable.

God did not intend the poor to suffer. Nor did God intend some men to live lives of luxury built on the cause of that suffering. It must then be God's will that this state of affairs would come to an end. If people came to believe that this was so, that love was more rewarding than hate, that giving was more pleasurable than taking, this world of theirs would be transformed into a world ready for God's earthly rule, built on the love of God for man and woman, on their love for him and on their love for one another.

In a sermon which addresses poverty, hunger and wealth, it is hardly surprising that debt is a recurring theme, one which Luke brings out more strongly, though in the Lord's Prayer it is Matthew who gives us the unequivocal 'Forgive us our debts as we forgive our debtors' (*Matthew* 6:12) while Luke relates God's forgiveness of our sins to our forgiveness of those in debt to us (*Luke* 11:4).

Debt was a burning issue in first-century Galilee, given unusual topicality because the very next year, 33 AD, would be *Yovel*, the Jubilee — the seventh Week of Years — when debts were to be cancelled, slaves liberated and land returned to its original owners.

In his attitude to debt, Joshua was speaking out in direct opposition to the most liberal of Pharisees, the school of the saintly Hillel, whose teaching he often echoes. Hillel was a compassionate man, and the idealism of the Jubilee's debt cancellation was too often abused in the increasingly sophisticated economic structure of Israel. If debts were cancelled on a seven-year cycle, everyone would insist on repayment before the seven years were up, or would refuse to lend money as the seventh year approached. This latter danger had been recognised by Moses, who warned against 'the evil thought' that 'the year of remission is near' as reason to refuse a loan (*Deuteronomy* 15:7–11).

To Hillel, this would mean hardship for the poor. So he came up with a measure called the *prosbul* (from the Greek *pros boule*, 'before the council'). Under this scheme, debts spanning a Sabbatical or Jubilee year were taken over by a *beth din*, a court. The proforma of a *prosbul* is preserved in the Talmud:

> I ……..………………….. transfer to you …………..………, judges at ……………………….., [my authority] to claim any debt owing to me from ………………………………….. at whatever time I choose.　　　(*Gittin* 36a)

Duly signed by judges or witnesses, the *prosbul* treated the debt as though it had already been paid, so it was unaffected by the seventh or forty-ninth year. The Jubilee debt law remained, but it was effectively evaded.

Unfortunately, Hillel's measure, intended 'for the better ordering of society', rebounded against the poor and benefited the rich. The poor could still be assured of a loan at any time, but their debts were not cancelled every seven years.

Hillel had provided the safeguard that the *prosbul* would only apply to debtors who owned land. This provision was easily evaded by rulings that a man would qualify for the *prosbul* if he had enough land to grow 'a stalk of carob' or owned 'a flowerpot with a hole in it' (so the pot could be considered as connected with the soil!). Even in a Jubilee year a creditor could demand payment and the court was required to recover the money or, if necessary, seize the debtor's property. Mortgages did not even need a *prosbul*. It was ruled that the Jubilee did not cancel them (*Gittin* 37a). Society was spared financial chaos every seven years at the price of an unrelieved debt burden on its poorer citizens.

Joshua vigorously opposed this situation. Time and time again he reiterated the debt theme of the Lord's Prayer, urging his listeners to give without expecting repayment, to share open-handedly, never turning away those in need:

> If you lend [to those] from whom you hope to receive, what thanks is owed to you? ... But love your enemies and do good, and lend, causing none to despair, and you will be greatly rewarded; and you will be sons of the Most High ...
>
> (*Luke* 6:34–5; see *Matthew* 5:42)

In parables and similes he spoke of a court stripping a debtor of every last *lepton* (cent), of imprisonment over debt, of enslavement over debt — images drawn from life in first-century Galilee (*Luke* 12:58–9; *Matthew* 18:23–35).

Joshua's attitude was clear. The Jubilee was a time of liberation and reclamation of birthright. What was the point of physical liberation — an end to physical slavery — when economic slavery was perpetuated? To preach in defiance of the *prosbul* in the year before the Jubilee would win Joshua many friends among the debt-laden peasants whose ability to repay would be further crippled by the no-farming provisions of the Sabbatical law. His views would be equally welcomed by the teeming poor of towns and villages. However, opposing the *prosbul* also guaranteed Joshua the enmity of those with everything to gain from maintenance of the existing debt structure in particular, those concerned with the nation's pre-eminent financial institution, the Temple in Jerusalem.

The great Shemaajah, teacher of Hillel, had advised, 'Do not press on the notice of those in power' (*Aboth* 1, 10). It was pharisaic wisdom which Joshua ignored, at his peril. His outspoken views on debt — so vividly stated in his inaugural sermon — must be seen as a factor in his coming fatal clash with the power elite of Jerusalem.

† † †

It is often said that the Sermon on the Mount or Plain paints a picture of the kingdom without putting forward any plan of how it is to be achieved. This is not true. The plan is built on two things — a commandment and a law. The commandment is to love unconditionally, to love even your enemies. The law is the Law of Moses. Joshua leaves no room for debate on this issue:

> Don't imagine that I have come to abolish the Law or [the teaching of] the Prophets. I haven't come to abolish them but to complete them. I tell you truly, as long as there is a sky and an earth, not a single dot, not a single stroke of the pen will disappear from the Law until all it set out to do has been done. So anyone who breaches even the most minor commandment and encourages others to do the same will be ranked as lowest in the kingdom of Heaven; but whoever observes the Law and teaches others to do the same will be ranked as great in the kingdom of Heaven. (*Matthew* 5:17–19)

According to Matthew, Joshua immediately follows this powerful testimonial for *Torah* with an attack on 'the scribes and Pharisees' — the canon lawyers and theologians intimately concerned with implementation of the law. 'For I tell you, if your righteousness is not greater than that of the scribes and Pharisees, there is no way you can enter the kingdom of Heaven' (*Matthew* 5:20). It is the first of many passages intended to show Joshua as bitterly opposed to *all* scribes and Pharisees, climaxing with a protracted tirade against them (*Matthew* 23:13–22; *Luke* 11:39–52). He certainly criticises some canon lawyer-landlords who 'devour widows' houses' (*Luke* 20:47) and Pharisees given to 'holier-than-thou' attitudes and 'straining out a gnat, but swallowing a camel' (*Matthew* 23:24). Pharisaism was equally critical of such men, dubbing them *hasid shoteh*, 'silly pietists' (*Sotah*, 21b.). The Talmud lists seven types of Pharisees and criticises all but one (*Sotah* 22a, 22b). We will see plenty of evidence that Joshua enjoyed good relationships with many Pharisees, was often treated by members of the fraternity with great respect and, at least once, with concern for his safety. In his Sermon, Joshua honours the Pharisaic tradition time after time, never more directly than in his statement of the so-called 'Golden Rule': 'Always do to others what you would like them to do to you; for this is the Law and [the teaching of] the Prophets' (*Matthew* 7:12; *Luke* 6:31). A generation before Joshua, the great Hillel had said 'What is hateful to you, do not do to your neighbours. That is the whole Torah; the rest is commentary. Go and learn it!' (*Shabbath* 31a).

In an immortal dictum on judging others, Joshua challenges his hearers to remove the beam from their own eyes before they try to remove the speck from their neighbour's eye (*Matthew* 7:15; *Luke* 6:37–42). The Talmud records of Rabbi Tarfon: 'If one said to him, "Remove the speck from between your eyes", he would answer, "Remove the beam from between *your* eyes!" (*Arakin* 16b).

At the core of Joshua's teaching is the rejection of material wealth and possessions:

> Do not hoard treasures on earth where moth and rust destroy and thieves break in and steal, but store treasures in heaven [i.e. with God] where moth and rust cannot destroy and thieves cannot break in and steal: for where your treasure is, there will be your heart.　　(*Matthew* 6:19–21; *Luke* 12:33–4)

The Talmud quotes King Monbas: 'My ancestors stored treasures here below, and I store treasures in heaven … in a place that can be reached by no human hand …' (*Baba Bathra* 11a).

Here, as elsewhere, Joshua goes further than the Pharisees:

> No-one can serve two masters; he will hate one and love the other or be devoted to one and despise the other. You cannot serve God and money!
> 　　(*Matthew* 6:24)

He later says that it is easier for a camel to pass through the eye of a needle than for a rich man to enter the kingdom (*Matthew* 19:24); and he declares: 'Unless you are prepared to give up all your possessions, you cannot be my disciple' (*Luke* 14:33). It is not surprising that this fundamental of his teaching has been ignored by most Christians in every age. It is asking too much, they say. It is impossibly idealistic. Albert Schweitzer suggested that it was part of an 'interim ethic' part of the end times. As it was. But so was all of Joshua's teaching. His extraordinary achievement is that so much of what he taught has nevertheless remained relevant.

✝✝✝

The distinguished Aboriginal leader, Pat Dodson, was taught public speaking by a blind man. He tells how his mentor once interrupted: 'I can't see what you're saying. Speak in pictures.' This is the way Joshua spoke; this was one of the great strengths of his teaching, especially in his favourite approach of teaching in parables, a classic technique of the Pharisees (a famous Rabbi is said to have devoted a third of all his teaching to parables).

The Greek word *parabole* means 'putting things side by side' and suggests a story in which one thing can mean another. (In his translation of the Gospels, Gaus calls parables 'metaphors'.) Typically, Pharisees used the parable (*mashal* in Hebrew) to illustrate a point for disciples. Immediately, Joshua's parables were different. They were usually not illustrations or allegories. They conveyed a central idea with emotional rather than intellectual force; and they were used when addressing ordinary villagers and town dwellers, 'to give them his truth, so far as they were able to understand it. He never spoke to them except in parables, *but he explained all things to his disciples privately*' (*Mark* 4:33–4).

Joshua was a born storyteller. A favourite approach was to ask, 'Which of you …?' and immediately the listener was challenged, involved. Joshua's vivid, pictorial stories are not about ideas to weigh and ponder but are designed to produce an immediate and individual response. He does not suggest a way to deal with a problem, but asks, 'How are *you* going to deal with this?' Not a matter of 'This is to show you what I mean,' but 'You tell me what this means.'

As Albert Nolan put it, 'They are not illustrations of revealed doctrines; they are works of art which reveal or uncover the truth about life'. Or, in Marcus Borg's words, they invite us 'to a different way of seeing, to different images for shaping our understanding of life'. It is obvious that Joshua left his parables unexplained which is why the Gospellers sometimes offer meanings that don't match the stories. Matthew provides three prime examples.

The Labourers in the Vineyard (*Matthew* 20:1–16) are hired at different times, but each receives a day's pay. Matthew quotes Joshua's famous 'one-liner': 'The last will be first, and the first will be last', which isn't really what the story is about — the even-handedness of God's grace.

The Wedding Banquet (*Matthew* 22:2–14) is about ungrateful guests replaced by people pulled off the streets. It does not relate, as Matthew claims, to 'Many are called but few are chosen'. Rather, a place in the kingdom is a privilege *available* to all; none gain it as a right.

The Ten Bridesmaids (*Matthew* 25:1–13) tells how five wise bridesmaids take oil for their lamps and five foolish bridesmaids don't. They all fall asleep and when the bridegroom arrives, the foolish ones have to dash out for more oil and are shut out of the wedding. 'So stay awake,' says Matthew, 'for you know neither the day nor the hour,' in spite of the fact that all ten fell asleep, whether they had oil or not.

These splendid mismatches were all selected by Canon David Edwards of Westminster Abbey. He, of all people, knew that an enormous amount has been written about Joshua's 'parabolic' stories and that scholars do not even agree on whether some of them are or are not parables. The whole point is that the stories were intended to be heard and reacted to, not explained even by the Gospellers. We must all read them and treasure these amazing windows into Joshua's world, and into his mind. (Unfortunately, we are likely to miss some sly Jewish humour which has been lost in translation, but should imagine the stories being told by a man with smiling eyes.)

Enjoy The Prodigal Son (*Luke* 15:11–32); The New Patch on the Old Garment (*Matthew* 9:16; *Mark* 2:21; *Luke* 5:36); The Sower and the Seeds (*Matthew* 13:3–8, 18–23; *Mark* 4:3–8, 14–20; *Luke* 8:5–8, 11–15); The Good Samaritan (*Luke* 10:30–7); The Lost Coin (*Luke* 15:8–10); The Tenants (*Matthew* 21:33–4; *Mark* 12:1–11; *Luke* 20:9–18); and that shrewd observation by an enthusiastic wine drinker, New Wine in Old Skins (*Matthew* 9:17; *Mark* 2:22; *Luke* 5:37–8). You might also like to read the closest approach to a parable in *John* (10: 7–16) and see if you hear Joshua's voice here, too.

Appropriately, according to Matthew, Joshua ended his great sermon with a parable, one which clearly sprang from his knowledge as a builder, and perhaps from something observed in his last, winter visit to hillside Nazareth:

> And everyone who hears these words of mine and acts on them will seem to me like a sensible man who built his house on rock. And the rain poured down, and floods rose, and the wind blew, and battered that house, but it did not fall, for its foundations were rock.
>
> And everyone who hears these words of mine and does not act on them is like a foolish man who built his house on sand. And the rain poured down, and the floods rose, and the wind blew, and battered that house, and it fell, with an almighty crash. (*Matthew* 7: 24–7)

CHAPTER 14

Mary with the Seven Demons

Of all the nonsense the Church has woven around the Gospels, none is sadder, sillier or at core more sinister, than the portrayal of Mary Magdalene as a former prostitute — at best, 'a woman of the city who was a sinner' — in an unnamed Galilean town-city, perhaps Nain. Chapter 7 of Luke's Gospel is the source of it all:

> One of the Pharisees invited Jesus to eat with him; and entering the Pharisee's house, he reclined at the table. And a woman of the city who was a sinner, knowing that Jesus was dining at the Pharisee's house, brought a phial of oil of myrrh and stood behind him, by his feet, weeping. She began to wet his feet with her tears, wiping them with her hair. And she kissed his feet, anointing them with the myrrh. But seeing this, the Pharisee who had invited Jesus, said to himself, 'If he were a real prophet he would know who and what this woman is who is touching him, because she is such a sinner.' And Jesus answered him ...
> (*Luke* 7:36–40)

Jesus then tells a brief near-parable. When two debtors have their debts cancelled (even among Pharisees, he casts the shadow of the *prosbul*), which of them will love the generous creditor more? The one with the bigger debt.

> ... Then, turning to the woman, he said to Simon, 'Do you see this woman? I came into your house, you gave me no water for my feet; but this woman has washed my feet with her tears and wiped them with her hair. You gave me no kiss, but ever since I came in she has been kissing my feet. You did not anoint my head with oil, but she has anointed my feet with myrrh. Because of this I tell you, her many sins have been forgiven because of the great love she has

shown. Where little is forgiven there is little love.'
And he said to her, 'Your sins are forgiven.'   (*Luke* 7:44–8)

It is a wonderful scene, a vivid and believable vignette which portrays Joshua's true attitude to forgiveness. He is not forgiving the woman's sins, as some of the dinner guests believe. Before he speaks to her directly, he tells Simon the Pharisee, 'Her many sins *have been* forgiven.' She is repentant and has physicalised her repentance in a display of generosity, humility and obvious remorse.

It is an intensely intimate encounter — more intimate than we imagine when our reading of *Luke* is coloured by paintings and dramatisations which have Jesus seated, with the woman kneeling at his feet.

This is a formal banquet in the style of the Graeco-Roman *triclinium*: three couches arranged in a 'U' shape, with food served on a table between them. The guests lie across the couches, feet away from the central table, leaning on the left elbow and eating with the other hand. The woman 'stood behind him, at his feet', kneeling to kiss Joshua's bare feet near the edge of the couch, her tears falling on them, her hair wiped across them. He continues to lie there on his side, looking down to her as she pours the fragrant oil on his feet and her fingers soothe it into his flesh. It is intimate, inescapably sensual.

The vividness of Luke's picture guarantees a lingering memory, a desire to know more. What happened to this unnamed woman when she started out on her new life? It is left to our imagination. And there lies the problem.

At the beginning of Luke's next chapter we find Joshua resuming his travels 'from town to town and village to village', accompanied by the Twelve ...

... and a number of women who had been healed of evil spirits and infirmities; Mary, known as Magdalene, from whom seven demons had been driven out, Joanna, wife of Herod's steward, Chuza, and Susanna, and many others, who were providing for him from their own resources.   (*Luke* 8:2–3)

Because Mary of Magdala (Mary Magdalene) is the only one of the women who plays any further role in the story, Christian tradition has merged her with the colourful penitent from a few verses earlier. Mary's 'seven demons' had nothing to do with sexual immorality. As we have seen, in the belief of the time, 'demons' were the cause of mental or physical illness. Joshua drove them out of her; she was cured.

Why fasten on Mary? Why not Susanna, the only woman mentioned by name whose link with Joshua is not defined or who is not described? It could be argued that this is because the link *has* been defined, she *has* been described in the immediately preceding scene. This is why she is named but never again mentioned.

If we adopt the Church's view that the first verses of *Luke* 8 are a continuation of *Luke* 7's 'sinful woman' story, Susanna seems a far more likely sequel candidate — with resonances of Susanna in the *Tanakh:* an attractive woman who is spied on by two lecherous elders while she is bathing, and when she rejects their advances, is unjustly accused of adultery and saved from stoning when Daniel cross examines her accusers (*Daniel and Susanna* 1–64). Of course, it's pure nonsense to make the link, but far less nonsensical than identifying Mary of Magdala as the fallen woman of the banquet.

The Church turned poor Mary into the patron saint of reformed sinners and lost women. She was so often portrayed as a weeping penitent that she gave the English language the word 'maudlin' (the medieval pronunciation of 'Magdalene') for mawkish, weepy sentimentality. In the eighteenth century, 'magdalenes' were institutions for the reform of prostitutes.

It is 120 years since a church scholar, the Abbé Constant Fouard, set out to offer some basis for the stories of Mary's 'immoral life' in his papally-approved work, *La Vie de N. S. Jesus Christ.*

> Of her sinful past we have no knowledge beyond a few legends in the Talmud, which speak of the beauty of Mary, the fame of her lovely hair, her wealth and her intrigues. Her husband was a doctor of the Law, Pappus son of Juda [*sic*]whose jealousy was so great that he was wont to keep her closely imprisoned whenever he left their home. The high-spirited Jewess soon broke away from this hateful restraint, joined forces with a gay officer of Magdala, and accompanied him to that town, where she led a life of such brilliant but unbridled indulgence that she has always kept the name of 'the Magdalene'.

It is true that passages censored from many manuscripts of the Talmud record rabbinical discussion about a woman called Mary (Miriam) who 'turned away from her husband' — that is, committed adultery (*Sanhedrin* 67a, cf. *Shabbath* 104b). It is mentioned in passing that this Mary was 'a dresser of women's hair', *megaddela neshaiya*. The similarity between *megaddela* and Magdala tripped the Abbé Fouard into identifying the errant hairdresser as Mary Magdalene.

The same Talmudic passages name Mary's husband as Pappus (or Pappos) bar Judah, who was a haggadist, almost 'a doctor of the Law', as Fouard described him, and another text confirms that Pappus was so suspicious of his wife that he locked her in the house when he went out (*Gittin* 90a). But Pappus was a contemporary of the revered Rabbi Akiba who played a leading role in the Bar Kochbar revolt of 132 to 135 AD. Pappus was actually imprisoned with Akiba when the gallant Rabbi was flayed alive by the Romans (*Berakoth* 61b).

The story of Mary the hairdresser was undoubtedly true but a century too late for her to have any place in the life of Joshua. It found its way into the Talmud only because this adulterous scandal involving a Mary blurred with tales of Mary the mother of Jesus and the Roman soldier Pantera. Here then are all the elements of Abbé Fouard's scenario — an adulterous woman called Mary, women's hair, a jealous husband, 'megaddela' and a soldier-seducer. It is perhaps coincidence that Fouard's story resembles Tolstoy's *Anna Karenina* published two years earlier.

Rabbinical writings provide one other piece of 'evidence' for Mary's 'immoral life', reporting: 'Magdala was destroyed by the Romans on account of its immorality' (*Lamentations Rabbah* 2:2). To take this as proof that Mary was a prostitute or a libertine would be on a par with assuming that anyone from Sydney was gay.

✝✝✝

Casting Mary as a reformed prostitute was only the beginning. The Church wove a complex web of fantasy around her which sprang, in part, from a 'harmonising tendency' — a shaky attempt to reconcile two Gospel versions of the one story.

In Chapter 11 of *John*, when Lazarus of Bethany is introduced with his sisters Martha and Mary, we are told: 'And it was Mary, who anointed the Lord with perfume and wiped his feet with her hair, whose brother Lazarus was sick' (*John* 11:2). This could easily be taken as a reference to Luke's story of the sinful woman at the banquet. However, in the very next chapter of *John*, Jesus arrives in Bethany on his way to the Passover and dines with Lazarus and his two sisters:

> Then Mary, taking a pound of expensive ointment made from pure spikenard anointed Jesus' feet and wiped them with her hair. And the house was filled with the scent of the ointment. (*John* 12:3)

It is obvious that Mary, sister of well-to-do Lazarus, is not a prostitute, and that Lazarus does not seem to be the Pharisee Simon. Yet, on the basis of this recycled incident and the groundless identification of Magdalene as Luke's sinful woman, Pope Gregory the Great (590 to 604) pronounced that Mary Magdalene was Lazarus's sister *and* the reformed whore. This

three-woman hybrid — still widely accepted — is only slightly less preposterous than a Coptic 'harmonising' creation which has Mary the mother of
Jesus as the daughter of 'Cleopa', born at the village of 'Magdalia', so she can
also be identified as Mary Magdalene and 'Mary of Cleopa'.

The legends of Mary's later life are a confusing blend of obvious fiction
and possible history. Consistently, she travels to France (according to one
version, in a rudderless boat) sometimes with her brother Lazarus and sister
Martha, sometimes with Jesus, sometimes with their baby, sometimes with
the skull of James the Younger. She leads a penitent and ascetic life, and as
she lies dying in the Maritime Alps, is miraculously transported to the
Chapel of St Maximin in Aix-en-Provence, where her relics are discovered in
1279. In a rival version, she is buried in Ephesus, after travelling there with
Mary the mother of Jesus and St John. A modest legend has her travelling to
Rome to denounce Pilate, and in one of the wilder flights of modern fancy
she is the author of 'Q', the collection of Jesus' sayings used by Matthew and
Luke. None of this brings us any closer to Mary of Magdala. If she was not the
reformed whore or the sister of Lazarus, who was she?

In spite of Bishop Spong's odd claim that 'no-one has ever been able to
identify such a town', neither Jewish nor Christian scholars hesitate to locate
Magdala at present-day Mejdel on the shore of Lake Kinneret, five kilometres
north of Tiberias. In Joshua's time it was one of the most important places in
Galilee, a city of perhaps 30 000, famous as a centre where fish were dried,
salted and pickled for export all over the Roman world, from Spain to Egypt.
There were also factories for the manufacture of *oxygarum*, a fish sauce widely used in Mediterranean countries. The town's name (*Migdal* in Hebrew,
Magdala in Aramaic) meant 'Tower'. The Talmud has two versions, *Migdal
Nunaiya*, 'Tower of Fishermen', and *Migdal Zabaiya*, 'Tower of Dyers', a reference to the blue, purple and scarlet dye made here from locally grown indigo
and fresh water shellfish. As well as eighty wool-weaving establishments,
Magdala was famous for its 300 shops supplying sacrificial pigeons and
doves, a trade which had earned the place its early nickname, 'The Village of
Doves'. (In Sholem Asch's charming description, 'the city was stained with
the dye of purple and flecked with the shadows of doves.') Magdala was also
a major boat-building centre. The famous 'Galilee boat' discovered in 1986
— a stripped-down first-century hull embedded in exposed mud flats — was
perhaps a relic of the industry.

This rich, bustling city was the home of Mary with the seven demons. Luke
gives us no clue to the nature of her illness, but the 'Bible number' of seven

demons suggests that the condition was severe. The anti-Christian writer Celsus, of the second century, says bluntly that Mary was 'crazy' and the eighth-century Moslem scribe, Wahb ben Numabbih, recorded that '[Jesus'] mother *and another woman whom he had cured of madness*' [my italics] were present at the crucifixion — a clear reference to Mary Magdalene. (The eighth century seems a long way from the first, but Moslem writers had access to early Syriac Gospels, some of which could have pre-dated our own.)

The next thing Luke tells us of Mary is that Joshua cured her. Freed of her mental torment, she followed him, like 'many' other women Joshua had healed. More than this, Luke makes it clear that Mary, like the others, was a patroness of Joshua. The women 'were providing for him from their own resources'. We know nothing of Susanna, but Joanna, wife of Herod's steward (household manager), Chuza, would have been a woman of substance. We assume that Mary Magdalene, too, was of independent means. Wild theories have been advanced. Magdala was wealthy (one of only three cities whose annual contributions had to be carried to Jerusalem in a wagon) and if Mary was well-to-do, her money had probably come from one of the town's staples — fishing, preserving, weaving, dyeing or boat-building. Perhaps she was the only child of a wealthy man; perhaps a widow ...

The Mary of Christian fantasy is sometimes shown in the sackcloth of a penitent, barefooted; sometimes in the flashy colours and filmy textures of an eastern temptress, adorned with cheap jewellery; sometimes gratuitously naked, often with red hair. Always, she is thought of as beautiful. As E. P. Sanders dryly comments: 'For all we know, on the basis of our sources, she was eighty-six, childless, and keen to mother unkempt young men.' This is possible, but it is not the impression created by a fragmentary passage in *The Gospel of Philip*, one of the Gnostic works found at Nag Hammadi. It probably dates from the third century:

> As for the Wisdom who is called 'the barren', she is the mother (of the) angels. And the companion of the (...) Mary Magdalene. (... loved) her more than (all) the disciples (and used to) kiss her (often) on her (...). The rest of (the disciples ...). They said to him, 'Why do you love her more than all of us?' The Saviour answered and said to them, 'Why do I not love you like her.'
>
> (*Gospel of Philip* 63, 31–6)

Another of these texts, written a century or so earlier, has Mary telling the disciples of a personal revelation shared with her by Jesus. Peter admits, 'Sister, we know that the Saviour loved you more than the rest of women' (*Gospel of Mary* 10:1–3), but later protests, 'Did he really speak with a woman without our knowledge, not openly? ... Did he prefer her to us?'

> Then Mary wept and said to Peter, 'My brother Peter, what do you think? Do you think that I thought this up myself in my heart, or that I am lying about the Saviour?'

> Levi answered and said to Peter, 'Peter, you have always been hot-tempered. Now I see you contending against this woman like the adversaries. But if the Saviour made her worthy, who are you indeed to reject her? Surely the Saviour knows her very well. That is why he loved her more than us.'

(Gospel of Mary 18:1–15)

In a Nag Hammadi document probably written before the end of the first century — about the same time as the Gospel of John — Mary is treated as one of the apostles. In the course of a remarkable conversation with Jesus, Judas and Matthew, Mary declares, 'I want to understand all things (just as) they are.' Jesus tells her, '(This) is the wealth of [those] who seek out life' (*Dialogue of the Saviour* 141, 14–16). The exchange illuminates a preceding description of Mary as 'a woman who understood completely' (*Dialogue of the Saviour* 139, 11–13).

The prominence given Mary in these passages is easily seen as a pro-feminist device to counteract the patristic and even mysogynistic leanings of early Paulian Christianity. Yet in the very text we've just looked at, Jesus urges, 'Pray where there is no woman.' And when, in the *Gospel of Thomas*, Peter says, 'Let Mary leave us, for women are not worthy of life', Jesus replies, 'I myself shall lead her in order to make her male, so that she too may become a living spirit resembling you males. For every woman who will make herself male will enter the kingdom of heaven' (*Gospel of Thomas*, Saying 114).

However one interprets these statements attributed the Gnostics' Jesus (to many scholars they are much less shocking than they seem), it is obvious that Mary's exalted role in the texts does not exemplify an attitude to women in general. Clearly, the Nag Hammadi material draws on a very early tradition that assigns Mary unique status — status which the Gospels have to acknowledge in the Easter story. It is Mary who comes to the tomb at dawn because she 'had not performed at the sepulchre of the Lord those things which women are accustomed to do unto them that die and are beloved of them' (the Apocryphal *Gospel of Peter* 12, 50–1). According to *John*, it is Mary who first sees the resurrected Jesus but does not recognise him until he speaks her name, then cautions her, 'Do not embrace me' (*John* 20:17).

To many Christians Jesus *must* be celibate — almost asexual (one suspects a hint of discomfort even at the reference to his circumcision). To them, any

144

suggestion of a physical relationship between Jesus and Mary Magdalene is tantamount to blasphemy. The fact remains that this relationship is indicated in a strong thread of textual evidence supported by a persistent legend which predated discovery of the evidence. While it is doubtful that theirs was the famous wedding at Cana, it is very likely that Joshua and Mary were married; otherwise her presence as a travelling companion would have been scandalous. And while Joshua was called 'Rabbi' as a respectful form of address, not strictly as a title, it would be very strange for an unmarried man to be accepted in such a role — a fact readily acknowledged by the prominent Catholic scholar, John P. Meier:

> The silence of the NT on the subject [of Jesus' marriage] arises from the fact that the earliest traditions about Jesus simply took for granted that Jesus was married.

In first-century Israel, it would be very strange to find any man in his late thirties who had not married. Celibacy — as opposed to abstinence — was not unknown to Judaism; but it was rare, confined to a few ascetics. Joshua was not ascetic. He shows himself to be remarkably at ease in the company of women, is ready to accept quite intimate physical contact with a notorious sinner and is quoted more than once as showing a relaxed and healthy attitude to nudity.

> 'When you disrobe without being ashamed and take up your garments and place them under your feet like little children and tread on them, then (you will see) the Son of the Living One and you will not be afraid.'
>
> (*Gospel of Thomas*, Saying 37)

> The Lord said, 'The governors (and) the administrators possess garments ... which do not last. But you, as children of truth, are not to clothe yourselves with these transitory garments. Rather, I say (to) you that you will become (blessed) when you strip yourselves!' (*Dialogue of the Saviour* 143, 15–24)

And in a closely related thought:

> The Saviour (said), 'The lamp (of the body) is the mind. As long as (the things inside you) are set in order ... your bodies are (luminous).
>
> (*Dialogue of the Saviour* 125, 18–21)

✝✝✝

Marina Warner has argued persuasively that Mary Magdalene's important role in the congregation of saints was almost demanded by the apotheosis of Mary the mother of Jesus as a virgin goddess.

The rise of the cult of Mary Magdalene through the high middle ages and Counter-Reformation keeps pace with the growth of belief in the immaculate conception of the Virgin. For the more Mary was held to be free of all taint of sin, actual and original, the less the ordinary sinner could turn to her for consolation in his weakness and the more he needed the individual saint whose own lapses held out hope for him.

To Warner, Magdalene, as 'the penitent whore', 'holds up a comforting mirror to those who sin again and again, and promises joy to human frailty'.

It is sad that she could not be revered by Christians simply as a woman loved, mind and body, by a man for whom human love represented, more than anything else, the key to a place in the kingdom; a woman who gave unconditionally, in gratitude and love; who devoted her wealth, however great or small, to Joshua's mission; who stayed with him through the agony of crucifixion and became the first human being to whom he offered proof that love such as his was not extinguished by death.

Ruins of ancient Tiberias lie by the shore of Lake Kinneret; beyond, Crusader walls and turrets mark the later city. In David Roberts's 1839 lithograph, snow-clad Mount Hermon is unrealistically close but this suggests the significant role it played in religious thought of Joshua's time. On its lower slopes he came to accept the role of Messiah.

White limestone ruins of the synagogue at Capernaum, photographed in the late nineteenth-century. A heart-shaped column base from one of its corners is at left foreground. Long believed to be the synagogue in which Joshua had preached, and reverently restored by Franciscans, it is now recognised as much later, though built on the exact ground plan of the house of worship that Joshua knew.

KEY 1. Lake Kinneret
     2. Hippos
     3. Tiberias
     4. Peter's House
     5. Jøshua's room
     6. synagogue

N Not to scale

Peter's house in lakeside Capernaum during Joshua's time there. The reconstruction of the house follows the ground plan discovered under the ruins of a fourth-century Christian basilica based on a first-century 'house-church' that had preserved and venerated the room occupied by Joshua. *Illustration by John Ward.*

CHAPTER 15

At the House of Simon Peter

The town of Capernaum symbolises a central mystery of Joshua's life the failure of his Galilee mission and the loss of 'many' disciples. The mission started at Capernaum in 30 to 31 AD; and here, probably on a spring morning in 32 AD, a mysterious event marked its end. Our one account of what happened is incoherent, unbelievable. While the town has given up many of its secrets in recent years, this one remains to be uncovered.

The name 'Capernaum' was a Roman form of the Hebrew *K'far Nahum*, Village of Nahum. The town was five kilometres north of Magdala on the north-western shore of Kinneret, where it curved across to form the top of the harp and receive the waters of the Jordan.

By Joshua's time it was a lively place of perhaps 1500 people, part fishing village, part frontier post, part stopping place on the *Via Maris*, the great caravan route from Damascus to Egypt. Sited on the border of Herod Antipas's Galilee and Gaulanitis, part of his brother Philip's tetrarchy, it had a customs station and was considered worthy of a Roman garrison — some eighty troops under a centurion. Their posting here was permanent enough to merit the building of a Roman-style bath house, and the centurion may have married a Jewish woman. He had built a synagogue for the town — perhaps using his troops for labour — a sound move for members of an occupation army trying to win goodwill. The synagogue was made of local black basalt — as was the rest of the town, which clustered along the lakeside for about 500 metres in a dark honeycomb of single-storey houses on a loose grid of streets and lanes which stretched back about 120 metres from the shore. In a later period, and probably in Joshua's time, there was a rough sea wall — little more than rocks dumped along the bank of the lake — and a stone jetty.

Such was the setting for the heart of Joshua's Galilee mission — a special place, even more special after his rejection by Nazareth. Three of the Twelve lived here — Simon Peter and Andrew, and Matthew who had held the despised position of revenue collector at the customs station (*Matthew* 9:9). If, as many believe, he was also the tax collector Levi of *Mark* 2:13–14 and *Luke* 5:27–8, then he was a son or brother of Joshua's stepfather Cleopas (Alphaeus) and therefore a stepbrother or uncle.

Matthew says that Joshua 'settled in Capernaum' and later calls it 'his own town' (*Matthew* 4:12–13). Mark tells us that when he returns there, word spreads that he is 'at home' (*Mark* 2:1). Mark and Luke imply that he lives at the house of Simon Peter. He goes there after a Sabbath visit to the synagogue (Mark writes as though the synagogue is almost next-door), is apparently still there in the evening and when he gets up before dawn and goes off to pray in solitude, and according to Mark it is Simon Peter who leads a group to find him (*Mark* 1:21–39; *Luke* 4:34–43). Mark speaks of 'the house of Simon and Andrew' (*Mark* 1:29) and Matthew, Mark and Luke say that Simon's mother-in-law also lives there (*Matthew* 8:14; *Mark* 1:29–30; *Luke* 4:38).

From the Gospels we see Joshua living in the home of Simon Peter, which is large enough to accommodate an extended family and might be close to the synagogue (though Capernaum was so small that this could probably apply to any house in town). After these few glimpses, the house of Simon Peter disappears for 350 years.

✝✝✝

Between 381 and 384, the remarkable pilgrim Egeria recorded: 'In Capernaum the house of the prince of the apostles has been made into a church with the original walls still standing.' Then, in 570 'The Piacenza Pilgrim' made a diary entry: 'We came to Capernaum where the house of St Peter is now a basilica.'

For centuries, even the site of the town was a mystery. It wasn't until 1866 that a pile of weed-choked ruins known as Tel Hum was identified as Capernaum. The remains of its synagogue were fairly easily recognised — handsome white limestone masonry and columns brightly contrasting with the scattered black basalt of the area. At first believed to be the centurion's synagogue attended by Joshua, it emerged that the building dated from a later period but was found in 1981 to be built on the foundation of the earlier basalt structure which Joshua knew.

It seems ironic that for more than half a century Christian attention was concentrated on the Jewish synagogue, while the Christian basilica built over Peter's house was not positively identified until the 1960s, when Franciscan archaeologists excavated an unusual octagonal ruin between the synagogue and the lake. They confirmed that it was a Christian church of the mid-fifth century and theorised that its shape — which matched the emperor Constantine's Church of the Nativity in Bethlehem — acknowledged this as a notable site. Below the basilica's mosaic-paved floor they found the ground plan of a fourth-century 'house church' based on a room which had formed the focus of the basilica, lying directly below its inner octagon. The house itself, classified as an *insula*, was almost identical to others excavated in the area — a rambling complex of rooms and courtyards built in about 63 BC from the inescapable black basalt. Yet in the first century — perhaps as early as 50 AD — the floor, walls and ceiling of this one room were plastered, *the only room in any of Capernaum's houses from this period to be treated in such a way.*

Until the room was plastered it had been used for normal domestic purposes, indicated by the remains of 'cooking pots, bowls, pitchers, jugs and storage jars'. After the plastering, only remains of storage jars and numerous small lamps were to be found. Over the next 300 years, in the course of at least two re-plasterings, countless inscriptions — religious graffiti — were scratched into the walls in Greek, Latin, Hebrew, Aramaic and Syriac. More than 130 could be recovered, messages like 'Lord Jesus Christ help thy servant' and 'Christ have mercy', with crosses of various types and even a roughly drawn boat. In what could be seen as wishful thinking, friar-excavators twice managed to read the name of Peter. True or not, this would prove nothing, any more than the discovery of some fish hooks among the domestic detritus could be imagined as evidence that the house's owners were fishermen.

Without depending on such clues, the archaeologists had demonstrated that a room in an ordinary Capernaum house had been venerated, probably by Jewish 'Christians', within perhaps twenty years of Joshua's time there. Quite apart from providing what has 'cautiously' been called, 'the earliest evidence for Christian gatherings that has ever come to light', the early Church's identification of the house as Peter's and the veneration of the room while most of the apostles were probably still alive, jointly support a conclusion that this was the house and the very room occupied by Joshua while he was in Capernaum. No site connected with his life or death has earlier or more impressive provenance — with the sole exception of the Temple in Jerusalem. Nowhere else can we trace his life so intimately; nowhere else can we come closer to the man.

✝✝✝

Peter's house was only 50 metres from the lakeside, on the left side of a street leading up to the synagogue. The street entrance opened into a courtyard and almost immediately on the left was the door of Joshua's room — the largest in the house, about 6 metres square. There were at least eight other rooms built unevenly around two courtyards, the whole complex covering an area of about 30 metres by 23. The walls were built from courses of unworked black basalt rocks fitted together without mortar and packed with smaller stones. Doorway and window frames were carved from basalt, the floor was paved with water-worn basalt creek stones. Even household equipment such as ovens, mortar and pestle, oil press and flour mill were of basalt. To relieve the relentless gloom of black rock and to provide maximum ventilation in Capernaum's stifling summers (for two months the average temperature was 30 degrees Celsius) the glassless windows were built close to the floor in pairs, sometimes in threes and fours.

The rooms had roofs of cross-hatched poles plastered with a marl of earth and straw or rushes. From the main courtyard, stone steps led up to the sun-baked earthen roof. Here, summertime booths of branches and cloth were set up, looking out to the lake with its colourful traffic of square-sailed fishing boats and larger craft carrying passengers and cargo past the mouth of the Jordan to Bethsaida, to the plateaued Decapolis shore and to Antipas's Tiberias, straight across the water on this crescent of coastline. Turn in the opposite direction and, only 25 metres away, the synagogue's gabled facade rose darkly above the intervening roofscape, facing Peter's house, the lake, and, of course, Jerusalem to the south.

This was the heart of Joshua's world for most of his ministry; a busy world he shared with Simon Peter and his wife and children, with Simon's mother-in-law and with Simon's brother Andrew, who probably also had a wife and family. If Mary Magdalene did not live here — and she probably did — she was certainly nearby, with the other disciples and the 'many' women who travelled with them. The interludes in Capernaum are exquisitely normal and domestic. You can see and hear them, touch and smell them.

There was a circular basalt oven against the western wall of the main courtyard where meals were cooked in fine weather. It is almost impossible not to see late sunlight shining across the black wall through thin smoke from the oven fire, to smell the char-grilled fish, taste the watered wine cooled in an unglazed jug, see the bread as it is broken apart in Joshua's hands, hear his blessing on the meal, listen to his stories while the sun dips behind the hills, and see him climb the steps to the roof for some precious solitude as the far shores of Kinneret and the permanent snows of Mount Hermon still glow with light from the western sky.

It is only at Capernaum that the Gospels follow Joshua through one complete day of his life. The sequence of events may be cut-and-pasted, but Mark and Luke set out to capture the busyness of his time in this community.

The day begins with Joshua and the disciples going up to the synagogue. It is sombre but handsome, the biggest of its time in Galilee — an impressive 12 metres high to the ridge of its gable and 24 metres in length. Its 18-metre width is divided by two rows of grey granite columns into a central nave and two broad aisles with stepped stone benches running their length. These are for elders and senior members of the synagogue. The rest of the congregation sit on rugs spread over the basalt-cobbled floor.

While Joshua is preaching with his usual calm authority (not like most preachers of the day who spent much of their time quoting prophets and sages in what could easily become a tedious display of learning), a voice echoes sharply between the stone walls: 'What are we to you, Joshua the Nazarene!'

It is 'a man with an unclean spirit', perhaps a well-known local character who is mentally disturbed. He approaches Joshua as he sits on the *bema*, perhaps in a basalt 'seat of Moses'.

'Did you come to destroy us?'

Joshua stands as the man comes closer, more and more agitated, pointing wildly. 'I know who you are! The Holy One of God!'

'Be quiet!'

Delivered with all Joshua's power and authority, those words would be like a blow from a fist, echoing as he stares into the man's eyes. Then, more quietly but with equal power, equal authority: 'Come out of him!'

The possessed man falls to the floor in convulsions, gives one last tortured shout, and is suddenly calm. One imagines him being helped by friends or welldoers as Joshua resumes preaching.

After the service, with Peter, Andrew and the others, Joshua walks down the street to Peter's house, anticipating a Sabbath midday meal prepared by Peter's wife and her mother, probably helped by some of the other women.

The meal is not ready. Peter's mother-in-law has been struck down with a 'burning fever' — a common complaint in Capernaum's oppressive, below-sea-level climate.

Joshua goes to the bed where she is lying, speaks sharply to the fever demon they both believe has entered her, then takes her by the hand and helps her up. He probably speaks quietly to her now, stroking her hand, calming her, assuring her that she needn't worry herself about the festive meal. She is soon able to busy herself, at least supervising the younger women, and probably as a matter of pride, she waits on them at the table.

That evening, as soon as the Sabbath has ended, a horde of people come to Peter's house, carrying or supporting their sick, their diseased and their possessed. As townsfolk pack the street outside Peter's door, Joshua performs his healing work.

Physically and spiritually, it is an exhausting night. He sleeps little, gets up before dawn, walks off into the stony rises beyond the town, and prays. He is still there when Peter and the others come looking for him in the morning.

Such was the beginning of the Galilee mission. There were many healings in Capernaum — the synagogue leader's daughter raised from the dead, the exorcism of many demons, the centurion's servant healed without Joshua even seeing the man. He preached in synagogues and performed healings and exorcisms in Chorazin, a few kilometres to the north, in Bethsaida, a little way across the lake, and throughout Galilee. But always he came back to Capernaum. Again he had somewhere to lay his head.

CHAPTER 16

The Curse on Capernaum

Something went wrong at Capernaum. Joshua was suddenly alienated from this heart of the Galilean mission, from the people of what had become 'his own town'. It was worse than his rejection by Nazareth; far worse. His home town's inability to accept him as a prophet had prompted regret and bitterness. His feelings against Capernaum would be poured out in white fury. He damned the place, called down its destruction.

Only John offers any explanation of what happened; and even in his account, the episode is smothered in a smoke screen of Paulian theology and Johannine long-windedness. In spite of this, the events form a discernible shape. John relates the Capernaum crisis to one of Joshua's nature miracles. Matthew relates this miracle directly to the death of John the Baptist; Mark describes the two events in sequence.

It was near Passover, the time of year which marked Herod Antipas's succession to part of his father's kingdom; the time when he would hold an anniversary banquet before going to Jerusalem for the festival. At last, perhaps on his own initiative, perhaps at the urging of Herodias, but certainly not because of Salome's dance, Antipas ended his long procrastination over the fate of the Baptist. Some of John's disciples came to Capernaum to tell Joshua of the murder.

Powerfully, Matthew gives no hint of the impact of this news on Joshua but simply says, 'And hearing this, he left secretly by boat for an isolated place.' (*Matthew* 14:13). His action can be read as private grief at the loss of a revered teacher (or a cousin, if we believe this detail). More credibly, to my mind, this secret embarkation from Capernaum — accompanied by the Twelve and almost certainly at night — shows Joshua's recognition of danger. Everything the Baptist had done, he had done. Everything the Baptist had said, he had said. His life was equally in jeopardy; and there was an even greater threat to all he was trying to achieve.

Joshua's way to the kingdom was through the commandment of love and true obedience to the Law of Moses honoured by Israel. Yet there was also the law of Rome. True, it could be personified in Capernaum's God-fearing centurion as benevolent, even generous. But inescapably, Caesar's rule could not coexist with the coming kingdom and must bow to the rule of God on earth. While Joshua believed that this was happening in God's way, in God's time (and the Capernaum centurion could be seen as offering hope of this), many others — even some of the Twelve — thought differently. If they believed the message of the Baptist and Joshua that the kingdom of God was about to become a reality, then how could they better prepare the way for God's rule than by throwing off the Roman yoke, *now*? Joshua must have realised that the Baptist's death could ignite a Messianic revolt.

With the Twelve, he sailed 5 or 6 kilometres across the top of Kinneret and came ashore near Bethsaida, beyond the eastern bank of the Jordan. It was a piece of country that the Bethsaida natives, Peter, Andrew and Philip, knew well, and it was in the tetrarchy of Philip, outside Herod Antipas's jurisdiction.

Matthew and Mark describe a crowd setting out in pursuit on foot and beating the party to their landing place. Luke and John offer a more likely version. Joshua and the Twelve arrive on the north-eastern shore and climb a hill. Perhaps hours later, John describes Joshua 'raising his eyes and seeing that a great crowd is coming to him' (*John* 6:5). One of the Fourth Gospel's admirers protests, 'The sentence is quite correct, though not well expressed … they did not arrive in a body *like an army on the march*' [my italics].

Everything suggests that this is precisely the way the crowd did arrive — like an army, but an army without a leader. Mark says that Joshua 'took compassion on them because they were like sheep without a shepherd' (*Mark* 6:34). This is an extraordinary echo of Joshua the Conqueror being appointed to command the Children of Israel in the invasion of Canaan. Moses prays for God to choose a new leader, 'so that the congregation of the Lord may not be like sheep without a shepherd' (*Numbers* 26:16–17). While Matthew numbers the crowd at '5000 men, beside women and children', Mark, Luke and John speak only of men. A little later, Joshua orders them to sit, 'rank by rank, in hundreds and fifties' (*Mark* 6:40). This resonates the ancient battle order of Israel, established by Moses in *Exodus* 18, reiterated in *Deuteronomy* 1, applied in *Maccabees* and imagined in the Qumran *War Scroll*. Mark says that Joshua 'began to teach them many things' (6:34); Luke is more specific: 'he spoke to them about the kingdom of God' (9:11).

Late in the afternoon, Joshua asks Philip, a local, where they can buy food for their supporters. Philip protests, 'Two hundred *denarii* worth of bread wouldn't be enough to give every man more than a few crumbs.' Another local, Andrew, announces that 'a young boy' (probably a Bethsaida lad he knows) has 'five barley loaves and two small fish'. He shrugs. 'But what good are they among so many?' (*John* 6:5–9).

Now Joshua orders the men to sit down in their military-style formation on the grassy slope and 'gives thanks' for the meal they are about to enjoy. This is a key moment. It would be unusual for men of Israel to walk out into open country like this without carrying any food. Yet, as the day wears on, each man may well suspect that his neighbours haven't been as prudent as him. There's enough for him in his satchel — bread, pickled fish, figs — but he's damned if he's going to let the clowns on either side of him gobble down his food.

But now they're all sitting down in their ranks and he sees the lad willing to share his five barley loaves and two fish, packed for him that morning by his mother. The loaves — probably what we'd call rolls — were the humblest of food (barley was referred to as 'animal fodder' in the Talmud); the fish would be salted, dried or pickled, little more than sardines. Yet the boy is willing to share his modest meal and here is Joshua thanking God for what they are all about to eat. And now he is breaking the rolls and the fish and his disciples are moving to hand them out.

Suddenly food starts to appear among the ranks — from satchels, from under cloaks, from small baskets — brought out by men who have been moved by the boy's gesture, perhaps embarrassed by it, regretting their own meanness and distrust. There is enough for everybody; more than enough. Supposedly, twelve small basketfuls of bread scraps are left over. The number of baskets, like the size of the crowd, are undoubtedly 'Bible numbers' (in a second version, the number of men shrinks by a thousand); but even with Western, twentieth-century concepts of truth and accuracy, statistics such as crowd numbers shrink or expand, depending on the allegiance of the person making the estimate. The point was that a big crowd had been fed in this isolated place. Whether Joshua had shown faith in God, in his own knowledge of human nature, or in both, the event was no less miraculous. Normal human selfishness had been overcome. Men had given and received and been enriched by sharing. It was remarkably simple, and always will be. Yet so often it needs a person like Joshua to make it happen.

† † †

What is the story about? We could say that it was simply contrived to provide the opportunity for a Moses-style nature miracle: manna from heaven, a miraculous feeding in the wilderness — as we've noted before, one which outdid the occasion when Elijah fed a hundred men with 'twenty loaves and fresh ears of grain' (*2 Kings* 4:42–4).

Yet, while differing in detail, all four Gospels tell the story. Matthew and Mark even record a second version, believing that it describes a separate miracle. Everything points to a solid core of fact, so compelling that it was left to speak for itself.

In three Gospels, the story ends here. Matthew and Mark have Jesus 'dismiss' the crowd, Luke simply cuts away to his next scene. To them, the miracle was the *raison d'être* for a grand tableau. We marvel and depart, leaving the climax of the Galilee mission a towering success. Bewilderingly, we will discover later that to Joshua it has been a failure. Only John looks into the heart of these events and lets us glimpse the seed of Joshua's sense of failure in his moment of triumph.

After the 'sign' of the loaves and fishes, John has the crowd hail Joshua: 'This truly is the Prophet, the one who will come into the world.' This may well have been what Joshua intended. Certainly, it was Mark's understanding of the event in his earliest account, with clear echoes of Moses and the Children of Israel on their way into the Promised Land; and, in all four Gospels, the outdoing of Elijah was implicit; Joshua's role was becoming more clearly defined — though in a way that deeply troubled him.

It is hardly coincidence that a large body of men had followed Joshua out to this lonely stretch of coast just after he had heard of the Baptist's death. Obviously, they too had heard of it. While John the Baptist lived, there was hope that he would be released. With his death, all hope was focused on the less prominent Joshua. The men had come out here wanting to believe, ready to follow. In surrendering their food, in following Joshua's teaching and giving up what was theirs, they had lost nothing. Yet this rejection of the material had only reinforced their conviction that here was a physical leader — a man who could satisfy their hunger for freedom as surely as this simple Messianic banquet had satisfied their need for food.

As they climbed to Jerusalem each year for the pilgrim festivals, in one of the Psalms of Ascent they sang of David's sons reigning over Israel 'for ever and ever', with God's promise:

> 'I will bless her with abundant provisions;
> Her poor I will satisfy with food.'   (*Psalm* 135)

This son of David was fulfilling that promise; the Baptist's death had led them to a Messiah. Gathered in their ranks, the army had found their leader. But, in a numbing moment, Joshua rejected the challenge:

> When Jesus realised that they were about to come and take him by force to make him a king, he left them, and climbed the hill, completely alone.
>
>   (*John* 6:15)

Only John reveals the Messianic hopes of the 5000 and Joshua's dashing of these hopes. If John is wrong, what are the alternatives? That the crowd had a nice day out and a free lunch, then went home? If not, then why had they gone out there? What were their expectations, and were they realised or frustrated? If realised, then their expectations matched Joshua's plans, and the mission was a success. If their hopes in him were frustrated, then they were out-of-phase with Joshua's plans, and his mission had failed. John's resolution of the episode answers both questions in a way which fits the preceding events and those that follow. The men's hopes were Messianic; Joshua would not or could not fulfill these hopes. He quite literally retreated from the demands of the situation. The sheep were again without a shepherd.

The Twelve and the horde of would-be followers might have watched that lonely receding figure until it was lost in a fold of the hillside. Then, disappointed, perhaps mystified, the crowd started to disperse into murmuring groups. Higher up the hill, Joshua could see the leaderless ranks breaking, straying. The sun was low in the sky beyond the lake, silhouetting the ominous cone of Mount Tabor.

With that inner voice again urging him to confront the awesome possibility of Messiahship, Joshua started to walk back around the coast towards Capernaum. Those men had been ready to accept him as a King Messiah. Could he imagine himself in that frightening role? If it was God's will, he must imagine it. But *was* this God's plan for him?

The sun set and, when Joshua didn't return, the Twelve decided he wanted to be alone, as he often did, so they set sail back to Capernaum. The moon was approaching full, the spring sky was probably clear, but while they were sailing or rowing across the dark water, a sharp south-westerly — a head wind — swept down on the lake. If they were under sail, they dropped it and started rowing. The wind strengthened to gale force and all they could do was hold the bow into it and row hard to maintain their course. If they tried to turn either way, they would be swamped.

By the time they had travelled 'twenty-five or thirty stadia' (some 5 or 6 kilometres) — almost the full breadth of the lake — they could no longer make headway and only frantic rowing could keep them headed into the gale. The crossing was taking so long that Joshua had walked around the northern shore to Capernaum. Finding that the Twelve hadn't returned, he continued along the shoreline until he sighted the plunging boat, the flailing oars.

When the disciples saw him ahead, walking *by* the water, he looked unearthly, a moonlit, wind-lashed figure, misted by spray from the waves that pounded the lake bank below his feet. He called out, 'It's me! (I am!) Don't be afraid!' The gale died as quickly as it had risen — seemingly, to the Twelve, as soon as Joshua had spoken — and they rowed the last few boat-lengths to shore. Keeping the bow into the wind had forced their landfall about 2 kilometres south of Capernaum. They picked up Joshua and rowed home along the shoreline in pre-dawn stillness. (*John* 6:16–21; *Matthew* 14:22–34; *Mark* 6:45–53)

At daylight, boats from Tiberias which had probably been forced on to the eastern shore by the same wind, sailed across to Capernaum carrying some of the men who had heard Joshua speak and had shared in yesterday's remarkable act of fellowship. They saw that the boat the disciples had used was there and came in search of Joshua.

It was obviously not the Sabbath, but when these men found him, Joshua seems to have taken them up to the synagogue, perhaps because Peter, Andrew and the rest of the Twelve were still asleep after their exhausting night voyage and pre-dawn arrival home. Men landing from the Tiberias boats would have attracted attention and perhaps some locals joined the group. Word spread and this spontaneous gathering seems to have become a symposium.

Joshua must have been in a strange state. The previous day had been a triumph, but a triumph tarnished by the images of earthly kingship that challenged him in the dying afternoon and during his tumultuous walk around the coastline. And he had come back here to the threat of Herod Antipas's Galilee, in sight of the place where the Baptist was probably murdered. The spectre of Messiahship was given a sword-edge of physical danger.

According to John, the discussion in the synagogue turned to the sharing of the loaves and fishes and Joshua spoke of the spiritual nourishment he offered through God's grace. The bread and fish had come to represent a parable in action.

The day before these very men had wanted him to accept the role of a Davidic king — a man to lead them physically into the kingdom of God. He wanted them to understand that every one of them held the key to the kingdom. Every one of them who had opened his heart to the commandment of love had helped create the Messianic banquet. Just as surely, every one of them could help create the kingdom. Yet they would never be able to see this as long as they insisted on separating the spiritual and the physical.

Like the other Gospellers with other parables, John feels compelled to explain — very, very badly — by putting words into Joshua's mouth, words John has plaited with his developing theology in half a century or more of sermonising while he 'employed an unwritten message' (Eusebius *History* 3, 24).

One of the group mentions the manna given to 'our fathers' in the wilderness. John's Jesus says, disturbingly, 'Moses has not given you the bread from heaven: but my Father gives you the true bread from heaven,' then goes on to deliver the first of John's famous 'I am' statements: 'I am the bread of life'. The Jesus of the Fourth Gospel is telling a gathering of Jews *in a synagogue* that the spiritual nourishment he offers is 'true'; while that offered by Moses was not.

The reliability of John's account crumbles. The man who has just rejected the role of Messiah now claims that he is superior to Moses the lawgiver, the spokesman of God. The voice of Joshua is being drowned out by John's Jesus, who announces: 'I have come down from heaven …'; Joshua continues: '… not to do my will but the will of him who sent me …' (*John* 6:38). Then the voice of Joshua is lost. 'And this is the will of him who sent me … that everyone seeing the son and believing him, shall have everlasting life; *and I shall raise him up on the last day*' (*John* 6:39–40).

The discourse eventually reaches an impossible climax:

> 'Anyone eating my flesh and drinking my blood has everlasting life. And I will raise him up on the last day. Because my flesh is really food and my blood is really drink. Anyone eating my flesh and drinking my blood lives in me and I in him.'
> (*John* 6:54–6)

No Jew could ever say such a thing. Of the 613 laws conveyed by Moses to the Jews, none was reiterated more often or more forcibly than the ban on partaking of blood — stated in *Genesis*, repeated twice in *Leviticus*, three times in *Deuteronomy* and again in *Samuel*. When Joshua's brother James sets down the minimum requirements for Gentiles wishing to become Christians, he will write that they are 'to abstain from pollution by idols, from fornication, from things strangled *and from blood*' (*Acts* 15:19–20; reiterated, *Acts* 15:29).

Christians protest that their Jesus is speaking symbolically; but to a Jew the symbol was as offensive as the reality. Christians protest that John is foreshadowing the sacrament of the bread and wine to be established at The Last Supper but John does not mention bread and wine in his account of The Last Supper and Christian Communion is not a prerequisite for 'everlasting life'.

Later we will try to explain why John needed to attribute such statements to his Jesus at this time. For the moment we can only accept that if there is a kernel of truth here, then Joshua said *something* that angered his audience and alienated him from the people of Capernaum.

John acknowledges the immediate shock waves, even among disciples who have by now joined the group in the synagogue. 'This is too hard,' they say. 'Who can listen to this!' John's Jesus hears them murmuring and asks, 'Does this offend you?' It is the ultimate rhetorical question. John tells us, 'From this time many of his disciples turned back and no longer walked with him'. His Jesus asks the Twelve, 'Do you want to go as well?' Peter replies: 'Your words are of everlasting life [to us]. We have come to believe and *know* that you are the Holy One of God' (*John* 6:54–69). Coming from Simon Peter *Barjona* after the previous day's triumphant rally, this would be highly believable. But if Jesus had just delivered John's 'drink my blood and eat my flesh' harangue, it would be as likely as Rome's College of Cardinals electing a Rabbi to be Pope.

✝✝✝

John provides no sequel to this strange episode; but, at a matching point in Mark's narrative, a party of Sadducee canon lawyers and Pharisees from Jerusalem arrive in Capernaum, perhaps summoned by local authorities. This was most unusual and an earlier instance of this in Mark's Gospel might represent another version of the same event. Here, there is a reference to Joshua's mother and brothers coming to see him in Capernaum but being forced to remain 'standing outside'. They cannot reach him; they must call to him, send a message to him. The building is packed and Joshua is described as having people sitting 'in a circle' around him. Credibly, this is a *beth din*, a religious court convened in the synagogue.

A semicircle of canon lawyers and perhaps the local Sanhedrin face Joshua, and a semicircle of onlookers and supporters sit behind him. Mark clearly doesn't understand the jurisdictional context of his material and there is no coherent account of a hearing. However, Joshua is accused of

160

'having an unclean spirit' being deranged and of casting out demons through the power of Beelzebul. He is derisive: 'How can Satan cast out Satan!' He launches a scathing attack on his accusers:

'Isaiah was right when he prophesied about you hypocrites! As he wrote: "These people honour me with their lips, but their hearts are far away from me. They worship me in vain. Their doctrines are commandments taught by men!"'

(*Mark* 3:22–35; 7:1–23)

If there was a formal hearing we are not told of its outcome; but clearly there was no finding of blasphemy or any other serious infringement of the Law (which would have been inescapable if Joshua had actually delivered the discourse reported by John). In fact some Pharisee members of the Jerusalem delegation could have advised Joshua to leave Galilee for his own safety in view of the Baptist's death. Antipas's stocks may have been high with Jerusalem's religious authorities after the affair of Pilate's votive shields; but the execution of a popular preacher without reference to a Sanhedrin was a discomforting reminder of Herod the Great's bloody excesses.

John makes it clear that Joshua did not attend that year's Passover in Jerusalem and there is a five-month gap in his account. Matthew and Luke tell us that Joshua and the disciples left Galilee and travelled into Gentile Phoenicia. When they returned, it was via Philip's tetrarchy and the Decapolis on the far shore of Kinneret. Joshua provides a bitter epilogue to the Galilee mission and his time at Capernaum:

'Woe to you, Chorazin, woe to you, Bethsaida! For if the miracles performed in you had been performed in Tyre and Sidon, they would have repented long ago in sackcloth and ashes. But I say to you, it will be more bearable for Tyre and Sidon on the day of judgement than for you. *And you Capernaum, have you been exalted to the skies? No! You will be hurled down to Hades; for if the miracles that were performed in you had been performed in Sodom, it would still be there today. But I say to you, it will be more bearable for the land of Sodom on the day of judgement than for you.*' [my italics] (*Matthew* 11:21–4; *Luke* 10:13–16)

It is an odd fact that all three towns damned by Joshua — Chorazin, Bethsaida and Capernaum — were obliterated so effectively that for centuries their sites were unknown. Gentile, corpse-impure Tiberias remained and became a great centre of Judaic culture — though re-sited a little to the north after destruction by earthquake. Of all the towns and cities that once surrounded Kinneret, only one remains on its original site — the supposedly sinful Magdala, home of Mary.

CHAPTER 17

Turning Point

The last year of Joshua's ministry is the most crucial and the most mysterious. It begins with the death of John the Baptist and ends with Joshua's death. It begins with a man who avoids being identified as the Messiah; it ends with a man who has accepted the title. It begins with a man who has declared peacemakers 'blessed' and has urged his followers to love their enemies and turn the other cheek if they are struck; it ends with a man who advises his disciples to arm themselves and who sanctions violent resistance. The year represents a redefinition of Joshua's role; a new understanding of what he believes to be God's purpose for him.

For a time, perhaps with the Twelve, Joshua seems to have been a fugitive in Gentile Phoenecia ('He wished no-one to know he was there'). Here, he provides another clear indication that his mission is only to Jews — in spite of his perceived failure in Galilee. When a Greek woman asks him to cleanse her daughter of 'an unclean spirit', he replies, 'First let the children be satisfied; it isn't good to take their bread and throw it to the dogs' (*Mark* 7:26–7). 'The children' are the Jews; 'the dogs' are the Gentiles. In spite of this almost chilling response he cures the girl.

After a dubious journey which loops needlessly down along the eastern shore of Kinneret (probably contrived by Matthew and Mark for their replay of the loaves and fishes miracle), Joshua and the disciples reach the city of Caesarea Philippi, to be the scene of a crucial moment in the ministry.

The city was some 40 kilometres north of Lake Kinneret, regally sited on the lower slopes of Mount Hermon. What happened there gains credibility from this seemingly inappropriate location. Nearby, the Jordan's major source gouted from a cavern that was a former shrine of the Graeco-Roman horned god Pan. The city of Paneas, named in honour of the god, had been rebuilt by Antipas's brother Philip and renamed Caesarea — 'Caesar's City' — in a display of loyalty to Rome. (*'Philippi'* — 'of Philip' — was added to distinguish the city from Herod the Great's seaport). It is here, or near one of its satellite villages, that Joshua asks his disciples, 'Who do men say that I am?'

The question is not a matter of curiosity, it is not rhetorical, it is atypical. The question reflects his dilemma, his quest to identify God's purpose for him, to define his role in establishing the kingdom. This has been the ongoing agony of his ministry. The disciples say that some believe him to be John the Baptist while others say he is Elijah or 'one of the prophets'. Joshua studies their faces. 'And you — who do *you* say that I am?'

It is Peter who speaks. 'You are the Messiah.' His words are illuminated in Christian lore as The Great Confession.

Joshua doesn't openly accept the title; but he doesn't deny it, either. He simply warns them (very sternly, in the Greek) 'not to tell anyone about him'. Then the discussion is briefly smothered in the to-be-repeated pattern of his telling them that he will be killed and will rise again on the third day — a pattern the Gospels themselves disprove. Visible through this theological veneer is the clear message that Joshua is reluctant to accept Messiahship in terms of the physical leadership that so many of his followers are seeking. This is obviously the sort of leadership that Peter is looking for and he takes Joshua aside to remonstrate with him.

Peter knows what Messiahship means — as do the other disciples; as does every Jew. Peter holds before Joshua the vision of human kingship inherent in all talk of the kingdom, just as 'the 5000 patriots' had done after the death of the Baptist, just as 'Satan' had done after the baptism. Joshua's reply rings through the millennia and acknowledges that he is painfully aware of this resonance.

'Get behind me, Satan!'

He is not calling Peter 'Satan' but is responding to that inner voice. Again the temptation has been held before him. God can let him *consider* the possibility of kingship — perhaps to test him. 'Satan' can tempt him to accept.

If there can be any doubt about the nature of Peter's reproach, Joshua lays it to rest with his next words to his friend: 'You're not considering what God wants but what men want!' (*Mark* 8:27–33).

Matthew and Luke follow Mark closely in recording this focal exchange, except that Matthew's Jesus wholeheartedly embraces the title of Messiah: 'Blessed are you, Simon *Barjona*, for flesh and blood did not reveal this to you, but my Father in Heaven.' He immediately appoints Peter as the 'rock' (a pun on his nickname), the rock on which 'I will build my church and the gates of Hades will not prevail against her' (*Matthew* 16:17–18). It is painfully obvious that Mark's version is more reliable and much earlier. It is then all the more frustrating when Mark abruptly jump-cuts to Joshua gathering a crowd including the disciples to deliver a remarkable address.

'If anyone wants to come with me, then he must deny himself and pick up his cross and follow me. Because anyone who wants to save his life will lose it. But if anyone loses his life for the sake of me and my teaching, then he will save it. What is the point if a man gains the whole word but destroys his soul? Or what can a man give in exchange for his soul? Because if anyone is ashamed of me in this adulterous and sinful generation, then *I* will be ashamed of *him* when I come in the glory of my Father with the holy angels.' (*Mark* 8: 34–8)

Joshua is telling the crowd that if they choose to follow him they must be prepared to face death on a Roman cross — to march to the place of execution with the crosspiece over their shoulders. They must be prepared to suffer the standard punishment of those who rebel against Roman rule. Suddenly, Joshua has publicly accepted the role of a Messiah. Suddenly, he is speaking like a leader of men who are about to risk their lives. In the whole 'unstated drama' this is the greatest single leap across a chasm of missing material.

Mark has probably cut-and-pasted a group of sayings into a single speech; most of them occur in other contexts in *Matthew*, *Luke* and *Thomas*. The point is that Mark has cut-and-pasted them into *this* speech built on the challenge to risk being crucified. It is easy to imagine the reference to crucifixion being provided by the Gospellers as an inspiration to Christians of their day facing the horrors of Roman persecution; or simply to foreshadow Jesus' death — prophecy with the wisdom of hindsight. Tellingly, it doesn't appear in John, probably the latest and certainly the most 'theological' of all the Gospels.

Perhaps most persuasively, the *Gospel of Thomas* associates the 'cross-reference' with unusual requirements for discipleship:

'Whoever does not hate his father and his mother cannot become a disciple to me. And whoever does not hate his brothers and sisters and take up his cross in my way will not be worthy of me.' (*Gospel of Thomas*, Saying 55)

The challenge to take up a cross is here linked to alienation within the family, which the Mishnah relates to the approach of the Messianic age:

> With the advent of the footfalls of the Messiah ... a son will revile his father, a daughter will rise up against [her] mother, a daughter-in-law against her mother-in-law, and a man's enemies will be the enemies of his household.
>
> (*Sotah* 9,15)

Embedded in Mishnaic reference to the awesome advance of the Messiah, the image of the cross gives a tactile, Judaic reality to what Joshua is saying — an affirmation that it does not refer to his coming death, to persecution or self-sacrifice, but to its relevance in first-century Israel as the fate threatening those who oppose Rome by following a Messiah. Perhaps it also bridges that chasm of transition between Joshua's ambiguous acceptance, among the Twelve, of a Messianic role, and this sudden, open challenge to those who would follow him.

In contemplating the death of the Baptist and its implied threat to him, perhaps he realised that — like 'the 5000 patriots' — he, too, had separated the physical and the spiritual; that the view from Mount Tabor comprised God's kingdom as surely as it included the domains of Antipas and Philip and the Gentile lands beyond them, reaching to the walls of Rome.

As soon as Joshua directly confronted the physical reality of Messiahship, that reality was inseparable from the smoke of burning Sepphoris and the hundreds of patriots nailed on roadside crosses, which were probably deeply etched images of his earliest memories.

Joshua ends his uniquely confronting address with a pledge:

> 'Truly, I tell you, some of you standing here will not taste death until you see the kingdom of God coming in power.'
>
> (*Mark* 9:1)

It is a pledge but also a definition. For some, it will happen in their lifetime *and* they will see it as flesh-and-blood dwellers of the earth. Perhaps it also suggests that others will die in the course of its becoming a reality.

Mark now specifies that six days pass before the next development in this abrupt turning point of the ministry. He then describes how Jesus takes Peter, James and John up 'a high mountain':

> And he was transformed before them. And his robes shone as white as snow, whiter than any fuller on earth could bleach them. And they saw Elijah and Moses speaking with Jesus. And Peter said to Jesus, 'Rabbi, I'm glad we're here; let us put up three tabernacles [or 'booths' or 'tents'] — one for you, one for Moses and one for Elijah' (he didn't know what to say, they were all terrified).

And a cloud overshadowed them and a voice came from the cloud, 'This is my beloved son, hear him.' And suddenly, looking around, they saw no-one else there; only Jesus was with them.   (*Mark* 9:28; *Matthew* 17:1–8; *Luke* 9:28–36)

To Christians, this is the Transfiguration; the word has taken on its own meaning. The Greek verb used to describe the effect, *metemorphothe*, tells us it was a metamorphosis, which perhaps brings us closer to what the Gospellers described — a vision in which Jesus was transformed.

'Rational' explanations are at hand: a break in the clouds, a shaft of sunlight (or moonlight) striking Jesus, mist wraiths swirling up like human figures, the Apostles' inspiration that these are Moses and Elijah, the 'luminous thought, so bright that it becomes a voice' confirming what they have come to believe — that their Jesus is indeed a Son of God, now granted the benediction of his heavenly Father. All this can give us logical comfort if we need it. More importantly, what does the vision *mean*?

Theories abound: that it represents an epiphany — a manifestation of supernatural or divine beings; in particular, that it evokes the epiphany of God to Moses on Mount Sinai. There is an echo of the six days passed by Moses and Joshua the Conqueror on the mount as they await God's instructions. Here, too, God speaks from a cloud that settles over the mountain (*Exodus* 24:16). Now Moses the Lawgiver and Elijah, Messenger of the Covenant, unite to attend the new Joshua as he prepares to re-enter the Promised Land. As Robert Funk neatly puts it, 'Epiphanies break through the crust of time in bringing together figures who lived in widely separated eras'. The story also evokes the prophet Malachi who compares God's messenger to a refiner's fire and a fuller's soap (*Malachi* 3:2).

The German scholar Bornkamm suggests that Peter, James and John are granted a preview of the risen Christ: 'They become for a moment witnesses of the coming glory of the Resurrection.' The American Crossan sees the placement of this post-Easter view as a Gospel creation: 'Jesus' resurrection-ascension accompanied by two heavenly beings was re-written as his transfiguration accompanied by Elijah and Moses'.

The Jewish scholar Hyam Maccoby offers another interpretation. To him, the Transfiguration is nothing less than 'a disguised, "spiritualised" account of Jesus' coronation'. This is why the six-day interval is so uncharacteristically stressed. Peter's salutation of Jesus as the Messiah is the Proclamation which initiates the coronation rite. Joshua's 'pick up the cross' address is given perhaps the next day, and six days after this comes the actual ceremony, a specified week after the Proclamation. It is carried out on a mountain in the tradition of Middle Eastern coronation ritual. Peter's odd remark about building 'tabernacles' might refer to the fact that Jewish kings were enthroned in a tabernacle or booth (Hebrew *sukkah*). The presence of Elijah relates to the role of a prophet (or someone representing a prophet) who carried out the anointing of the king:

> The presence of Moses in addition can perhaps be explained by the fact that Jesus was the culminating Messiah, and was himself a prophet, so Moses himself, the greatest of all the prophets, was required to assist at the coronation.

Maccoby's ingenious theory is supported by the apparent location of the incident. Tradition points to two possible sites, Mount Tabor or Mount Hermon. Tabor was in the heart of Antipas's Galilee and had a village on its summit at this time. In spite of this, the Church chose to venerate Tabor as the Transfiguration site, perhaps because it was more accessible than Hermon and closer to other landmarks in the life of Jesus. All logic points to Hermon as the site — which explains Peter's Great Confession at Caesarea Philippi — and neglected evidence supports the choice.

Jews attached apocalyptic significance to a site known as Abel-Mayin, between the source of the Jordan and the summit of Hermon. The cave that had once honoured the horned god of the pagans represented Hades, while the three dazzling peaks of Hermon touched heaven. Both Enoch and Levi received divine messages at this site (*Enoch* 13:7; *Testament of Levi* 4Q, 13, frag. 1) on the flanks of the mountain which had become 'a literary figure in Jewish apocalyptic thought to which all the great revelations of their history were referred'. This was the perfect site for the revelation of Joshua as Messiah; the nearby sacred mount itself provided the appropriate location for the coronation of Joshua as a Davidic king. Whether, as Maccoby believes, there was an actual ceremony which was 'spiritualised' in the Gospel accounts or whether there was a vision or dream of the event shared or (more credibly) jointly interpreted by the three Apostles in terms of a coronation, the significance of the incident is unaltered. In the eyes of Peter, James and John, their Joshua was transformed; 'changed into another man' (*Samuel* 10:6), a man reconceived by God (Psalm 2:7). To them he was now the King Messiah.

CHAPTER 18

Not Peace but a Sword

Soon after Joshua accepted the role of Messiah, Luke tells us that he 'set his face to go to Jerusalem' (*Luke* 9:51). Luke's Greek captures a mood of decision, determination and — perhaps because we know what is to come — a sense of destiny.

According to Luke, Joshua heads for Jerusalem via Samaria, with scouts travelling ahead 'to make ready for him'. Because this party of Jews is travelling to Jerusalem, apparently for a festival, a Samaritan village refuses them hospitality. James and John show how they earned the nickname 'Sons of Thunder' as they ask, 'Lord, do you want us to call fire down from the sky to destroy them, just as Elijah did?' Joshua cools the hotheads; yet soon after, when he invites a new disciple to follow him and the man asks for time to bury his father, Joshua answers harshly: 'Leave the dead to bury their dead. You go out and proclaim the kingdom of God!' (A theory that the man was really asking permission to wait until his ailing father died is unconvincing and does not mitigate the stoniness of Joshua's response.)

Another new follower who asks leave to say goodbye to his family, gets the cold reply: 'No-one who puts his hand on the plough and then looks back is fit for the kingdom of God' (*Luke* 9:57–62).

In writing that Joshua 'set his face to go to Jerusalem', Luke may have intended the verbal link to Isaiah, when the loyal servant of the Lord declares, 'I have set my face like flint' (*Isaiah* 50:7). This is a new Joshua, a less compassionate, even ruthless Joshua. This is the man who will soon announce:

I came to cast fire on the earth; if only it were already alight! But I have a baptism to go through and how I am under pressure until it is over! Do you think
I came to give peace to the earth? No, I tell you, rather division. For from now
on, five in a single house will be divided — three against two and two against
three ... (*Luke* 12:49–52)

He goes on to speak of the family disruption which the Mishnah associates
with the 'footfalls of the Messiah'. Matthew found similar material in the 'Q'
document and drew from it an even more startling declaration: 'I did not
come to bring peace, but a sword!' (*Matthew* 10:34). Here, again, Matthew
relates this surprisingly violent statement to the Mishnah's picture of strife-
torn families as a sign of the Messiah's approach. And again, it is in this
strongly Judaic and Messianic context that Joshua points to the threat of the
Roman cross:

Any man loving his father and mother more than me is not worthy of me; any
man loving his son and daughter more than me is not worthy of me. Any man
who does not pick up his cross and follow me is not worthy of me.
(*Matthew* 10:37–8)

Joshua is demanding more than piety, more than loyalty, more than zeal. He
is demanding zealotry. Attempts to dismiss these statements as 'retrojections'
of the crucifixion and the future persecution of Christians ignore the bloody,
wood-and-iron reality and relevance of the cross to Joshua's Jewish listeners.

It is true that, in mentioning the cross, Joshua is considering his own
death; but not as a predestined, inescapable event; he is foreshadowing its
possibility. In the same way, when he spoke of the cross to his followers, Luke
had him say, 'If anyone wants to follow me, let him deny himself and pick up
his cross *every day* (*Luke* 9:23). Obviously, he was not saying that a follower
must walk to his execution every day or even suffer every day. He meant that
the follower must be prepared to face the daily *threat* of death and suffering
— as he himself was doing.

As John Howard Yoder saw it, 'The believer's cross must be, like his
Lord's, the price of his social nonconformity. It is ... the end of a path freely
chosen after counting the cost.' And in another passage: 'The cross of Christ
... was the political, legally to be expected result of a moral clash with the
powers ruling his society.'

Here, a nagging question must be faced: could it be only a *moral* clash
with the ruling powers? Could the kingdom possibly be achieved without
physical conflict; and was this why Joshua had held back from accepting the

role of Messiah? It was probably a major reason. Yet now he acknowledges that the coming of the kingdom will be associated with violence; he speaks of fire on the earth, the sword, houses divided. *The Gospel of Thomas* offers particularly vivid evidence of this acceptance:

> Jesus said, 'The kingdom of the Father is like someone who wanted to kill a powerful man. In his own house he drew his sword and stabbed it into the wall to find out whether his hand could carry it through. Then he killed the powerful man.'　　　　　　　　　　　*(Gospel of Thomas*, Saying 98)

It is in this new and unsettling context of violence that Joshua speaks of a revolution in Jewish society: 'The last will be first and the first will be last' (*Matthew* 20:16; cf. *Mark* 10:31). Some try to see this as a proclamation of equality; yet there is still a first and last — literally, a new order, totally different from what has existed until now. Joshua is speaking of a reversal of traditional positions, the inversion of Jewish society so clearly foreshadowed in his sermon on mount or plain. The pyramidal social structure of first-century Israel will be turned upside-down. The handful of men who enjoy wealth and power at the golden apex will be swung to the bottom of the structure, overshadowed by the huge mass of people making up its base and bulk.

In the Gnostic *Dialogue of the Saviour*, Judas protests: 'The governors dwell above us so it is they who rule over us.' No, says Joshua. 'It is you who rule over them!' (138, 49–50). The first three Gospels offer a similar message; the disciples expect a new hierarchy and are seen bickering about their positions. Joshua says that none of them will be tyrants 'like the rulers of the Gentiles', and, 'Whoever wants to be great among you, let him be your servant. And whoever wants to be first among you, he will be your menial' (*Matthew* 20:27–8): cf. *Mark* 9:33–7; *Luke* 9:46–8; *Matthew* 18:1–5). Yet, as we have seen, he will also promise them thrones as judges over the twelve tribes of Israel (note this: *twelve* judges, meaning that Judas *Sikarios*, supposedly a preordained traitor, is also preordained as a judge in the kingdom). Again remember that this is no kingdom of the clouds; it is the reign of God over a perfected earth.

Luke surprises us. After his Jesus sets his face to go to Jerusalem, we discover that this is not the last, fatal journey to the Holy City. Chapters 7 to 10 of *John* seem to describe this earlier visit. John's Jesus has missed Passover in the spring of 32 AD but now goes to Jerusalem for Tabernacles — the great autumn festival. He goes there, 'not openly but as it were in secret', travelling alone after 'his brothers' have left on their pilgrim journey. According to most modern texts of *John*, on this visit to Jerusalem Joshua has his encounter with the woman accused of adultery — a memorable episode in his ministry. After spending a night on the Mount of Olives ...

> ... at dawn he returned to the Temple, and all the people came to him and he sat down and taught them. And the scribes and Pharisees brought to him a woman who had been caught in the act of adultery; and standing her between them, they said to him: 'Teacher, this woman has been caught in the act of adultery; and in the Law, Moses commanded that such a one should be stoned. So you, what do you say?' They said this as a trap, so they might have grounds to accuse him. But, bending down, Jesus wrote in the earth with his finger. And when they kept on questioning him, he straightened and said to them" 'The one of you who is sinless, let him dash the first rock on her.' And, again bending down, he wrote in the earth. But having heard this, they left, one by one, starting with the older men. And Jesus was left alone, with the woman still standing there. And, straightening, he said to her: 'Woman, where are those who accused you? No-one condemned you?' And she said, 'No-one, Lord.' And Jesus said to her: 'Neither do I condemn you. Go, and sin no more.'
>
> (*John* 8:2–11)

Because this story provides such a luminous and intensely human glimpse of Joshua, it is disturbing to find that it doesn't appear in the earliest manuscripts of *John* and is sometimes found at the end of *Luke*'s Chapter 28. It has been called a 'floating' or 'orphan' story. Even in those texts of *John* where the passage does appear, it seems wrongly placed. Joshua couldn't 'write in the earth' while he was in the Temple; the whole area was paved. Yet, as A.N. Wilson remarks with a fine eye for those touches that help define a character, 'It is one of the most remarkably naturalistic details in the entire Gospels'. One believes strongly that this is an *observed* detail, perhaps a personal mannerism, which conveys the calm power of Joshua's reaction to the hostile 'Jerusalemites' who have produced the adulterous woman while ignoring the man who is equally guilty.

Edersheim, the devout nineteenth-century scholar, and today's hard-headed Jesus Seminar are in rare agreement on the story; both reject it — but with regret. To Edersheim, 'It contains much of which we instinctively feel to be like the Master, both in what Christ is represented as saying and as doing.'; while the Seminar's Fellows 'assigned the [spoken] words and story to a special category of things they wish Jesus had said and done'.

The story reaches to the heart of Joshua's attitude to the Law and sublimely captures his empathy for those who have 'missed the mark' — to a degree that defies attempts to see it as a literary creation. This foundling episode could have an honourable lineage. Joshua's readiness to forgive adultery might have offended some sections of the early Church which enshrined Paul's anti-sexual obsessions. This could have led to censorship and later reinstatement of the passage — albeit in the wrong place or the wrong Gospel. It is also possible that the incident was salvaged from the vanished *Gospel According to the Hebrews*. Reinstated, salvaged or even invented, it stands as a superb vignette.

Without including this incident, Joshua's time in Jerusalem is almost bizarrely eventful. He preaches in wildly Johannine style, twice evades mobs who try to stone him, twice slips away from other hostile crowds, escapes arrest by the Temple Guard who are acting on the orders of the Sanhedrin, and has an exchange with canon lawyers and Pharisees which involves elements of a trial:

'The Pharisees said to him, "You gave evidence about yourself. Your evidence is not true"' (*John* 7:13) — a clear reference to the rabbinical principle: 'A person is not accredited [to testify] about himself,' (*Kethub* 2,9), a principle which, as Edersheim points out, was apparently applied only in *judicial* cases. Jesus counters with the arguments that, as required by Jewish law, he has two witnesses — himself and his Father — a thoroughly Johannine response which, in this case, is also highly rabbinical. The very rabbinical canon which rejected personal testimony also directed that such testimony should be credited if supported by one other witness. Jesus also tells his accusers: 'You judge according to the flesh' (John 7:15). Was he appearing before a *beth din* — or even before the Great Sanhedrin? Was there a judgement? If so, we are not told of it. The exchange is made the excuse for sermonising in John's usual extravagant mode, and the flashes of legal argument stand out like black-and-white documentary footage cut into an overblown biblical epic.

The most remarkable feature of this action-packed visit to Jerusalem is that John's Jesus seems to spend three months in the city; he arrives for Tabernacles in October and is still there for the Feast of Dedication in December. Threatened by angry, even murderous, mobs, and by a hostile Sanhedrin with Temple Guards on the alert, this seems all but impossible. Intriguingly, we are told nothing of how the three months were passed and shouldn't ignore the possibility that Joshua was imprisoned after the trial that may underlie part of John's text.

This opens up a hornet's nest of further possibilities. Maccoby, who does not recognise a trial in John's account, nevertheless believes that Jesus was imprisoned at the time of Tabernacles. This follows from a line of scholarship which argues that Jesus' triumphal entry to Jerusalem on Palm Sunday, supposedly less than a week before his death at Passover, actually took place at the Feast of Tabernacles some six months earlier. There are clues aplenty to support this provocative concept.

The palm branches waved by the welcoming crowd, which gave Palm Sunday its name, were a significant feature of the Tabernacles ritual, as were the ready-to-hand branches of trees all over the city, used in the making of booths for the festival. The fruitless fig tree, cursed by Jesus soon after his arrival in Jerusalem, could not be expected to bear fruit in spring at Passover time, but would normally carry figs in autumn, the season of Tabernacles. The crowd's cry of '*Hosanna* (save us)', with other quotations from Psalm 118, formed a special part of the Tabernacles liturgy which reached its climax on the Day of the Great Hosanna with priests reciting Psalm 118:25 while they circled the Temple altar seven times in procession.

Perhaps most persuasively, Jesus' entry to Jerusalem on an ass's colt evoked Zechariah's image of the Messiah and the prophet's constantly reiterated theme of Tabernacles as a festive symbol of Messianic triumph.

Maccoby believes that Jesus was arrested at Tabernacles, imprisoned until the Passover, then crucified; and this is the major flaw in the argument (others will be noted later). Why hold Jesus prisoner for almost six months, then *choose* to execute him at Passover? This was a volatile time when Jerusalem was packed to explosion point and when Galileans and Israel-at-large were most prone to violent outbursts of religious patriotism. This problem is highlighted in the Gospels. According to Mark and Matthew, when Jerusalem's religious authorities plot the death of Jesus, they stress, 'but not during the Passover festival, in case it causes a riot' (*Matthew* 26:4–5; *Mark* 14:1–2).

It could be argued — though Maccoby ignores the possibility — that Jesus was actually crucified at the time of Tabernacles or soon after and that the spring crucifixion date was subsequently adopted by the Gospellers as more appropriate (and more attractive to the Gentile world because, as Maccoby points out, it coincided with the death and resurrection rites of Adonis, Attis and Osiris).

Against this, it could be said that the other considerations made the date so unlikely that, unless the events leading up to the crucifixion demanded it take place at Passover, the choice would be very hard to believe. Also, while Jewish sources rarely agree with Christian belief concerning the life of Jesus, on this point they concur — that he was executed at Passover time (*Sanhedrin* 43a).

Slavonic and Romanian texts of Josephus seem to offer a solution to the mystery. They claim that Jesus was arrested, placed on trial before Pilate *and released*, prior to a second arrest and trial which led to his execution by Jewish authorities. Could this mean that he was arrested at Tabernacles, tried, released, then arrested again five months later, to be retried and crucified? It could mean this, but only if we can trust the material.

> Pilate ... sent for the wonder worker [Jesus] and questioned him and recognised that he was a benefactor and neither a robber nor a malefactor nor even a rebel or an imposter eager for rule [or 'covetous of kingship']. He therefore let him go free again [according to the Slavonic version, 'because he had healed his dying wife'] and Jesus continued his calling. When still more people flocked to him, the Scribes [or 'teachers of the law'] were overcome with envy ... They therefore took him prisoner and brought him to the governor Pilate.

The fact that these are late, Christian rewrites of Josephus, designed to ease the guilt on Pilate and lay it squarely on the Jews, is advertised when the Scribes proceed to bribe Pilate with thirty pieces of silver and he gives them Jesus to be crucified. This Christian bowdlerising proves no help in solving the 'Tabernacles' mystery but, as we will see later, its very clumsiness helps to reveal a vastly different story underlying the passage.

It seems most likely that the Tabernacles journey to Jerusalem represented a reconnaissance by Joshua. Obviously intended as a low-key visit (which would hardly allow a 'triumphal entry'), it led, almost inevitably, to a confrontation with the 'Jerusalemites' that might have involved appearance before a court. He may have then left the capital, passed some time in Judaea, and returned to Jerusalem for the Feast of Dedication — and renewed friction. This much is possible and credible.

In addition to this broad scenario, John's colourful account can be relied on for several details — whether or not they can be safely allocated to this three-month period. Joshua's teaching had made him a marked man; the Jerusalem religious authorities regarded him with growing hostility; and normal festival crowds did not see him in the same Messianic light as the people of Galilee — all of which meant that a major mission to Jerusalem would be very dangerous.

According to Luke, it is now that Joshua returns to Galilee or the tetrarchy of Philip and gathers the Seventy — the broader group of disciples who seem to make up the Sanhedrin of the coming Kingdom. The Seventy are briefed by Joshua and sent out in pairs to the towns and villages he will pass through on his projected mission-journey to Jerusalem. Any town or village that will not receive them is cursed by Joshua in precisely the same terms as Capernaum.

The Seventy return with glowing reports of their reception and speak of driving out demons in Joshua's name. He tells them, 'I saw Satan falling from heaven like a bolt of lightning!' (*Luke* 10:18). He has driven out a personal demon. Now that he accepts Messiahship as the will of God and understands why the view from Mount Tabor demanded contemplation, that inner voice is meaningless. How can he be 'tempted' to accept the will of God? Perhaps he realises that to see the possibility of Messiahship as a temptation was an expression of his own doubts. It could be a rationalisation of a perfectly understandable fear that he would not be able to meet the demands of this awesome role; or it could represent a sane, self-preserving hesitation to accept it. Joshua was a man, and men are always capable of such self-deception, though only the most self-critical are capable of recognising it. The 'temptation' to kingship was in fact a challenge — one he has now accepted. 'And he travelled through cities and villages, teaching, and always advancing towards Jerusalem' (*Luke* 13:22).

Mark offers an oddly-phrased comment on the journey: 'And Jesus went before them and they were apprehensive [or 'overwhelmed'] and, following, they were afraid' (*Mark* 10:32). Matthew and Luke don't hesitate to describe the disciples' shortcomings yet omit this detail from their accounts — a strong hint that Mark's original text said that it was *Joshua* who was apprehensive, even overwhelmed, by this last phase of the mission — again a very understandable, human response.

Joshua travelled down through the Decapolis and Peraea, then crossed the Jordan to Jericho, the last major centre before the climb through the Judaean Wilderness to Jerusalem. Here, a blind beggar hailed him as 'Son of David', a Messianic title (*Luke* 18:38). In spite of the Messianic setting of this mission, in spite of Joshua acknowledging his Messiahship among the Twelve, this is the first time he is seen publicly accepting the title — here in Judaea, the domain of Pontius Pilate. Like Joshua the Conquerer, he has led his followers across the Jordan and now, symbolically, he has conquered Jericho, from which 'a great crowd followed him' (*Matthew* 20:29).

Before he left Jericho for the last leg of the journey, Joshua told an extraordinary parable. A nobleman must travel to another country to be granted a kingdom. Before his departure, he gathers ten of his followers and gives each of them one *mina* (more than three months' wages), with the instruction, 'Invest, until I return'. Then he sets out, to be followed by a deputation declaring that his people do not want him as their ruler. On his return, one of his retinue has earned ten *minas* and is given control of ten cities; another has earned five *minas* and is given authority over five cities; until one follower tells him that he has wrapped the single *mina* in a cloth and guarded it carefully, because he knows his lord to be a harsh and miserly man. The newly crowned king is furious. The cautious subject's *mina* is given to the man who had earned ten ...

> 'Because I tell you, to those who have, it will be given. And from anyone who does not have, everything will be taken. But those enemies of mine — who didn't want me to reign over them — bring them here and slaughter them before me.' And after saying this, [Jesus] led them on their way, up towards Jerusalem. (*Luke* 19:12–28; cf. *Matthew* 25:14–30)

This, Luke tell us, was a parable Joshua intended for the disciples, 'because he was near Jerusalem and they thought that the kingdom of God was about to reveal itself' (*Luke* 19:12). Luke does not explain what Joshua meant to convey; but to blunt men like the Twelve, at whom the parable was aimed, the message must have been clear enough — perhaps very much as it seems to a blunt modern mind: 'He who dares most for me, wins most. He who dares to oppose me, dies.'

So he led the way along the 40 kilometres of road that wound up through the naked white and brown hills of the *Midbar Yehuda* towards the cloud-forming spine of the range where Jerusalem lay. Here he would face the enemies who did not want him to reign.

Perhaps that very day, on the far side of the range, the most formidable of those enemies, Pontius Pilate, was approaching Jerusalem from the opposite direction, mounted as befitted a Roman knight, possibly accompanied by his wife riding in a litter, and escorted by a detachment of soldiers. They would provide a bodyguard for Pilate in Herod the Great's palace, joining the 2000-odd men of the reinforced garrison which already manned the Antonia, ready to crush any outburst of religio-patriotic zeal among the hundreds of thousands of pilgrims streaming into the Holy City or setting up camp on the surrounding slopes.

Joshua climbed steadily towards Jerusalem, leading the eighty-two disciples, the women, other followers from Galilee and the Jericho contingent. The Slavonic and Romanian texts of Josephus later claimed that he could marshal '150 ministers [or "pupils"] and a multitude of people [or "many of the lower classes"].' Sossianus Hierocles, a third-century prefect of several provinces including Egypt, said that Joshua led 'as many as 900 men' engaged in what he called *latrocinia* (Lactantius, *Institutiones* 5, 3). The word's normal meaning is 'highway robbery', which seems preposterous until we realise that *latrocinia* is used by Josephus as a technical term to describe the activities of Jewish patriots in the war against Rome. Perhaps this translation seems equally preposterous until we examine the events of the coming week.

CHAPTER 19

The Uprising

Why was Joshua taking his Messianic mission to Jerusalem for the Passover of 33 AD? The choice of *year* is obvious. This was *Yovel*, the Jubilee — the year of liberation and the reclamation of ancestral land — the perfect time to see the kingdom established. But the Jubilee would not begin until five days before the Feast of Tabernacles, on the Day of Atonement. Why advance on Jerusalem for the Passover, five months earlier?

It may have been Joshua's original intention to make his entry coincide with Tabernacles; if so, something happened to alter his plans. In the last week of his journey down the Jordan Valley, as the month of Adar (mid-February to mid-March) drew to its close, there was an eclipse of the sun — on 19 March, according to our calendar. In rabbinical teaching, a solar eclipse was an ill-omen for pagans, who worshipped the sun and lived by a solar calendar (*Sukkah* 29a). Israel's life was regulated by the phases of the moon. True, some argued that if the eclipse was in mid-heaven, like this one, then the ill-omen would extend to the whole world.

> But when Israel fulfils the will of the Omnipresent, they need have no fear of all these [omens] as it is said, 'Thus said the Lord; "Learn not the way of [Gentile] nations, and be not dismayed at the signs of heaven, for the nations are dismayed at them." ' [*Jeremiah* 10:2] The idolators will be dismayed, but Israel will not be dismayed.   (*Sukkah* 29a)

The moon of Israel had eclipsed the sun of Rome. In perhaps the most extraordinary detail of the event, it was the Passover moon that had accom-

The Danish artist Carl Bloch
captures the ethereal quality
of the 'Transfiguration' vision
that was 'shared or (more
credibly) jointly interpreted'
by Peter, James and John. The
event has been explained in
many ways. Most importantly,
it marked the acceptance of
Joshua as the Messiah by this
inner circle of the disciples.

The story of The Good Samaritan, who helps a man
beaten and stripped by robbers, is perhaps the best
known of Joshua's parables — stories which set out to
convey an aspect of his teaching in vivid images that
did not need literal explanation. The Gospellers
sometimes misinterpreted them, an interesting symbol
of Joshua's message being altered, even in the
documents that recorded it.

Doré's engraving of Mary Magdalene shows her as a mourning penitent — a popular image in religious art which also associates her, as here, with a skull. Usually explained as a symbol of death, the skull may have greater significance. In some legends, Mary carries to France the skull of Joshua's brother, James. According to others, it is the skull of Joshua — which would deny the physical resurrection and the Ascension. Doré's cavernous darkness honours the mystery.

The incident of the woman caught in the act of adultery (shown here in one of Hofmann's Gospel illustrations) provides one of the most impressive moments in the Gospel of *John* (8:2-11). Yet it is missing from the earliest manuscripts, seems to be wrongly placed in those manuscripts where it does appear and sometimes pops up in manuscripts of *Luke*. It is rarely considered that this could represent an early case of Church censorship; that Joshua's readiness to intercede on the woman's behalf offended those sections of the early Church which regarded sexuality as sinful. The passage was 'lost' and later retrieved.

plished this portent. The very next evening the Temple's silver trumpets signalled the new moon which began the Passover month of Nisan and a beacon fire on the Mount of Olives flashed the news from mount to mount across the land.

Passover, on 15 Nisan, would mark the beginning of the holy year and celebrate the Children of Israel's liberation from Egyptian bondage, the beginning of the journey to claim their holy land.

Even without knowing the astronomical link between the two phenomena, Joshua could not have been given a clearer sign that this was the time to move on Jerusalem — *if he saw the eclipse*. But we know he didn't. The eclipse was visible only in a 'window' which extended from below the equator to slightly above it, across an area of ocean which included no land mass. However, it was observed, probably from a ship or ships, and recorded by the second-century chronicler Phlegon of Thralles who dated it to 'the fourth year of the 202nd Olympiad' — 32–33 AD — and noted that it was followed by an earthquake which caused considerable damage in Nicea. This was exactly a fortnight before Joshua's death and it is hardly surprising that, by the time the earliest Gospels were written, both phenomena had come to be associated with the Crucifixion — especially in view of the prophet Joel's prediction. He told how: 'The earth quakes, the heavens tremble, the sun and moon grow dark' as the Lord advances at the head of his army 'on the great and terrible day of the Lord' (*Joel* 2:10–11, 31).

The darkening of the sun preceding Joshua's death, as described by Matthew, Mark and Luke, occurs between the sixth hour and the ninth hour — between noon and 3 pm — the time of the unseen eclipse two weeks before. John's eyewitness account of the Crucifixion does not mention it.

Whatever impact the solar eclipse had on the Gospels, Joshua knew nothing of it. If he *had* intended to enter Jerusalem at Tabernacles, there is a far more prosaic explanation of his decision to advance the date.

Luke records that during the mission down the Jordan Valley, 'some Pharisees came to Joshua, saying, 'Get away from here; Herod wants to kill you!'. His reply is defiant: 'Go and tell that fox [I suspect that Joshua would have called him a jackal] that today and tomorrow I cast out demons and on the third day my work will be complete.' He speaks bitterly of Jerusalem as 'the city that kills the prophets and stones those that are sent to it,' and sends Antipas the message: 'You will not see me until you say, "Blessed is the one who comes in the name of the Lord" ' (*Luke* 13:31–5). This is the verse of Psalm 118 immediately following Tabernacles' 'Great Hosanna', an apparent challenge that he intends to enter Jerusalem in time for the festival.

Much or all of the dialogue in this exchange may be Luke's, but the event itself — Joshua being warned *by Pharisees* of Herod Antipas's wish to kill him — is one of those stubborn facts that has elbowed its way through a sleeve of anti-Pharisee propaganda. Significantly, it was earlier on this same journey that Mark recorded Joshua's attack on Antipas's marriage, when he declared that, if a woman divorced her husband and remarried, she had committed adultery. As we've seen, this situation was impossible under Judaic law but reflected Herodias divorcing Herod Boethus to marry Antipas — a union now damned by Joshua as adulterous (*Mark* 10:12). He was following in the Baptist's steps with dangerous fidelity.

In the light of the Pharisees' warning (which only confirmed what he had obviously suspected ever since John's murder), Joshua must have realised that he couldn't afford to wait until the Feast of Tabernacles. Some people were saying that he was 'the Baptist raised from the dead'. Understandably, when Herod had heard this, earlier in the mission, he was 'perplexed ... And Herod said, "I beheaded John, but who is this I hear such things about?" And he wanted to see him.' (*Luke* 9:9).

One way or another, Antipas was determined to lay this ghost of the Baptist, and if Joshua fell into his hands during the next six months — even if only to be held prisoner — the mission would be ended. So Joshua could choose to leave Antipas's territory, return to the Decapolis or the tetrarchy of Philip, perhaps take refuge in Samaria or Phoenecia for six months ... or he could do the last thing anyone would expect: enter Jerusalem for the Passover and inaugurate the kingdom. As Joshua says on this journey:

> If the master of the house had known at what hour the thief was coming, he would have been on watch and would not have let his house be broken into. So be prepared; because the Son of Man will come at a time you don't expect.
>
> (*Luke* 12:39–40)

†††

Perhaps seven days before Passover, on the afternoon of 7 Nisan, Joshua and his band of followers reached the village of Bethany on the south-eastern slopes of the Mount of Olives, only three kilometres from Jerusalem. According to John, this was the home of Martha and Mary who may have had a brother called Lazarus (though Luke writes as though the two women lived in a village much further from the Holy City).

A tomb excavated in 1952 on the Mount of Olives, near the road from Bethany to Jerusalem, contained an ossuary — a stone casket of human bones — inscribed, 'Martha and Mary'. It may be coincidence, but the linking of the two names in death, at this location, is persuasive.

Martha and Mary were friends of Joshua who had probably given him hospitality many times in the past on his visits to Jerusalem. Mary — often and illogically identified as Luke's sinful woman *and* Mary Magdalene — was clearly a disciple and is described sitting at Joshua's feet, the traditional position of Pharisaic pupils before their teacher. It also seems that the family were people of substance, who might have owned olive groves or fig orchards which thrived here on the fringes of the rain from Jerusalem's clouds.

It may have been Mary who performed a significant role in what was now a royal progress to Jerusalem. At some point — according to John soon after arriving at Bethany, while Mark says later in the week — Joshua was anointed with spikenard, a rare and expensive perfumed oil imported from India. In John's account, Mary anoints Joshua's feet and wipes them with her hair in a confusing replay of Luke's sinful woman at the home of Simon the Pharisee. Mark described an unnamed woman breaking open an alabaster jar of spikenard and pouring it on Joshua's head during a meal at the Bethany home of Simon the Leper. Both accounts agree that the quantity of oil used was worth 300 *denarii* — almost a year's wage for a labourer.

Mark's account strongly suggests a ceremonial anointing, a fact which is obscured by Jesus announcing: 'She has anointed my body in preparation for its burial.' The Gospels demonstrate very clearly that Jesus' repeated predictions of his death, burial and resurrection are later embroideries of the story. We are left with a princely anointing on the slopes of the Mount of Olives, a site which plays a recurrent role in Jewish tradition and ceremony and was in fact named in the Mishnah as the Mount of Anointing (*Rosh Hashannah* 2, 4).

This is perhaps the evening meal of the Sabbath — the beginning of Sunday in Jewish reckoning. The anointing inaugurates and defines the coming day's events. Joshua has laid his plans for the arrival in Jerusalem and it is not hard to recognise his major inspiration. Throughout this last week of his life he shows a fixation with the book of the prophet Zechariah. He constantly quotes it, alludes to it and, most obviously, on this day re-enacts a key passage from it. Zechariah provides the Messianic scenario for Joshua's time in Jerusalem — even for a development which was not part of the original plan.

So, on the Sunday, Joshua sets out with his followers on the last few kilo-metres of the journey, along a road which winds up across the Mount of Olives, following the right shoulder of a curving pass. Just below the crest, the village of Bethpage is scattered on the opposite slope. Joshua sends two disciples ahead to fetch an ass colt which they will find tethered at the road-side. Joshua tells them: 'Untie it and bring it here. And if anyone asks you, "Why are you doing this?" say, "The Master needs it," and he will send it straight away' (*Mark* 11:1–4).

Everything happens as Joshua has described it — open to interpretation as prophecy, or pre-planning complete with a pre-arranged and cleverly ambiguous password.

The disciples throw some cloaks across the colt's back and Joshua mounts it, then leads the procession up across the summit, turning out of the pass to see Jerusalem revealed below them in morning sunlight — the Temple daz-zling white and ablaze with gold, the Antonia brooding close beside it. Few men confront their destiny in a moment of such spectacle, embodying two such dominant symbols.

This is the prelude to the 'Triumphal Entry' on what is called Palm Sunday. Every detail of the event has been challenged, the event itself dis-missed as Gospel fiction or derided as an insignificant detail of Joshua's journey distorted to become the fulfilment of Zechariah's prophecy his unforgettable picture of Messianic triumph:

> Rejoice greatly, you daughter of Zion!
> Shout joyously, you daughter of Jerusalem!
> Look, your king is coming to you,
> Victorious and triumphant,
> Gentle and riding on a donkey,
> On a colt, the foal of a donkey.
> He will sweep away the chariots from Ephraim
> And the war horses from Jerusalem
> And the battle bow will be broken,
> He will proclaim peace to the Nations,
> His domain will stretch from sea to sea
> And from the river to the ends of the earth.   (*Zechariah* 9:9–10)

This entry to Jerusalem is the great obstacle in the way of those Jewish and Christian scholars who insist that Joshua never accepted the role of Messiah. It is equally an obstacle in the way of Christians who accept the Gospels as truth but cannot believe that Jesus ever claimed *physical*

Messiahship; that he ever intended to rule as a Davidic king over an earthly kingdom. Even the Gospels, in recording the incident, carefully avoid some links with Zechariah's image of the King Messiah.

Matthew quotes Zechariah's description but pointedly omits 'victorious and triumphant' and ignores the picture of the Messiah's universal kingdom. John gives a more heavily edited version which even avoids 'gentle' (*John* 12:15). The obvious fact that the Zechariah prophecy was 'inconvenient', strongly suggests that it was fastened on by Joshua, rather than the Gospellers. Mark's description of the Triumphal Entry is almost certainly the earliest. He seems unaware of the echoes of Zechariah.

> And many spread their garments on the road and others cut branches from trees and scattered them in his way. And those ahead of him and those following cried out, 'Hosanna! Blessed is the one coming in the name of the Lord! Blessed is the coming kingdom of our father David in the name of the Lord! Hosanna in the highest!' And Jesus entered Jerusalem and went into the Temple. (*Mark* 11:8–11)

Matthew's account follows Mark closely except that, oddly, he has Joshua riding an ass *and* a colt. Also, the cries of Joshua's band now include, 'Hosanna to the son of David!' (*Matthew* 21:6–9). Luke doesn't mention branches being strewn and, while he has the procession calling 'Hosanna!', he again varies the cries: 'Blessed is the coming one, the King, in the name of the Lord. Peace in heaven and glory in the highest places!' (*Luke* 19:36–8). Tellingly, John describes the scene from the viewpoint of Jerusalem:

> Hearing that Jesus is on his way to Jerusalem, a great crowd took [the change of tense is typical of John] branches of palm trees and went out to meet him; and they were calling, 'Hosanna! Blessed is the one coming in the name of the Lord, the king of Israel!'

According to John, it is only after being hailed as the king of Israel that Jesus finds the ass colt and rides it. John is carefully avoiding any suggestion that Zechariah's description of the Messiah's coming has inspired the staging of the entry — or that it is the members of Jesus' party who hail him with Messianic titles. John quotes the essence of the passage from Zechariah, then comments:

> His disciples were not aware of this at first. But when Jesus was glorified, then they recalled that these things had been written of him and that they had done these things to him. (*John* 12:16)

John seems to protest too much. Everything suggests that the partisan group had set out to proclaim Joshua's Messiahship by helping him realise Zechariah's prophecy, by singing their hosannas and by strewing garments in front of him, as the Israelites had done before a newly anointed king (2 *Kings* 9:13).

Each Gospeller takes the acclamation a step further. Mark's crowd speaks of 'the coming kingdom of our father David'; Matthew's people cry, 'Hosanna to the son of David!'; Luke's band call Joshua 'the coming one, the king'; and John's people of Jerusalem hail Joshua as 'the king of Israel!'.

Even if the actual demonstration matched Mark's earliest and most restrained version, it was still unmistakably Messianic, stamped as such by the cry of 'Hosanna!', which means 'Save us!' — even though there is some confusion over its use. 'Save us in the highest!' or 'Save us to the son of David!' are very unlikely, suggesting that the cry, as recorded in Hebrew or Aramaic, was imperfectly understood by Gentile translators — even that the paraphrase of Psalm 118 may have involved the Aramaic form '*Osh ha'na*', which has the shading of 'Free us!'

It is true, as Maccoby stresses, that 'Hosanna!', in the context of *Psalm* 118:25, was an integral part of the Tabernacles liturgy and that palm branches, too, featured in this festival. But Psalm 118 was also part of the *Hallel*, a cycle of psalms sung at all the pilgrim festivals; and note that only John mentions *palm* branches. Also, it must be recognised that Psalm 118 is much more than a plea for rescue and a song of praise for the redeemer. Like the passage of Zechariah which inspired the staging of Joshua's entry, the psalm is also a song of victory and a very militant one:

> With the Lord on my side, I am not afraid,
> What can any man do to harm me? …
> Gentile nations pressed around me,
> In the name of the Lord I cut them down.
> They swarmed around me like bees,
> They blazed like a fire of thorns,
> In the name of the Lord I cut them down.
> I was almost overcome, close to falling,
> But the Lord came to my aid.
> The Lord is my strength, he is my song,
> He has become my salvation.   (*Psalm* 118:6, 10–14)

If Joshua's followers sang or recited this Psalm as he rode into Jerusalem, probably through a gate immediately below the Temple, its impact on the volatile Passover crowds packing the city's streets is easily imagined. For

Christians, 'Hosanna!' is a sort of religious 'Hooray!'. To those crowds, 'Hosanna!' meant precisely what it said: 'Save us!' or even 'Free us!'.

We are by now familiar with the Gospel device of identifying and even inventing incidents or details which can be matched with 'Old Testament' prophecies; but this case is different. Joshua is making a deliberate choice to enter Jerusalem in a way which conforms to a prophecy and is therefore recognisably Messianic. And he is doing this during the lead-up to the Passover festival that has provided the seedbed for more than one revolt in the near past. He has a ready-made crowd poised in that heady stratum between celebration and riot, preparing to celebrate Israel's delivery from an earlier bondage. In this time of past glories recalled and illuminated by religious fervour, the humiliating ritual of retrieving the high priest's vestments from the Antonia has just been enacted. The garments are undergoing purification after their pollution by Roman custody (Josephus *Antiquities* 18,4,3). They will shine in renewed glory at this festival, never again to be returned to pagan hands — just as the people of Israel will be liberated from the spiritual exile (*galus*) of pagan domination; and Joshua's appointment of the Twelve as judges over the restored tribes of Israel will signal the nation's return to its pre-exile glory.

Joshua the fugitive has chosen this week of all weeks to enter Jerusalem, in a way that will attract the attention of priests, Sadducess, Pharisees, the people and the Romans. He is no longer a fugitive. His claim to the Messiahship is no longer a secret.

✝✝✝

According to Mark, Joshua went straight to the Temple. He perhaps dismounted at the foot of the broad bank of steps below the southern wall to enter by the twin Huldah gates; or, more dramatically, he rode another sixty metres to the foot of the monumental staircase that mounted in three turning flights to the lofty western entrance of the Royal Stoa.

This was probably his destination. The magnificent basilica, two hundred metres long, with its soaring central nave flanked by rows of columns, served as a huge bazaar for the festival crowds weaving through the open colonnade of the northern aisle on their way to and from the Court of the Gentiles. The Stoa was, in Kathleen Ritmeyer's description, 'a scene of frenzied commercial activity':

> At the tables of moneychangers, the pilgrim exchanges coins bearing the image of Caesar for silver shekels without the forbidden graven image. Women who

have recently given birth are crowded at the stalls nearby haggling over the price of the doves and pigeons they will sacrifice in gratitude for the happy conclusion of their pregnancies. Those who successfully complete a purchase walk away bearing small cages. Oxen and sheep to be sacrificed are also offered for sale; the smell of their droppings permeates the entire area.

This day, bleating lambs would be on offer by the thousands in preparation for Friday's Passover sacrifices. What happened next was probably part of Joshua's original plan.

> And Jesus went into the Temple of God and threw out all those who were selling and buying there; and he overturned the tables of the moneychangers and the benches of the dove sellers.   (*Matthew* 21:12–13; *Mark* 11:15; *Luke* 11:45)

John gives a fuller account of what is almost certainly the same incident.

> And there in the Temple he found those selling oxen and sheep and doves, with moneychangers also sitting there. And making a whip out of ropes, he drove them all out of the Temple — sheep and oxen and moneychangers — pouring out the money and overturning the tables. And to those selling doves he said, 'Get these things out of here! Don't make my Father's house a place of business!'   (*John* 2:14–16)

We are not seeing a spontaneous outburst of anger. Nothing had changed since Joshua's previous visit here less than three months before. This was a demonstration directly related to the Triumphal Entry — an action carried out under the authority of Messiahship — which all the Gospels identify as the issue at stake here — authority (*Matthew* 21:23; *Mark* 11:27–8; *Luke* 20:1–2; *John* 2:18). What was Joshua trying to achieve by this violence? John's mention of palm branches immediately evokes the purification and rededication of the Temple by Judas Maccabee after its desecration by Antiochus and the Syrian Greeks:

> Carrying garlanded wands and flowering branches as well as palm-fronds, they chanted hymns to the One who had so triumphantly achieved the purification of His own Temple.   (2 *Maccabees* 10:7)

Judas's inaugural eight-day festival, closely based on Tabernacles, became the Feast of Dedication. It featured a procession in which the 'hosanna' from Psalm 118 was chanted and branches of palms and other trees were waved, reminding us that John's welcoming crowd carry their palm fronds while, in the other Gospels, the members of Joshua's party simply scatter branches in his path. Yet John makes no link between the triumphal entry and the 'cleansing' of the Temple which, according to his Gospel, happened some three years earlier at the very beginning of the ministry, immediately after the Cana miracle. It seems likely that John deliberately separated this incident from the events leading up to Joshua's death. And with good reason.

As N.T. Wright said, 'if Jesus did *not* want to be thought of in any way as a Messiah, the Entry and the action in the Temple were extremely unwise things to undertake.' One could add that if the Gospellers did not want to portray their Jesus as an earthly Messiah, these were extremely unwise things to report — or, as some would have it, to invent.

An attack on Temple activities, as described in the Gospels, would have attracted the immediate attention of the Temple Guard, if not Pilate's festival reinforcements. (An incident involving the 'Apostle' Paul [*Acts* 21:30–2] shows how quickly Roman troops intervened when a scuffle broke out in the Temple environs.) Yet no such intervention is described. The only reaction recorded by the Gospels is a demand to know by what authority Joshua behaved in such a way. He is supposedly able to preach in the Temple for the best part of two days. Mark tells us 'all the crowd was astonished at his doctrine' (*Mark* 11:18), but only briefly quotes his teaching — a comment on the 'cleansing': 'Was it not written, "My house shall be called a house of prayer for all nations"? But you have made it a den of thieves' (*Mark* 11:17). It is usually pointed out that Joshua is quoting *Isaiah* 56:7 and *Jeremiah* 7:11. Yet these are also clear references to Zechariah's picture of the Messianic age when:

> all who survive of the nations that have oppressed Jerusalem will go up, year after year, to worship the King, the Lord of Hosts, and to keep the Feast of Tabernacles ... *and there will no longer be traders in the Temple of the Lord of Hosts on that day*. [my italics]   (*Zechariah* 14:16, 21)

Here, in the book's closing words, in its final, vivid impression on the reader, is the clearest motivation for the attack on the Temple. Joshua is again living out the Messianic scenario provided by Zechariah.

Most modern scholars agree that the 'cleansing' is a symbolic action, while disagreeing on what it symbolises. Joshua is not trying to abolish the Jewish custom of sacrifice; he has already sanctioned it and within days will express his wish to eat a sacrificed Passover lamb with his disciples. He is not symbolically destroying the Temple; he later *predicts* its destruction but also its rebuilding — clearly by God under his Messiahship. In attacking the traders, he is hitting out at practices barred from the Temple in the days of the kingdom. This is a parable in action. Joshua has *said* that the kingdom of God is here. Now he demonstrates its reality; he creates the fact. And in doing this he is posing a direct challenge to his enemies — more direct than is usually imagined.

According to the Mishnah, 'forty years before the destruction of the Temple', about 30 AD, the Sanhedrin was 'expelled' from the Chamber of Hewn (or 'Polished') Stone 'and took its seat at the *Hanuyot*' (*Sanhedrin* 41, 2; *Abodah Zarah* 8, b). This was the Royal Stoa. The council met in a semicircular, half-domed 'apse' at the far, eastern end of the Stoa, separated only by a partition from the scene of Joshua's attack on the traders and dealers. There is no evidence that the Sanhedrin was actually in session during the incident; but the fact that this disturbance erupted virtually on the doorstep of the council chamber makes non-intervention of the Temple Guard even harder to believe.

In fact, the Gospels provide evidence that there was a violent clash of some kind, involving at least one death, and that, probably as a result of this clash, Joshua again became a fugitive, forced into a last desperate attempt to inaugurate the kingdom.

Five days after this incident, at least four men awaited execution. One is reported 'chained with the rebels who had committed murder in the uprising' (*Mark* 15:7). Two others are identified as *lestai* — partisans or freedom fighters (*Mark* 15:27). The Romans treat Joshua as their leader (*John* 19:18) and he later promises one of them a place with him in paradise (*Luke* 24:43).

It is not hard to imagine what happened. Joshua's eviction of the traders and dealers triggers a clash between his supporters and Temple personnel, and perhaps with disgruntled pilgrims trying to buy their Passover lambs and do necessary business with the moneychangers. His followers and sympathetic pilgrims may be numerous enough to hold off the Temple Guard while he 'astonishes' the crowd with talk of the kingdom, the *prosbul*, the Baptist, the earth-shaking 'footfalls of the Messiah' — perhaps even predicting destruction of the Temple ('Do you see these huge buildings? There is not one stone standing on another stone that will not be torn down.') (*Mark* 13:2)

With their Jesus in sight of the huge, golden grapevine glittering across the façade of the Temple, Matthew, Mark and Luke have him deliver his Parable of the Tenants — the story of share farmers left in charge of a vineyard who beat and kill the messengers sent to collect the owner's due portion of the crop. Eventually, the master of the vineyard sends his son, who is also killed, belatedly prompting his vengeance and the transfer of the vineyard into more worthy hands. The symbolism is clear. In Isaiah's words:

The vineyard of the Lord Almighty
Is the house of Israel.   (*Isaiah* 5:7)

The brutal and greedy tenants are the Temple establishment; the ill-treated messengers are the prophets. The murdered son is of course Jesus — though this is probably a 'wisdom of hindsight' embellishment of Joshua's original parable. Matthew and Luke, however, draw from their 'Q' source an extraordinary corollary to the story. Their Jesus quotes *Psalm* 118:22:

> 'The stone that the builders rejected
> Has become the head of the corner.'

In rabbinical teaching, this cornerstone represents David, who was overlooked by Samuel and Jesse but went on to become the greatest of all kings (*Midsrash Hagadol, Deuteronomy* 1:17). Thus identifying himself as a Davidic king, Jesus declares:

> 'Everyone who falls on that stone will be broken in pieces; but anyone it falls
> on will be crushed.'   (*Luke* 20:18)

Though uttered by the Gospels' Jesus, who is supposedly about to sacrifice himself, this chimes with the Davidic reference as a clear statement of Joshua's sense of victorious destiny, especially as it paraphrases a rabbinical adage of the pot that falls on a stone or has a stone fall on it. 'In either case, woe to the pot' (*Esther Rabbah* 7, 10). To the Rabbis, the stone is Israel; the pot is their foreign oppressors.

This display of Messianic defiance sets the scene for a memorable exchange. Whether or not it happened during Joshua's brief occupation of the Temple area, it strikes to the very core of the issues at stake here — authority and allegiance. Acting with the authority of his God, in allegiance to his God, Joshua has challenged the authority of the Temple establishment on this holy mount. In challenging them, he also challenges the authority of Caesar to whom *they* owe allegiance.

Someone — perhaps an *agent provocateur* — asks: 'Is it or is it not lawful for us to give tribute to Caesar?'

It is a very dangerous and very topical question. The next year, 34 AD, is a census year, with tax payable to Rome. If Joshua supports the payment of these taxes, he will alienate every patriot in his audience. To speak against it will represent treason against Caesar. As the crowd awaits his reply, he asks to see a *denarius*, then displays it.

'Whose image and inscription is on it?'
'Caesar's.'

Joshua's reply is characteristically enigmatic. 'Then give back to Caesar the things that are Caesar's; and the things that are God's to God' (*Luke* 20:22–5).

Luke tells us, 'They could not condemn his speech before the people. And having marvelled at his words, they said nothing' (*Luke* 20:26).

Unlike Joshua's enemies, theologians have had much to say over the millennia about this reply, all of which only underlines the dazzling ambiguity of the statement. American scholar Ben Witherington comes as close as any to a definitive interpretation: 'Give back to Caesar his worthless coin, and give to God your wholehearted and undivided allegiance.' Joshua challenges his audience to confront the question, 'Who is Lord?'.

Perhaps as described by John in an earlier incident, the Jewish Temple Guard are swayed by the power of Joshua's preaching; but the Roman troops move in, inflaming the religious patriotism of the crowd. Opposing Jewish factions may clash, Zealots seize the moment, the disturbance is suddenly 'the uprising' and blood is spilt.

In the chaos of violent movement — men, women, children, animals and traders scattering among the columns of the Stoa — Joshua manages to escape, as he has before, this time screened by tough Galileans, while the Romans restore order, leave casualties strewn on the paving and hustle their prisoners across the Court of Gentiles, into the Antonia.

Some see the Temple incident erupting into a full-scale military engagement between Zealots and Roman soldiers. Eisler imagines the rebels holding out in a fortified tower of the city wall until it is toppled by the Romans — the mysterious fall of 'the tower of Siloam' in which eighteen people died (*Luke* 13:1–6).

While few believe that Jesus' Messianic demonstrations led to a pitched battle on such a scale, there are clues that Josephus's *Antiquities of the Jews* originally portrayed Jesus' connection with a failed or aborted insurrection. The heavily Christianised *Testimonium*, Josephus's account of Jesus' ministry and execution, is immediately followed by the statement, 'About the same time, another sad calamity put the Jews into disorder' (*Antiquities* 18,3,4,). This link sits strangely with the tranquil *Testimonium* but is quite appropriate to the account of Jesus' ministry found in the Slavonic Josephus, particularly to an obvious fragment of the original text stranded among the Christian amendments which were intended to stigmatise the Jews and ease Pilate's guilt:

> And there assembled unto [Jesus] of ministers one hundred and fifty and a
> multitude of the people. Now when they saw his power, that he accomplished

whatsoever he would by (a) word, and when they had made known to him their will that he should enter into the city and cut down the Roman troops and Pilate and rule over us, he disdained us not [in a more credible version, 'he heeded not']. And when thereafter knowledge of it came to the Jewish leaders … they went and communicated it to Pilate. *And he sent and had many of the multitude slain.* [my italics]

Even without this evidence, it is clear that Joshua's attempt to proclaim his Messiahship had ended in bloodshed. A number of men were in Roman hands, facing almost certain execution. If the Sanhedrin was not already sitting, it quickly convened.

John or his editors have isolated this crucial session from the clash in the Temple. According to him, the council is thrown into crisis mode by the raising of Lazarus and the sensation it causes among the people of Jerusalem (events unknown to the other Gospels). Members of the Sanhedrin declare:

> 'If we let him go on like this, everyone will believe in him and the Romans will come and take away our place and our nation.' (*John* 11:48–50)

As a reaction to the miracle, this is unconvincing; but, as the Jewish scholar Isidore Epstein acknowledges, in the context of Messianic rebellion the discussion rings true. Especially convincing is the potent argument put to the council by Caiaphas:

> 'It is better for us that one man should die for the people rather than the whole nation perish.' And he said this not on his own behalf, but, being high priest that year, he predicted that Jesus was to die for the nation; and not just for the nation, but to reunite the scattered children of God. (*John* 11:50–2)

This is a surprisingly sympathetic portrayal of Caiaphas's motives and views, which match those of other Jewish leaders with the welfare of Israel at heart. Trying to dissuade the Jews from war with Rome, King Agrippa later told his people, 'It is absurd to make war with many for the sake of one' (Josephus, *Wars* 2,16,4). The high priest Ananus spoke in similar terms against the Zealots and declared: 'It is probable one may hereafter find the Romans to be supporters of our law, and those within ourselves the subverters of them' (*Wars* 4,3,10). To Caiaphas, it is better for Joshua to die than for some futile Messianic rebellion to plunge the Jewish people into war with Rome — a war that could only mean the destruction of the Jewish nation and the destruction of its Temple — the destruction of Judaism as it had existed since the time of Solomon. Of course, he is right; and the decision is taken.

The Chief Priests and the Pharisees gave orders that if anyone knew where [Jesus] was, he should provide the information so they could arrest him.

(John 11:57)

Noting John's one obvious distortion (characterising the Sanhedrin as 'the Chief Priests *and the Pharisees*'), he has accurately described the council's almost inescapable response to the Triumphal Entry and the Cleansing of the Temple. In Rabbi Dr Epstein's words: 'Theirs was *the duty* to order the arrest of any persons suspected of plotting against Rome'. Robin Lane Fox, Reader of Ancient History at Oxford, is an often irreverent critic of the Gospels as history, but considers this order of the Sanhedrin ...

> ... beautifully explained by the outlawing, or proscribing, of wanted criminals which local authorities practised elsewhere in cities and towns of the Roman Empire. Criminals' names were posted, and Roman subjects would be encouraged to denounce them, as we can see from first-hand papyri on this topic which survive in Roman Egypt.

By decree of Jerusalem's Sanhedrin, Joshua was proclaimed an outlaw.

CHAPTER 20

The Valley of Decision

Joshua was again a fugitive. John does not show the cause, but says bluntly: 'He went away and hid himself' (*John* 12:36). Matthew, Mark and Luke, who do show the cause, ignore this result but later show its impact on the activities of Joshua and the disciples. The four Gospels orbit around a dark core — a carefully avoided fact that will soon reveal itself.

This is perhaps the most spectacular and obvious divergence of the Gospels from the events of Joshua's life. They imply that his entry to Jerusalem and the 'cleansing' of the Temple are so spectacularly successful and attract such general support that no-one dares to act against him. The Sanhedrin must plot his death by some clandestine manoeuvre; Pilate and the Romans are simply not an issue. Yet, if the Gospels are to be believed, in proclaiming Messiahship Joshua and his supporters are already guilty of *crimen laesae majestatis*, treason against Caesar ('Blessed is … the king of Israel') — a capital crime in the eyes of Rome. Even ignoring the skirmish in the Temple, the alleged supinity of Joshua's enemies is simply unbelievable.

After the violence which inevitably broke out after his attack on the Temple traders, Joshua probably escaped back to Bethany. Below the mountainside village, the waterless gullies and ridges of the *Midbar Yehuda* would have offered harsh sanctuary until he could safely emerge and be lost among the hordes of Passover pilgrims returning to Galilee the following week. But traditionally Joshua did not follow this course. In Christian imagination he simply passed the next few days until it was time for him to die.

Jesus had given his disciples highly detailed predictions of his trial, death and resurrection (including a particularly unlikely six-phase version (*Mark* 10:33–4) which has been described as 'reading like a printed programme of a Passion Play'.

Joshua, on the other hand, did not know God's plan for him — least of all the appalling idea that he should serve as a human sacrifice to atone for the sins of mankind. No Jew — and no Christian with any love and respect for God — could imagine such a thing. Joshua did not spend the coming days in preparation for death. He made a final attempt to interpret God's will and to carry out what he saw as God's plan for the kingdom.

Joshua probably knew of his outlawry almost before the Sanhedrin's decree was promulgated. John Mark, who was not known as a disciple, could travel to Bethany without attracting suspicion, carrying the news perhaps given to him by Nicodemus, the sympathetic Sanhedrin member. To any man but Joshua, the situation would have seemed hopeless. His supporters were scattered, he faced the combined power of Jerusalem and Rome. Yet to accept defeat would be to deny everything he believed about God's plan for him. And that was unimaginable. So he must have spent many, many hours contemplating the events of 'Palm Sunday' and their meaning.

He had entered Jerusalem in a way that proclaimed his Messiahship; he had driven traders from the Temple in confirmation of Zechariah's prophecy. Yet the whole thing had lost direction, erupted into profitless violence — pain, death and imprisonment — with the threat of crucifixion for the men taken by the Romans. Perhaps as he pondered that failure he came to believe that he had misinterpreted God's will. The Triumphal Entry to Jerusalem heralded the Day of the Lord but did not accomplish it. A temple free of traders was not a signal of the kingdom's arrival, but an effect of its existence. He had planted the seed and tried to harvest too hastily. And there was the answer, locked in the seed: the power of God waiting to be released for the benefit of his people.

Joshua's parable of the kingdom being like a mustard seed is often quoted; the smallest of seeds, mustard, grows to be one of the largest plants. Immediately before this, Joshua had said:

> 'The kingdom of God is like a man who throws seed on the ground and who sleeps by night and rises by day and the seed sprouts and grows and he doesn't know how ... but when the grain is ripe he wields the sickle, for the harvest time has come.' (*Mark* 4:26–9)

The seed is planted by humankind, the crop produced by God, then harvested by humankind. Yet in Joshua's attempt to inaugurate the kingdom, he had sown the seed and wielded the sickle, without letting God raise the crop. How clearly he saw it now, and how clearly he heard God speak — first perhaps in the words of the prophet Joel, in the very passage which was implicit in this parable. Then again in the words of Zechariah and in the words of David. It was all so obvious now; but now there was so little time to achieve so much.

Joshua's kingdom image of the seed and the harvest carries a seemingly peaceful message of God's bounties to his people — until the harvest symbol is related to the passage of Joel it carefully echoes, when God announces through his prophet:

> 'Let the Nations heed the summons
> And advance to the Valley of Jehosophat
> For there I shall sit in judgement
> On all the Nations around us;
> *Wield the sickle,*
> *For the harvest time has come;*
> Go tread the grapes
> For the wine press is full;
> The vats overflow,
> for their wickedness is great.
> Multitudes, multitudes
> In the Valley of Decision!
> For the Day of the Lord is near,
> In the Valley of Decision.' [my italics] (*Joel* 3:12–14)

In Joel's resounding poetry, God judges (Jehosophat means exactly that), and his people crush the Nations like grapes in a wine press; their blood overflows. The Valley of Jehosophat, site of this God-given victory — also called the Valley of Decision — is the Kidron Valley.

The book of the prophet Zechariah is constantly quoted by Joshua in this last week of his life. Immediately after a passage cited in his last night on earth, there are terrible images of cosmic warfare. Jerusalem is brutalised by Gentile conquerors, and the survivors of the genocide are consigned by God to a furnace to be refined and tested like silver and gold. They call on God's name and he answers: 'These are my people!'

> Then the Lord will go out and fight against those Nations as he fights on a day
> of battle. That day his feet will stand on the Mount of Olives, which faces
> Jerusalem to the east; and the Mount of Olives will be torn apart to the east

and to the west by a huge valley ... then the Lord my God will come and all the holy ones with him ... and the Lord will become King over all the earth; and on that day the Lord will be one and his name will be one. (*Zechariah* 14:3–5, 9)

For Joshua's Triumphal Entry he descended the Mount of Olives and crossed the Kidron Valley to the Holy City — a route that led to failure and retreat. Now he sees that the Mount of Olives and the Kidron are not the route, they are the destination. Here, God will strike down the enemies of Israel, the enemies of his Messiah.

Immediately, Joshua must think of Gethsemane which lies on the rim of the Kidron Valley and on the western slope of the Mount of Olives, facing Jerusalem. Here, the two prophecies converge.

The name 'Gethsemane' means 'Oil Press' and the place is described, only by John, as a garden or orchard. Early Christian traditions fastened on a grove of eight ancient olive trees and a nearby cave with a circular hole cut in its roof and rock-cut gutters below it, which could be related to oil production. John tells us that Joshua and the disciples often used the garden site and it is feasible that, as an olive grove, oil press, or both, it belonged to the family of Martha and Mary. Such details are unimportant. The site perfectly matches the area where Joel and Zechariah prophesied that the destruction of Gentile forces would take place; the very name 'Gethsemane' resonates with Joel's gory image of their being crushed — to a remarkable degree; it means, literally, 'wine press of oil'. It is here that Joshua and the disciples will choose to face the enemies of Israel. Here, God will come to their aid, as Zechariah promised, 'and all the holy ones with him'.

This was the dream of Qumran's holy warriors, who imagined an all-powerful angelic army joining them in a final battle against the Romans. Qumran's Dead Sea Scrolls spoke of the forces being led by the archangel Michael, but also by Melchizedek, the baffling priest-king of ancient Jerusalem who had achieved immortality in the eyes of some first-century Jews, including the Qumran sect and at least some Judaeo-Christians.

To the men of Qumran, Melchizedek was a key figure in the Jubilee of the Last Days. It was Melchizedek who would restore to the people of Israel what was rightly theirs, who would 'exact the vengeance demanded by God's Law' and 'establish a righteous kingdom' (11Q13).

There is no indication that Joshua or his followers saw Melchizedek in this specific role; but the New Testament's *Epistle to the Hebrews* regards the priest-king in a similar exalted light and calls Joshua 'a second Melchizedek' (*Hebrews* 7:15). The writer makes the identification five times in two chapters, stressing that God has made Joshua 'a priest forever in the order of Melchizedek', words familiar to Joshua from God's great promise of victory to King David:

> 'You are a priest forever,
> in the order of Melchizedek.
> The Lord is at your right hand;
> He will strike down kings
> on the day of his wrath.
> He will condemn the Nations;
> He will strew the earth with carcasses;
> He will scatter heads across the world.'
>
> (*Psalm* 110:4–6)

As a Melchizedek figure, David stands side by side with God on his Great and Terrible Day, the 'mighty surge of sacred violence' that purges Israel of pagan domination. Joshua knows the inviolate pledge that the Lord 'keeps faith with his Anointed, with David *and his heirs* forever' (*Psalm* 18:50). If he is the Messiah, the Lord will honour that sacred vow and be at his right hand on the Day of Wrath to strike down his enemies. And even if Joshua is tempted to doubt his Messiahship, he can still believe in divine forces marshalling to face his enemies. A hundred and thirty years earlier, when Judas Maccabee of Galilee and his men faced the huge army of the Gentile Timotheus, they had prayed for God to show himself 'the enemy of their enemies, the adversary of their adversaries, as the Law clearly states':

> And as the battle was raging, the enemy saw five magnificent men appear in the sky, riding horses with golden bridles. They put themselves at the head of the Jews. Surrounding Maccabaeus and protecting him with their own armour, they kept him safe from harm while they showered arrows and thunderbolts on the enemy; until, blinded and bewildered, they broke and ran in total confusion.
>
> (*2 Maccabees* 10:29–30)

As he faces his enemies, Joshua later declares: 'Do you think that even now I can't call on my Father and have him send me more than twelve legions of angels?' (*Matthew* 26:53). In context, the statement seems like bravado, yet this is what Joshua passionately believes; and it is this belief that shapes his actions in the coming days.

To twentieth-century Christians, such ideas are fantastic. At best, belief in them seems impossibly naïve — religious gullibility carried to a preposterous extreme. At worst it seems to suggest a psychotic inability to distinguish between reality and allegory. Yet to a Jew of the first century whose life had been devoted to belief in the Tanakh, not to believe in the intervention of angelic armies would have represented denial of faith. And as we have seen, time and time again, Joshua was a product of his time; he not only believed in the legendary Queen of Sheba, but he believed she would return on the Day of Judgement (*Matthew* 12:42). The Tanakh was the voice of God, speaking through Moses and his prophets; and God did not lie. How could Joshua believe in the literal truth and accuracy of these extraordinary prophecies about the Mount of Olives and the Kidron Valley? It would have been unthinkable not to.

Most Christians will rebel at the idea of their Jesus contemplating such divine carnage. They will cling to the 'gentle Jesus, meek and mild' of the childhood prayers, the soulful man of a thousand prints and religious statues, the good shepherd tending his sunset flock — anything but the dynamic leader of men sprung from the race of warriors who, within a century, would shake Rome to her arrogant foundations with an impossible three-year war of independence led by another Son of David hailed as Messiah.

We have already seen that Joshua accepted the inevitability of violence in his Messianic mission. And if this seems incompatible with his blessings on the peacemakers who were guaranteed the kingdom, both Joel and Zechariah paint wonderful pictures of the peace that will follow the Great and Terrible Day of the Lord.

'In that day, the mountains will run with sweet wine and the hills flow with milk; every stream bed in Judah will brim with water' (*Joel* 3:18). 'Once again old men and women will sit in the streets of Jerusalem, leaning on their staffs because of their great age and the streets of the city will be filled with boys and girls at play' (*Zechariah* 8:4). The land will thrive in an eternal spring, 'farmers will sow in peace, the vine will yield its fruit, the soil its crops, and the heavens their dew' (*Zechariah* 8:12). Jews of the Dispersion will be brought back to Jerusalem and Gentiles will flock to worship in the Temple. All this will be won by an end-of-days battle in the place of judgement, the Valley of Decision.

With this shining vision of God's great design, Joshua now sets out to achieve it. We will reconstruct his plan and see it confirmed in its execution.

CHAPTER 21

Mysteries of The Last Supper 1

The first day of The Feast of Unleavened Bread falls on a Sabbath this year, 33 AD. Everything must be accomplished by the sixth day of the week, Friday, no more than three or four days ahead. Most of the disciples are probably scattered among the encampments of Galilean pilgrims. Joshua plans to gather them for a special meal in Jerusalem before they all go to Gethsemane. Christians will recognise this as The Last Supper, without considering that the event is in any way mysterious; yet mysteries abound. Why did it happen? When and where did it take place? And, perhaps the greatest mystery of all, what happened during it?

Joshua's decision to emerge from hiding and join the disciples in Jerusalem — a walled city where he would be vulnerable to recognition and arrest — seems foolhardy. It would be much safer for the disciples to join him at Bethany. Clearly, the question of physical safety was outweighed by other factors which Joshua considered far more important. The decision to meet in Jerusalem was dictated by the prophecies that shaped his plan and by the specific site in the city which was available for the occasion.

Six weeks later, the disciples were living in an 'upper room' at the house of John Mark's mother (*Acts* 1:13). There can be little doubt that this was the same 'upper room' used as a venue for The Last Supper. Perhaps surprisingly, an impressive case can be mounted to show that the traditional site in Jerusalem is authentic — marking a house used by the Jerusalem congregation until the destruction of the city in 70 AD, then rebuilt as a Judaeo-Christian synagogue which formed the nucleus of successive Christian churches.

The venerated *Cenaculum* ('Upper Room') is on so-called Mount Zion, the western hill of Jerusalem. When the mid-first-century writer of *Hebrews* declares, 'You are come to Mount Zion ... the general assembly and church of all the firstborn' (*Hebrews* 12:22), he may be speaking symbolically, but still refers to an actual site, just as, in the same passage, 'the heavenly Jerusalem' refers to an actual city.

Even though the original Zion, David's city, had been on the opposite, eastern hill, Joshua — like his near-contemporary, the historian Josephus — believed that Mount Zion was this higher, western ridge, Jerusalem's affluent Upper City, crowned by Herod's Palace which supposedly marked the site of King David's citadel (*Antiquities* 7,3,1). To this day, a remnant of Herod's Palace is called the Tower of David. For Joshua, it was worth any danger to meet the disciples here because this was decreed as the starting point for his second journey to Messiahship.

The prophet Joel had described the loyal remnant marshalling 'on Mount Zion and in Jerusalem' for the final confrontation with Israel's enemies in the Valley of Decision (*Joel* 2:32). Zechariah had said:

> The Lord will shield the people of Jerusalem so that on that day the feeblest among them will be like David, and the house of David will be like God, like the angel of the Lord at their head. (*Zechariah* 12:8)

And God had told David in his 'Melchizedek' promise of victory:

> 'The Lord sends out from Zion
> your powerful sceptre.
> Rule, in the midst of your enemies.' (*Psalm* 110:2)

How clearly it all confirmed that he should lead the disciples to the place of divine judgement from John Mark's home on Mount Zion — scarcely 200 metres from what he believed to be David's citadel, yet truly in the midst of his enemies; the palace complex was now occupied by Pontius Pilate.

Their gathering has to be carried out with great care to avoid arrest or confrontation before they have reached their destination on the slopes of the Lord's mountain by the Valley of Decision, where Joshua and his men must confront the enemies of Israel. Those enemies will be Romans; the Levitical Temple Guard have no jurisdiction outside the city. Only one gap in the plan remains — how to contrive a confrontation with the Romans on the prophesied site.

It is impossible to imagine Joshua's first reaction to the news of his outlawry; but very soon he must come to accept it as inevitable. And when he does, he realises that here, too, the voice of God can be heard. This, too, is part of God's plan as he now recognises it.

John Mark could respond to the Sanhedrin's proclamation by informing on Joshua and leading the arresting troops to Gethsemane; but he is known to, or perhaps even related to, the high priest who lives near his mother's house, and he is too vulnerable to retribution if anything goes wrong. Peter, John and James, the leading disciples, are too blunt, too headstrong for this mission. James the Younger, Joshua's brother, is a saintly man, of great courage and loyalty, but lacking the qualities to carry off such a critical deception.

The next logical choice is between Joshua's Zealot twin brothers, Judas and Simon. Joshua chooses Judas, perhaps because Simon is already widowed, with a child or children to care for. Of his four brothers, Joshua may have the closest relationship with Judas; clearly, he is prepared to place great trust in him. Perhaps because of the very qualities that make the other leading disciples less suited to the role — too impulsive or less temperamentally and psychologically fitted for such a revolutionary strategy — Joshua does not tell them of the part Judas will play in his plan. Their protests and his explanations can come later.

As he prepares to return to Jerusalem on Thursday evening for the meal with his disciples, does it occur to him that it was opposite Gethsemane, from the pinnacle of the Temple, that he had been tempted to hurl himself down and prove for all to see that he was the expected Messiah? Now, four years later, he accepts that only such a display of divine power will firmly establish his Messiahship and institute the kingdom of God.

Perhaps it also strikes him that Gethsemane lies opposite Mount Moriah where Abraham was about to sacrifice his son Isaac when God provided a ram to die in the boy's place (*Genesis* 22). God required only the *willingness* of Abraham to kill his beloved son. Now Joshua will prove his willingness to die, while believing that God will save him. The act still demands exemplary courage and faith. Joshua will demonstrate both. So he approaches The Last Supper with a bewildering amalgam of emotions.

He has reached the end of the journey made with the loyal Twelve. They all face a night of inconceivable challenge before they emerge in the dawn of the kingdom. He faces the threat of ugly and violent death. Like every brave, sane man in such a situation, he is prepared to die, but hopes to live.

As he crosses the Mount of Olives and walks down the stepped road past Gethsemane and through the shadows of the Valley of Decision, the sky is still luminous behind the towers of Herod's palace on the western skyline of Mount Zion. Jerusalem's winding, tumultuous streets are darkening in the creeping chill of an early spring night. It is impossible to imagine Joshua's thoughts of what tomorrow may bring.

✝✝✝

The arrangements for Thursday evening's meal with the disciples underline the need for secrecy. Joshua has given precise instructions to Peter and John:

> 'Go into the city and you will meet a man carrying a jar of water [an identifying signal, because this was normally a woman's work]. Follow him. And wherever he enters, say to the owner of the house, "The Teacher says, 'Where is the guest room where I can eat the Passover with my disciples?'" And he will show you a large upper room *that has been spread and made ready*. Get everything ready for us there.' [my italics]   (*Mark* 14:13–15)

Inescapably, this briefing, with its recognition device and pre-arranged greeting formula, is reminiscent of wartime fugitives in an occupied country being conducted to a safe house by members of the Resistance. This is precisely what it was.

Note Joshua's mention of the Passover. Matthew, Mark and Luke believed that this was to be the Passover meal, on the evening of 'the First Day of Unleavened Bread when the Passover lamb is sacrificed'. They have been confused by their Hebrew or Aramaic sources, and by the Jewish reckoning of days from sunset to sunset.

The lamb was sacrificed during the afternoon of Passover, the Fourteenth Day of Nisan, and eaten at the evening meal which marked the beginning of 15 Nisan — the first day of the Feast of Unleavened Bread (*Leviticus* 23:5-6). This was a day of great solemnity. 'On the first day there will be a sacred assembly: you are not to do your daily work' (*Leviticus* 23:7). This year, the first day of the feast, 15 Nisan, fell on a Sabbath, making it doubly sacrosanct. It is inconceivable that the extraordinary activity of the next twenty-four hours could take place on such a day.

John's account makes it clear that this meal was on the evening of 13–14 Nisan, Thursday 2 April of 33 AD in the Julian Calendar. It could not be a Passover meal because it lacked the lamb which would be sacrificed the following afternoon. It was a ceremonial banquet convened by Joshua for the specific purpose of initiating this second attempt to establish the kingdom. (The earliest portrayals of the meal in Christian art show Joshua and the disciples eating bread and fish — a Messianic banquet perhaps foreshadowed in the 'Miracle of the Loaves and Fishes'.) To Christians, The Last Supper marks, above all, Jesus' establishment of the Eucharist, the sacrament of Christian Communion. And it did, though the very core of the sacrament, as we know it, is a travesty of what happened that evening.

Most Christians are surprised to discover that the earliest description of The Last Supper was written by the 'Apostle' Paul, some twenty-two years after the event:

> The Lord Jesus on the night he was betrayed took bread and, giving thanks, he broke it and said, 'Take, eat, this is my body which is broken for you. Do this in remembrance of me.' In the same way with the cup, after eating, he said, 'This cup is the New Covenant in my blood. As often as you may drink it, do this in remembrance of me.'
> (*1 Corinthians* 11:23–5)

If this seems in any way ambiguous, Paul has already said:

> 'The cup of thanksgiving that we bless, is it not a partaking of the blood of Christ? The bread that we break, is it not a partaking of the body of Christ?'
> (*1 Corinthians* 10:16)

We have already seen the shock waves among the disciples supposedly caused by John's Jesus saying at Capernaum that his followers must eat his flesh and drink his blood; we have seen the total rejection of such a concept in Mosaic Law; we have also seen James the Younger identify the consumption of blood as one of the few practices that would bar a Gentile from membership of the Christian brotherhood. How then can Joshua institute a symbol of this abhorrent act as a memorial rite? What is Paul's source? We imagine that he received an eyewitness account from Peter or other surviving apostles when they described the evening's events (note the reference to betrayal). Yet Paul is quite specific that his account was from Jesus, presumably in a vision. 'I received from the Lord what I passed on to you' (*1 Corinthians* 11:23).

Many Christian scholars are uncomfortable with this claim and suggest that Paul really means that the information was from Jesus via eyewitnesses. However, in other epistles Paul goes out of his way to insist that his knowledge of Jesus and his teaching was not communicated to him by any human agency; it was the result of direct revelation from the resurrected Jesus (*Galatians* 1:11–12; *Ephesians* 3:2–5).

Writing many years later, Matthew, Mark and Luke closely follow Paul's account (*Matthew* 26:26–8; *Mark* 14:22–4; *Luke* 22:19–20). (Though Luke's original version — possibly preserved in the Codex Bezae and the Old Latin — appears to have followed the Jewish form with the cup preceding the bread and with no reference to the wine as blood. Later, a second cup described as 'the new covenant in my blood' was interposed *after* the bread and the 'words of institution' were added: 'Do this in remembrance of me' — both additions apparently introduced to make Luke's account follow Paul's version more closely.)

Then we come to John. We are dealing with our nearest approach to an eyewitness account. In it, Joshua washes the feet of the Twelve, sends Judas on his mission of 'betrayal' and talks for two solid chapters. *There is no mention of the bread and wine.*

We know that, from the earliest days of Christian congregations, a form of Eucharist was practised. In 1873 an eleventh-century codex of 120 pages was discovered in the library of the Patriarch of Jerusalem. It contained copies of the Epistles of Clement and Barnabas and, perhaps most notably, *The Teaching (Didache) of the Apostles* which provides the earliest known Christian liturgy, including the celebration of the Eucharist:

> At the Eucharist, offer the eucharistic prayer in this way. Begin with the chalice. 'We give thanks to thee, Father, for the holy Vine of thy servant David, which thou hast made known to us through thy servant Jesus. Glory be to thee, world without end.'
>
> Then over the broken bread: 'We give thanks to thee, our Father for the life and knowledge thou has made known to us through thy servant Jesus. Glory be to thee, world without end.
>
> 'As this broken bread, once dispersed over the hills, was brought together and became one loaf, so may thy Church be brought together from the ends of the earth into thy kingdom. Thine is the glory and the power, through Jesus Christ for ever and ever.' (*Didache* 2,9)

There is no reference to the bread and wine as the flesh and blood of Jesus. Yet this liturgy dates from an age when the possible attendance of 'Prophets' and 'Apostles' is provided for, titles used by the primitive Church in the earliest days of Paul's missionary journeys (*1 Corinthians* 12:28). The *Didache* is confidently dated to the second half of the first century, before some of the Gospels were written and probably before any of them were in their final form.

The *Didache* Eucharist is strongly Jewish and reflects a *Kiddush* (Sanctification), a simple, Friday mealtime ceremony involving wine and bread which was offered as a thanksgiving for the creation and the gift of the Sabbath. It was also performed on the eve of festivals and opened with the head of the table taking a cup of wine and saying over it: 'Blessed are you, the Lord our God, who created the fruit of the vine.'

It is clear why, in one passage, Paul refers to the Eucharist as 'the Cup of Thanksgiving (or Blessing)'. Later he calls it 'The Lord's Supper' (*kuriakon deipnon*), a title he has adopted from pagan mystery cults which were becoming increasingly popular in Rome. The associations were so offensive that the Church fathers soon favoured 'Eucharist', a Graeco-Roman word which means 'Thanksgiving', acknowledging the original Judaic nature of the sacrament.

Paul's use of 'The Lord's Supper' might seem an unfortunate coincidence or a momentary lapse of taste. In fact, it points to the very source of Christian Communion as we know it — a source far removed from Joshua's act of thanksgiving at The Last Supper.

CHAPTER 22

Mysteries of The Last Supper 2

Joshua, as an observant Jew, could not possibly advocate symbolic eating of his flesh and drinking of his blood. How then was it possible for Paul, educated as a Pharisee under the great Gamaliel, to initiate this travesty? Let us not forget that, in Paul, we are dealing with the man who said: 'To the Jews, I became a Jew so that I might win over the Jews ... to the weak, I became weak so that I might win over the weak. I have become all things to all men so that, by any means, I might save some' (*1 Corinthians* 9:20, 22). Again ... 'I did not burden you, but being crafty, I took you by trickery' (*2 Corinthians* 12:16). And perhaps most startlingly, 'In every way, whether in pretence or in truth, Christ is proclaimed' (*Philippians* 1:18).

As a man whose writing shows the influence of Greek philosophy and drama, Paul clearly subscribed to Plato's notion of 'the noble falsehood' — permissible distortion of the truth in pursuit of what was perceived as a noble end; and Paul obviously saw release from Judaic law as a noble end. In spite of Joshua's teaching that the Law was inviolable, Paul could say, 'Christ rescued us from the curse of the Law' (*Galatians* 3:13) and 'Christ is the end of the Law' (*Romans* 10:4) — a claim he makes in eight separate passages, another of which states: 'Do not let anyone judge you in eating or in drinking or with regard to a feast or the new moon *or of Sabbaths*' [my italics] (*Colossians* 2:16). It becomes clear that Paul was using the name of Jesus to sanction a personal agenda of separating Christianity from Judaism. His account of The Last Supper probably marks the most audacious ploy in this campaign.

It is small wonder that some Jewish scholars doubt Paul's Pharisaic background. For our purpose, a careful reading of Paul's letters to the Romans, Colossians, Galatians and Ephesians reveals his complex and baffling attitude to Judaism — an attitude which, in its dichotomy of acceptance and rejection, has endured in Paulian Christianity to this day.

In the first century, Judaism offered the pagan world a monolithic structure of tradition which reached back to what were perceived as the beginnings of humankind and traced a developing relationship with God. It offered a tapestry of vivid characters and fabulous events, a rigid and admirable moral code — in fact, many features which Graeco-Romans found attractive. But its image of God was often daunting to them, its complex and ever-elaborated framework of law — especially dietary law — was too restrictive and frequently irrelevant to the Roman way of life. Circumcision seemed quite out of the question.

Joshua, beside his incomparable moral, social and ethical teaching, had expressed a more intimate image of God and God's relationship with men and women. Despite a strongly conservative strand, Joshua showed a liberalism in his approach to Judaism which offered greater freedom and flexibility; he reconciled the essential truths of Judaic law and philosophy with an intensely egalitarian and humanistic approach at odds with the rigid, judgemental and increasingly self-protective elitism of the priestly caste — and with the legalistic excesses of *some* Pharisees.

There were problems. Joshua preached a way of life that demanded rejection of material wealth; and in religious observances with his followers he offered no magic, no mystery, no secret rites, no exotic settings, no splendid trappings. Outside the Temple and the synagogues, there were only groups of men and women in their everyday dress, meeting in humble homes and in the open air, following age-old Jewish forms of prayer and thanksgiving. In essence, Joshua offered a form of liberal Judaism — simple, homely, unadorned.

Primitive 'Christianity', for all its beauty, power, truth and its deep foundation of Judaism, lacked the glamour of the 'mystery' cults which were gaining strength in Rome, as enthusiasm declined for the worship of the old Roman gods in passive public ritual.

The cult of the Egyptian goddess Isis could offer a ten-day initiation ceremony which climaxed with a re-enactment of the death and resurrection of Isis's husband Osiris. Resurrection was a popular theme of these cults, as was the birth of a deity from a woman impregnated by a god.

Most popular of all the Roman mystery cults was Mithraism — worship of the god Mithras (the name meant 'Friend'), first recorded as a Mesopotamian divinity of the fourteenth century BC and evolving through the next millennium, across Persia, India and Asia Minor, as an attractive deity of goodness, truth and light.

By the first century, Mithraism and sun worship ran in close and sometimes confusing parallel. The cult offered a well-developed moral code and was based on the central idea of light versus darkness, good versus evil — with a militant message of its members doing battle in the cause of good and advancing through a fraternal hierarchic structure that has been compared to that of Freemasonry. Mithraism had forms of baptism and communion; its parallels with Christianity have often been noted. This similarity was not coincidental.

The 'Apostle' Paul's home province of Cilicia, north of Cyprus, was a stronghold of Mithraism (it was from here that the religion was carried to Rome by prisoners of war in 67 BC) and scholars have detected echoes of the cult in Paul's writings. He may have considered committing himself to Mithraism; or he may have simply studied the cult which would prove Christianity's greatest rival for eventual acceptance as the state religion of Rome. Either way, the conclusion is almost inescapable that Paul adopted a central element of the Mithraic liturgy as the key to his transformation of Christianity into a religion that would be more attractive to non-Jews and, most specifically, to Romans.

Second-century Christian scholars recorded that Mithraism observed a Lord's Supper remarkably similar to Christian Communion. Tertullian called it 'a devilish imitation', Justin Martyr spoke of 'a certain formula' closely resembling the Eucharistic liturgy; but all trace of the rite had disappeared from the Mithraic texts which survived the sect's outlawry when Rome became Christian in the fourth century. Even Last-Supper-like wall paintings of Mithraism's sacred meal were defaced by fourth-century Christians. The 'certain formula' survived, however, in a medieval Persian text of the teachings of Zoroaster, a Persian prophet and mystic of the sixth century BC, who influenced the development of Mithraism. Its phrasing is uncomfortably familiar:

'He who will not eat of my body and drink of my blood, so that he will be made one with me and I with him, the same shall not know salvation.'

As the Mithraic authority Maarten Vermaseren comments, 'though of later date, it seems to confirm Justin's assertion'. The formula also matches everything we know of Mithraic ritual. Eating the flesh and drinking the blood of a sacrificed bull had played a significant role in the worship of Mithras for countless centuries. In the view of respected scholars, 'The bull was Mithras who had offered himself as a sacrifice ... and the believer then consumed the divine body and drank his blood.'

It defies logic to suggest that first- and second-century followers of a 1400-year-old religion — then enjoying enormous success throughout the Roman Empire — needed to copy the liturgy for their ancient sacred meal ritual from the newly-established Eucharist of a sect which Rome barely tolerated or actively persecuted. We must also reject the implications of Justin and Tertullian that the centuries-old Mithraic rite had been inspired by 'the Devil' or 'the wicked devils' to counter the impact of Christ's teaching.

Coincidence is out of the question, as is the idea that *Joshua* adopted the concept from Mithraism. Given Paul's Hellenistic background, his demonstrated desire to make Christianity more attractive to the Graeco-Roman world (note references in his letters to 'mysteries' and 'initiation'), his curiously ambivalent attitude to Judaism and his exposure to Mithraic doctrine, it was clearly his hand that introduced this pagan element to the Eucharist via his vision or revelation. Demonstrably, it did not come from Joshua; it was the conscious or subconscious product of Paul's complex mind. And so Paul — who is quoted in most Christian churches more often than Jesus and who has been credited with writing a third of the New Testament — took a simple, domestic expression of thanksgiving and fellowship and turned it into a symbolic act of cannibalism. He had created a central rite for Christianity which gave it the aura of a mystery cult and, at the same time, provided a wedge that would help to split its followers from Judaism. Immediately, we think of the alienating discourse which John attributed to his Jesus in the synagogue at Capernaum:

'He who eats my flesh and drinks my blood has everlasting life ... he who eats my flesh and drinks my blood lives in me and I in him.'   (*John* 6:54, 56)

The significance of the paraphrased Mithraic formula in its non-Eucharistic setting (and with its non-Eucharistic theology) is profound. If it had been interpolated in the Gospel by Paulian Christians, why here and not in John's account of The Last Supper? Clearly this accretion is John's own; he acknowledges that it is repugnant to Jews and that it alienates many disciples. Why did he write it?

It seems most likely that, by the time John wrote his Gospel, very late in the first century, the Mithraic communion rite had become so inextricably a part of Gentile Christian ritual, that John felt unable to disown it totally without discrediting Christianity itself. Instead, he set out to confront, and perhaps compensate for, its profound and shocking impact on Jews, while unwilling to let it intrude on his account of Joshua's last meal with the Twelve. In fact, while he was obviously aware that Joshua's characteristic blessing of the wine and bread — as performed at The Last Supper — had become the basis of the Christian Eucharist, John pointedly avoided any reference to it. This extraordinary gap in his account is persuasive evidence that, in his momentous Passover *Kiddush* in the upper room, Joshua did not identify the bread and wine as symbols of his flesh and blood.

We have established what did *not* happen at The Last Supper. What did happen is less clear. First, we must discard the traditional Leonardo da Vinci image of Jesus and the Twelve seated in wide screen format at a large table. It is clear from the Gospel accounts that this was a formal *triclinium* with fourteen men reclining on three couches, arranged as three sides of a square, to eat from large dishes set on a central table or tables.

While custom varied as to the placing of diners on such occasions, the Gospels and the Talmud enable a partial reconstruction of the way Joshua and the disciples were positioned. As the most distinguished person at the meal, Joshua probably took a central position on the middle couch, leaning on his left elbow. Studying the Gospel accounts, many have concluded, correctly, that 'the beloved disciple' reclined at Joshua's right, where he could be described as 'leaning [back] on Jesus' chest' to speak with him (*John* 13:23). (Some artists have tried to accommodate this detail while showing

Two great artists portray the two events that defined Joshua's Messiahship — the triumphant entry to Jerusalem on 'Palm Sunday' and the 'cleansing' of the Temple. Rubens's seventeenth-century vision of the entry (left) captures a quality that is rare in paintings of the occasion. This is not the bright and joyous event shown in much religious art. It is challenging, forceful, fateful, as befits a Messiah liberating his people. According to Mark, the entry was immediately followed by an attack on the traders and moneychangers in the Temple, depicted (below) in Gustave Doré's handsome engraving, which, if anything, downplays the chaos created by Joshua's action. Both incidents sit strangely with the reconstructed, otherworldly Jesus of Christian tradition.

A nineteenth-century German engraving (above) of Joshua washing the disciples' feet at the Last Supper — a detail preserved only in John's eyewitness account. An unhaloed Judas lurks in the background, soon to leave on his errand of 'betrayal' and (right), he prepares to hang himself, a detail mentioned in only one Gospel and contradicted in *Acts* — both accounts attempting to explain the 'disappearance' of Judas Iscariot.

Plockhorst's nineteenth-century drawing, 'The Son of Man coming in the clouds of heaven', is an unusual portrayal of the Gospels' Jesus leading an angelic army. Here, the enemy is Satan. Joshua — like the 'holy warriors' of the Dead Sea Scrolls sect — seems to have envisaged a similar scene, though in terms of a cataclysmic end-of-days battle against Israel's earthly enemies, the Romans.

Bida's powerful drawing shows Peter's remorse after having 'denied' Joshua in the courtyard of the High Priest's palace. The rooster at top centre reminds us that this is the fable in which a cock's crow marks the third denial prophesied by the Gospels' Jesus. The fable obscures the fact that Peter had shown great courage in following his master into this enemy heartland. To admit here that he was a disciple would have been suicidal. Only the unlikely prophecy impugns his bravery.

Joshua's trial before Jerusalem's Sanhedrin, described in three Gospels and imaginatively re-created by James Tissot (right) in his *Life of Christ*, was impossible on a feast day, on the eve of a feast or the eve of a Sabbath. According to John's eyewitness account, the only Jewish examination of Joshua was at an informal appearance before the emeritus high priest, Annas, shown (below right) in van Honthorst's superb seventeenth-century painting, known for many years as 'Christ Before Pilate'.

This scrap of papyrus (below) is the earliest known fragment of a Gospel — from John's eyewitness account of Joshua's trial before Pontius Pilate. The words are from chapter 18, verses 31 to 34. Handwriting dates the fragment to about 130 AD, only thirty or forty years after the Gospel was first written and less than 100 years after the events described here. It is preserved in the John Rylands Library of Manchester University.

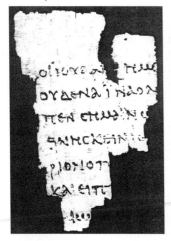

In 1496, part of the titulus supposedly set on Joshua's cross was found during repairs to the vaulted roof of the Church of Santa Croce in Rome, a building traditionally linked with St Helena who found the 'True Cross' in Jerusalem. (Above), the relic as it looks today, and (below) a nineteenth-century drawing of the all-but-illegible inscription. (Bottom) a reconstruction of the complete titulus, 'Jesus of Nazareth King of the Jews' in Hebrew, Greek and Latin, with the existing section marked. In an unusual detail, the Greek and Latin are written right to left, matching the Hebrew.

It is hard to believe that this grandiose structure in Jerusalem's Church of the Holy Sepulchre could possibly be the tomb of Joshua; and David Roberts's 1839 view suggests his detachment. Yet recent archaeological discoveries and a persuasive body of research indicate that vestiges of the original rock-carved tomb have survived here.

The Crucifixion, as portrayed in a segment from a famous Munich cyclorama of the late nineteenth century. The reconstruction is realistic enough though it sites the event at 'Gordon's Calvary' — a miniature plateau near Jerusalem's Damascus Gate. This was a popular Protestant theory of the period that endured well into the twentieth century.

A nineteenth-century engraving of 'the beloved disciple' taking Mary the mother of Joshua to his home highlights a vital clue to his identity. This wouldn't have happened while Joshua still hung on the cross, as shown here, but the Gospel of *John* stresses that it was less than an hour after his death. The artist, unlike many Christians, correctly concludes that the beloved disciple's home was in Jerusalem.

Joshua's body being prepared for burial was a popular subject for religious art. As in this version by the Renaissance artist, Solario, Mary and the disciples usually carry out the sad task; or, at the very least, are there to mourn. The less acceptable Gospel account of burial by two Pharisee members of Jerusalem's Sanhedrin, without any involvement by family or friends, matches all available evidence of Jewish interment of execution victims.

the diners seated at a table, and have John lolling rather boozily against Jesus' chest.) This position at Joshua's right — 'below him' in Talmudic terms — is usually regarded as a place of honour, which it was, an appropriate position for John Mark, acting as host at an all-male gathering in the home of his widowed mother. However, according to Jewish custom, the *most* honoured place at the table was on Joshua's left, 'above him'. The Gospels suggest that this place was taken by Judas, where Joshua could hand him a piece of dipped bread — an awkward action if he were any further away. Also, in handing him the bread, Joshua was observing the place-of-honour protocol. Was this detail artificially created by a Gospel need for some contact between Joshua and Judas? Perhaps; though, as a brother of Joshua, and senior in his own right as treasurer of the group, Judas merited a 'high place' at any time. And this night he had a crucial role to play during the meal. With Judas at his left shoulder, Joshua would have felt that he could speak to his brother without being overheard. He was wrong.

Peter was able to signal John Mark and was in a position where he was the first to have his feet washed by Joshua — probably at the far end of the right-hand couch, diagonally opposite John Mark. The positions — and even all the names — of the remaining nine disciples can't be established with certainty, in spite of some very confident attempts.

Andrew, John and James the Older were possibly next to Peter, with Simon the Zealot at the top of the right-hand couch and/or next to his twin brother Judas (together in life as they are always placed in otherwise varying lists of the Twelve). James the Younger could have been on John Mark's right, at the left-hand end of the central couch, with the remaining five disciples along the left-hand couch (*Berakoth* 46b; *Tosephta Berakoth* 5; *j.Ta anith* 68a).

It is often pointed out that this meal has echoes of the Qumran sect's Messianic Banquet (1QSa or 1Q28a). 'The heads of the clans (or "thousands") of Israel' sit before 'the Messiah of Israel' with 'each man in his order of dignity' and the Priest-Messiah blesses 'the first-fruits of bread and wine'.

In reconstructing Joshua's meal with the disciples, the blessing of the bread and wine as a Passover *kiddush* was undoubtedly the major piece of ceremony — with a traditional reference to the coming festival as a symbol of liberation, 'the season of our freedom' — a theme given new meaning by Joshua's conviction that this Passover will see the coming of the kingdom, perhaps before dawn, a re-creation precisely in the spirit of the festival. The afternoon sacrifice of the lambs will have a new and joyous significance and, with sunset, the Passover meal will inaugurate the first Sabbath of the kingdom, an eternal Sabbath of peace, justice, prosperity and universal homage to God.

This is truly a Last Supper intended not as the last meal of Joshua's earthly life but as the last meal he will share with his disciples in a world ruled by men.

Luke, who visited the Jerusalem congregation, recorded a tradition that Joshua said he would not eat the Passover 'until it is fulfilled in the kingdom of God' (*Luke* 22:16). Even in Mark's brief, early account, after giving thanks for the wine, Joshua announces: 'I say to you sincerely that I will not drink of the fruit of the vine again until the day when I drink it in the kingdom of God' (*Mark* 14:25).

John Dominic Crossan says that, with these words, Joshua 'prophesies his coming death'. Even E. P. Sanders, a New Testament scholar well-versed in Jewish belief, can comment: 'The saying makes it highly probable that Jesus knew he was a marked man'. Like Crossan, Sanders here equates the kingdom with Jesus' death; he sees it as a 'heavenly' realm. Yet the Twelve, who supposedly have been told repeatedly that Joshua is in Jerusalem to be tried and executed, show very earthly concern for their positions in the imminent kingdom, and after giving a homily on service, Joshua tells them:

> 'You are the ones sharing my trials with me. And I appoint a kingdom to you as my Father appointed it to me, so you can eat and drink at my table in my king-dom; and you will sit on thrones judging the twelve tribes of Israel.'
>
> (*Luke* 22:28–30)

If Joshua is predicting his imminent death when he speaks of eating and drinking in the kingdom, is he also predicting the imminent death of the Twelve? Obviously not. So why do Crossan and Sanders, perhaps America's leading 'Jesus' scholars, see Joshua's eating and drinking as post-resurrec-tion? Because, like the Gospellers, they know he is about to die. But *he* does not know this; and neither do the Twelve. Like every other Jew of their time, they look to God's kingdom on earth. This is what The Last Supper is about.

In view of this expectation, one of Joshua's great concerns is to curb the mundane ambitions of the Twelve, who have such vital roles to play in the transformed world. This is why he insists on washing the feet of the thirteen guests, a parable-in-action of the kingdom where the first will be last and the last first. The leader is performing a menial task, the teacher is offering his pupils a final, vivid lesson in humility and service (*John* 13:2–16).

Matthew, Mark and Luke do not mention the foot-washing. In fact, the four Gospels agree on only one detail of what took place at this meal: that

Jesus predicted his betrayal by one of the Twelve (and, according to John, actually identified Judas as his betrayer). Along with every other aspect of the Betrayal narrative, this almost certainly didn't happen. The story is so firmly imbedded in the Christian montage of the Passion that it seems one of its most solid foundations. Yet it is a collage of sometimes contradictory components built on a surprisingly illogical situation which in itself challenges the unanimity of the Gospels.

We have already noted Luke's record of a tradition that, at The Last Supper, Jesus promised thrones to all twelve disciples as judges of Israel. And the early *Gospel of Peter* mentions the Twelve meeting in the week after the crucifixion, 'weeping and ... in sorrow' (*Gospel of Peter* 14, 59). Neither source knows of Judas's defection. In fact, even the earliest reference to the Betrayal does not mention him.

You will recall that Paul introduces his seminal account of The Last Supper by saying: 'The Lord Jesus, on the night he was betrayed ...' One thing is immediately noticeable. Paul uses the Greek *paradidomai* which means 'to betray' *or* 'to hand over', 'to deliver up.' The word occurs several times in Gospel accounts of what happened in the next twelve hours and the King James Version flicks from one translation to the other. Judas 'betrays' Jesus; Jewish religious leaders 'deliver him up' to Pilate. There is nothing in Paul's reference to show which meaning he intends. It is possible that Paul is referring to Jesus being 'handed over' to the Jewish authorities; or even 'handed over' by them to Pilate. This may well have been the genesis of the story of Judas's betrayal.

There was probably a mysterious tradition of Judas being in some way involved in the arrest (Peter says that he 'was a guide for the men who arrested Jesus' [*Acts* 1:16]). Of course, this was what Paul meant by 'betrayal'; Judas was the betrayer! Yet Judas was also the loyal twin. So then there needed to be two Judases, which meant that, because there was really only one, Judas the betrayer had to be accounted for; he had to disappear. In three Gospels — Mark, Luke and John — he does just that. He vanishes from the story without explanation. Matthew, however, feels compelled to explain. So Judas is overcome by remorse and hangs himself. Eventually, in *Acts*, Luke also decides that the story needs an end, so he tells how Judas bought a field with his blood money, fell down in it and his bowels gushed out. The harmonisers rush in and declare that he hanged himself, the body hung until it decomposed, then fell to the ground and burst open.

It is clear that no-one knew what happened to Judas the betrayer. He vanished without trace because he never existed. Clearly, Judas the Twin was appalled by what happened to Joshua and, after some little time, left the Twelve. If indeed he was the Judas who wrote *The Epistle of Jude* — identifying himself as 'brother of James' — he spoke of the Apostles as though he was not one of them. By that stage, he wasn't; his place in the Twelve had been taken by Matthias. But he remained a loyal 'servant' to his dead brother and, as we have noted, probably died a martyr's death with his twin, Simon, to become St Jude the Obscure.

If this explanation of the Judas 'Betrayal' story seems fanciful, a comparison of the four Gospel accounts shows clearly that the basic *idea* of Judas betraying Jesus has been freely dramatised in successive versions.

Mark's earliest Gospel account represents a first stab at the story. He merely says that Judas goes to the high priests to betray Jesus. No motive is suggested and Judas is promised 'silver' *after* he has made his offer: he will wait for the right moment to act (*Mark* 14:10–11). At The Last Supper Jesus predicts his betrayal and curses his betrayer (14:17– 21). Judas (identified as 'one of the Twelve', as though we haven't heard of him before) arrives with the arresting party and kisses Jesus as an identifying signal (14:43). One suspects that Mark's original version did not mention Judas until his appearance at the arrest.

In *Matthew* 26:14–16, Judas asks for money *before* offering to betray Jesus and is given thirty pieces of silver, a detail inspired by *Zechariah* 11:12, which enables Matthew to show yet another prophecy fulfilled. After Jesus' Last Supper prediction of betrayal, Judas compounds his treachery by protesting: 'Surely not me, Lord' (26:25). Judas again identifies Jesus with a kiss, but the day after the arrest is remorseful. He throws the money into the Temple (Zechariah 11:13, another prophecy fulfilled!) and hangs himself. The money is used to buy the Potter's Field which is called the Field of Blood two prophecies for the price of one (*Zechariah* 11:13 and *Jeremiah* 19:6). Matthew summarises the process by cobbling together a final prophecy supposedly from *Jeremiah* (*Matthew* 27:9–10).

Luke blames Satan for instigating Judas's treachery and, like Mark, has the priests give him an unspecified amount of money *after* he has offered to betray his leader (*Luke* 22:3–6). Luke also has Judas kiss Jesus at the arrest. His account closely follows Mark's. It seems that the 'Q' source he shared with Matthew said nothing of the Betrayal.

John again blames Satan and has Jesus openly incriminate Judas at The Last Supper. Announcing that he will hand bread to his betrayer, he immediately gives a piece to Judas (*John* 13:21–30). When the arresting party arrives,

Judas is with them but does *not* identify Jesus with a kiss.

Conflicting details apart, the story is bizarre. The Gospel's Jesus is supposedly dying in fulfilment of his destiny as a sacrifice to redeem humankind. He knows how, when and where he will die; he knows that Judas will betray him. Judas is helping him accomplish his redemptive death; yet Satan must enter into Judas to make him carry out his part in the divine plan, and further, Jesus curses his betrayer.

John Mark, while being the only Gospeller able to provide an eyewitness account, was not one of the Twelve and was therefore least likely of all the men present to be aware of Judas's true role that evening. Later, he absorbed the 'Betrayal' tradition and embroidered it into his account. Yet he also gives us apparent glimpses of what actually happened.

John Mark was perfectly placed to hear a crucial exchange between Joshua and his brother — when Joshua turned aside to hand Judas a piece of dipped bread and said quietly: 'What you are to do, do quickly' (*John* 13:28–9). John explains:

> None of those reclining at the meal knew why he said this to him; for some of them thought that, because Judas had charge of the bag of money, Jesus was telling him, 'Buy what we need for the feast,' or that he should give something to the poor.   (*John* 13:28–9)

It is doubtful that anyone but John Mark heard what Joshua said to Judas. They would notice only that their treasurer left the meal immediately after his brother had spoken to him while offering a piece of bread dipped in the main dish. If this had followed Joshua announcing that he was about to identify his betrayer by handing him some bread, the disciples' reactions to the exchange and to Judas's departure would have been very different. The story makes nonsense of itself.

John Mark has produced a particularly awkward blend of what actually happened and what *would* have happened if his all-seeing, all-knowing Jesus had cued Satan to enter Judas and initiate the train of events leading to his crucifixion.

At this stage it is impossible to say whether the Gospel version of the Judas story sprang from ignorance of the facts or from a need to protect Judas the Twin from the repercussions of his well-intentioned role in the events of Thursday night; but the latter seems far more likely.

Judas did what was required of him with love for his brother, in total devotion to the Messianic mission and at risk to his own life by luring Roman troops to an intended disaster in the Valley of Decision. His role as an accomplice was enough in itself to demand secrecy while he remained in Israel. By the time he was safe from Roman retribution, the 'cover' story of Judas the betrayer had taken on its own life and Judas the Twin was a respected but oddly mysterious figure whose sons and grandsons would carry on his tradition of devotion to the memory and teaching of Joshua.

In spite of the apparently contrived obscurity of Judas and the Passover strategy he was involved in, a few fragments of that earth-changing plan have survived. Luke, again drawing on a Jerusalem tradition unknown to Matthew and Mark (and probably avoided by John), ends his account of The Last Supper with a remarkable exchange:

> And he said to them, 'When I sent you out with no purse, satchel or sandals, did you lack anything?' And they said, 'Nothing.' Then he said to them, 'But now, if you have a purse, take it. The same with a satchel. And if any of you lacks a sword, let him sell his garment to buy one.' ... And they said, 'Lord, look, here are two swords.' And he said to them, 'That is enough.'   (*Luke* 22:35, 36, 38)

Attempts to explain this passage include the notion that Joshua is speaking ironically and the disciples don't understand (his 'That is enough!' is supposedly said in exasperation or resignation). Another theory proposes that this is prudent advice for missionaries about to be turned loose in a hostile world (when two swords among a scattered Twelve would be of distinctly limited value).

The logical explanation of the passage — that the disciples are about to face a situation in which they need to be armed — fits perfectly in the actual context of the Jerusalem meal and its aftermath. In the coming clash with the Roman force in the Valley of Decision, two swords will be enough because the angelic warriors will be at their side, shielding them from harm and crushing their enemies.

✝✝✝

Judas has left on his critical mission to 'inform' on the outlawed Joshua and lead his enemies, the enemies of Israel, to their fate. An indeterminate time later, Joshua and the eleven leave the Upper Room and probably take their farewell of John Mark at a courtyard gateway.

As the Gospels make clear, it is a bitterly cold night — typical of highland Jerusalem in mid-Nisan. Accepting the traditional, artificially tranquil version of the night's events, few bother to query why the group leave the warmth and safety of the Upper Room (which accommodates all the disciples some six weeks later) to go and spend the night on the chill slopes of the Mount of Olives within sight of the highest tower of the Antonia. Of course, there is a pressing reason to do this. We know that Joshua must not be arrested anywhere but Gethsemane. This is his place of destiny, ordained by Zechariah and Joel. So again he risks recognition to move through the moonlit streets of Jerusalem, perhaps to leave the city via the nearby Essene Gate, and lead the disciples down a track which runs along the flank of the Hinnom Valley to the south-east corner of the city wall. There, the Kidron Valley opens before them, its newly whitewashed tombs brilliant under the Passover full moon, with thousands of tents crowded on the slopes among the trees, lit by fires or feebly glowing from inner lamplight. The twelve men head for the stone bridge that leads across the Kidron to Gethsemane.

Behind the walls of the city above them, Judas has perhaps seen the high priest, Joseph Caiaphas, at his mansion not far from John Mark's home, to reveal that he knows where to find the proclaimed outlaw, Joshua. Probably carrying a letter of authority from Caiaphas and escorted by one of the high priest's staff called Malchus, Judas is sent to Caiaphas's brother-in-law, Jonathan bar Annas, who controls the Temple Guard. If Jonathan is willing to try and arrest Joshua with his own men (which would not suit the plan), Judas can warn of the thousands of Galileans — notorious troublemakers — camped around Gethsemane. Probably, no such prompting is needed. There has already been one minor uprising this week and Jonathan sees clearly that this is no mere police action; it is a job for Roman soldiers.

In the Antonia fortress abutting the Temple, a cohort of between five hundred and eight hundred men is mobilised under a military tribune. There is no need to hurry. The later the hour, the more likely that the outlaw and his followers will be asleep, with less chance of escape or resistance. Eventually, carrying torches and accompanied by Judas, Malchus and a detachment of Jonathan's Temple Guard, the cohort marches out of the fortress, across a bridge over a moat-like pool, and strikes down towards Gethsemane. The tribune, an imperial figure in moulded bronze breastplate, is probably mounted and accompanied by some of the garrison's Samaritan cavalrymen in case fast pursuit is needed.

In Roman military annals, this foray of provincial auxiliaries, led by veteran Roman centurions and the tribune, would be seen as a piffling exercise. Yet it was about to leave a momentous mark on the world.

CHAPTER 23

Arrest and 'Trial'

What happened in Gethsemane — whether it was a garden, grove, oil press or cave — reveals the purpose that guided Joshua's actions during these last hours of freedom. In a famous Gospel scene, 'the Agony in the Garden', Matthew, Mark and Luke show Jesus praying to be relieved of the gigantic burden he has accepted. Mark sets the pattern which is closely followed by the other two.

> He said to the disciples, 'Sit here while I pray.' And he took Peter, James and John with him; and he was overcome by fear and a great distress. And he said to them, 'My soul is sorrowful to the point of death. Wait here and keep watch.' And continuing a little way, he fell to the earth and prayed that, if it were possible, this hour might pass him by. And he said, 'Abba, Father, everything is possible for you; take this cup from me. But [let it be] not what I want, but what you want.
>
> (*Mark* 14:32–6)

The prayer would be totally believable if 'the cup' represented the awesome responsibility of initiating God's judgement and the unleashing of divine carnage here in the Valley of Decision. Any man would hesitate to face such a task; he would seek confirmation that this was indeed God's will, and pray that it wasn't. But the prayer is supposedly delivered by the Gospels' Jesus, a divine being who has come to earth to die in atonement for the sins of mankind and is hours from that culminating, sacrificial death. 'This cup' inevitably echoes The Last Supper's cup of wine over which Mark has just shown his Jesus saying: 'This is my blood of the New Covenant which is being poured out for many' (*Mark* 14:24). Earlier, on the way to Jerusalem, Mark's Jesus has said: 'Even the Son of Man did not come to be served but to serve, and to give his life as a ransom for many' (*Mark* 10:45). Now he is asking for his blood not to be shed; for his life not to be a ransom.

Luke tends to downplay the concept of Jesus' death as an atoning sacrifice but makes more of his torment than do the other Gospellers. Immediately after the Gethsemane prayer, Luke says:

> And an angel appeared to him from heaven, giving him strength. And, now in agony, he prayed more urgently. And his sweat was like drops of blood falling down onto the ground. (*Luke* 22:43–4)

Luke is using a powerful poetic image to convey the depth and pain of Jesus' turmoil; his sweat falls *like* drops of blood. Yet there have been attempts to show that, in rare cases, blood can actually pass through the pores of the skin. It's hard to see the point of such literalism when the scene is clearly a work of imagination. There is no-one to overhear the prayer and record it. Jesus is alone; the disciples, who are 'a stone's throw' away, have fallen (almost instantly) asleep. He goes to them three times and must wake them three times, just as Peter will deny him two or three times before the cock has crowed once or twice — depending on which Gospel we follow. This is the stuff of fables. More to the point, the Gethsemane fable shows the Gospels' Jesus trying to revoke the New Covenant which is to be sealed with his blood; it shows him second-guessing on the brink of a destiny fulfilled. The fable is unworthy of him.

While Luke dilutes the fable though heightening the agony, John ignores both. He describes Joshua and the disciples going to Gethsemane, then moves immediately to the arrival of the arresting party. Unlike the other Gospellers, John does not describe the scene from the viewpoint of Joshua and the Eleven. It is as though we travel to Gethsemane with the cohort. Perhaps this is precisely what John Mark did.

From the upper room, he could have noticed unusual activity between Caiaphas's house and the Temple, or been alerted to it by the household's female gatekeeper, perhaps Rhoda of *Acts* 12:13. He could have investigated and seen the detachment of the Temple Guard crossing to the Antonia, heard the shrill notes of a Roman *cornu* mustering the cohort, then hurried down through the Susa Gate below the Temple to watch the torchlit ranks of auxiliaries marching across the Kidron bridge towards Gethsemane. Perhaps he recognised Judas walking ahead of the mounted tribune, to record: 'So Judas comes there, guiding the cohort and the officers of the chief priests and Pharisees, all carrying torches and lanterns and weapons' (*John* 18:3).

Matthew, Mark and Luke portray the arresting party as 'a large crowd with swords and clubs, from the chief priests and the scribes and the elders' (*Mark* 14:43), making it sound almost like a lynch mob. John, however, is quite specific that this is a *speira* — a cohort, led by a *chiliarchos* — 'a commander of a thousand', a military tribune. Translations often cloak this forbidding force with words like 'detachment', 'party' and, at best, 'military unit'. In the Graeco-Roman world of the first century, a cohort was a cohort.

It is probably about midnight as Judas leads the party up the stepped roadway from the Kidron bridge, horses perhaps to either side of the paving, the soldiers' hobnailed sandal boots clashing on the rock, marching briskly. No point in stealth with hundreds of families camped all over the hillside. Just get the job done as soon as possible, before too many of them have woken up.

In these last moments, is Judas tempted to doubt his brother's strategy? It would be so easy to lead the cohort past the turn-off to Gethsemane, then claim that he has been confused by new campsites that have sprung up since afternoon, giving Joshua a chance to reconsider, to abandon this apocalyptic climax to the mission. But, whatever his doubts or fears, Judas follows the plan, signals to the tribune that they have reached their destination, and, as the centurions deploy their troops, he leads the way towards the dozen men who stand waiting, facing them, facing the moon approaching its zenith above Jerusalem. Joshua is probably very calm, very still, on the brink of a moment that he believes will change the world forever, as indeed it did.

In *Matthew*, *Mark* and *Luke*, the arch-traitor Judas kisses Jesus to identify him for the arresting officers. John tells a very different story. Jesus sees Judas and the soldiers approaching.

> Then, knowing everything that was to happen to him, Jesus went out and said to them, 'Who are you looking for?' They answered, 'Jesus the Nazarene'. Jesus said to them, 'I am [he]'. And Judas the betrayer was with them. And when he said 'I am [he]', they stepped back and fell to the ground.　　(*John* 18:4–6)

The recoil and fall is an embarrassing touch which should not be allowed to discredit John's account. He may be trying to convey the impact of the exchange as he experienced it. Quite unrealistically, but powerfully, he replays it. The question is asked again:

> 'Who are you looking for?'
> 'Jesus the Nazarene.'
> 'I told you that I am [he].'

The moment oscillates in time, following or preceding itself, and John's Jesus is serenely in command of men and events, just as he commanded the forces of nature when he stood in the swirling spray of Lake Kinneret. Now, as then, John has his Jesus identify himself by saying simply, 'I am', echoing God's reply when Moses asks his name (*Exodus* 3:13–15).

One feels strongly that this is a moment when John Mark saw Joshua and here tries to convey not what he said but what he *was* — a striking figure by moonlight and the flicker of hostile torches, utterly confident in the power of his affinity with God — a power John Mark would transfer to the storm on Kinneret and to other moments he hadn't seen, all consecrated by this fragment of time when he saw Joshua transformed by a passionate belief that he stood as the instrument of divine justice.

✝✝✝

In their accounts of Gethsemane, all the Gospels agree on two points: that Judas was with the party and that there was armed resistance to the arrest, although only Luke has made any earlier reference to the disciples being armed. Now he writes:

> And, seeing what was about to happen, those around him said, 'Lord, shall we strike with the sword?'
>
> (*Luke* 22:49)

It is an extraordinary question, far more extraordinary than most appreciate. Joshua and his eleven disciples face a huge armed force. Even given the fact that they are surrounded by hundreds, perhaps thousands of encamped pilgrims roused from sleep by the arrival of the cohort, it would be futile for the disciples to attempt resistance with their two swords. So their question, 'Shall we strike?' seems almost ludicrous.

The most remarkable thing about this defining moment is that Joshua does not answer his disciples. He does not forbid them to use their pathetic weapons — two *machairai*, shortswords, little more than daggers — against an entire Roman cohort equipped and armed ready for battle. Yet, if we understand Joshua's strategy, the reason is clear. The men wielding those two swords — probably Peter *Barjona* and Simon the Zealot — will not fight alone. By striking the first blows against these massed enemies of Israel's Messiah, they will trigger the promised battle of the End of Days — here in the ordained battleground on the western slope of the Mount of Olives, the Lord's Mountain; here on the rim of the Valley of Decision where a divine army will join them to slaughter the men of the Nations.

The question is asked of Joshua; he says nothing. The two disciples have his tacit approval to strike. Malchus, from Caiaphas's staff, probably moves to make the arrest on behalf of the Sanhedrin. It is Peter's sword that flashes in the torchlight — a vicious chop at the side of Malchus's head. It hacks off his right ear. Perhaps the man screams, perhaps he feels only the shock of the blow. And the moment hangs like the steam of a last breath. It is a nightmarish moment, but a worse nightmare is yet to come.

Peter, as a holy warrior, has struck the first blow in defence of his Messiah, signalling the full force of God's vengeance. But there is only an unfortunate man with blood gouting from where his ear had been and twelve men with two swords facing hundreds of soldiers. In this numbing hiatus Joshua knows that, for whatever reason, God is not coming to save him with angelic armies under Michael or Melchizedek. In spite of the Eleven, in spite of the Seventy, in spite of the hundreds of Galileans probably ready to hurl themselves against Roman swords and javelins, he is alone.

✝✝✝

The Gospels do not agree on what was said at this point. As we will see, there was little time for speech, but pieces of the truth *may* be retrievable. Matthew, Mark and Luke have Jesus ask: 'Have you come out with swords and clubs to arrest me, as though I am a revolutionary (*lestes*)?' (*Mark* 14:48; *Matthew* 26:55; *Luke* 22:52) — a question which effectively confirms that Roman soldiers make up most of the arresting party. It would be very odd to put such a question (even rhetorically) to a party of Temple officials and Levitical police.

Matthew gives his Jesus the longest speech. After Peter has struck at Malchus, Jesus begins: 'Put your sword away! All those who take up a sword will die by a sword' (*Matthew* 26:52).

This has been treated as a timeless and universal truth, which was obviously not the intention. It is a warning, directed at the disciples and the surrounding Galileans here in Gethsemane and perhaps at anyone else who might try and use armed force against Rome at this Passover. Joshua has not suddenly repudiated Israel's warrior tradition. He has recognised that a man who takes up a sword in *his* cause, at this time, will fight alone. And, whether

222

or not he actually says so, he probably realises why. He continues:

> 'Do you think that even now I can't call on my Father and have him send me
> more than twelve legions of angels? But then, how would the scriptures be ful-
> filled that say it must happen this way?' (*Matthew* 26:53–4)

What does this mean? Is Matthew's Jesus saying that he cannot call for
rescue by angelic armies because he must suffer and die in accordance with
later Christian interpretations of biblical prophecy shaped by the hindsight
wisdom of his imminent death? Or could he be saying that he must not
appeal for help, that any rescue in fulfilment of prophecy can only be God's
initiative? Could there be a recognition here that he has succumbed to the
temptation of tempting God, challenging him to come to the aid of his
Messiah? — even a terrible thought that the non-intervention by divine
forces represents a denial of his Messiahship?

Whether or not Matthew is conscious of any ambiguity, he ends by leaning heavily and unconvincingly towards an acceptance of arrest by Jesus as
the realisation of prophecy, and an announcement: 'All this has happened so
the scriptures of the prophets may be fulfilled,' even though, a mere twenty
verses before, he has been fervently praying for a different end to the story.

✝✝✝

Weighing it all, even though there may be glimpses of the truth here, it seems
clear that Joshua could scarcely do more than call for an end to resistance
before he was bound and led away. Everything points to urgent departure.
Peter had seriously wounded one of the party yet there was no retaliation
and he was not arrested; in fact, all the disciples escaped (and 'deserting him,
they all fled'), including the mysterious young man who managed to run
away, naked, leaving his linen 'cloth' or 'garment' in the hands of the party
(*Mark* 14:50–2).

In the traditional picture of the arrest, Peter's immunity from retribution
and the all-but-uninterrupted flight of the other ten is almost inexplicable. It
is obvious that the surrounding pilgrims played a key role. Some of them
would have been supporters of Joshua but most were probably just Galileans
living up to their provincial reputation as hotheads, easily inflamed by this
midnight display of Roman provocation. They either physically attacked the
soldiers or posed such a threat that the tribune was more concerned with the
safe return of his prisoner than the pursuit of Peter, the disciples and the others through a hostile crowd. The cohort closed ranks around Joshua and the

Temple party with an impenetrable wall of shoulder-high shields and swiftly withdrew to Jerusalem. It is significant that Joshua was tied before being led away. Then, as now, such restraint suggested an arrest involving the threat of escape or rescue.

Picture the five-hundred-plus soldiers hurrying their prisoner across the Kidron Valley, back towards Jerusalem, through increasing numbers of pilgrim families roused from sleep by the ruckus and probably followed by a riotous Galilean mob. This scene, in itself, would demand prompt action by Jewish and Roman authorities and explain the summary executions which followed, in spite of this being such a critical and sensitive time. There may, however, have been further justification for such sudden and untimely retribution.

The Slavonic and Romanian texts of Josephus describe Jesus (identified only as 'the wonder worker') gathering his 150 supporters and the 'great crowd of the lower orders' on the Mount of Olives. One reconstruction of the original text speaks of Pilate having 'many of the multitude slain' after the followers of 'the wonder worker' have 'flocked into Jerusalem ... uttering blasphemies alike against God and Caesar', clearly the Palm Sunday disturbance. However, the Slavonic version places the killing of 'the wonder worker's' rank-and-file supporters immediately before his arrest, with the implication that the clash occurred on the Mount of Olives.

Given the timing and setting of Joshua's arrest by the cohort, a massacre is all too easy to believe. Joshua's call to end resistance against the Romans would have been immediately obeyed by the disciples, but it could have been ignored, or even unheard, by hundreds of others clamouring around the arresting force. The auxiliaries would have simply cleared a path with their javelins and swords, prompting an explosion of anger, futile resistance and more killing.

Was this the basis of an earlier, unexplained reference in Luke to 'the Galileans whose blood Pilate had mixed with their sacrifices' (*Luke* 13:1) — meaning that the deaths occurred while they were on a Passover visit to Jerusalem, or that they died among the lambs they had ready to sacrifice the following afternoon? Even without such a clash, the authorities now held the man responsible for the earlier Temple fracas; his arrest had been violently resisted; one of the official party — a member of the high priest's staff — had been seriously wounded and there had been at least a threat of further violence from a large, anti-Roman crowd. At least four men were now in custody after the week's tumult. However undesirable it may have been to contemplate executions in the volatile climate of Passover, an example had to be made of these rebels before the unrest developed into something more serious and before the majority of the pilgrims dispersed, carrying with them a message of unpunished rebellion. It had to be today — on the Friday — or after the feast, in a week's time. On balance, the executions must happen today, and the sooner the better.

✝✝✝

The Gospel stories of Jesus' trial agree on only two basic facts — that he was taken to the high priest, Caiaphas, and that Caiaphas handed him over to the Roman prefect, Pontius Pilate, who then conducted a particularly reluctant inquiry which resulted in Jesus' crucifixion. Into this basic structure the Gospels weave varying and often contradictory details, all of which have two basic intentions — to show that 'the Jews' wanted to kill Jesus and that Pilate wanted to spare his life.

One other detail is attested by all four Gospellers: that Peter was at the high priest's house while Jesus was held there and that he denied any connection with the prisoner.

Mark, as usual, sets the broad pattern. Jesus is taken to the house of Caiaphas 'and all the chief priests, elders and scribes convened there' (*Mark* 14:53). Later confirming that this gathering is 'the whole Sanhedrin', Mark tells us that 'they sought evidence against Jesus to execute him' and examined 'many' witnesses who gave contradictory evidence. Jesus, Mark tells us, 'was silent and said nothing'. Eventually Caiaphas asks: 'Are you the Messiah, the son of the Blessed?' Jesus replies, 'I am. And you will see the Son of Man sitting at the right hand of Power and coming with the clouds of heaven!'

At this, Caiaphas tears his garments (a recognition of blasphemy, *Sanhedrin* 56a) and asks the court: 'Why do we still need witnesses? You heard the blasphemy. What is your opinion?' The verdict is unanimous: 'they all considered him worthy of death'. Now, 'some' of those present 'started to spit at him and cover his face and beat him with their fists, saying, "Prophesy!" And the Temple guards slapped him.' So much for the Jewish trial. 'And as soon as it was morning all the Sanhedrin bound him and led him to Pilate' (*Mark* 14:55–15:1).

This account by Mark — which is closely followed by Matthew — is simply fantastic. No Jewish trial could begin at night (*Shabbath* 9b) and the verdict in a capital case had to be reached in daytime (*Sanhedrin* 4,1). A guilty verdict in a capital case could not be pronounced on the day of the trial and the Sanhedrin could not hear a capital case anywhere but at its appointed meeting place (*Abhodah Zarah* 8b). Nothing Mark's Jesus said before the court could qualify as blasphemy ('The blasphemer is punished only if he utters [the divine] name', *Sanhedrin* 55b, 56a).

Luke — obviously after some research on the subject — avoids most of Mark's implausibilities. His Jesus is taken to Caiaphas's home, but there is no trial there. Luke covers the night hours by telling us: 'The men in charge of Jesus mocked him and beat him' (*Luke* 22:54). Then, '*as day broke*, the elders of the people, the chief priests and the scribes gathered and led him to the Sanhedrin' [my italics] (*Luke* 22:66).

Examined by the court, Jesus avoids admitting that he is the Messiah. However, to a final question, 'Are you the Son of God?' he declares: 'You say [so] because I am!' The members of the Sanhedrin react: 'Why do we need more witnesses? We heard it from his own mouth!' (*Luke* 22:67–71).

There is no tearing of garments, no pronouncement of blasphemy. And, in admitting sonship with God, Luke's Jesus is not saying that he is the Messiah; he is merely accepting a title that had been applied to King David but is not, in itself, exclusively Davidic or Messianic. So Luke's Sanhedrin now lead Jesus off to Pilate without pronouncing a verdict — and apparently without reaching one.

Luke has cleverly avoided three of Mark's blunders: Luke's Sanhedrin has not met at night, it has not convened away from its usual meeting place and it has not pronounced a 'guilty' verdict on the first day of the trial. But his version is still critically flawed. A trial could not be held on a feast day, on the eve of a feast or on the eve of a Sabbath (*Beitsah* 36; *Babha Qamma* 113a). According to Matthew, Mark and Luke, this is the First Day of the Feast of Unleavened Bread; according to John, it is the Passover. According to all four, it is the eve of the Sabbath. On this day, by every conceivable criterion, a Jewish trial of Joshua is impossible.

John offers a credible account of what happened in the hours after Joshua's arrest. He is first taken, not to Caiaphas, but to the home of the emeritus high priest, Caiaphas's father-in-law, Annas. It is possible that this wily, old, grey eminence of the Temple faction is trying to avoid the coming disaster — a crucifixion on the day of Passover and the possible Galilean/Zealot backlash which is the dark side of his son-in-law's 'kill-one-save-many' philosophy. Certainly Annas does not seem concerned with existing or pending charges against Joshua, has him untied and questions him 'about his disciples and about his teaching'.

Joshua, however, is uncooperative. He tells Annas: 'I spoke openly to the world. I always taught in synagogues and in the Temple where Jews gather and I said nothing in secret. Why question *me*? Question the people who listened to me. They know what I said.'

This is a far cry from the dialogue John usually supplies for his Jesus. It has a steely ring of truth to it. Too steely for the Temple guard at Joshua's side; he hits him. 'Is this any way to answer the high priest!'

Joshua turns on the guard. 'If I said something that was wrong, prove it was wrong. But if I spoke the truth, why do you hit me?' (*John* 18:19–23).

If Annas has had any thought of saving Joshua from what is to come, he abandons the idea. The man is another rebellious Galilean; another Maccabee, another Judas of Gallilee; magnificent in his way, passionate, courageous, but impossible. So he will send this prisoner to his son-in-law, Joseph Caiaphas, knowing that, if anything is to be done this day, then there is only one possible line of action open to Caiaphas: send the Nazarene to Pilate. And perhaps, just this once, Annas knows exactly what Pilate will do.

For seven challenging years, Caiaphas has served under Pilate as high priest, always vulnerable to replacement but surviving a series of bitter chess games fought out between Jerusalem and Caesarea. There were two losses for Pilate — the affair of the Roman standards beside the Temple and the provocative replay with votive shields outside Herod's palace. Then came a confrontation when Pilate seized some Temple funds to finance a water supply project. Faced with a protesting mob, Pilate turned his soldiers loose on them, dressed as civilians and armed with daggers and clubs. Many dissidents died. At last Pilate had a victory (Josephus, *Antiquities* 18,3,2; *Wars* 2,9,4).

Scarcely eighteen months earlier everything changed. Pilate's patron Aelius Sejanus, de facto ruler of Rome, was finally outsmarted in his campaign to gain the crown. Tiberius uncovered his plot, won over the praetorian guard and had Sejanus strangled. He then launched a reign of terror — the murder, forced suicide or imprisonment of every ally, every friend of the toppled arch-traitor.

As the months passed, Sejanus's protégé, Pontius Pilate, had at last grown to feel safe, here in Jerusalem, so far from Rome. Then when the Mediterranean sea lanes reopened at the end of winter, the first mails brought news of a renewed tide of Tiberian vengeance. All Sejanus's accomplices still held in prison were being strangled, their bodies dumped on the Gemonian steps beside the Tiber and left to rot (Tacitus, *Annals* 6,18). As knights and patricians alike battled to prove their loyalty to Tiberius by ferreting out new accomplices of Sejanus, Pilate knew that a false move could cost him his position; return to Rome could cost his life.

Pontius Pilate was vulnerable. And, this night, Joseph Caiaphas was about to take charge of a prisoner who had caused trouble and must cause no more. Under Jewish law, no solution was possible on this day of Passover, this Sabbath eve. So Annas had Joshua bound again and sent him to Caiaphas, in full knowledge that his son-in-law would let Pontius Pilate solve both their problems.

It was still dark when Joshua arrived at Caiaphas's near-palace on the slope above the Temple, with its courtyard and pillared porches and mosaic floors. Here, there would be no impossible gathering of the Sanhedrin, no impossible trial. Just a passing of time until the Temple's silver trumpets signalled the first glimpse of the sun. Then Caiaphas would take Joshua up the hill to the sunlit crest of Mount Zion where Pilate had set up his *praetorium* in the palace of Herod the Great (Philo, *Embassy to Gaius* 39,306; Josephus, *Wars* 2,14,8).

This is the totally believable story as we have it from John — John Mark, the beloved disciple, who was now waiting for dawn in the courtyard of Caiaphas's mansion with a group of servants and Temple guards warming themselves around a charcoal fire. He and Peter had followed Joshua here. John was known to the servant girl on the gate, and, probably against his better judgement, had managed to get Peter inside.

It was touchy. One of the servants, a relative of Malchus who had lost his ear at Gethsemane, was there when it happened and thought he recognised Peter. Of course Peter swore and bluffed it through; and stayed there. But this was as far as he dared to go. Already his thick, Galilean accent had attracted attention; by daylight he would be even more recognisable. Only John Mark, the unknown disciple, friend of the high priest, could risk going with the party that would take Joshua to Pilate — then follow him to the end of the journey (*John* 18:15–18, 24–8).

CHAPTER 24

'Caesar's Friend'

Herod the Great's palace, now Pontius Pilate's praetorium, was even bigger than the Temple, a miniature walled city of kingly apartments, colonnaded courts and gardens, all dominated by three huge, square towers of white marble. It was approached across a raised terrace (*Gabbatha*, 'High Place') with an imperial view down across the Valley of Cheesemongers to the sprawl of the old city and the Temple on its lower mount. (Josephus, *Antiquities* 1,21,2;15,9,3; *Wars* 5,4,3–4).

Here, Joshua was handed over to the Romans and taken inside. John tell us, 'The Jews did not enter the praetorium so they could avoid defilement and be able to eat the Passover' (*John* 18:28). This seems a nice detail of Jewish belief that again advertises the specialised knowledge of John Mark; but surprisingly, it is not accurate. Certainly, any priests involved in the afternoon sacrifices would not jeopardise their ritual purity by entering a Gentile or heathen building. For the others, however, entering Gentile premises would mean, at worst, that they were ritually unclean *only until sunset*. They would then bathe in a *mikveh* and eat Passover. There was some slight danger of corpse impurity which demanded seven days purification, but supervision of the building by a Jewish servant was considered enough to waive this concern (*Oholoth*, 18,7; *Toharoth* 7,3).

This detail is far from trivial. John Mark seems to be artificially separating the Jewish party from the proceedings in the praetorium. His motive for this may be clarified by the fact that he has pointedly isolated Caiaphas from the previous night's events. According to John, there was no interaction between the high priest and Joshua; his house merely provided a holding place until the early morning, when, John tell us, 'they took Jesus *from Caiaphas* to the praetorium' [my italics] (*John* 18:28). John has thus dissociated the high priest from everything that follows, never mentions his name again and now contrives to have the Jewish officials stay outside Pilate's palace. This leads to a bizarre situation in which Pilate questions Jesus while trotting in and out of the building to argue with the Temple party gathered en masse on the *Gabbatha*, a clumsy process easily corrected by having Jesus held outside the building where there was a *bema*, a probably semi-permanent 'seat of judgement' (Josephus, *Wars* 2,14,8).

John's unlikely portrayal of shuttle magistracy must be seen as the unhappy marriage of two opposing scenarios. On the one hand he follows the other Gospellers in their basic intention — to show that 'the Jews' wanted to kill Jesus and that Pilate wanted to spare his life. On the other hand he continues to distance Caiaphas from what happens — and in doing this, he must physically distance all Temple officials from the proceedings in the praetorium. If he showed any priestly dialogue with Pilate during his examination of Jesus, it would be preposterous not to have Caiaphas present.

John Mark's aim seems clear. As the only Gospeller who could possibly know what happened in the praetorium, he is concealing the fact that the essential dialogue concerning Joshua, the debate as to whether he would live or die, was between two men — Pontius Pilate and Joseph Caiaphas. John's 'complex and confused' account is designed to shelter his onetime friend and transfer all guilt — Pilate's *and* Caiaphas's — to 'the Jews'.

It is generally recognised that the Gospels blacken the Jews and whitewash Pilate in the later context of 'gentilising' Jesus' movement. Thus the Jews find Jesus guilty under Jewish Law of a capital offence he has *not* committed (blasphemy), then hand him over to Pilate who is reluctant to convict him under Roman law for a capital offence he *has* committed (treason against Caesar). Given this degree of distortion, can we hope to retrieve an accurate picture of the trial from our sources? We can certainly try.

Comparing Matthew, Mark and Luke, we see how each has manipulated varying details within a basic structure. As historian Robin Lane Fox sees it, 'There are three separate paintings worked in three different ways from a broadly similar framework', later concluding, 'Harmony is a misguided method: if we want the truth, we have to choose one of the three paintings or none'. In a balanced study of the trial narratives, Fox leans to John as the only true primary source, the only eyewitness account. Fox's conclusion — and the qualification he places on it — are equally to be respected: 'My inclination is to follow the Fourth's framework but reject its motivation, the one being primary, the other of the author's shaping'. Regarding that motivation, we have already noted John's obvious concern to obscure Caiaphas's key role and the resulting outdoor/indoor setting of the trial. Aware of this and of John's broad conformity to the Gospels' 'policy', we can follow his account, better armed to trace what happened in the praetorium of Pontius Pilate that Friday morning.

✝✝✝

The basic situation is clear enough. John Mark, while obscuring Caiaphas's role in the Roman trial, has already had the high priest state his attitude in unequivocal terms.

> 'It is better for us that one man should die for the people rather than the whole nation perish.' And he said this not on his own behalf, but being high priest that year, he predicted that Jesus was to die for the nation: and not just for the nation, but to reunite the scattered children of God.   (*John* 11:50–2)

This remains Caiaphas's position, now with the added pressure of achieving this necessary death almost immediately. Yet his hands are tied. Within Jewish Law he can do nothing until after the feast, which lasts for seven days. There is a further complication: many pilgrims will leave after the third day, with the Galileans almost certainly among them — the very people who need to learn from the fate of Joshua. Only Pilate can carry out the execution today.

Typically, Roman governors were reluctant to become involved in questions of Jewish Law, especially in its political ramifications (cf. *Acts* 24,25). Pilate, of course, was not typical. His approach to the Jews was abrasive and antagonistic. From the start, he had set out to challenge and, in fact, 'to abolish' their Law (Josephus, *Antiquities* 18,3,1); but that was Pilate as an arm of Sejanus's insidious power and notorious anti-Semitism. Now, that former source of power has become a source of vulnerability. In dealing with a Jewish politico-religious problem, Pilate faces the same dilemma as any other governor, and from a far weaker position. In the past, he has overreacted from a position of strength. On this crucial Friday, his overreaction from a position of weakness will produce atypical and unpredictable behaviour. We know that Caiaphas wants Joshua to die; could Pilate want him to live?

Matthew has a story that, during the examination of Jesus, the prefect's wife (named in early tradition as Claudia Procula or Procla) sends him a message:

'Have nothing to do with that honest man, for I have suffered a great deal today because of a dream about him' (*Matthew* 27:19). It is true that the influence of Roman governors' wives on their husbands' decisions was a notorious problem in the provinces (Tacitus, *Annals* 3, 31–2), though Matthew's lone report of this intercession should be treated with wariness. It seems an attempt to counter the fact that, normally, Pilate wouldn't lift a finger to save some provocative Galilean preacher — especially a preacher who has been involved in at least one violent disturbance and has made some claims to Messiahship. There is, nevertheless, a very strong motive for Pilate to oppose Joshua's execution today: *Caiaphas wants it.* The high priest, via his brother-in-law, has already involved Pilate's troops in Joshua's arrest. They were probably the reinforcing 'festival' cohort assigned to the Temple, which could be employed without reference to the prefect. It is unlikely, however, that this licence would extend to an operation not only outside the Temple, but outside the city. Caiaphas probably overstepped the mark, providing a source of resentment, another spur for the prefect to oppose him this morning.

After seven years of bitter game-playing, Pilate knows his opponent. And he has probably gained enough insight into Jewish belief and practice to know that, on this occasion, Caiaphas, too, is in a weak position. He cannot ask the prefect to execute a man who has challenged the authority of the Temple or upset the Sadducees or ruffled the most legalistic of the Pharisees. These are religious matters — Jewish, not Roman. Caiaphas can, however, *expect* the prefect to execute a man who has caused a riot for which at least three men already await execution, a man whose arrest was violently resisted and, above all, a man who has been hailed by his followers as a King Messiah.

Each man may well think that he has the advantage over the other in this encounter; their antagonism is obvious from the very opening of the trial in John's account (*John* 18:28–19:16). The prefect is magisterial: 'What charge do you bring against this man?'

Caiaphas, almost unarguably the Temple spokesman, answers obliquely, provocatively: 'If he wasn't a criminal, we wouldn't have brought him to you!'

Pilate is in no mood for Jewish *chutzpah* and immediately attacks the high priest's weakest point. 'Take him and judge him by your own law!' He knows that Caiaphas can't do this. If he could, he wouldn't be standing with his prisoner in the Roman praetorium on the day of Passover.

Caiaphas's response, as reported by John, is extraordinary. John has not described an impossible Jewish trial and an impossible verdict of blasphemy. But, days before, he has shown Caiaphas announcing that Joshua should die.

Now, there is no question of a trial; the high priest simply tells Pilate: 'It isn't lawful for us to put a man to death.'

This point has been hotly debated through the years. The evidence seems clear that the Jews could put men and women to death for offences against *religious* Law (Josephus, *Against Apion* 25,31). Gentiles — even Romans — could be executed for profaning the Temple (Josephus, *Wars* 6,2,4); adulterers could be stoned to death (*John* 8:7–11); a priest's daughter found guilty of adultery could be burnt at the stake like a witch (*Sanhedrin* 52b); the first Christian martyr, Stephen, was later stoned to death (Acts 6:8–8:1), as was Joshua's brother James (Josephus, *Antiquities* 20,9,1), probably by the same murderous Sadducean court that burned the priest's daughter. Some of these executions have been called 'lynchings'. If this is what they were, then in *most* cases, Jewish religious 'lynchings' were allowed by Rome.

In effect, Caiaphas claims that he is not seeking Joshua's execution for a religious crime; it is a political matter. John tries to avoid this fact, but Luke provides the Jewish indictment:

> 'We found this man perverting our nation and saying not to pay taxes to Rome and claiming that he is the King Messiah.'　　　　　　　　(*Luke* 23:2)

While trying to present the trial as an investigation of religious issues, John (like all the Gospellers) acknowledges the major political charge against Joshua by having Pilate ask him at the outset: '*Are* you the king of the Jews?'

Josephus makes it clear that a claim to the title of 'king' was associated with Jewish rebel activity. He records that 'as the several companies of the seditious lighted upon any one to lead them, he was created a king immediately in order to do mischief to the public' (Josephus, *Antiquities* 17,10,8). Pilate's question to Joshua is like a Second World War German military governor asking a citizen of an occupied country: 'Are you the leader of the Resistance?' Joshua's reply suggests that the indictment has been communicated privately to Pilate or perhaps given to him in written form: 'Is this your own idea or did others tell you this about me?'

This is precisely in the spirit of Joshua's response to Annas, and has much the same effect on Pilate. He snaps back: 'Am *I* a Jew? It is *your* people — even your chief priests — who have brought you to me. *What have you done?*'

Joshua proceeds to answer the original question. Now we hear his realisation of the situation he faces, and, perhaps, the more terrible realisation: why he is in this situation.

'My kingdom isn't of this world. If my kingdom *was* of this world, my supporters would have fought to prevent me being turned over to the Jews. But *now* my kingdom isn't from here ...' (John's Jesus being turned over to 'the Jews' is rather like King Charles 1 being turned over to 'the English'. John probably means 'the Jerusalemites' — the Temple faction).

John proceeds to indulge himself with some characteristic verbal embroidery but has Joshua deliver a tacit admission of Messiahship, which all the Gospels show him making before Pilate:

> 'You say I am a king. For this I was born. And for this I came into the world: that I should bear witness to the truth. Everyone who is concerned with the truth hears my voice.'

Here, in spite of a characteristic ambiguity, Joshua speaks like John. The embroidery is like a curtain across the scene; yet shapes are visible. Joshua says something that convinces Pilate he is dealing with a man whose life has been passionately dedicated to a search for truth. Pilate has had few dealings with honest men; and even the murderous Tiberius Caesar was occasionally disarmed by honesty. Pilate may consider Joshua's dawning recognition of an unworldly kingdom as impossibly deluded, while also accepting that this is the truth as he *now* sees it. The prefect's reaction can be read as sneering or cynical; or it can tell us that he is challenged by something he sees in this extraordinary man, *this enemy of Caiaphas*. Pilate's response has a chiselled edge of reality,

'What *is* truth?'

The prefect turns to the high priest and gives his verdict: 'I cannot find this man guilty on a single count.'

At this point, John's account crumbles into Gospel orthodoxy. Joshua has, effectively, confessed to the most serious charge brought against him. Pilate has chosen to ignore that confession and deny Caiaphas's bid for a quick execution. He could defend the decision on the grounds that the prisoner brought before him is simply a harmless crank who has irritated the Jewish religious authorities; he offers no threat to Caesar or Rome. Yet, having supposedly delivered his verdict, Pontius Pilate, a man with supreme power in the province, answerable only to Caesar, seeks to achieve Joshua's release not on the basis of that verdict, but supposedly in accord with a *Jewish* custom of releasing a prisoner at festival time.

Nothing is known of such a custom in any source outside the Gospels and even one of the Gospels rejects the idea. The most reliable manuscripts (and translations) of Luke omit the King James Version's *Luke* 23:17 — 'And he had to release one [prisoner] to them at the feast.' In Luke's original text,

Pilate offers to flog Jesus and release him but the crowd spontaneously ask for the release of Barabbas, 'a man who had been imprisoned for rebellion and murder' (*Luke* 23:25), one of at least three arrested after 'the uprising' (*Mark* 15:7) which had followed Joshua's attack on the Temple. Mark's earlier Gospel says nothing of Jesus being flogged as a condition of the release offer (which here seems to be *Pilate's* festival custom) but Mark's crowd, too, clamour for Barabbas. Matthew's Pilate also seems to follow his own convention of granting a festival amnesty and offers to release either Jesus or Barabbas. The crowd chooses Barabbas (*Luke* 23:13–19, 25; *Matthew* 27:15–20; *Mark* 15:6–11).

Confusion over the release of Barabbas extends to the man himself. Early manuscripts of *Matthew* 27:16 call him *Jesus* Barabbas — and this compounds the problem (or, some insist, solves it). 'Barabbas' could represent *Bar Rabba* (or *Rabban*), 'Son of the Master' (or 'Teacher'), or *Bar Abba*, 'Son of the Father'. 'Abba' could also be used as an honorific title and — by Joshua — as a name for God. So, who is Jesus Barabbas? Theories abound, some of them fanciful.

According to Eisler, he is 'the son of a venerable doctor of the law' accidentally caught up in 'the uprising'; for Brandon, he is a prominent figure in Jesus' own movement, arrested at the same time. Eisenman sees Jesus Barabbas as Jesus' 'alter ego or double' and parallels Pilate's release of Barabbas with his release of Jesus as described in the Slavonic Josephus.

To the Jewish scholar, Maccoby, Barabbas is Jesus himself — Jesus Son of Abba — and he suggests that the Gospels present a garbled version of the Jewish crowd calling for *Jesus'* release. For Crossan, Barabbas personifies the Zealots who fought each other for control of Jerusalem when the city was besieged by the Romans in 68 AD. The people's choice of 'an armed rebel over an unarmed saviour' represents 'a symbolic dramatisation of Jerusalem's fate'. This 'Gospel fiction' view is supported by Funk. 'Barabbas … in *Mark* 15:7 is certainly a fiction, as is Simon of Cyrene, the father of Alexander and Rufus, in *Mark* 10:46'. Such certainty may prove presumptuous.

Australians have provided the most colourful theories. Joyce identifies Barabbas as the son of Jesus and Mary Magdalene and suggests that the story as we have it is 'a distorted echo' of behind-the-scenes bargaining which saw Jesus take his son's place as the condemned man. To Thiering, Barabbas is the disciple Thaddeus (really the Messianic rebel Theudas, formerly The Prodigal Son) and his name means 'Servant of Abba' — Abba, in this case, being the heir presumptive to the Temple high-priesthood, Caiaphas's brother-in-law, Jonathan.

In perhaps the most plausible scenario, Barabbas is simply a crowd-pleasing activist whose release can cause some embarrassment to Pilate but none to the Temple. The incident *could* be a total invention to reinforce the picture of heartless Jews and humane prefect, though acceptance of the name *Jesus* Barabbas would make it far less likely to be an invention.

In view of the unresolvable problems of the Barabbas incident, it is perhaps not surprising that this element completely disrupts John's account. After Barabbas is released, Pilate — for no apparent reason — sends Joshua to be flogged.

In Mark and Matthew, Pilate has Jesus flogged as a first step in the process of crucifixion. In Luke, Pilate *speaks* of flogging as a punishment to precede Jesus' release. The problem is that, in Roman practice, a flogging could be either a prelude to execution or a punishment in itself. John *later* implies that Pilate intended to have Joshua flogged as an alternative to the crucifixion being demanded by the Jews. If this is the case, there seems to be a critical breakdown in communication.

Before crucifixion, a prisoner was given a particularly severe flogging, an outwardly brutal practice with a strange humanity to it. The more the victim was weakened by whipping, the shorter the time he could survive worse torture on the cross. All evidence suggests that the soldiers charged with flogging Joshua treat him as a crucifixion victim. He is stripped and viciously scourged — probably by two flagellators, one right-handed, one left-handed, wielding two-thonged whips with little lead dumbells (*plumbatae*) or pieces of bone at the end of each thong. This is the Roman *flagrum*, nicknamed 'the scorpion'. After an incalculable time, Joshua's back, buttocks, chest and legs are covered with a cross-hatching of twin rips to the flesh. Only twenty-five lashes by each flagellator would inflict a hundred wounds. Pilate's soldiers then untie their prisoner, plait a crown of thorns and force it onto his head, drawing more blood. They put a purple robe on him, jeering: 'Hail, the king of the Jews!', while others strike him. It is all completely in character as a prelude to crucifixion. These are the men who crucify victims in unusual positions, 'by way of jest' (Josephus, *Wars* 5, 11, 1).

Bloodied, weakened and perhaps a figure of strange dignity in the contemptuous costume, Joshua is taken back to Pilate and the Temple party. Because Pilate continues to oppose 'the Jews', John's account suggests that Pilate had not intended it to be the especially brutal pre-crucifixion beating; if so, Pilate would hope that this degree of bloodshed could satisfy Caiaphas and his allies. John tells us that the prefect gestures, 'There, the man!'

It isn't enough. Caiaphas has determined that 'the man' must die. It is not a question of cruelty or vindictiveness. It is about the survival of a caste and a class and a people — *perhaps* in reverse priority, but, to Caiaphas, inseparable. So there is more talk, more unlikely exits and entrances by the prefect.

The Gospels have a Jewish crowd screaming: 'Crucify him!' without explaining why. Matthew has Pilate wash his hands and declare: 'I am innocent of this man's blood. *You* can see to it!' The crowd yells back: 'His blood be on us and on our children!' (*Matthew* 27:24–5). This is bad enough, but Luke goes even further in this blatant process of sanitising Pilate's role and vilifying the Jews. Three times the prefect tells the bloodthirsting mob that he cannot find Jesus guilty. He speaks of a flogging *but doesn't carry it out*. He even sends his prisoner to Herod and it is the Jewish tetrarch who lets his soldiers abuse Jesus and then puts a 'brilliant' robe on him before sending him back to Pilate. According to Luke, the Romans are not even guilty of the pre-crucifixion indignities (*Luke* 23:1–25).

In John's account it is 'the high priests and the Temple officers' who demand crucifixion (*John* 19:6). Significantly, John has more than once characterised the Sanhedrin as 'the chief priests and Pharisees'. Yet, according to his account, Pharisees play no part in this day's proceedings. Jewish and Christian scholarship supports his picture. Epstein comments: 'The Pharisees stood aloof from the whole affair.' Sanders concurs: 'According to the evidence, they had nothing to do with these events.' More than ever, with an apparent boycott of the trial by the Sanhedrin's only populist group, the Jewish mob screaming for blood seems a Gospel creation. Increasingly, the picture emerges of a select group centred on Caiaphas — priests, Sadducees and Temple officers — pressing their case before Pilate to produce what the Jewish historian Jost calls 'a private murder committed by burning enemies'.

In the weakest moment of John's account, the men from the Temple tell Pilate: 'We have a Law and according to our Law he should die because he has made himself Son of God,' introducing a spurious and irrelevant religious element which supposedly frightens Pilate. This is almost certainly a Gentile corruption of John's text. His Gospel does not mention a divine conception and, as a Jew, he knows that 'Son of God' is a Davidic title that could not possibly merit death under the Law. The statement leads nevertheless to a remarkable exchange.

When Joshua refuses to answer Pilate's questions, the prefect snaps in frustration: 'Don't you know that I have the authority to crucify you? and the authority to let you go?' Joshua's reply seems baffling: 'You wouldn't have one shred of authority over me unless it had been given to you from above. *So the one who handed me over to you is guilty of a greater sin'* [my italics] (*John* 19:11).

Theologians turn themselves inside out dealing with this speech. Pilate's authority is from Caesar. Who had 'handed over' Joshua to Pilate? Caiaphas or Judas. Yet neither of these had anything to do with Caesar. Process of elimination leads to an awkward result. Only one possible source of Pilate's authority had also delivered Joshua into the prefect's hands, or 'betrayed' him. The guiltier party is God. It is a very human, very understandable reaction; but one we cannot believe that John intended. Perhaps it's a case of John's bad Greek failing to convey what he meant …

After even more of John's contrived comings and goings on the part of Pilate, we hear a voice apparently inside the praetorium. It is supposedly the voice of 'the Jews' who clamour outside; but the words we hear are not those of men howling for blood. This is unmistakably the voice of Caiaphas:

> 'If you release him you are not Caesar's friend. Anyone who makes himself a king, speaks against Caesar.' (*John* 19:12)

The historian, Sherwin-White, a specialist in Roman law, sees here, 'a convincing technicality'. To him, the statement 'recalls the frequent manipulation of the treason law for political ends in Roman public life, and uses a notable political term — *Caesaris amicus* ["Caesar's friend"] — to enforce its point.'

Three years before this, in 30 AD, when many believe that Joshua stood before Pilate, those words would have had little effect. Pilate did not need to be considered Caesar's friend when he was Sejanus's friend. But now, in this spring of 33 AD, that 'notable political term' summons images of the bodies rotting on the Gemonian steps until they are raked into the Tiber, to be replaced by more bodies of Sejanus's friends (Tacitus, *Annals* 6,18).

Caiaphas has won. But note that he has won, not on the spurious grounds of blasphemy supposedly introduced in an eleventh hour change of strategy (*John* 19:7); Pilate could release a blasphemer and remain Caesar's friend. Caiaphas has won on the grounds of Messiaship, which has been revealed in this trial, for the first time in the Gospels, as a political issue — one that is potent enough to threaten even the Prefect of Judaea.

John ends his account of the trial by resigning himself to the same regrettable ambiguity as Matthew, Mark and Luke. 'So he handed him over to *them* so he could be crucified' [my italics] (*John* 19:16). Predictably, Luke goes furthest. 'He handed Jesus over to them to do with as they wished' (*Luke* 23:28).

Pilate handed his prisoner over to no-one but his own soldiers. Joshua was in Roman hands and remained in Roman hands for a Roman execution of a kind almost exclusively reserved for rebels against Rome and runaway slaves. Joshua was probably dressed in his own clothes again, and, against all portrayals in art, literature, film and drama, the crown of thorns might have been removed.

He would be nailed and/or tied on the *crux humilis* after being marched to the place of execution outside the city, carrying the *patibulum*, the cross-beam, on his shoulders. He would also have a *titulus*, a sign proclaiming his crime, hung around his neck, later to be set on the cross. This sign gives us the final definition of the proceedings that had occupied much of the morning. Matthew has it proclaim: 'This is Jesus king of the Jews' (*Matthew* 27:37), while Mark and Luke have simply, 'King of the Jews', with Luke adding that it was in Hebrew, Latin and Greek (*Mark* 15:26; *Luke* 23:38).

John records that Pilate personally worded the sign. It reads: 'Jesus of Nazareth the king of the Jews' (in religious art often shown as INRI, initials of the Latin form). John agrees that it is in three languages — a sizeable board — and tells how 'the Chief priests' object and ask Pilate to alter the wording to: 'This man claimed, "I am king of the Jews."' Pilate won't budge. He gives himself one last, rather sad victory and pronounces: 'What I have written, I have written' (*John* 19:19–22).

The varying details of the sign's wording change nothing. The Gospels are unanimous in what it tells us: that their Jesus was charged with a crime against Rome, that he was found guilty of that crime under Roman law and is about to suffer slow death by a specifically Roman form of torture. The guilt for the death is Pilate's. The case for his defence presented or created by the Gospels is weaker than that of a war criminal who pleads that he was acting under orders. Pilate was under no-one's orders. Prompted eventually by pure self-preservation, he had accepted the advice of a man with a very specific agenda, which, while certainly suiting the interests of the priests and Sadducees, also considered the best interests of the Jewish people.

In the end, Caiaphas's advice was probably also in the best interests of Pontius Pilate. If the prefect had refused to crucify Joshua out of sheer adversarial stubbornness, his action would have been almost indefensible in terms of his duty to the emperor. Any man, however deluded, who claimed kingship in a province governed by Rome, was indeed speaking against Caesar. Joseph Caiaphas could look Pilate in the eye, allowing himself perhaps the slightest trace of a smile, and declare: 'We have no king but Caesar' (*John* 19:15).

Many modern scholars insist that Joshua did not claim Messiahship — that he was framed on this capital charge by Pilate and the Jews. If so, it is very odd that the first Christians and the Gospellers reacted to this miscarriage of justice by taking the key piece of false evidence against their master — that he claimed to be the King Messiah — and adopting it as his title. Every Christian who called his Jesus 'the Christ' was accepting and confirming the purported lie that justified his execution. To the unscholarly mind it seems an unlikely way to behave.

Joshua was marched out of the praetorium and across the *Gabbatha* down to the street running below it towards the city's western *Gennath* ('Garden') Gate. The Via Dolorosa ('Way of Sorrow'), *Jesus'* route to crucifixion as revered by Christians, starts on the other side of the Temple mount at the site of the Antonia fortress (where it was imagined that the trial took place) and runs virtually in the opposite direction. Its Stations of the Cross, marking incidents in the Passion story, were only finalised in the nineteenth century and are often Apocryphal (Jesus falling, seeing his mother, having his brow mopped by St Veronica, etc.). If these sites had existed, they would now be buried 20 or 30 metres below the detritus of two millennia and the rubble of Joshua's Jerusalem, which was totally destroyed thirty-seven years after his death.

Joshua's painful journey to death, struggling along the street with the rough, 20-kilogram beam across his lacerated shoulders, seems lost forever, never more than at Easter when the devout, with touching piety and emotion, follow the wrong route from fictitious station to fictitious station, investing this 'unhistorical' course with its own special sanctity. Yet in this last decade of the millennium, Joshua's neglected way to the cross and Jesus' Via Dolorosa have dramatically intersected — not at a place, but in an incident.

The Fifth Station of the Cross is at the corner of Jerusalem's King Solomon Street where the Via Dolorosa strikes west towards the Church of the Holy Sepulchre. Here, a small chapel preserves on its wall a stone bearing what is claimed to be the miraculous imprint of Jesus' hand, supposedly marking the place where he fell and where the Romans made Simon of Cyrene carry his cross. The traditional explanation of the incident — that Jesus had been exhausted by the flogging — is highly credible, though Mark does not mention Jesus falling. He simply says:

> And they brought him out [of the praetorium] to execute him. And they forced a passer-by coming from his field, Simon of Cyrene, *Father of Alexander* and Rufus, to carry his cross. [my italics]　　　　　　　　　　　　　　　(*Mark* 15:21)

During excavation of a Jerusalem building site, a white limestone ossuary was found, inscribed in Greek, 'Alexander son of Simon of Cyrene'. The detail of the crucifixion story that is confirmed by this inscription seems unimportant, even trivial; yet this is the very reason why it is impressive. There is no theological reason to show that Jesus was unable to carry his cross. It is simply an incident that might illuminate whether or not he was given a brutal pre-crucifixion flogging, though no Gospel uses it to make this point. It is unrelated, unexplained, merely recorded — except by John, perhaps because the detail seems to diminish the stature of his Jesus by betraying human weakness. And this is the point.

The ossuary inscription quietly affirms that, contrary to the views of many modern scholars — and of a prominent US churchman — we are not dealing here with a ghastly fairytale cobbled together from a collection of biblical prophecies supposedly describing the death of a 'suffering Messiah'. We are dealing with the real death of a real man, as real as the bones of Alexander, son of Simon, who might have been there that Friday two thousand years ago; who certainly would have heard his father tell how he had been dragooned into carrying a condemned man's crossbeam in a Roman execution procession.

Priest-archeologist Jerome Murphy-O'Connor has commented: 'The Via Dolorosa is defined by faith, not by history.' Jesus' way to the cross is symbolised by the Fifth Station's miraculous handprint in stone. *Joshua's* last journey is symbolised by the touchable reality of the ossuary's roughly incised inscription. It seems to offer a firmer foundation for faith.

CHAPTER 25

The Place of the Skull

The Roman crucifixion squad marched Joshua some 200 metres along Jerusalem's paved streets and out through the Gennath Gate, set at the end of a short stretch of east-west city wall where it right-angled to the north — a reversed 'L' facing out to a large, sunken area of level ground, some of it taken up by orchard and garden.

The developing city had avoided this place because, for 600 years, it was a quarry for high-grade *meleke* limestone. It had been abandoned about 100 years before, and, according to archaeologist Virgilio Corbo, given a layer of reddish-brown soil to cover the geometrically pitted rock floor and provide an area for cultivation. In another theory, the soil accumulated naturally over the century and seeds were spread by winds and birds. Some cereal crops grew here, with olive, fig and carob trees.

Roads from the north, west and south converged on the Gennath Gate, but in spite of the levelled ground and trees, this was probably not a popular camping place for pilgrims. Tombs were cut into the western cliff-face of the quarry, and, opposite them, by the higher eastern scarp, which was also honeycombed with tombs, an outcrop of poorer-grade limestone had been left by the quarrymen. It loomed among the bare fig trees, the evergreen carobs and olives — a blunt, grey-white knob 13 metres high, with two cavities near its base like the dark eye-sockets of a skull. This forbidding feature blighted the site and earned it its name — The Place of the Skull, or simply, The Skull, Hebrew *Gulgoleth*, Aramaic *Gulgulta*, rendered in the Gospels as Golgotha. The Latin translation, *Calvaria*, gives us Calvary, the name by

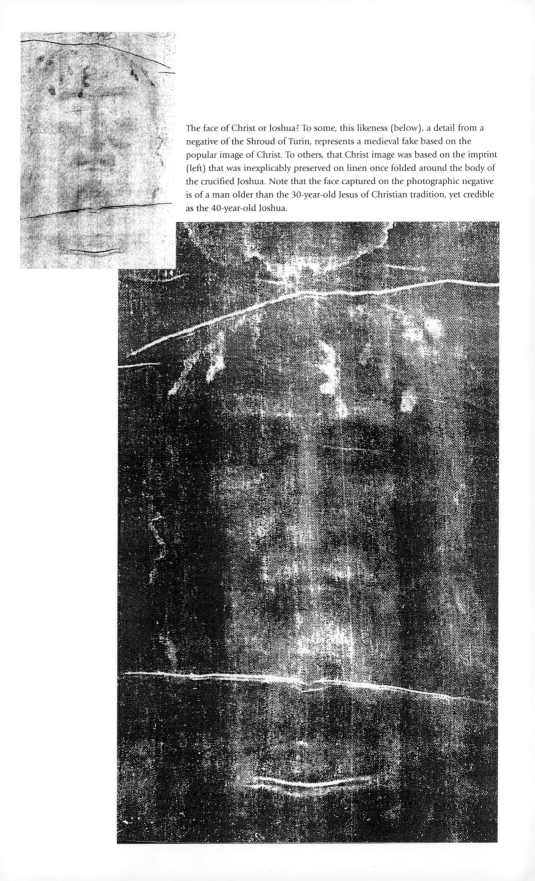

The face of Christ or Joshua? To some, this likeness (below), a detail from a negative of the Shroud of Turin, represents a medieval fake based on the popular image of Christ. To others, that Christ image was based on the imprint (left) that was inexplicably preserved on linen once folded around the body of the crucified Joshua. Note that the face captured on the photographic negative is of a man older than the 30-year-old Jesus of Christian tradition, yet credible as the 40-year-old Joshua.

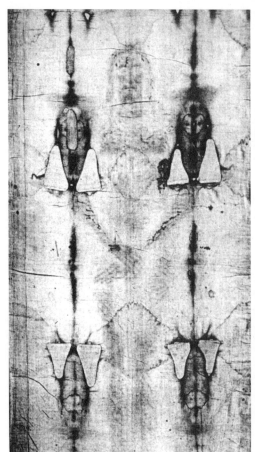 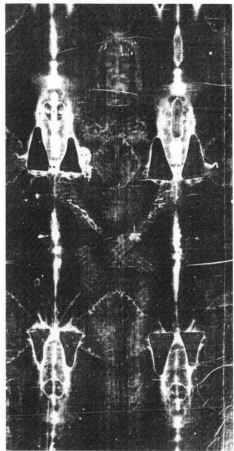

At left, the frontal image from the Shroud of Turin (slightly intensified), showing pale, yellow-brown discolorations, bloodstains and partially-repaired scorch marks from a 1532 fire. In 1988 this remarkable artifact was apparently exposed as a medieval forgery when the cloth was carbon-dated to the thirteenth or fourteenth centuries AD. Yet no-one has satisfactorily explained how even the most brilliant medieval artist could create a perfect negative. When the shroud is photographed in black-and-white, the negative reveals the totally realistic image seen at right.

The seventeenth-century artist Della Rovere painted the enshrouding of Jesus to illustrate the creation of the Shroud of Turin images. Apart from the grieving women on hand (and the involvement of a typically clean-shaven John), the reconstruction is plausible.

which most Christians know the place where Jesus died.

In spite of the popular view, there is no evidence that this was Jerusalem's usual killing field. Crucifixions were carried out wherever the crime had been committed or in a place where passers-by could ponder the fate of those who defied the rule and law of Rome. Golgotha qualified on the second count — and it was close to the praetorium, only about 150 metres north-west of the Gennath Gate.

At the gate or near The Skull, the squad probably met a party of soldiers bringing the other condemned men from the Antonia — at least two of them, possibly more. John simply tells us, 'they crucified him and two others with him, one to either side and Jesus in the middle' (*John* 19:18). These were *lestai* — rebels, freedom fighters.

Luke says that Jesus and the two *lestai* were 'under the same sentence' — *en to auto krimati* (Luke 23:40). Eisler argues that the phrase means 'on a similar charge'. This apart, Romans were methodical and the arrangement of the three victims is significant, a fact recognised by Matthew Henry whose reverent eighteenth-century commentary touches historical truth in a way he did not intend:

> He was crucified in the midst between two thieves (*sic*), as if he had been the worst of the three. He was not only treated as a transgressor, but numbered with them, the worst of them. (Henry on *Luke* 23:33)

The Romans were treating Joshua as a rebel leader, executed with at least two of his 'followers'. In purely historical terms, these crucifixions at Golgotha on Friday 3 April, 33 AD, were virtually indistinguishable from countless thousands of others carried out in the land of Israel during the Roman occupation. For this reason, by Talmudic times when Joshua's life had assumed a new significance as the focus of an increasingly hostile Gentile sect, authentic traditions were hard to recover and often clouded with polemic. Nevertheless, in a rabbinical discussion Joshua is recalled as 'a revolutionary' (*Sanhedrin* 43a), there is an allusion to his kingship and to his being crucified as a *listis,* Hebrew for 'robber', echoing the Greek *lestes* (*Tosephta Sanhedrin* 9, 7). And he is confused with a robber chief called Ben Netzer, 'a robber among kings and a king among robbers' (*Bereshith Rabba* 76).

It becomes clear why none of the Twelve could be here — or the Seventy. It was not a matter of being fainthearted. It was a matter of staying alive — not being nailed to crosses as known followers of a condemned rebel.

John Mark, respectable young man about town, with no telltale Galilean accent to betray him, could risk following his master to this final scene. His account of what happens is mercifully unadorned. The other Gospellers have stories of the Jerusalem crowd, the scribes, priests and even the two *lestai* mocking Jesus. They are sad and fantastic products of the same enmity which coloured the more extreme rabbinical traditions. In John's eyewitness account, there are no mockers. The only onlookers he mentions, apart from himself, are Joshua's mother, Mary, her unnamed sister and Mary Magdalene. And, of course, the Roman auxiliaries, who, after the wretched guardroom horseplay at the scourging, seem to conduct the actual execution with more humanity — though we must be wary of the other side of the Gospel medal, as when Matthew, Mark and Luke show the centurion in charge of the executions declaring that Jesus was 'the Son of God' (*Matthew* and *Mark*), or in *Luke*, 'an innocent man' (often translated as 'a righteous man' or even 'the Righteous One'), a preposterous contrast with the insults and derision of 'the Jews' (*Matthew* 27:54; *Mark* 15:39; *Luke* 23:47).

All the Gospellers edge around the inescapable fact that their Jesus was tortured to death by Romans. Mark suggests that 'they' offer Jesus 'wine mixed with myrrh' (*Mark* 15:23). The ambiguity may be unintentional. This was a Jewish custom intended to blunt the agony to come, the wine and myrrh (or incense) paid for by the *charburat ir*, a charitable organisation of Jerusalem women (*Sanhedrin* 43a). Mark tells us that Jesus declined the opiate and the execution proceeded.

Joshua was stripped naked and stretched on his back on the ground, arms extended along the crossbeam. A nail was driven through each hand at the very base of the palm — a hand-forged iron spike 15 cm to 18 cm long, square-sectioned with a flat, round head and tapered straight to an ice-pick point. A single hammer blow would drive that point between four small carpal bones and below or through a transverse carpal ligament. Second and subsequent blows would force the bones apart and drive the nail down into the wood, convulsing Joshua's thumb across his palm in a reflex action as a flexor muscle and the median nerve of the hand were damaged, causing, in the words of twentieth-century surgeon Henri Barbet, 'the most horrible pain'. With both Joshua's hands nailed to the crossbeam, it was lifted, dragging him upwards, clear of the ground, and attached to the *stipes*, the upright post — perhaps even a tree trunk (the word *stipes* can mean precisely that and the only crucifixion victim whose bones were ever recovered — outside Jerusalem in 1968 — had been hung on an olive trunk. Five *New Testament* passages speak of Jesus being crucified on a 'tree'.)

Joshua's full weight was borne by the two nails, the injured nerves stretched over them, again in Barbet's words, 'like the strings of a violin on their bridge'. In his agony, Joshua would have been almost unaware of his feet being nailed to the *stipes*, probably crossed one over the other, with a single spike hammered into the upper instep and through both feet into the wood. At least he could relieve the pain of his hands and the suffocating strain on his chest by taking some of the weight on that third spike — though at the cost of another source of pain and a cramping stress on partly bent legs. These torments could be relieved by letting himself sag back again on his outstretched arms ... and so it went on for several hours. As Seneca would write, 'Those condemned to such a death lose their life drop by drop.' (*Epistulae* 101,14).

In John's taut account of this death on the cross, Joshua speaks only a dozen words, most of them during an exchange directly involving John Mark.

> Then seeing his mother and his beloved disciple standing nearby, Jesus says to his mother, 'Woman, here is your son.' Then he says to his disciple, 'There is your mother.' *And from that hour*, the disciple took her into his own home. [my italics]   (*John* 19:26)

Mary would have a husband and four surviving sons to look after her, but at least three of the sons and possibly her husband were fugitives and her only home was in distant Galilee. The exchange is the clearest possible indication that 'the beloved disciple' we identify as John Mark lived nearby, that he could provide a home for Mary, here in Jerusalem, and that he had the means to care for her. It will emerge that Mary Magdalene also finds shelter with him and that Peter is already in hiding at his house.

Joshua's cross was attended by a *quaternion* — a four-man squad. John tells us that his clothes were shared among them, as acknowledged in Roman Law (*Digest* 48,20,6); but when it came to his tunic, because it was a priestly garment, 'seamless, woven from the top in one piece', the soldiers said: 'Let's not tear it up; we'll throw dice to see who gets it' (*John* 19:23-4a). This is a convincing detail, but unfortunately John proceeds in Matthew-like vein to tell us that this was, 'so the scriptures could be fulfilled, which said, "They divided my garments among them; they cast lots for my garments" ' (*John* 19:24b; *Psalm* 22:18).

Psalm 22, according to many scholars, is the actual source — or at least the major source — of the crucifixion story. Even when it is not actually cited by the Gospellers to show 'prophecy fulfilled', it foreshadows details of the narrative, as in the passage:

All who see me, mock me,
they wag their heads and sneer:
'He trusted in the Lord,
let the Lord save him.
If the Lord thinks so much of him,
let him rescue him.'   (*Psalm* 22:6b–8)

Matthew, Mark and Luke's heartless and derisive Jewish onlookers also 'mock' and 'sneer'. They too 'wag their heads' and say, 'He trusted in God, let him rescue him if he wants to' (*Matthew* 27:39–44; *Mark* 15:29–32; *Luke* 23:35–9).

It seems that there are two alternatives: either the Psalm foreshadowed the death of Jesus to an impressive degree, or the Gospellers shamelessly adopted details from this and other Psalms and from the Prophets to lend theological weight to this ugly event; a first step in taking this unexpected and disastrous end to the story and turning it into the climax of Jesus' life as foretold by David and the Prophets.

There is another explanation. The *Tanakh* was the major influence on Joshua's thought processes. We overhear rabbinical discussion in the Talmud and marvel at the facility with which lore and Law is illuminated by scripture. There is always a passage at hand to support a point of view on the most obscure of topics. This was the Pharisaic tradition in which Joshua's whole approach to life had developed; the tradition by which his journey to Golgotha had been shaped.

Here, nailed to a cross in these last tortured hours of consciousness, one question would burn: 'Why?' No man could have tried harder, or more passionately, to discover God's intention for him; no man could have devoted himself more faithfully to carrying out that intention; no man could have shown greater faith, in placing his life in God's hands as he had done. He had not sought Messiahship; he had avoided the role as long as was humanly possible. In the end, he had accepted it as his destiny only because this was where God had led him. Yet *this* was the end of it. His Messiahship proclaimed on a board nailed to the trunk above his head, his humanity proclaimed by the flesh nailed to wood below it. Could this be what God intended for the Son of David? If he was not the Messiah, he had misunderstood God's will. Perhaps he saw that now.

Yet that would mean that God had some other plan for him — otherwise his whole life had been dedicated to this obscenity; and how could such butchery be God's will? In this darkest moment of his life, Joshua found expression for his torment in a bitter paraphrase of the opening words of *Psalm* 22, words written by David in what seemed *his* darkest hour. Matthew and Mark recorded the cry as it was uttered: *'Eli, Eli, lama sabachthani?'*, and translated it in the words of the psalm: 'My God, my God, why have you forsaken me?'

For centuries, that cry has disturbed Christians. It seems the ultimate expression of human doubt, human aloneness, human despair — the ultimate definition of Joshua's humanity. Yet it understates the depth of his alienation.

The Psalm has *asavtani* — 'forsaken me'. Joshua's cry ended with, *sabachthani* — 'slaughtering me', as in *Deuteronomy* 12:21: 'you shall slaughter (*sabachta*) of your herd and flock'. Attempts to turn the cry into an Aramaic transliteration of the psalm simply obscure the fact that this expression of primal despair accused God of something more than abandonment; it accused him of this atrocity: 'My God, my God, why are *you* slaughtering me?'.

John, of all people, would have known what Joshua said. He did not record it. Perhaps it was obliterated from his memory as something *his* Jesus would not say; and so did not say it. Luke, too, rejected it as inappropriate to his picture of Jesus.

One thing is clear. Even in the form of the direct quotation from *Psalm* 22, 'the cry of derelection' could not be a Gospel creation. It seems here that we are dealing with Gospel truth; and having paraphrased the psalm's beginning, Joshua's quotation (or paraphrase) of its last line with his last breath would be perfectly believable from a devout Jew.

Perhaps it is only to be expected that once Joshua had quoted *Psalm* 22, it would be searched for other insights into those last hours of his life, encouraging further links with scripture.

In a challenging collision of prophecy and fact, all the Gospels agree that, as he hung on the cross, Jesus was offered or given vinegar to drink — a clear echo of *Psalm* 69 (which resonates with Psalm 22:14–15, a powerful portrayal of the agony of thirst).

> They gave me poison to eat,
> And when I was thirsty,
> They gave me vinegar to drink.   (*Psalm* 69:21)

Luke has the soldiers offer Jesus vinegar while they are mocking him; it is portrayed as an act of cruelty (*Luke* 23:36). According to Matthew and Mark, when Jesus gives his cry of despair, an unspecified man runs to fetch a sponge filled with vinegar and offers it on a reed or stick (*Matthew* 27:48; *Mark* 15:36).

Apparently supporting the scenario of what Crossan calls 'not history remembered but prophecy historicised', John tells us that when his Jesus calls, 'I am thirsty,' it is 'so that the scriptures may be fulfilled'. John then describes a spongeful of vinegar being impossibly raised to Jesus' mouth on hyssop, a spriggy, mint-like plant which could never support such a weight (*John* 19:28–9). Deepening our suspicion of John's account, hyssop was used for sprinkling lamb's blood in the inauguration of the Passover (*Exodus* 12:22). This dubious scene is abruptly transformed when 'hyssop' is recognised as a mistranslation — a confusion between *hyssopos*, hyssop, and *hyssos*, a javelin. (Intriguingly, in Hebrew, javelin is *hanith* and a reed is *kaneth*, suggesting the possibility of a similar confusion in Mark's source.)

Immediately it is clear why vinegar was offered. *Posca*, vinegar-and-water, was the normal refreshment of Roman soldiers; it has been said, 'The Roman army marched on vinegar'. When Joshua said he was thirsty, one of the auxiliaries went to their jug of *posca*, soaked some into a sponge, impaled it on a javelin and raised it to Joshua's lips. As Leonard Cottrell comments: 'he was performing a charitable act. It was his own standard drink'. We are back to the reality of the *quaternion* assigned to this wretched duty and it becomes easier to see John making the link to scripture rather than scripture providing the inspiration for the incident.

There is a problem in trying to see the crucifixion as either a pastiche of prophecies or as a sequence of events recorded precisely as they happened. The alternatives are not mutually exclusive. Given the fact that Joshua was crucified (and the greatest advocates of 'Gospel fiction' seem to concede that much), there are certain inescapable details of the crucifixion process that can be linked to passages from the Psalms and Prophets. The fact that the Gospellers eagerly fastened on these links does not mean that the details are fictitious.

In most cases, a crucified man was 'pierced' and people would 'look at him' (*John* 19:37; *Zechariah* 12:10). In the course of several hours he would become thirsty. Vinegar was the most readily available drink from a Roman execution squad and the sponge on the javelin is a particularly convincing detail. Given that the victim's clothing was the perquisite of the executioners, some means of dividing up that clothing was inevitable. Yet all this does not justify a blanket classification of the Gospel's crucifixion story as historically factual. While it is true that 'the cry of dereliction' is almost inconceivable as fiction, the mocking Jews and marvelling centurion are equally hard to accept as fact. It is not a case of 'either … or' — least of all in *John* (who omits both of these extremes). His surprisingly restrained and highly credible narrative is nevertheless characterised by four direct scriptural allusions in the space of fourteen verses, with three repetitions of the formula, 'that the scriptures might be fulfilled'. This is John's frame for his picture of the crucifixion — an elaborate and distracting frame. His picture does not need it and deserves respect in its own right.

John does not tell us when Joshua was crucified or how long he hung on the cross. He reports that Pilate 'delivered' Joshua to crucifixion while he was in the praetorium at 'about the sixth hour', about midday (*John* 19:14–15). Mark places the actual crucifixion three hours before this at the third hour — about 9 am — and has Jesus die soon after the ninth hour — 3 pm (*Mark* 15:25, 34–7). Some scholars simply transfer Mark's time of death to John's account and have Jesus die, supposedly after only three hours on the cross, airily ignoring the fact that Mark's Jesus had survived for six hours.

According to John's time frame, Joshua could have been nailed to the cross by about 12:30 pm. At that very time, in the Temple beyond the white cliffs of the quarry and the western wall of the city, the sacrifice of the tens of thousands of Passover lambs began (*Pesachim* 5,1). It is often suggested that John adjusted his timing of the crucifixion to symbolise Joshua's sacrificial death. It is hard to believe that he would have contrived this without mentioning either the time or the sacrifices; he was not given to such subtlety. John, the inveterate sermoniser, does not even give Joshua anything approaching a last speech, though his last words may be taken as a quotation from the last sentence of Psalm 22.

According to John, the end came very simply, immediately after Joshua had sucked the *posca* from the sponge:

> Then when Jesus had taken the vinegar, he said, 'It is finished.' And, bowing his head, he gave up his spirit.
>
> (*John* 19:30)

It is magnificently anti-climactic. It is also very real. Theories swirl around the moment like flies. The death comes too soon; crucified men could last for days; the vinegar is drugged, part of a plot to fake death and rescue Jesus — all easily answered. Men *could* last for days, when they were *tied* on the cross and/or given a *sedile*, a seat-or-saddle-like support to ease the suffocating strain on chest and arms. With only nailed feet and hands to support him, a man weakened by brutal flogging and tortured by damaged median nerves would lose consciousness comparatively quickly. Once he fainted and hung by his arms without respite, he would soon die from a combination of circulatory failure and suffocation. As for the drug, unless the Roman army was part of the plot, the theory cannot work. As with every form of capital punishment in every age, the soldiers would guard against their prisoner being given anything to eat or drink that might contain poison and spoil the ritual and the deterrent spectacle of execution.

Given Joshua's extraordinary ability to transmit healing energy — ability acknowledged by his most bitter critics — it is hardly surprising that when the only two alternatives were prolonged agony or death, he simply chose to surrender his own life force — as graphically described by John. In 'bowing his head', Joshua let himself hang forward, increasing the strain on arms and chest, then 'gave up his spirit', or, precisely as written by John, 'gave up his breath', his *pneuma*.

Because John had avoided the terrible cry of despair, the issue of Joshua coming to terms with what was happening to him did not arise. Luke, too, had omitted that unsettling admission of his Jesus feeling alienated from God. Yet one senses that he knew of it and sought some sign of Jesus becoming reconciled to his fate; in effect, becoming reconciled with God. Luke achieved this with a final prayer, a line from a psalm, which captures superbly the simple acceptance of death portrayed by John — almost as though, while he was in Jerusalem, Luke the historian had spoken with John Mark and drawn on his memory of that moment.

In his cry of despair, Joshua had called on *Eli*, the sometimes fearful God of Israel, as though all those years of loving God, all those years of sonship to a loving Father, were obliterated by this appalling ordeal he had been abandoned to. Then, eventually, like almost every human being suffering a protracted death, Joshua came to accept what was happening. He could not hope to understand; but he was no less a son of the Father, and, if he felt alienation, it had sprung from him, not from God. In accepting this incomprehensible event as the divine will, he again embraced God.

As a child, he had learnt a simple prayer which acknowledges the universal and timeless fear of going to sleep and never waking again. Now — perhaps remembering his own words, that unless men and women could be like children they would never enter the kingdom — he offered up that nightly childhood prayer. Joshua the man, like Joshua the child, let himself slip into oblivion with the renewed conviction that his spirit could leave his body, safely in the hands of a loving Father:

'Abba, into your hands I commit my spirit.'   (*Luke* 23:46; *Psalm* 31:5)

There was no fear of the darkness that closed around him, no anger, and at last no pain. Joshua joined his earthly father in death; he and his heavenly Father were reconciled.

✝✝✝
_____

Joshua probably died in late afternoon, his body slumped on the central cross between the two *lestai* as they continued their struggle to live and the shadow of the western quarry face reached among the trees towards the crosses.

Because the day that would begin at sunset was not only a Sabbath but also the high holy day of the festival, Pilate was asked to expedite the death of the day's crucifixion victims so their bodies could be taken down from the crosses before Friday had passed. He agreed to allow the *crurifragium*, one of the two standard procedures to hasten death by crucifixion (*John* 19:31–2).

The prefect's order was conveyed to the supervising centurion, and the execution squad smashed the legs of the two *lestai*, probably with a heavy mallet. Unable to relieve the strain on arms and chest, they could no longer fight for blood and breath. (The same 'merciful' end was apparently inflicted on the only crucifixion victim whose bones have been recovered. His shin bones had been shattered.)

Motionless on his cross between the two dying men, Joshua seemed to be dead. To make sure, one of the soldiers took a javelin and thrust the long blade up into his side (*perforatio*, the second standard procedure). John Mark was watching. He tells us:

> And blood and water came straight out. And the one who saw that happen is giving this evidence. He knows that he speaks the truth so that you, too, may believe.   (*John* 19:34b–5)

And we do believe John Mark, even though he proceeds to tell us:

> These things happened so that the scriptures might be fulfilled: 'Not a single bone of his will be broken.' And again, a different passage of scripture says: 'They shall look at the one they have pierced.'
>   (*John* 18:36–7; *Psalm* 34:20; *Exodus* 12:46; *Zechariah* 12:10)

Theories surround the blood and water that ran from the javelin wound, the phenomenon so firmly attested by John Mark. They are symbols of the Eucharist and baptism; they are proof that Jesus was alive because a corpse cannot bleed; they are proof that he was dead and his blood had decomposed; proof that the javelin had pierced his lung but missed vital organs, allowing him to survive.

Dr Henri Barbet, whose 70-year-old research on crucifixion has never been discredited, saw the flow of 'blood and water' as evidence that the javelin blade had punctured the pericardial sac — which contained clear serum (hydroperi-cardium) — and the right auricle of the heart — which contained blood. He experimented twice with syringes and twice with a knife blade, each time producing a flow of blood and clear liquid from a dead body.

What happened next is obscured in a tangle of theories and images. The classical image is the *Pieta* (Piety or Devotion), the crucified body lifted down from the cross as Mary mourns over her son in the midst of grieving male and female disciples. It defies the Gospel account, as does the polar extreme provided by modern scholarship — John Dominic Crossan's image of Jesus' body 'left on the cross or in a shallow grave barely covered with dirt and stones', to be eaten by scavenging dogs.

Between these opposites, the thickest cluster of theories surround various plots to save Jesus from death, some supposedly engineered by Jesus himself. Sometimes a drug has been administered to produce a death-like state. In every case, Jesus is rushed from the cross to a tomb where he is treated for his injuries, given an antidote or resuscitated, then carried away by dark to emerge as a resurrected Messiah and/or raise a family, dictate the Gospel of John, accompany Paul to Rome, die there (or in Kashmir) of old age or meet a violent but triumphant death among the defenders of Masada.

The place of burial varies almost as wildly. Jesus' tomb (if he has one) is west of Jerusalem near Golgotha, east of Jerusalem in the Kidron Valley near Gethsemane, north of Jerusalem at 'Gordon's Calvary' or 20 kilometres east of Jerusalem at Qumran by the Dead Sea.

All the Gospels agree that a man called Joseph of Arimathea approached Pilate for permission to bury Jesus' body. Matthew calls him 'rich', Mark and Luke identify him as a member of the Sanhedrin, with Mark adding that Joseph was 'eagerly awaiting the kingdom of God', demonstrating that he was a Pharisee. This is strongly supported by John who does not identify Joseph as a councillor or a Pharisee but has him accompanied at the burial of Jesus by Nicodemus, Pharisee member of the Sanhedrin (*Matthew* 27:57-8; *Mark* 15:43-5; *Luke* 25:50-2; *John* 19:38-9).

Joseph's involvement — a rich man burying Jesus — is rejected by many scholars because it is seen as 'fulfilment' of the prophecy: 'He was given a grave with the wicked and his death with the rich' (*Isaiah* 53:9), even though no Gospel cites this verse — and for good reasons. Isaiah — like most prophets — saw 'the rich' as automatically 'wicked'. It is simply a case of characteristic

Jewish repetition; and, if one wanted to press the point, also the exact reverse of what happened to Jesus. Some of the scholars who reject the rich Joseph and his role believe that the Apocryphal *Gospel of Peter*'s account of Jesus' death was the original source of the Gospel stories. According to *Peter*, 'Joseph, the friend of Pilate and of the Lord' asks for the body (*Gospel of Peter* 2,3). Apart from confirming Joseph's involvement, the passage indicates that he was wealthy; Pilate would hardly be the friend of a poor Jew.

Joseph, from the obscure town of 'Arimathea' (perhaps er-Ram, 8 kilometres north of Jerusalem on the Nablus road), has become the butt of several theories, some inevitably connected with a rescue plan. Schonfield, adopting a theory of Eisler, suggests that the name, 'Joseph of Arimathea' is fictitious, based on the Jewish name of the historian Josephus (Joseph bar Mattathia) or on the Greek form, *Josepou Matthias*, apparently because the whole incident echoes a passage in Josephus's autobiography in which he recognises three friends who have been crucified and asks the Roman general Titus to spare their lives. Two die, but one responds to treatment and survives (Josephus, *Life*, 75). To Donovan Joyce, Joseph from Areimeh, near Capernaum, is Mary's former husband, burying her son's body (his nephew!) in a family tomb. To Thiering, Joseph is Jesus' brother James as well as the recurring 'rich man' of parable and narrative.

There is no good reason to doubt that Joseph and the part he played in the burial of Joshua are accurately described in the Gospels, matching, as they do, what we know of the disposal of Jewish execution victims in the first century.

There was nothing out-of-the-ordinary in Joseph's request to Pilate. In fact, it would have been completely aberrant if Joshua's body — and those of the *lestai* — had not been taken from the crosses *and properly interred* before sunset. Mosaic law was specific:

> When a man is convicted of a capital offence [under Jewish Law] and his body hung on a tree [after execution], you must not leave his body on the tree overnight; you must bury it the same day. (*Deuteronomy* 21:22–3)

Even an ultimate transgressor of Jewish Law was buried in a tomb and by the *beth din* that had sentenced him.

> And they did not bury him in his ancestral tomb. But two burial places were prepared by the *beth din*, one for those who were decapitated or strangled, and the other for those who were stoned or burned. When the flesh was completely decomposed, the bones were gathered and buried in their proper place [the family tomb]. (*Sanhedrin* 46a)

When such treatment was extended to murderers, adulterers, false prophets, blasphemers, idolators and breakers of the Sabbath, it is obvious that the bodies of men who had died under Roman law — often as Jewish patriots — would be treated with equal or greater dignity. Josephus tells us:

> The Jews used to take so much care of the burial of men, that they took down those that were condemned and crucified, and buried them before the going down of the sun. (Josephus, *Wars* 4,5;2)

This makes it clear that the procedure followed by Joseph was normal — as was Pilate's permission for the removal and interment of Joshua's body. The *lestai* would have received similar treatment — though probably not from Joseph and Nicodemus.

The involvement of the two Sanhedrin members in Joshua's entombment could suggest that even in the case of Roman executions, a *beth din* accepted responsibility for burials — a possibility borne out by the fact that Joshua's mother and Mary Magdalene played no part in the process but simply followed Joseph's party to the tomb, and observed the interment, planning to return later. Much is made of the fact that the onset of the Sabbath prevented their involvement. Luke tells us that the women 'prepared spices and ointment and rested on the Sabbath according to the commandment' (*Luke* 23:56). Yet the Mishnah is quite specific that on the Sabbath it was permissible 'to make ready all that is needful for the dead body *and anoint it and wash it*' [my italics] (*Shabbath* 23,5). Certainly, if the two Marys prepared Joshua's body they could not eat that evening's Passover meal; yet it is almost unbelievable that this would stop them performing this last service for a man they loved. It is far more credible that the interment was a Roman concession to Jewish belief, carried out as an official procedure under Roman military supervision, and family members were not allowed to take part.

There were three unusual features of Joshua's burial as reported by the Gospels. Joseph bought a linen shroud for the interment (*Mark* 15:46) and, according to *John* 19:39, Nicodemus provided 'about 100 *litrae*' — some 34 kilograms — of mixed myrrh and aloes (7 kilograms more than the amount used at the burial of the great Pharisee, Gamaliel). Both were credible gestures by men of some wealth who respected Joshua and regretted or even resented his execution, instigated as it was by Sadducees, at Roman hands.

Perhaps the most unusual detail of the burial was that Joseph of Arimathea provided his own rock-cut family tomb which, until then, had not been used. It was a generous and reverential act. It was also expedient. If ancient tradition and modern archaeology are correct, Joseph's tomb — apparently in a walled

'Garden of Joseph' — was one of those cut into the western quarry face only some 40 metres from Golgotha, and sunset was rapidly approaching.

The actual handling of Joshua's body was undoubtedly carried out by servants — perhaps Gentiles. (A Jew exposed to corpse impurity would have to undergo seven days' purification and could not share that evening's Passover meal with his family — although he could eat a specially sacrificed Passover lamb exactly one month later). Joshua's body was removed from the cross — a bloody procedure because of the huge nails involved — and carried to Joseph's tomb.

The tomb and its surroundings were almost totally destroyed by pious vandalism (and a Christian-hating Caliph) over a span of more than sixteen hundred years. Its all-but- unrecognisable vestiges are now housed in a grandiose structure that forms the centrepiece of Jerusalem's Church of the Holy Sepulchre and defies belief in the site. In spite of all this, intensive archaeological work on the tomb and its environs has established its authenticity — certainly that it was revered as Jesus' burial place from the earliest days of the Jerusalem congregation — and it has been possible to reconstruct its original form.

The entrance in the white cliff face opened into an antechamber about three metres by two, cut from the rock. A doorway led to an inner burial chamber of about the same size — dimensions specified in the Mishnah (*Babha Bathra* 6, 8). An *arcosolium* was cut into one wall — a bench long enough to hold a body, with an arch carved out above it. Here, a corpse would lie until it was dehydrated. It would then be placed in one of the *khokhim* (literally, 'ovens'), narrow, deep, oven-shaped recesses carved in another wall, and left there until only bones remained, for storage in an ossuary.

Contrary to almost everything written on the subject of Joshua's burial, there was no obligation for his body to be washed. In fact to do so would have violated Jewish burial custom as applied to victims of violent death involving loss of blood. In the preceding six or eight hours the blood from innumerable wounds had collected on his flesh, including what the Mishnah called 'life-blood', shed at the moment of death. According to Jewish Law, if the 'mingled blood' amounted to only 'a quarter of a *log*' (about 0.07 of a litre), then the body had to be buried with the 'life-blood' still on it (*Zebahim* 3,1; *Oholoth* 1–3; *Niddah* 7a and b). For this reason — and because the preparation of a corpse for burial was an intimate act usually performed by the closest female relatives — it seems most likely that, as theorised by students of the Shroud of Turin, the myrrh and aloes mixture was spread on the linen and it was folded over Joshua's naked, unwashed body on the limestone bench of the *arcosolium*.

The burial party left the now-fragrant tomb and a huge stone disc like a mill wheel, a *golel*, was then rolled ponderously into position along a carved-out slot, completely blocking the entrance. The sun was probably setting, the first three stars of the Sabbath would soon appear. Joseph, Nicodemus and their helpers hurried away, the watching women and John Mark began their sad walk back to the house with the upper room on Mount Zion. In gathering dusk, the soldiers of the *quaternion* packed up their weapons and, tools, their jar of *posca*, and with each man carrying his share of Joshua's clothes, headed back to the city, to the warmth and rough camaraderie of the Antonia.

The Passover full moon had risen a few minutes after sunset. Now, in deep dusk, it appeared above the Mount of Olives beyond the eastern wall — a chilling sight. Probably blood-red through smoke from the feast's tens of thousands of cooking fires, the moon was disfigured by a dark crescent gouged from its orb in a partial eclipse.

Any eclipse of the moon was 'a bad omen for Israel', according to the Pharisee sages, and 'if its face is red as blood, a sword is coming to the world', while some said that if it occurred at sunset, 'the calamity ... hastens on its way' (*Sukkah* 19a). Who could imagine the catastrophe foreshadowed by an eclipse of the Passover moon in the very hour that Jerusalem and its quarter of a million guests prepared to eat the *seder*?

The portent was unlikely to disturb Caiaphas, Annas and their coterie. They were aware of the sages' dire pronouncements on eclipses but, as Sadducees, probably had greater faith in the prophet Jeremiah's view that such 'signs of heaven' should alarm Gentile nations, not Israel (*Jeremiah* 10:2). If the eclipse caused the Temple faction any concern it was because, in coinciding with the death of the latest prophet of their doom, this phenomenon might further unsettle Jerusalem's Passover pilgrims — always volatile, and pushed closer to the edge by the week's Messianic disturbance. If Caiaphas and his father-in-law discussed the matter, they would not let it tarnish their Passover meal; but later perhaps the problem should be addressed ...

Contrary to Christian legend, Joshua's rock-closed tomb was left unguarded that night. Whatever happened or did not happen behind the *golel* in the next twenty-four hours would reverberate to eternity.

CHAPTER 26

Empty Tomb

Friday evening's entombment of Joshua by the Pharisees, Joseph and Nicodemus, is our last glimpse of the man. Up to this point, it has been possible to trace his life through birth, ministry, bid for Messiahship, arrest, trial and execution. Now, suddenly, the trail is lost.

Christians joyfully insist that, on the contrary, the great climax of the story lies ahead; and this is unarguable. Yet that climax, that supreme fulfilment of destiny revolves not around Joshua but around the Gospels' Jesus; it involves not the man but the semi-mythological creation of almost a century's development. As biographer A. N. Wilson sees it: 'We have reached the point in our narrative where we must abandon our efforts to pursue "what really happened". Subjectivity is the only criterion of Gospel truth'. The honoured American scholar, E. P. Sanders, must admit: 'The resurrection is not, strictly speaking, part of the story of the historical Jesus, but rather belongs to the aftermath of his life'. German theologian, Gunther Bornkamm, goes further: 'The event of Christ's resurrection from the dead, his life and his eternal reign, are things removed from historical scholarship. History cannot ascertain and establish conclusively the facts about them as it can with other events of the past.' And further still ... 'We are to understand the Easter stories ... as testimonies of faith, and not as records or chronicles'. Clearly, that faith had to be built on the fact of Jesus' resurrection, so it is surprising when Professor Bornkamm dismisses as 'obviously a legend' the one piece of physical evidence that supports the story — discovery of Jesus' empty tomb by the women on Sunday morning.

The indefatigable American Bishop Spong sees the whole resurrection story (like almost every other aspect of Jesus' life) as a pious myth, this one the inspiration of Peter. In attacking Spong's views, Australian Bishop, Paul Barnett, describes how Jesus died on Friday and his tomb was found to be empty at dawn on Sunday ... 'But praise be to God the Risen One appeared to, was seen and heard and handled by, many witnesses for the next forty days. *On this edifice the whole truth of Christianity stands or falls'* [my italics]. It is eloquent of the resurrection problem that, in this crucial proclamation of faith, Dr Barnett has included a statement that is not supported by any Gospel (Jesus' resurrection appearances lasting for forty days) and another statement that rests on one very dubious verse (*Matthew* 28:9, in which the risen Jesus is 'handled').

In the face of all this, should we simply abandon the search for historical truth and follow the path of what Robert Funk criticises as, 'privileging the resurrection' — exempting it from historical investigation, or do we examine the evidence and see what it can tell us? In his dedicated quest for the physical realities of Jesus' life, biblical archaeologist John Wilkinson discourages such an exercise in this case: 'Any attempt to disentangle a sequence of tangible or "objective" events from the resurrection narrative is bound to fail simply because it is inappropriate. Such events are out of reach for the reason, simple and profound, that they are indescribable.' Yet every Gospel describes them. It seems then that the Gospellers are not describing events, they are describing *an event* — the resurrection. They are determined to show us that it happened, even though it cannot be defined in terms of the experiences of specific witnesses in specific places at specific times.

Even the millennial message of the Archbishop of Canterbury, Dr George Carey, states:

> While we can be absolutely sure that Jesus lived, and that he was certainly crucified on the cross, we cannot with the same certainty say that we know he was raised by God from the dead.

Rather than facts, we are confronting *the* fact of resurrection. When we seek to verify this fact, supposedly one of the most powerful arguments in support of it is the resurrection faith — the post-Easter conviction of Christ's followers that he had been raised from the dead. That faith had to be based on something that happened in these people's lives, something that convinced them that Jesus had risen; but unless that something was describable as an event or events, unless it could be recorded and chronicled, it was no more than an idea, a conviction. This is dangerously close to saying that the resurrection faith created the resurrection fact — the 'Elvis lives!' phenomenon on a cosmic scale.

One is reluctant to repeat the exercise of comparing the Gospel accounts of appearances by the resurrected Jesus and discovering that they fail to agree with each other. However, Christians who don't read the Gospels are blissfully unaware of these disagreements and have a very clear picture of what happened. From childhood they have been familiar with a well-established collage of images and incidents put together from the four Gospels and *Acts* (usually omitting Paul's earlier list of resurrection appearances, because they differ from those in the Gospel accounts and simply cloud the issue). This popular harmony, synthesised from extraordinarily unharmonious elements, impels us to conduct yet again the examination which Christian scholars admit to be unprofitable — with good reason. Frankly, Gospel evidence for the resurrection is an unholy mess.

✝✝✝

No two Gospels agree on who found Jesus' tomb to be empty. In Mark it is the two Marys and Salome, in Matthew only the two Marys. Luke writes of at least five women, including the two Marys and Joanna, while John has the discovery made by Mary Magdalene, alone.

The Gospellers continue to disagree on details of the phenomenon itself. Mark's three women find the stone rolled away from the entrance to the tomb and, on entering, they see 'a young man dressed in a white robe, seated at the right-hand side.' In Matthew, the two Marys are approaching the sealed tomb when there is an earthquake and an angel descends to roll away the stone, then sits on it. Luke's women find the tomb open and empty; 'two men in shining robes' appear. In John's account, Mary Magdalene also finds the stone rolled back and the tomb empty; but there is no young man, no angel, no two men in shining robes — at least, not on this first visit.

Before going any further with this variable story we must ask what the women are doing here, apparently at daybreak (or before daybreak or after sunrise) on the Sunday. Mark and Luke say that they have waited until the Sabbath is over to anoint Jesus' body. Two points: as we've seen, they *could* have anointed the body on the Sabbath, and, quite apart from this, for Jews the Sabbath had ended some twelve hours earlier, at sunset on Saturday. Why wait until dawn on Sunday? Obviously because, to Gentile authors, this marked the beginning of the day after the Sabbath.

Matthew avoids both these blunders. His women come simply 'to see the tomb' and seem to arrive on the evening of (or 'late on') the Sabbath, 'at the beginning of the first day of the week'. (Matthew's word for 'beginning' is literally 'dawning', but Luke used the same word to describe the 'beginning' of the Sabbath on Friday evening.) Restrictions on Sabbath travel *could* have delayed the visit — if the women's accommodation was more than half a Sabbath journey from Golgotha.

John again offers the most plausible account. Without apology, he has Mary Magdalene arriving at the tomb 'early on the first day of the week while it was still dark'. According to the Mishnah, this conformed to the time ('within three days') when a body should be viewed to make sure that death had been correctly established (*Semachoth* 8). The first signs of putrescence would be something that Mary was prepared to confront alone, sparing Jesus' mother from this sad duty. Before following John's account further we will trace the diverging trails of the other Gospels.

Mark's young man in the white robe tells the women:

> 'Don't be alarmed. You're looking for Jesus the Nazarene who was crucified. He has been raised; see where they laid him. But go and tell Peter and the disciples that he is going ahead of you to Galilee. You'll see him there, just as he told you.'
>
> And hurrying out, they fled from the tomb, trembling and in great excitement. And they said nothing of this to anyone; because they were afraid.
>
> (*Mark* 16:6–8)

And this is Mark's last word on the resurrection — an empty tomb and not a single glimpse of the risen Jesus. Another twelve verses have been added to the Gospel by another author at a much later date, comprising a sketchy round-up of resurrection appearances (culled from Luke's account, written ten to twenty years later), climaxed by a bizarre catalogue of powers promised to believers and a perfunctory mention of Jesus ascending into heaven (again derived from Luke). The entire passage is an embarrassment, still printed as the end of Mark's Gospel, but universally discredited (*Mark* 16:9–20).

Matthew embellishes Mark's basic account. First he claims that 'the chief priests and Pharisees' go to Pilate (*but not until the morning after the crucifixion*) and ask to have the tomb guarded because of the danger that Jesus' disciples might steal the body that night in 'fulfilment' of his prophecy: 'After three days I will rise'. Pilate tells them: 'You have a guard, go and make it as secure as possible.' A watch is established — members of the Temple Guard or *perhaps* festival reinforcements — and the *golel* is sealed. (Even though

Matthew is the only Gospeller to mention the guard, Christians fasten on this detail as convenient for their purpose, while usually ignoring Matthew's other additions.)

Apparently, that evening, as the two Marys approach, the guards are terrified into a state of collapse by the earthquake and the appearance of the angel who rolls the stone away, sits on it and makes precisely the same announcement as Mark's 'young man': Jesus has been raised and will appear to the disciples in Galilee. Note that, according to Matthew, Jesus has disappeared from the tomb before the rock is rolled away. This is clearly designed to deny the possibility, inherent in Mark's account, that someone had taken the body and the young man in white was merely *claiming* that Jesus had been 'raised' and would reappear in Galilee. In line with this policy of caulking the holes in Mark's story, Matthew now gives us what is probably the earliest Gospel resurrection appearance one which is usually ignored in the popular montage. The two Marys hurry from the tomb, 'frightened and overjoyed', and are on their way to tell the disciples when Jesus meets them and says, 'Hello!' Matthew tells us that the two women 'seized his feet and worshipped him.' There seems little point in the appearance; Jesus simply repeats the angel's message.

Next, Matthew tells us how members of the guard report what they have witnessed and are given 'silver' to spread the story that, while they were asleep, Jesus' disciples came and stole his body. (If Pilate hears of this, the members of the Sanhedrin promise to 'persuade him' and protect the guards from repercussions.) An appearance of Jesus to the Eleven on a mountain in Galilee is given sketchy treatment, complete with a highly Paulian 'commission' to make disciples of 'all nations' — further advertised as a very late addition by its inclusion of the sole Gospel reference to the awkward doctrine of the Trinity — bread-and-butter to theologians, but, by any normal standards, monotheism stretched to breaking point (*Matthew* 28:1–20).

We are left with a strong conviction that the original tradition available to Matthew included only the empty tomb and the announcement to the women. The additional material reeks of apologetics or tries to justify a Gentile mission that was alien to Joshua's teaching. Even if we can accept the addition of the guards, the earthquake and the rock-rolling angel, if the women visiting the tomb had seen the resurrected Jesus it is inconceivable that Mark would have omitted this detail from his first telling of the story.

Everything changes with the appearance of the Gospel written by Luke, sometime travelling companion and biographer of Paul. Every detail of Matthew and Mark's stories — except the basic fact of the empty tomb — is contradicted or omitted. In Luke's version, 'two men in shining robes' do *not* tell the women that Jesus will see his disciples in Galilee, and Luke sets out, quite pointedly, to show how such a mistaken idea arose. Luke's 'men' remind the women that Jesus announced, 'while he was still in Galilee', that he would rise on the third day. The women (who do not see the risen Jesus) describe their experiences to the disciples, who dismiss the story as 'an idle tale'; but Peter runs to find the tomb empty and sees the burial cloths lying in their place. He leaves, 'amazed at what had happened' — his reaction and those of the others sitting oddly with Jesus' repeated prophecies of his death and resurrection (doubly odd because Peter's visit to the tomb seems, in itself, a later addition to Luke's original).

Luke goes on to relate the impressive story of Cleopas and his unnamed companion meeting an unrecognised Jesus on the road to Emmaus. Only when Jesus breaks bread do they realise who he is. He vanishes. They return to the disciples and learn that Jesus has been seen by 'Simon'. Jesus appears to the group, invites them to touch his wounds (there is no indication that they do), then eats some grilled fish and honeycomb before he leads them to Bethany and is 'carried up into heaven' (*Luke* 24:4–51).

This is the body of evidence for the resurrection provided by the first three Gospels. 'The agreeable trio' have failed to agree. The inconsistencies are spectacular — though, to some, encouraging in their naiveté. Much is made of the discrepancies involving the women and the man/men/angel. Far more interesting is Luke's studied rejection of the promised Galilee appearance and his placement of the Ascension *on the night of the resurrection day*. This time-scale clashes head-on with the broad sketch of resurrection encounters given in *Acts*, which was also written by Luke:

> After his execution he gave them infallible proof that he was alive, *appearing to them during forty days* and speaking about the kingdom of God. [my italics]
>
> (*Acts* 1:3)

As Jesus speaks to the Eleven on 'the Mount of Olive Grove', Luke tells us, 'He was lifted up and a cloud obliterated him from their sight' (*Acts* 1:9).

More than any other varying detail of the resurrection accounts, this discrepancy in the duration of the phenomena defines our problem. To E.P.Sanders, it ranks among those variations which 'are not difficult to explain':

> The author of Luke-Acts was an artistic writer, and he thought that repeating himself was not good style. Therefore, the risen Lord was with the disciples for only a few hours in Luke and for forty days in Acts.

Such is the reliability of the evidence we are examining. Variations in numbers, names, places and even the nature of the phenomena seem to depend on nothing more than the taste of the particular author. We are dealing with a milieu where, in writing about a truth, individual stories do not have to be true; that much is clear. But when story after story emerges as a literary creation, confidence in the core truth must be shaken. If no two writers can agree as to what happened, one must suspect that nobody knows, or that nothing of the kind took place. Can John help us here, as he has been able to help in the past? In his account of the resurrection, will we come closer to the factual nucleus of the story, or find ourselves sitting through another religious pageant with more sermonising? Here are the events of Sunday, 5 April, as described in the words (and in the original Greek, mixed tenses!) of John Mark:

> Early on the first day of the week, while it is still dark, Mary Magdalene comes to the tomb; and sees that the stone has been moved away from the tomb. Then she runs and comes to Simon Peter and the beloved disciple and says to them, 'They've taken the Lord out of the tomb and we don't know where they've put him!'

> Then Peter and the other disciple went out and came to the tomb. They ran, the two of them, and the other disciple ran faster than Peter and arrived at the tomb. And, bending down, he saw the linen lying there; but he didn't go in. Then Peter arrives after him and entered the tomb. And he sees the linen lying there. And the facecloth (*soudarion*) which was around his head was not lying with the linen, but away from it, rolled together in its own place. So then the other disciple, the one who had reached the tomb first, also entered; and he saw and believed.

> Because they were yet to know the scripture [saying] that he must rise from the dead, the disciples then returned home. But Mary stood crying outside the tomb. Then, still crying, she bent to look inside the tomb and saw two angels in white, one sitting at the head and the other at the feet, where the body of Jesus had lain. And they say to her, 'Woman, why are you crying?'

> She says to them, 'Because they have taken my Lord and I don't know where they've put him.' And as she is speaking, she turned and sees Jesus standing there, without knowing that it is Jesus.

> Jesus says to her, 'Woman, why are you crying? Who are you looking for?'

> And, thinking it is the gardener, she says to him, 'Sir, if you carried him away, tell me where you put him, and *I* will take him.'

Jesus says to her, 'Mary ...'

Turning to him, she said to him, 'Rabboni!', which means, 'My Master!'

Jesus says to her, 'Don't embrace me because I've not yet gone up to my Father. But go to my brothers and tell them I go up to my father and your father and my God and your God.'

Mary Magdalene came to the disciples, bringing word that she has seen the Lord and that he told her these things. *(John* 20:1–18)

Here, in John Mark's 'happening' Greek, is our closest approach to a first-hand account of an appearance by the resurrected Jesus. Several things mark it out as worthy of special consideration. First, even though Simon Peter and John Mark himself are featured in the story, it is Mary Magdalene who plays the central role and actually sees Jesus, after generating the entire sequence of events by her pre-dawn visit and her discovery of the open tomb and missing body. The detail of the two disciples running to the tomb and John Mark arriving first but not entering, is convincing. The description of the grave cloths with the *soudarion* rolled in its place is also persuasive. After the changing parade of man/men/angel images from the earlier Gospel accounts, the two white-clad angels provide nothing but 'religious' imprimatur and seem curiously out-of-place. In blunt contrast, the encounter with Jesus is very powerful. Mary does not immediately recognise him, vividly suggesting the sense of altered state confirmed by his, 'Don't embrace me ...' Perhaps, above all, the resurrected Jesus being mistaken for a gardener stamps this narrative with a mundane reality that is totally unexpected in such a context.

If John stopped here, we could readily believe that this is the resurrection as he experienced it and as he heard of it from Mary. Staying at John Mark's home with Jesus' mother, Peter and perhaps other disciples, Mary leaves in the fore-dawn to visit the tomb, arrives back breathless to tell what she has seen, then follows well behind John Mark and Peter as they run to investigate. Tired, confused, tearful, she stays behind at the tomb to be consoled by her encounter with Jesus, or even, perhaps, with her beloved Joshua. Unfortunately, John doesn't stop here.

That evening, as the disciples gather behind locked doors 'for fear of the Jews', Jesus appears and says, 'Peace to you.' He displays 'his hands and side' and tells them, 'Just as the Father has sent me, I send you.' He then breathes on them to impart the Holy Spirit and with it the power to forgive sins. No mention is made of how long Jesus stays with them and whether he leaves or disappears. Judas Thomas (the Twin) is absent for his brother's appearance to the disciples and refuses to believe unless he can see the wounds for himself and put his fingers into the nail holes and his hand into the javelin gash. 'Doubting Thomas' is born. Eight days later, with all the disciples again behind locked doors, Jesus appears and, as in Luke's account, *invites* Judas Thomas to touch the wounds:

> And Thomas answered him, saying, 'My Lord and my God.' Jesus said to him, 'Because you have seen me Thomas, you believed. Blessed [are those] not seeing and [yet] believing.' (*John* 20:28–9)

(Judas's, 'My Lord and my God', stamps the scene as a theologico-literary creation. No disciple of Jesus could have said such a thing in 33 AD. Some sixty years later, when John Mark was committed to deifying his master, he had become capable of this noble falsehood.)

An unspecified time later, Peter, John Mark, Judas and four others have spent an unsuccessful night fishing on Lake Kinneret and, at daybreak, see Jesus on the shore. Even when he speaks, they don't realise who he is until a 'miraculous' catch of 153 fish triggers their recognition. When they come ashore, Jesus is already cooking fish on a charcoal fire. He invites them to eat with him and gives them bread, then fish. Jesus seems to sanction Peter's primacy of the infant 'church' (ignoring the first twenty-seven years of leadership by James) and obliquely predicts Peter's martyrdom — both details suggesting late inspiration. Peter then indicates John Mark and asks Jesus, 'Lord, and what about this one?' (there is a strong sense that John Mark of Jerusalem is an outsider in this Galilean setting). Jesus replies, 'I want him to wait until I come; what [is that] to you? You follow me.' (John 21:1–24)

Read the passage. Especially in the last exchange of dialogue you will hear an old man speaking — just as you may have glimpsed the play of muscles in Peter's naked body or smelt the cooking fish in the earlier verses. You feel that our author is recalling a long-lost daybreak, reaching back to vivid images of his youth. He says nothing of an Ascension. He leaves us simply with a powerful, shining picture of Jesus alive. It seems a flashback to an earlier time in the ministry (echoing the 'miracle' in *Luke* 5:1–10), an affirmation — after all the sermonising and ecclesiastical embroidery — that Jesus actually lived.

And yet, perhaps because of this very quality, as evidence for the resurrection the story is less than totally persuasive, especially after John's two other carefully staged and reverently scripted set-pieces with the disciples. There is the uncomfortable suspicion that this is another example of a disarranged codex manuscript — an incident that found its way from Jesus' earthly life into these post-Easter chapters and has been confirmed in this position by some judicious editing. And, while the initial encounter between Mary Magdalene and Jesus is far and away the most credible of all the Gospels' resurrection appearances, how could this have been omitted by Mark from his seminal story of the two Marys discovering the empty tomb? There have been attempts to dovetail the two accounts — Mary first arriving before daybreak, then bringing Peter and John Mark and coming back for a third visit after sunrise accompanied by Jesus' mother and Salome; but this is pure desperation. Once again, 'harmony is a misguided method'; again, there are four 'separate paintings' and 'if we want the truth, we have to choose one of the ... paintings or none'.

There is one more piece of evidence to examine — evidence that is independent of the Gospels and earlier — the *First Epistle to the Corinthians*, written by Paul in about 55 AD. It contains a brief summary of resurrection appearances — which hardly clarifies the picture. As we have seen, the earliest Gospel tradition dealt only with the women who found the tomb empty. Paul omits the women completely — underlining the point often made by Christian commentators that it was an *inconvenient* detail to have Christ's resurrection discovered by a woman, a pair of women or a group of women, whose testimony was not acceptable as evidence, under Jewish law.

In chronological order, Paul records:

> He appeared to Cephas [Peter], then to the Twelve. Then he appeared to more than five hundred brothers at the one time, most of whom are still with us, but some have fallen asleep. Then he appeared to James, then to all the Apostles. And last of all, like a delayed birth, he also appeared to me.
>
> (*1 Corinthians* 15:5–8)

Several points emerge. Paul is the only scriptural authority for Peter seeing the risen Jesus apart from the other disciples, for the appearance to 'the five hundred' and to James (although a reunion between the two brothers is movingly described in a fragment of the *Gospel According to the Hebrews*). The only point at which Paul's account tallies with the Gospels is in having Jesus appear to the Twelve (not the Eleven; for Paul, Judas is still a member of the group).

What are we to make of it all? Because the resurrection has come to be seen as the central fact of the Gospels (one writer calls it 'The Central Event of

Universal History'), Christians' largely uncritical acceptance of this garbled chronicle is disturbing. Our sources cannot agree on the most mundane details. While there are some examples of incidents adopted from one account to be sketched or embellished in another, it is more common to find details ignored and even contradicted. There seems no line of evidence.

The justly respected C.H. Dodd comments: 'the continuous narrative which ran from the account of the entry into Jerusalem to the discovery of the tomb is now broken. We have something more like a number of detached incidents.' Dodd notes a degree of artificiality in Luke's and John's attempts to create a cohesive story and speaks of the resurrection events as, 'sporadic, elusive, evanescent'.

One is reminded forcibly of the inaccurate, over-coloured and contradictory stories that can circulate about an event before official and/or eyewitness accounts are available. Yet we are here looking at Christian records of Christian events recorded by Christian witnesses, many of whom remained available for more than thirty-five years in places where these events had taken place.

We are asked to believe that, although a Christian 'Church', which included some of the Twelve, was soon based in Jerusalem, those resurrection appearances that occurred there — and which formed a basic tenet of the Christian faith — could not be recorded with even the degree of unanimity seen in accounts of the crucifixion. In these, details vary from Gospel to Gospel, but the broad shape of the story is common to all four; generally, they complement rather than contradict. Yet when we proceed to the resurrection only days later, our sources are suddenly in disarray, in spite of the fact that the same witnesses are involved and the key locations of both events are within a few kilometres of each other, with the two basic sites — Golgotha and the tomb — today under the one roof.

The almost self-evident explanation of the problem is that we are dealing with two entirely different exercises in reportage — something that most Christians are prepared to admit. But what caused the difference?

In the crucifixion, we have a basic fact — the death of Jesus — described via a sequence of events, *some* of which can be explained as 'prophecy fulfilled', some of which could be derived from the inescapable nature of this form of execution and some of which seem drawn from specific details of this man's death. It would have been far more convenient for the Gospellers if 'the Jews' had stoned Jesus to death for blasphemy; the basic fact of Roman crucifixion strongly argues for foundation on an actual event. Many details — the *titulus*, the absence of the disciples, the awkward timing, the burial by

Pharisees — support a conclusion that these accounts are built on a factual grid rather than a framework of desirable theological elements. In direct contrast, examination of the detail of the post-crucifixion stories does *not* support our belief in the basic fact of resurrection. It is here that the great difference lies. To understand why the all-important events of the resurrection can be recorded in such a cavalier way, with such divergent detail, we must examine that central event, its significance to Jesus' followers, then and later, and to Jesus' enemies across the same span of time. Here, the solution to the mystery can be found.

✝✝✝

Grasping at the one fact common to all the stories, some Christian commentators challenge us to explain the empty tomb as anything but proof of the resurrection. There is a far more pressing question to answer. How do we know it existed? Outside Christian Gospels and apocrypha, the empty tomb is unknown to history. Even the Epistles fail to mention it.

If Jesus' body had disappeared the day after his crucifixion, the incident *might* have rated a mention in Pilate's report, which was seen by the Christian writer, Justin, early in the second century. But no such report now exists. We have some ludicrous, late forgeries and the fractionally more impressive *Acts of Pilate* or *Gospel of Nicodemus*, (which has the Roman standards bowing to Jesus of their own accord at his trial!). In this work, members of the tomb guard report to the Jewish leaders and recite Matthew's story of the earthquake and the fearful angel. When the 'rulers of the synagogue and the priests and the Levites' declare (rather too conveniently): 'As the Lord liveth, we believe you not,' the soldiers reply: 'So many signs saw ye in this man and ye believed not, how then should ye believe us? Verily ye swear rightly, "as the Lord liveth", for he liveth *indeed*.'

It is in a group of Coptic, Ethiopic and Arabic documents — some attributed to the great Pharisee Gamaliel — that we find the most elaborate explorations of the empty tomb. Pilate investigates the disappearance of Jesus' body and finds the grave cloths. He is then shown a well in the garden where the Jews have found the body of a crucified man. Joseph and Nicodemus claim that this is the body of one of the crucified 'thieves'. When the Jews insist that the body is that of Jesus, Pilate declares: 'It is right to lay his body in his own tomb.' But when the 'thief's' body is placed in Jesus' tomb, it returns to life and proclaims the truth. It is easy to dismiss the tale as preposterous. It is perhaps harder to admit that it also represents only a slight extension of the process we can recognise in the Gospels.

Perhaps the most impressive Gospel evidence for the existence of the empty tomb can be found in the account of the Jewish leaders bribing the guards to say the body was stolen by disciples — explaining a story supposedly current in the 70s or 80s when Matthew was written. But this could be simply a literary device to encourage our belief in the core phenomenon — that there was an empty tomb to be explained. It would be strange if the resurrection narratives were free of literary devices when these occur so freely in both Testaments. Certainly, rabbinic literature offers no record of, or counterblast to, the empty tomb, suggesting that the story did not achieve early, wide currency outside the Christian community.

Justin Martyr reported, however, in his second-century *Dialogue with Trypho*, that Jewish authorities were spreading the claim that Jesus' body had been stolen by his disciples; and the medieval *Toledoth Jeshu* came up with a garbled tale that Judas stole the body and sold it to the Jewish priestly faction for thirty pieces of silver. Both stories seem inspired by the Gospels rather than an independent Jewish tradition of the empty tomb.

While the evidence hardly justifies a conclusion, either way, it can be said that the disappearance of Jesus' body is the most credible feature of the resurrection narratives; in fact, as we've noted, it was the *only* feature of the earliest Gospel account.

If there was an empty tomb, its discovery by Mary Magdalene (with or without one or more of the other women) is highly believable. Whether or not the burial cloths were lying in place, as described by John, is much harder to say. The myrrh used to anoint the body (or coat the cloth) was a gum resin; removal would have been awkward and a curious exercise to undertake. Clearly, the shroud and *soudarion* left lying on the limestone shelf were intended to show that no human agency was involved. Yet, without human involvement, why was there any need for the stone to be rolled away?

According to Matthew, Jesus has left the tomb while it is still sealed by the stone, yet the women can grasp his feet. In John's account, soon after leaving the tomb Jesus seems able to pass through locked doors, but according to Luke, he proceeds to eat fish and honeycomb. A week later he again appears behind locked doors. In providing these details, the Gospellers aggressively refuse to let us identify the risen Jesus as either a 'ghostly' apparition *or* as a physical being. Luke's Jesus on the road to Emmaus is markedly different from the living man and he can disappear; but he can break bread. John's resurrected Jesus on the shores of Kinneret is also unrecognised. He can bring bread and fish to the lakeside and kindle a fire. This time he neither appears nor disappears. The Gospel evidence is totally split between Jesus appearing in a spiritual form or materialising as a tangible, physical body, able to perform physical acts.

Peter is illuminating, and refreshingly blunt on the subject. Writing in the mid 60s, some thirty years after Jesus' death, he speaks of Jesus 'being put to death in the flesh but made alive in the spirit' (*1 Peter* 3:18). There seems no doubt here that the resurrection was a spiritual phenomenon.

Paul, too, gives no hint of a physical resurrection. He does not claim to see Jesus; he sees only, 'a light from heaven', and hears his voice (*Acts* 9:3–4; 26:12–14). He describes the encounter as 'a heavenly vision' (*Acts* 26:19), yet, to Paul, this experience differs from the others only in being 'last of all'. Paul portrays Jesus' resurrection as the prototype of all those to come — 'the first fruit of those who have died', and goes on to say of resurrection, 'It is sown a physical body, but raised a spiritual body' (*1 Corinthians* 15:20, 44). It is hardly surprising that some attempts to define Paul's description, 'a spiritual body', embrace the baffling array of characteristics attributed by John and Luke to the resurrected Jesus even though Paul's sole recorded encounter with 'the Risen One' was a vision involving only a light and a voice.

In fact, Paul specifically denies the physicality of the resurrected body. While Luke's Jesus tells the disciples: 'A spirit does not have flesh and bones as you see me having' (*Luke* 24:39), Paul declares: 'As we bore the image of the earthly man, we shall also bear the image of the heavenly man … *flesh and blood cannot inherit the kingdom of God*' [my italics] (*1 Corinthians* 15:49–50).

Peter and Paul provide an impressive consensus. Yet if we relate these two early views with the original Gospel account, we find an immediate contradiction. The only resurrection phenomenon described by Mark is the *physical* disappearance of Jesus' body from the tomb. How can we equate this with what Peter and Paul clearly saw as a *spiritual* resurrection? We are speaking of two quite different phenomena. And this may well reach to the core of the mystery.

If Jesus' body disappeared from the tomb, many explanations can be put forward; the problem is not nearly as daunting as most Christian commentators pretend. The earliest theory is in fact advanced by Mary Magdalene. She suspects that 'they' have removed the body and, when she mistakes Jesus for 'the gardener', asks him if *he* has carried the body away. Her question inspires two bizarre offshoots. Tertullian, lawyer and theologian of the late second and early third centuries, refers to a story that 'the gardener' removed Jesus' body from the garden tomb 'that his lettuces might not be damaged by the crowd of visitors' (*De Spectaculis*, 30); but this is heavy-handed irony, an early theological joke. Equally heavy-handed, but far from a joke, is the *Book of the Resurrection of Christ by Bartholomew the Apostle*, written in perhaps the fifth century. Here, the gardener, Philogenes, tells Mary how he had removed the body at the instigation of 'the Jews' (who feared its theft, presumably by the disciples) and re-interred it in a tomb near his vegetable garden. As he returned at midnight, planning to carry the body away and anoint it, he witnessed the resurrection — a spectacular involving 'all the orders of angels', complete with Jesus riding 'the chariot of the Father'. The Apocrypha authority M. R. James shows some restraint in saying that the work is 'better described as a rhapsody than a narrative'.

If we accept the 'gardener' theory simply as representing human intervention, that intervention, the theft of Jesus' body, could have been carried out by someone acting on behalf of the Romans, the Sadducees or the disciples — and without any great difficulty, since the mounting of the guard seems a dubious detail.

A Roman disentombment could have represented second thoughts by Pilate or independent action by an individual or group who considered that the prefect had not acted in the best interests of Rome in allowing a Jewish burial. The tomb offered a site for veneration, a focus for anti-Roman, anti-establishment ferment. By removing the body, the threat was defused.

We are left with a situation in which those responsible for the theft could have come forward and exposed the Christian 'myth' of resurrection. Two points: if the body was removed without Pilate's authority, the perpetrators would be unlikely to admit what they had done. On the other hand, if the action was officially inspired, Pilate held the means to discredit Christianity by exposing its great focus as a hoax perpetrated on these gullible Jews *by him*!

All this, however, presupposes that the disappearance of the body virtually coincided with the emergence of the resurrection as a lynch-pin of the Christian religion — whereas, until the fall of Jerusalem in 70 AD, or very close to it, the only Gospel account records the empty tomb as the end of the story. While it points to a reappearance by Jesus in Galilee, Mark left no account of this reappearance — or any other. Yet Luke shows Peter making the resurrection the centrepiece of his famous Pentecost sermon in Jerusalem only fifty days after the crucifixion — and demonstrating (rather unconvincingly) that the raising of Jesus had been prophesied by David (*Acts* 2:14–36). There are very early elements in this sermon; but this is clearly not one of them. The speech is constructed like all of Luke's speeches, and, as we will see, the ideas it presents are largely those of Paul.

It is also important to note that, at this stage, we are not speaking of the emergence of a new religion. While we refer conventionally to the Jerusalem 'Church', we are in fact speaking of a group of observant Jews in daily attendance at the Temple (*Luke* 24:53; *Acts* 2:46) who did not equate Jesus with God, and who, while losing the cherished dream of his Messiahship, still retained his teaching, his inspiration, his unparalleled view of man's relationship with God.

Perhaps within this mourning congregation there emerged inspiriting stories of Jesus' presence being felt or even seen, stories of his inspiration reaching out to the disciples in audible messages of support and encouragement. If Mary Magdalene spoke of seeing her beloved master, nobody would have doubted her, any more than they would have doubted James and Simon and Cleopas. This was comforting to hear, beautiful to experience; but they would do no honour to their revered Rabbi by making such experiences the whole point of his life. The idea would have seemed ridiculous. It was his teaching that mattered; it was what he had told them and shown them of love and faith and obedience to God and sharing, that guaranteed his enduring place in their lives. It was his life that shaped their ongoing devotion, not echoes, reflections of that life after his death. Of course, these would have been treasured, but not as tenets of faith, not as central to their beliefs.

If Paul's letters pre-date the Gospels — and almost every modern scholar believes they do — it was outside Jerusalem that these uncodified, as yet unrecorded experiences, perhaps no more than rumours, began to assume a new significance; what may have been initially, to the Jerusalem congregation, a disturbing significance. *It is this tension that informs and illuminates the elusive, almost haphazard development of the resurrection narratives.* The broad variations in the accounts, the discrepancies in numbers, names, places and times are characteristic of stories carried over long distances, repeated second and third hand. This is almost certainly what they were.

The disciples and the members of the Jerusalem congregation had direct memories of Jesus, his enduring reality, at the very least, the *sense* of his presence to sustain them, in the very places where he had walked and eaten with them, where he had lived and died. But for the distant Jewish and Gentile enclaves visited by Paul and his acolytes, ten, twenty, thirty years after the crucifixion, there was no such dynamic, no similar sense of continuity of person and place. What was *implicit* in the faith of the Jerusalem congregation had to become *explicit* to satisfy the evangelical needs of Paul, Silas and the rest. Paul who had never encountered the living Jesus yet preached his Gospel for three years before he had spoken with any of the disciples (Galations 1:15-20) — focused on the resurrection as the sacred nucleus of his reinvention of Christianity.

> If Christ has not been raised, then our preaching is useless and your faith is also useless … if Christ has not been raised, you are still in your sins.
>
> (*1 Corinthians* 15:14, 17)

It was Paul's man Luke who provided, in his Gentile-orientated work of 70 to 80 AD, the first significant Gospel material on appearances of the resurrected Jesus. Yet by then Jerusalem was rubble after the Jewish revolt. *If* the empty tomb had resulted from a Roman theft of the body — even if the phenomenon had become linked with highly coloured stories of a Messianic prophet and healer who had reappeared briefly after his death — the believers in such tales were scattered, defeated. Pockets of physical resistance like Masada and its Zealot garrison posed a far more significant threat. The empty tomb was a non-issue.

A similar scenario applies to the theft of the body by Sadducees. There seems clear evidence of a factional rift in the Sanhedrin over the crucifixion of Jesus. The Pharisees had taken no part in the events surrounding the trial; and two of their Sanhedrin members had buried the executed man with some display of reverence. This, in itself, could be seen as a strong motive for the opposing Sadducees to disinter the body and so eliminate a rallying point, a physical focus for conflict that could threaten their cherished *status quo* and the stability of Israel.

This tactic becomes even more credible when the execution and burial were immediately followed by the Passover moon's eclipse — an omen with powerful potential to reignite the Messianic zeal of the dead man's followers. If Sadducees stole the body, by the time a slowly developing pattern of belief in Jesus' resurrection took clear shape as a threatening force, the Temple — and the Sadducees with it — had ceased to exist.

We are left with the possibility that a disciple or disciples engineered the theft of Jesus' body, not necessarily intending to perpetrate a hoax, perhaps merely considering it inappropriate that members of the Temple establishment should stake this claim on their beloved master. Feelings ran high on such matters, as they still do in the Middle East; recall the bizarre battles for the body of the Ayatollah Khomeini.

It is *possible* that the Twelve knew of, or sanctioned the removal of Jesus' body from the tomb; or it could have been taken by an individual or small group acting without their knowledge. Either way, it was an event they could come to see as heralding, endorsing, proclaiming a great truth. The essence of Jesus, his words, the power of his presence, his very life spirit had endured among them. As we have already seen many times, accuracy and truth are not inseparable to the Middle Eastern mind. The story behind the empty tomb did not need to be 'accurate' in order to be 'true'. If it served to strengthen the truth of Jesus' inspiration to his followers, if it helped to physicalise their feelings of his ongoing influence, then it was fulfilling God's purpose and helping perpetuate Jesus' work. They were not living a lie in embroidering this and the other resurrection stories spreading through the Dispersion and the Gentile world. They were breathing life into a truth.

The empty tomb became the physical symbol of a spiritual reality.

And so accounts of the resurrection became more elaborate, more intricately woven between the physical and spiritual, more determined to defeat rational explanation, and further and further removed from whatever had really happened. They became what Plato called 'noble falsehoods'; but the central truth remained inviolate a truth the disciples would be prepared to die for.

Innumerable Christian scholars argue that the 'post-Easter faith', generated by the resurrection, was the transforming power that 'turned Peter and the other disciples from being cowards into fearless leaders of the Christian movement'. This is made the most potent argument for the reality of the resurrection. Much is made of the 'fainthearted' Eleven (who generally receive a bad press from the Gentile-aimed Gospels). Yet it would have been suicidal for them *not* to go into hiding during Jesus' trial and execution and immediately afterwards. True, Peter sanely 'denied' Jesus at Caiaphas's home; but he was there! Of all the disciples, he was the most wanted man after his attack on Malchus, yet he followed the arresting party into the very heart of enemy territory. Hardly cowardice. It was simply a question of surviving and showing his courage later to greater effect.

It is important to recognise that the death of a great leader and/or a great teacher does not automatically obliterate his leadership or his teaching. In innumerable cases throughout history, a leader's stature — and even his influence — has grown after his death, often at the hands of supporters who gain their own strength, authority and power in the process. Such men —

from Socrates, King Arthur and Robin Hood to Lenin and Mustapha Kemal Attaturk — were not resurrected. In death, they achieved a level of immortality as symbols of a people or a movement or even an idea. If men are great enough or the ideas they represent are good enough, their deaths do not prevent their impact extending far beyond a lifetime.

To suggest that only the resurrection could have empowered the disciples and laid the foundations of Christianity is to devalue everything that Jesus was and everything that he said and did during his life.

The disappearance of Joshua's body from the tomb — or the need to claim that such a thing had happened — must be seen as the point of transition between Joshua and Jesus.

A physical resurrection posed an array of problems, some of which were evident to the first promulgators of, or believers in, such a doctrine. If Jesus was physically resurrected, then he was available again to lead his disciples, physically; to continue his ministry with startling new power and authority — representing the physical embodiment of the eternal life he promised. But he did not continue to lead, to minister, to teach, to heal. So the Ascension — be it on the day of the resurrection or forty days later — became essential. And this, in turn, demanded the physical assumption of his body into heaven. It is hardly surprising that Christians teetered confusedly between promises of a spiritual or a physical resurrection for believers. A bodily resurrection became the expectation of many Christians — a doctrine enshrined in the feverish climax of *Revelation* with its promise of the thousand-year reign of Christ and the martyrs as the prelude to the new heaven and a new earth with the new Jerusalem as its jewel.

The physical kingdom of God, prophesied by Zechariah and looked-to by Joshua, had been hijacked by theology to form yet another contradictory element in the amalgam that became Christianity — a structure in which each new building block of doctrine demanded further complication, further illogicality, climaxing with the ultimate paradox — that Jesus was wholly man and wholly God.

Yet it had all started with something as physical and enigmatic as an empty tomb that had held the body of an executed Messianic rebel called Joshua.

We cannot ignore the so-called 'swoon' theory — that Jesus was not dead when placed in the tomb and could therefore reappear, alive. The classic Christian response is that it would be 'impossible' for Jesus to survive the ordeal of crucifixion and appear almost immediately afterwards in apparently normal condition. However, as Rod Sangwell points out, it seems 'anomalous' to believe in clinical death followed by resurrection and yet reject the possibility of near-death followed by remarkably rapid revival and recovery.

It if is permissible to compare different degrees of *impossibility*, I would think that the former is more impossible than the latter.

The 'swoon' theory has appeared in many and varied forms over the last two hundred years — sometimes in terms of a rescue (often by Essenes, taken for angels in their characteristic white garb), sometimes in terms of a cosmic hoax contrived by Jesus himself. The aftermath is always the problem with these theories, and ironically, the same problem faced those who first advanced the notion of a 'physical' resurrection. What happened to Jesus? Why did he then abandon his disciples (or in Thiering's scenario, sanction Paul's bowdlerising of his teaching)?

One of the 'Essene' stories, supposedly translated by a German Mason from an ancient letter, was published in 1873 as *The Crucifixion by an Eye Witness*. In it, Jesus dies soon after his rescue from the tomb (a detail echoed by Schonfield in 1961 and Lemesurier in 1981). Purely as a way of avoiding the theological point of resurrection, this is almost plausible; though it does nothing to explain the resurrection phenomena, apart from the empty tomb and angels. In every other version, Jesus is revived from the 'swoon', slips away into virtual obscurity and dies at Masada, in Rome, Kashmir, Japan, etc. The most effective argument against these fantasies is that, in having a living Jesus leave his Messianic mission to Israel uncompleted, they fail to fit the facts of his life and character as we can perceive them. Many Christians will find it hard to accept that the concept of a bodily resurrection — even when followed by Ascension and Assumption — fails equally to fit these facts, and for precisely the same reason.

In the end, we arrive back at our starting point. We will believe what we want to believe, irrespective of evidence; irrespective of semantics, sophistry and cynicism; irrespective of argument that springs from passionate conviction or from little more than academic ambition and intellectual arm-wrestling. Human beings are impelled to believe in *something* and display the same impulse whether they believe that something to be a truth or denial of a truth. The resurrection gives free reign to both options. The empty tomb remains a dark and enigmatic void or the symbol of a shining realm beyond death.

It is important to understand that Joshua's appearance or non-appearance after death, to family and followers, made no difference to the nature of his life, the quality of his teaching or the magnificent act of faith embodied in his death. Equally, it could be said that *Jesus'* physical resurrection, as described in the Gospels, served no useful purpose apart from lending strength to doctrines unsupported by his life and teaching (if we ignore, as we should, the unsupportable prophecies). His promise of immortality needed no such stunts to be credible. When his reluctant bid for Messiahship had failed, resurrection did nothing to revive that claim. *If* his death was intended as a sacrifice, its value was not enhanced by his rising. (In fact, his supposed foreknowledge of resurrection devalues the sacrifice.) Eventually, the phenomena of the resurrection and the then-necessary Ascension serve only to balance the Nativity — to deny Jesus' humanity at the end of his life, just as it had been denied at the beginning.

The recognition of Jesus as a man — as Joshua — does not diminish him. Quite the reverse. It makes his life all the more remarkable and meaningful. Belief in him as an exceptional human being empowers all other human beings in the search to understand their place in God's universe. Comprehending the real nature of Joshua's sonship to God inspires every man and woman to reach towards a similar intimacy — and show similar impatience with 'holier than thou' hypocrisy. Of course Joshua spoke of his *Abba* — 'my beloved Father'; but Joshua also urged his followers to pray: '*our* beloved Father'. These were not intended as hollow words. For all human beings they represent the simple key to a relationship with God, with Joshua, and with each other.

Bibliography

Translations of primary sources which include significant commentary are listed here. All primary authorities, including Biblical and rabbinical sources, are cited in the text. Secondary sources and articles from periodicals are identified in the Notes.

Achtemeir, Paul J., ed., *Harpercollins Bible Dictionary*, San Francisco, 1996

Allegro, John M., *The Dead Sea Scrolls*, Harmondsworth, 1956

Armstrong, Karen, *The First Christian*, London, 1983
— *A History of God*, London, 1995
— *A History of Jerusalem*, London, 1996

Asch, Sholem, *The Nazarene*, London, 1949

Assfy, Zaid, H., *Islam and Christianity*, York, 1977

Avi-Yonah, M., *The Jews Under Roman and Byzantine Rule*, Jerusalem, 1984

Ayerst, W., *The Hope of Israel* (Messianic doctrine in the Targumim), London, 1885

Baigent, Michael, and **Richard Leigh**, *The Dead Sea Scrolls Deception*, London, 1991
— and **Henry Lincoln**, *The Messianic Legacy*, London, 1987

Barnett, Paul, *Bethlehem to Patmos*, Carlisle, 1998
— *Is the New Testament History?*, Carlisle, 1998
— with **Peter Jensen** and **David Peterson**, *Resurrection — Truth and Reality*, Sydney, 1994

Barrett, C. K., *The New Testament Background: Selected Documents*, London, 1957

Bear, Magdalen, *Days, Months and Years*, Stradbroke, 1989

Biddle, Martin, *The Tomb of Christ*, Stroud, 1999

Bishop, Jim, *The Day Christ Died*, London, 1975

Borg, Marcus, *Meeting Jesus Again for the First Time*, New York, 1994
— and **N. T. Wright**, *The Meaning of Jesus*, San Francisco, 1999

Bornkamm, Günther, *Jesus of Nazareth*, London, 1973

Brandon, S. G. F., *The Trial of Jesus of Nazareth*, London, 1968

Brod, Menachem M., *The Days of Moshiach*, K'far Chabad, Israel, 1993

Brown, Raymond E., *The Death of the Messiah*, 2 Vols, London, 1994

Browne, Lewis, ed., *The Wisdom of Israel*, London, 1955

Bruce, F. F., *Jesus and Christian Origins Outside the New Testament*, London, 1974

Busch, Fritz-Otto, *The Five Herods*, London, 1958

Comay, Joan, *The World's Greatest Story*, London, 1978

Corbo, V., *The House of St Peter at Capharnaum*, Jerusalem, 1972

Cornfeld, Gaalyah, *The Historical Jesus*, New York, 1982

Cottrell, Leonard, *The Great Invasion*, London, 1958

Crossan, John Dominic, *Jesus, a Revolutionary Biography*, San Francisco, 1994
— *The Historical Jesus*, North Blackburn, Aust., 1991

Daniel, Orville E., *A Harmony of the Four Gospels*, Grand Rapids, 1996

Dimont, Max I., *Jews, God and History*, New York, 1962

Dodd, C. H., *The Founder of Christianity*, London, 1971

Downing, Barry H., *The Bible and Flying Saucers*, London, 1977

Drane, John, *Introducing the New Testament*, Tring, 1986

Drazin, Michael, *Their Hollow Inheritance*, Jerusalem, 1990

Dunn, James, D. G., *The Evidence for Jesus*, London, 1986

Edersheim, Alfred, *The Life and Times of Jesus the Messiah*, 2 vols, Grand Rapids, 1967

— *Sketches of Jewish Social Life*, Peabody, 1994

— *The Temple, Its Ministry and Services*, Peabody, 1994

Edwards, David L., *What Is Real in Christianity?*, London, 1972

— *Jesus for Modern Man*, Glasgow, 1975

Eisenman, Robert, *James the Brother of Jesus*, London, 1997

Eisler, Robert, *Jesus the Messiah and John the Baptist*, London, 1931

Epstein, Isidore, *Judaism*, Harmondsworth, 1979

Evans, Adelaide Bee, *The Children s Friend*, Warburton, Victoria, n. d.

Ewert, David, *From Ancient Tablets to Modern Translations*, Grand Rapids, 1983

Fouard, Abb Constant, *The Christ the Son of God*, London, 1958

Fox, Robin Lane, *The Unauthorised Version*, London, 1992

Funk, Robert W., *Honest to Jesus*, Rydalmere, 1996

— and Roy Hoover, eds, *The Five Gospels*, New York, 1993

Gaster, Theodore H., *The Scripture of the Dead Sea Scrolls*, London, 1957

Gaus, Andy, trans., *The Unvarnished Gospels*, Brighton, 1988

Grant, Michael, *The History of Ancient Israel*, London, 1997

Grant, Robert, *A Historical Introduction to the New Testament*, London, 1974

Green, Jay P., *Interlinear Greek—English New Testament*, Grand Rapids, 1980

Grollenberg, L. H., *A Shorter Atlas of the Bible*, London, 1959

— Jesus, London, 1978

Habershon, A. R., *Exploring in New Testament Fields*, London, n.d.

Harris, Anthony, *The Sacred Virgin and the Holy Whore*, London, 1988

Hart, J. Stephen, *A Companion to St John s Gospel*, Melbourne, 1952

Haskins, Susan, *Mary Magdalen Myth and Metaphor*, New York, 1995

Hastings, James, *Dictionary of the Bible*, Edinburgh, 1924

Henshaw, T., *New Testament Literature*, London, 1963

Herford, R. Travers, *Christianity in Talmud and Midrash*, Westmead, 1972 (Facsimile London 1903 Edition)

Herklots, H. G. G., *A Fresh Approach to the New Testament*, London 1950

Hoare, Rodney, *The Turin Shroud Is Genuine*, London, 1994

Hoehner, Harold W., *Herod Antipas*, Cambridge, 1972

Hughes, David, *The Star of Bethlehem Mystery*, London, 1981

James, Montague Rhodes, *The Apocryphal New Testament*, Oxford, 1986

Jeremias, Joachim, *Jerusalem in the Time of Jesus*, London, 1976

Johnson, Luke Timothy, *The Real Jesus*, New York, 1996

Joyce, Donovan, *The Jesus Scroll*, London, 1975

Keller, Werner, *The Bible as History*, New York, 1982

Kersten, Holger, *Jesus Lived in India*, Longmead, 1991

— and Elmar R. Gruber, *The Jesus Conspiracy*, Shaftsbury, 1995

Klausner, Joseph, *The Messianic Idea in Israel*, London, 1956

Klingaman, William K., *The First Century*, London, 1991

La Sor, William Sanford, *The Dead Sea Scrolls and the New Testament*, Grand Rapids, 1972

Lemesurier, Peter, *The Armageddon Script*, Shaftsbury, 1981

Maccoby, Hyam, *Revolution in Judaea*, London, 1973

— *The Mythmaker*, London, 1986

— *Judaism in the First Century*, London, 1989

— *Judas Iscariot and the Myth of Jewish Evil*, New York, 1992

Macklin, Robert, *The Secret Life of Jesus*, Sydney, 1990

Mason, Steve, *Josephus and the New Testament*, Peabody, 1992

Meier, John P., *A Marginal Jew*, 2 Vols, New York, 1991, 1994

Merrill, Selah, *Galilee in the Time of Christ*, London, 1885

Meyer, Marvin W., *The Secret Teachings of Jesus*, New York, 1986

Milik, J. T., *Ten Years of Discovery in the Wilderness of Judaea*, London, 1959

Miller, Madeline and J. Lane, *Encyclopedia of Bible Life*, London, 1957

Morgan, Rex, *Perpetual Miracle*, Manly, Aust., 1980

Morison, James, *Who Moved the Stone?*, London, 1983

Moshe, Beth, *Judaism's Truth Answers the Missionaries*, New York, 1987

Muggeridge, Malcolm, *Jesus Rediscovered*, Glasgow, 1981

Murphy-O'Connor, Jerome, *The Holy Land*, Oxford, 1992

Nineham, D. E., *Saint Mark*, Ringwood, Aust., 1983

Nolan, Albert, *Jesus Before Christianity*, London, 1987

Olmstead, A. T., *Jesus in the Light of History*, New York, 1942

Osband, Linda, ed., *Famous Travellers to the Holy Land*, London, 1989

Palmer, Joseph, *The Central Event of Universal History*, Sydney, 1918

Parkes, James, *A History of the Jewish People*, Harmondsworth, 1969

Peters, F. E., *Judaism, Christianity and Islam*, Vol. 1, Princeton, 1990

Picknett, Lynn, and Clive Prince, *Turin Shroud*, London, 1994

Prajnanananda, Swami, *Christ the Saviour and Christ Myth*, Calcutta, 1984

Radin, Max, *The Jews Among the Greeks and Romans*, Philadelphia, 1915

Reban, John, *Inquest on Jesus Christ*, London, 1967

Richards, N. J., *The First Christmas*, London, 1975

Richardson, Alan, ed., *A Theological Word Book of the Bible*, New York, 1950

Rinaldi, Peter M., *The Man in the Shroud*, London, 1978

Robinson, James M., ed., *The Nag Hammadi Library*, San Francisco, 1990

Romer, John, *Testament — The Bible and History*, Sydney, 1996

Russell, D. S., *The Jews from Alexander to Herod*, Oxford, 1988

Sanders, E. P., *The Historical Figure of Jesus*, London, 1995

Schofield, Guy, *Crime Before Calvary*, London, 1960

Schonfield, Hugh, *The Passover Plot*, Shaftesbury, 1961 (1996)

Schneerson, Menachem M., *I Await His Coming Every Day*, New York, 1991

Schweitzer, Albert, *The Quest of the Historical Jesus*, London, 1956

Scobie, Charles H., *John the Baptist*, London, 1964

Shanks, Hershel, *Understanding the Dead Sea Scrolls*, New York, 1993

Sherwin-White, A. N., *Roman Society and Roman Law in the New Testament*, Oxford, 1969

Simkins, Michael, *The Roman Army from Caesar to Trajan*, London, 1983

Sox, David, *The Shroud Unmasked*, Scoresby, 1988

Spong, John Shelby, *Rescuing the Bible from Fundamentalism*, San Francisco, 1991
— *Born of a Woman*, San Francisco, 1992
— *This Hebrew Lord*, San Francisco, 1993
— *Resurrection — Myth or Reality?*, San Francisco, 1994
— *Liberating the Gospels*, San Francisco, 1996

Staniforth, Maxwell, and Andrew Louth, eds., *Early Christian Writings*, London, 1988

Stern, David H., trans., *Jewish New Testament*, Jerusalem, 1990

Talmage, T. de Witt, *From Manger to Throne*, Philadelphia, 1890

Thiede, Carnsten Peter, and Matthew D'Ancona, *The Jesus Papyrus*, London, 1996

Thiering, Barbara, *The Gospels and Qumran*, Sydney, 1981
— *Jesus, the Man*, London, 1993
— *Jesus of the Apocalypse*, Moorebank, 1995
— *The Book That Jesus Wrote*, Moorebank, 1998

Treves, Sir Frederick, *The Land That Is Desolate*, London, 1913

Umen, Samuel, *Pharisaism and Jesus*, New York, 1963

Unterman, Alan, *Dictionary of Jewish Lore and Legend*, London, 1997

Vardy, Peter, and Mary Mills, *The Puzzle of The Gospels*, London, 1995

Vermaseren, M. J., *Mithras, the Secret God*, London, 1963

Vermes, Geza, *Jesus and the World of Judaism*, Philadelphia, 1984
— *Jesus the Jew*, Philadelphia, 1985
— *The Dead Sea Scrolls in English*, London, 1995

Walsh, Michael, *Roots of Christianity*, London, 1986

Wand, J. W. C., *First Century Christianity*, London, 1937

Warner, Marina, *Alone of All Her Sex*, London, 1990

Wells, G. A., *The Jesus Legend*, Chicago, 1996

Werblowsky, R. J. Z., *Encyclopedia of the Jewish Religion*, London, 1967

White, Kristin E., *A Guide to the Saints*, New York, 1992

Wijngaards, John N. M., *The Homeland of Jesus*, Great Wakering, 1979

Wilcox, Robert K., *Shroud*, London, 1978

Wilkinson, John, *Jerusalem as Jesus Knew It*, London, 1978

Wilson, A. N., *Jesus*, London, 1993

Wilson, Ian, *The Turin Shroud*, London, 1978
— *Jesus: the Evidence*, London, 1985
— *Holy Faces, Secret Places*, New York, 1991
— *Are These the Words of Jesus?*, Oxford, 1990

Wise, Michael, Martin Abegg Jr and Edward Cook, *The Dead Sea Scrolls — a New Translation*, San Francisco, 1996

Witherington, Ben, *The Jesus Quest*, Downers Grove, 1997

Wright, Tom, *The Original Jesus*, Oxford, 1996

Yoder, John Howard, *The Politics of Jesus*, Grand Rapids, 1983

Young, Brad H., *Jesus the Jewish Theologian*, Peabody, 1995

Notes

PREFACE

Jesus and the dead dog: Ian Wilson, *Are These the Words of Jesus?* pp. 112–13.

1 THE SEARCH FOR AN EYEWITNESS

Early dating of *Matthew*: Thiede and d'Ancoma, *The Jesus Papyrus*.

Apocryphal Gospels: James, *The Apocryphal New Testament*.

The Gnostic Gospels etc.: *The Nag Hammadi Library*, ed. Robinson.

***John* as earliest Gospel**: J.A.T. Robinson, *The Priority of John*, London, 1985; 'dead-heat with Mark': Barnett, *Is the New Testament History?*, p. 66; *John* dictated by Jesus: Thiering, *The Book that Jesus Wrote*. Intriguingly, in an earlier work (*Jesus the Man*) Dr Thiering had *John* written by 'Phillip the Evangelist' (p. 102) under the sponsorship of John Mark (p. 541), who emerged in her next book (*Jesus of the Apocalypse*) as 'an uncircumcised Gentile' (p. 35), the Apostle Bartholomew (p. 76), the centurion of Mark's and Luke's Gospels (p. 150) and 'the freedman Eutychus who drove Agrippa I's chariot' (p. 234).

'Authorial creativity' in the Gospels conceded: Johnson, *The Real Jesus*, p. 108; 'complete reshuffling of the pieces', *ibid.*, p. 32.

***John* as a 'disarranged codex'**: see Bultmann's rearrangement of the Gospel, q. Robert Grant, *A Historical Introduction to the New Testament*, pp. 160–1.

Jesus Seminar on actual words of Jesus: Funk and Borg, eds, *The Five Gospels*.

Schonfield's views on *John*: *The Passover Plot*, pp. 115, 292; Jacobs's assessment: *Jewish Encyclopedia*, Vol. 7, pp. 160, 165.

Evidence that John died with James: Henshaw, *New Testament Literature*, pp. 148–9; Muratorian Fragment, *ibid.*, pp. 432–4.

John's 'barbarous' Greek: Edwards, *Jesus for Modern Man*, p. 19.

2 THE BIRTH OF JOSHUA

The Jupiter/Saturn conjunction: Holden, 'The Wise Men from the East', *F.A.A. Journal* (Federation of Australian Astrologers), April/July 1975, reprinted Dec. 1986; Smit, 'Jesus was a Virgo?', *F.A.A. Journal*, Sept. 1987; see also, Hughes, *The Star of Bethlehem Mystery*; Keller, *The Bible as History*, pp. 361–9.

Dates for reappearance of Halley's Comet: Richard Allen, research assistant, Melbourne Planetarium; Magi journey to Rome: Robert Grant, *op. cit.*, p. 305; Spong, *Born of Woman*, p. 94.

Only Solomon's line to inherit kingship: Drazin, *Their Hollow Inheritance*, p. 118.

'God can do anything …': Moshe, *Judaism's Truth Answers the Missionaries*, p. 17.

'The historical Mary' not pursued: Warner, *Alone of All Her Sex*, p. XXII; 'totally defined by men': Spong, *op. cit.*, p. 214; rape theory: *ibid.*, pp. 162–3.

Luke's census story dismissed: Fox, *The Unauthorised Version*, p. 30. For a more sympathetic investigation of the Quirinius controversy: David J Hayles, 'The Roman Census and Jesus' Birth', *Buried History*, (Journal of the Australian Institute of Archaeology) Dec. 1973 and March 1974. (Surprisingly, Hayles does not mention Tertullian's testimony of a registration during the Syrian governorship of Saturninus.)

'No space in the room': Murphy–O'Connor, *The Holy Land*, p. 207.

The Flight to Egypt: Capistram Heim, 'Traditions About the Holy Family in Egypt', *Holy Land Review*, Winter 1986, p. 186.

3 JOSHUA'S WORLD

The major sources for the earlier part of this chapter were Josephus and the Old Testament. Major secondary sources consulted were: Dimont, *Jews, God and History*; Michael Grant, *The History of Ancient Israel*; Epstein, *Judaism*; Comay, *The World's Greatest Story*; Parkes, *A History of the Jewish People*.

The Old Testament as History: It is outside the aim of this background sketch to note the swarm of controversies surrounding the vexed question of the Old Testament as history. Romer, *Testament*, and Fox, *op. cit.*, offer highly readable surveys. We cannot, however, ignore the Aramaic inscription from the ninth century BC discovered at Tel Dan, Israel, in 1993. It includes a reference to *bytdwd*, 'The House of David' — the first archaeological evidence of the royal line that lay at the core of Messianism and was central to Joshua's role. See Francis I. Anderson, 'I Have Called You by Name' (Walter J. Beasley Memorial Lecture) in *Buried History*, June 1998, which includes a thirty-item bibliography on this important find.

Antiochus as perpetrator of 'history's first religious persecution': Avi-Yonah, *The Jews Under Roman and Byzantine Rule*, p. 3. This work was valuable for the latter part of the chapter, as were: Russell, *The Jews from Alexander to Herod*; Klausner, *The Messianic Idea in Israel*; Cornfeld, *The Historical Jesus*; Busch, *The Five Herods*; Maccoby, *Judaism in the First Century*; Radin, *The Jews Among the Greeks and Romans*; Edersheim, *Sketches of Jewish Social Life* and *The Temple*; Hoehner, *Herod Antipas*; Merrill, *Galilee in the Time of Jesus*.

Joseph and his sons as builders at Sepphoris: M. & L. Miller, *Encyclopedia of Bible Life*, pp. 99, 167; hypocrites and colonnaded streets: Richard A. Batey, 'Sepphoris, an Urban Portrait of Jesus', *Biblical Archaeology Review*, May/June 1992; Jesus as 'poor carpenter' or 'of the burgher class': Piers Crocker, 'Some Old Chestnuts Revisited', *Buried History*, Dec. 1997.

Midrash 'splits the rock of Torah': Unterman, *Dictionary of Jewish Lore and Legend*, p. 134.

Joshua as a Pharisee: Umens, *Pharisaism and Jesus*; Maccoby, *Revolution in Judaea*, and *The Mythmaker*; Young, *Jesus the Jewish Theologian*. See also Jesuit scholar Daniel J. Harrington's 'The Jewishness of Jesus', *Bible Review*, Spring 1987.

Roman soldiers as Joshua knew them: Simkins, *The Roman Army from Caesar to Trajan*, pp. 12–21, 34.

Industries of Galilee: Avi-Yonah, *op. cit.*; Roman pattern of regional development: Neil Asher Silberman, 'Searching for Jesus — the Politics of First-Century Judaea' and Eric M. Meyers, 'Galilee in the Time of Jesus', both in *Archaeology*, Nov./Dec. 1994. 'Debt became endemic', Yoder, *The Politics of Jesus*, p. 68.

4 PRIVATE AND PUBLIC LIVES

Hasidim use 'Abba' for God: Vermes, *Jesus and the World of Judaism*, pp. 40–2, and *Jesus the Jew*, pp. 210–12 — views firmly opposed in Witherington, *The Jesus Quest*, pp. 108–9.

In unravelling the mystery of Cleopas and 'the other Mary', my conclusions (reached in 1987) are broadly supported by Eisenman, *James the Brother of Jesus* (who devotes almost a quarter of the work's 1000 pages to sorting out Mary's and Joseph's family). He leans, however, to the likelihood of Cleopas and Joseph being the same man ('Joseph', as Jesus' father, is, to Professor Eisenman, 'a total gloss', *op. cit.*, p. 931).

'Cleopas's house' as a building of the eighth or ninth century AD: Murphy–O'Connor, *op. cit.*, pp. 392–4.

The career of Sejanus is from Tacitus and Suetonius. For an excellent, compact account of his career: Klingman, *The First Century*, Chapters 8, 10, 15, 16.

5 PILATE AND 'THE ABOMINATION'

'The Gospels' portrait ... separated from real time ...': Romer, *Testament*, pp. 177–8.

For bull and boar as emblems of the Tenth Legion permanently stationed in Syria: Radin, *op. cit.*, p. 281.

Daniel, 'a fiction and a fake': Fox, *op. cit.*, p. 336.

Description of Assyrian advance interpreted as Messiah's approach: Wise, Abegg & Cook, *The Dead Sea Scrolls — a New Translation*, p. 210. 'Torturing sense and meaning': Fox, *op. cit.*, p. 336. Allegro's counter-view: *The Dead Sea Scrolls*, p. 94.

6 HOLY WARRIORS

Hanan as the Baptist: Kohler, q. Eisler, *The Messiah Jesus and John the Baptist*, p. 242. Theory adopted by Eisenman: *op. cit.*, p. 366. Earlier Eisenman theory, the Baptist as Zadok (Sadduc): Baigent & Leigh, *The Dead Sea Scrolls Deception*, p. 207. Thiering's views on the Baptist as Teacher of Righteousness, etc., *The Gospels and Qumran* and *Jesus the Man*. Eisler concurs: *op. cit.*, p. 254. Thiering's theories damned: Johnson, *op. cit.*, p. 30.

The Baptist as an Essene: Allegro, *op. cit.*, p. 165.

Dead Sea Scrolls texts: cf. Wise, Abegg & Cook translations, *op. cit.*, and Vermes, *The Dead Sea Scrolls in English*. Because there is no standard titling of the Qumran documents, I cite their usual coding — the number of the cave where they were found (1Q, 5Q, etc.), followed by the document's identifying letter or number. The identification 'Geniza A' (or 'B') shows that this was a more complete text found in the Geniza (a sort of lumber room for religious texts) of a Cairo synagogue in 1896.

Professor Grant's comments on the War Scroll (1QM): Robert Grant, *op. cit.*, pp. 266–7.

Theories on the origins of Qumran summarised: Hershel Shanks, 'The Qumran Settlement — Monastery, Villa or Fortress?', *Biblical Archaeology Review*, May/June 1993. The 'monks' as 'holy warriors': Wise, Abegg & Cook, *op. cit.*, p. 125. *Sicarii* as only named users of the Qumran calendar, *ibid.*, p. 34.

Benedictus as 'Maccabean battle song': Winter, q. Yoder, *op. cit.*, p. 600.

7 'MY BELOVED SON'

Baptism: Romanian Josephus and Mandaean *Book of John* on night baptism, q. Eisler, *op. cit.*, p. 600. For early Christian baptism, Hippolytus, *The Apostolic Tradition*, q. Walsh, *Roots of Christianity*, p. 195. The rite, 'awe-inspiring': St John Chrysostom, *ibid.*, p. 192.

8 THE VOICE OF SATAN

Tradition of Temptation site not known before twelfth century: Murphy–O'Connor, *op. cit.*, p. 372.

Messiah, 'the ultimate Jewish monarch': Schneerson, *I Await His Coming Every Day*, p. 34.

'Mount Tabor' fragment of *Gospel According to the Hebrews* 'strongly Aramaic in its form':

Jacobs concurs with Jerome, *Jewish Encyclopedia*, Vol. 7, p. 161. 'Bargain with the Devil has to be fulfilled': Muggeridge, *Jesus Rediscovered*, p. 73.

9 'RUFFIANS OF THE DEEPEST DYE'

Judas Thomas as Jesus' twin, suits Gnostic agenda: Robinson, *op. cit.*, pp. 199–200. *Gospel of Barnabas* forged by 'renegade from Christianity to Islam': James, *op. cit.*, p. 22. (The Prophet believed that Jesus was not actually crucified and Moslem scholars have proposed that a 'simulacrum' suffered crucifixion in his place. See Bruce, *Jesus and Christian Origins Outside the New Testament*, p. 178).

The presence of Joshua's brothers among the Twelve has been pursued most recently by Eisenman, *op. cit.*, and earlier by Maccoby, who first proposed in his *Revolution in Judaea*, 1973, (Appendix 3) that Judas was a brother of Jesus — a thesis that forms the core of his *Judas Iscariot and the Myth of Jewish Evil*, 1992.

Earthly kingdom as 'eyewitness report of the way Jesus had been heard': Yoder, *op. cit.*, p. 60.

Herodias urges Antipas to petition Caesar: Schofield, *Crime Before Calvary*, pp. 100–1.

10 SALOME UNVEILED

Jerome and Nicephorus on treatment of the Baptist's body: Fouard, *The Christ the Son of God*, p. 155.

Antipas's fear of rebellion justified by Gospel accounts of the Baptist's mission: Sanders, *The Historical Figure of Jesus*, pp. 92–3. Slavonic Josephus's account of John's teaching ('no mortal ruling over you', etc.): Appendix, *Josephus*, Vol. 3, *Loeb Classical Library*. Political or military threat of the Baptist theorised: Barrett, *The New Testament Background: Selected Documents*, p. 190. This concept rejected: Scobie, *John the Baptist*, p. 89.

Vermes's 'thirty-year campaign' to deny that Jesus 'spoke of himself as "Son of Man" in a Messianic or apocalyptic sense', began with a paper delivered at Oxford in 1965, immediately after his arrival. See, Vermes, *Jesus and the World of Judaism*, pp. 89–99 and *Jesus the Jew*, pp. 163–8 and 188–91. Son of Man as 'supreme eschatological judge', Flusser, q. Young, *op. cit.*, p. 243, part of a balanced discussion on the issue. See also Witherington, *op. cit.*, pp. 94–8. Joshua is not named in the cited Talmudic passage, but as Herford comments (*Christianity in Talmud and Midrash*, p. 62), 'that it refers to Jesus there can be no possibility of doubt'.

11 THE POLITICS OF MIRACLES

Denial of Joshua using 'faith healing': Richardson, *A Theological Word Book of the Bible*, p. 153.

'Nature miracles' by later Christians: Herford, *op. cit.*, pp. 114–15. Cana miracle as 'passing of the old covenant': Warner, *op. cit.*, p. 16. God of Jesus, 'another and higher': Edersheim, *The Life and Times of Jesus the Messiah*, Vol. 1, p. 363.

Cana 'Christianised a popular tale': Robert Grant, *op. cit.*, p. 330.

'Charming idyll': Olmstead, *Jesus in the Light of History*, p. 64.

Cana wedding of Simon the Zealot: Romanian Josephus, q. Eisler, *op. cit.*, p. 600.

St Augustine on miracles: q. Richardson, *op. cit.*, p. 152.

Appolonius raises bride from death: q. Funk & Hoover, *op. cit.*, p. 437.

'Secret Gospel of Mark': Ian Wilson, *op. cit.*, pp. 175–6.

'Our first lawgiver is risen' prompts comment from Thackeray: Appendix, *Josephus*, Vol. 3, *Loeb Classical Library*.

'Veteran Kinneret fisherman' on the 'miraculous' haul of fish: Mendel Nun, 'Cast Your Net Upon the Waters', *Biblical Archaeology Review*, Nov./Dec. 1993. 'The pillow' in the stern: Shelley Wachsmann, 'The Galilee Boat', *Biblical Archaeology Review*, Sept./Oct.

1988. 'Revealing description of a Kinneret storm': Linda Osband, ed., *Famous Travellers to the Holy Land*, pp. 86–7.

Greek god 'in a bad mood': Sanders *op. cit.* p. 155

'Roman imperialism as demonic possession': Crossan, *Jesus, a Revolutionary Biography*, p. 90.

12 NOWHERE TO LAY HIS HEAD

Talmud on Nicodemus (Naqdimon): Herford, *op. cit.*, pp. 92–3.

Synagogue services of the first century: Maccoby, *Judaism in the First Century*, pp. 62, 70–1; Olmstead, *op. cit.*, pp. 61–3; Edersheim, *Sketches of Jewish Social Life*, pp. 244–5, 239–40.

Isaiah 60:17 to 61:6 as the reading from the Prophets for the sixty-second Sabbath: Olmstead, *op. cit.*, p. 62. (Because of his preferred chronology, Olmstead dates the incident to the previous occurrence of the passage, three years earlier, in 28 AD) cf. Maccoby, *op. cit.*, p. 70.

13 A SERMON SOMEWHERE

'A wonderful expression of Jewish philosophy': Alex Emanuel, 1956

'the key to the ... Sermon on the Mount': Yoder, *op. cit.*, pp.119–20.

Pat Dodson's blind mentor quoted: Martin Flanagan, Melbourne *Age Good Weekend*, 15 Jan. 1997.

Parables 'uncover the truth': Nolan, *Jesus Before Christianity*, p. 122. 'A different way of seeing ...': Borg, *Meeting Jesus Again for the First Time*, p. 74. 'Splendid mismatches': Edwards, *What Is Real in Christianity?*, pp. 118–19.

14 MARY WITH THE SEVEN DEMONS

Mary's 'immoral life': Fouard, *op. cit.*, p. 133.

Pope Gregor's 'three-woman hybrid': Warner, *op. cit.*, pp. 348–9. Coptic 'harmonising' of all the Marys: James, *op. cit.*, pp. 87–8; Legends of Mary's later life, death: Warner, *op. cit.*, pp. 224–36; White, *A Guide to the Saints*, p. 277.

Mary travels to Rome to denounce Pilate: James, *op. cit.*, p. 117. She is the author of 'Q': Harris, *The Sacred Virgin and the Holy Whore*, p. 278. Magdala unidentified: Spong, *op. cit.*, p. 196. The city 'dyed ... and flecked ...': Asch, *The Nazarene*, p. 295.

Mary was 'crazy': Celsus, q. Robert Grant, *op. cit.*, p. 372. 'Woman ... cured of madness': Wahb ben Numabbih, q. Bruce, *op. cit.*, p. 178. Mary was 'eighty-six ... childless ...': Sanders, *op. cit.*, p. 75.

'Prominent Catholic scholar' on Joshua's marriage: Meier, *A Marginal Jew*, Vol. 1, p. 334.

Mary, as 'penitent whore ... holds up a comforting mirror ...': Warner, *op. cit.*, p. 235.

15 AT THE HOUSE OF SIMON PETER

Capernaum: Sources for the archaeology of Capernaum, apart from personal inspection, are: Corbo, *The House of St Peter at Capharnaum*; Wilkinson, *Jerusalem as Jesus Knew It*; Frederick Joseph, 'Capharnaum: Its History and Description', *Holy Land Review*, Summer 1975. And from the *Biblical Archaeology Review*: James E. Strange & Hershel Shanks, 'Has the House Where Jesus Stayed in Capernaum Been Found?' (Nov./Dec. 1982) and 'Synagogue Where Jesus Preached Found at Capernaum' (Nov./Dec. 1983); also, John C. H. Laughlin, 'Capernaum from Jesus' Time and After' (Sept./Oct. 1993). For a rather lofty dismissal of the Peter's House site, see Romer, *op. cit.*, pp. 171–2.

16 THE CURSE ON CAPERNAUM

Joshua's followers not 'like an army on the march': Hart, *A Companion to St John's Gospel*, p. 94. Bishop Hart also provides a highly practical reconstruction of the disciples' voyage across Kinneret after the feeding of the 5000 (p. 99), borne out and augmented by two of my friends with wide experience of small craft in high winds — Ron Shaw and Andrew Swanson.

17 TURNING POINT

The '5000 patriots': Dodd, *The Founder of Christianity*, p. 143. Mishnaic reference to family strife with the approach of the Messianic Age, q. Brod, *The Days of the Moshiach*, p. 14.

The Transfiguration as 'the coming glory of the resurrection': Bornkamm, *Jesus of Nazareth*, p. 171. As 'Gospel creation': Crossan, *The Historical Jesus*, p. 386. As '"spiritualised" coronation': Maccoby, *Revolution in Judaea*, p. 167. Presence of Moses: *ibid.*, p. 168.

Mount Hermon, 'a literary figure in Jewish apocalyptic thought …': Allegro, *op. cit.*, pp. 142–4.

18 NOT PEACE BUT A SWORD

The cross, 'the price of social nonconformity' etc.: Yoder, *op. cit.*, pp. 97, 132.

The adulterous woman, a 'floating' or 'orphan' story: Funk & Hoover, *op. cit.*, p. 426. Joshua writing in the earth, 'remarkably naturalistic': A. N. Wilson, *Jesus*, p. 153. 'Rare agreement' on the story: Edersheim, *The Life and Times of Jesus the Messiah*, Vol. 2, p. 163; Funk & Hoover, *op. cit.*, p. 426. I am grateful to Alida Sewell for pointing out that Joshua's opponents produced the woman while ignoring the man who was caught with her and equally guilty (Letter, *Buried History*, Dec. 1997).

Personal testimony inadmissible in *judicial* cases: Edersheim, *op. cit.*, Vol. 2, p. 169. Theory that Joshua was arrested at Tabernacles, executed six months later: Maccoby, *Revolution in Judaea*, pp. 175 ff. Slavonic and Romanian texts of Josephus describing trial *and release* by Pilate: *Josephus*, Vol. 3, *Loeb Classical Library*, p. 650; Eisler, *op. cit.*, pp. 601–2.

'150 ministers (or pupils)': *ibid.*, *Loeb*, p. 645; Eisler, p. 601. 'Led as many as 900 men': Lactantius, q. Eisler, *op. cit.*, p. 9.

19 THE UPRISING

Solar eclipse on 19 March 33 AD: Smit, *op. cit.*, *F.A.A. Journal*, Sept. 1987, pp. 16–17; confirmed, Zelko Karlovic, former manager of the Melbourne Planetarium, who provided additional detail. Phlegon's account: quoted by Eusebius in his *Chronicle of Jerome.* Eisler, *op. cit.*, p. 297, cites Eusebius but discounts this report on the grounds of his preferred chronology. He is aware only of the total eclipse of 29 AD, as is Wells (*The Jesus Legend*, pp. 43–6) who accepts that a second historian, Thallus, also recorded the eclipse. cf. Bruce, *op. cit.*, p. 30.

'Martha and Mary' ossuary near Bethany: Grollenberg, *A Shorter Atlas of the Bible*, pp. 177, 186.

The Royal Stoa as a livestock bazaar: Kathleen Ritmeyer, 'A Pilgrim's Journey', *Biblical Archaeology Review*, Nov./Dec. 1989.

'Entry and action in the Temple …unwise': N. T. Wright, q. Witherington, *op. cit.*, p. 231.

Sanhedrin meets in 'apse' at the end of the Royal Stoa: Kathleen & Leen Ritmeyer, 'Reconstructing the Temple Mount in Jerusalem', *Biblical Archaeology Review*, Nov./Dec. 1989; Cornfeld, *The Historical Jesus*, pp. 149–55.

Rabbinical adage of pot falling on stone: Young, *op. cit.*, p. 155.

Slavonic Josephus account of Pilate's attack on 'multitude': *Josephus*, Vol. 3, *Loeb Classical Library*, pp. 649–50.

Sanhedrin's reaction suggests rebellion: Epstein, *Judaism*, p. 106; their duty to arrest plotters against Rome: *ibid.*; cf. Josephus, *Wars*, 2,4,8; Sanhedrin order concerning Joshua matches outlawry procedure: Fox, *op. cit.*, p. 300.

20 THE VALLEY OF DECISION

Identification of the Kidron Valley as the Valley of Jehosaphat is based on ancient tradition which had made it (and the western slopes of the Mount of Olives) a popular place for burials since pre-Exile times. The dead would be close to the place of God's judgement and would not have far to travel for their resurrection (Unterman, *op. cit.*, p. 149). Joshua, like all Jews of his day, would have accepted that prophecies concerning the Valley of Jehosaphat — the Valley of Decision — would be realised in the Kidron.

Archaeology of Gethsemane: Wilkinson, *op. cit.*, pp. 125–31; Murphy–O'Connor, *op. cit.*, pp. 132, 135. The existing olive trees postdate Joshua's time but may have sprung from the original root stock after the slopes had been cleared during the siege of Jerusalem in 70 AD.

Jesus' last days: Many scholars have considered it possible or likely that Jesus looked to divine intervention in this final confrontation. Robert Grant asks, 'Did he die in the mistaken belief that God was soon to intervene? … some of his sayings point in this direction.' (*op. cit.*, p. 288); and Sanders, while believing that his Jesus anticipates death, concedes: 'Conceivably, he thought that God would intervene before he was arrested and executed.' (*op. cit.*, p. 264). I am totally persuaded by Maccoby's thesis that the events surrounding Joshua's last days were shaped by his belief that the prophecies of Zechariah and Joel would be fulfilled in the Kidron Valley (*Revolution in Judaea*, pp. 183–96; Note 9, p. 304). I differ only on questions of detail.

21 MYSTERIES OF THE LAST SUPPER 1

Site of The Last Supper: The 'impressive case' that the traditional site of The Last Supper is authentic: Bargil Pixner, 'Church of the Apostles Found on Mt. Zion', *Biblical Archaeology Review*, May/June 1990. Israeli archaeologists, Pinkerfeld and Avi-Yonah, identified an ancient synagogue on the site. Benedictine archaeologist Pixner argues persuasively that it was a Judaeo–Christian structure because its niche to hold the Torah was oriented towards the site of the crucifixion, not towards the site of the Temple. Neither Wilkinson (*op. cit.*, pp. 168–70) nor Murphy–O'Connor (*op. cit.*, pp. 111–12) recognise remains of a synagogue, but Wilkinson is prepared to accept the site as authentic. Encouragingly, the building is now shared by a Jewish synagogue on the ground floor and the Christian-venerated 'Cenacle' above it.

The antiquity of the *Didache* and its earliest Eucharist liturgy: Staniforth & Louth, eds, *Early Christian Writings*, pp. 188–9; cf. Crossan, *Jesus, a Revolutionary Biography*, p. 130).

22 MYSTERIES OF THE LAST SUPPER 2

Surviving Mithraic texts: Barrett, *op. cit.*, pp. 102–4).

'The certain formula': Cumont, q. Vermaseren, *Mithras, the Secret God*, p. 104. See also: Baigent, Leigh & Lincoln, *The Messianic Legacy*, pp. 104–6. 'Respected scholars' on believers consuming the body and drinking the blood of Mithras: Kristensen and Loisy, q. Vermaseren, *op. cit.*, p. 103.

Placement of disciples at The Last Supper: Edersheim, *The Life and Times of Jesus the Messiah*, Vol. 2, pp. 207–8, 492–5; Wijngaards, *The Homeland of Jesus*, pp. 84–5. I depart from both versions.

Jesus 'prophesies his coming death': Crossan, *op. cit.*, p. 129; 'knew he was a marked man': Sanders, *op. cit.*, p. 264.

Jesus' 'That is enough' response to the mention of two swords: Brown, *The Death of the Messiah*, Vol. 1, pp. 269–70.

Jonathan bar Annas controls the Temple Guard: Jeremias, *Jerusalem in the Time of Jesus*, pp. 162, 196; Note 165, p. 197.

23 ARREST AND TRIAL

'Reconstruction' of original text of Romanian Josephus has 'many of the multitude slain' on Palm Sunday: Eisler, *op. cit.*, pp. 464–7; Slavonic Josephus places clash immediately before arrest: *Josephus*, Vol. 3, *Loeb Classical Library*, p. 650.

The trials of Jesus: It would be tedious to list the literature on the trials of Jesus. Among the major studies (not included in the bibliography) are: Winter, *On the Trial of Jesus*; Wilson, *The Execution of Jesus*; Cohen, *The Trial and Death of Jesus*; Blinzler, *The Trial of Jesus*; Rivkin, *What Crucified Jesus?*; Slayan, *Jesus on Trial*. Relevant works from the Bibliography include: Brandon, *The Trial of Jesus of Nazareth*; Brown, *The Death of the Messiah*; Sherwin-White, *Roman Society and Roman Law in the New Testament*.

24 'CAESAR'S FRIEND'

'One of the three paintings or none': Fox, *op. cit.*, pp. 301–2; 'follow John's framework but reject its motivation': *ibid.*, p. 304. Roman governors wary of Jewish Law: Sherwin-White, *op. cit.*, p. 195. Joshua's brother James and priest's daughter probably killed by 'same murderous Sadducean court': note by Isidore Epstein on Sanhedrin 52b in the Soncino Press edition of *The Babylonian Talmud*. 'Are you the leader of the resistance?': Sherwin-White: *op. cit.*, p. 24. Theories about Barabbas: Eisler, *op. cit.*, p. 474; Brandon, *op. cit.*, p. 102; Eisenman, *op. cit.*, pp. 178, 403; Maccoby, *Revolution in Judaea*, pp. 208–19; Crossan, *op. cit.*, p. 143; Funk, *Honest to Jesus*, p. 235; Joyce, *op. cit.*, pp. 104–8; Thiering, *Jesus the Man*, pp. 109, 534.

Pharisees not concerned in condemnation of Joshua: Epstein, *Judaism*, p. 107; Sanders, *op. cit.*, p. 269.

'A private murder ... by burning enemies': Jost, q. Edersheim, *The Life and Times of Jesus the Messiah*, Vol. 2, p. 555.

'Not Caesar's friend' seen as 'a convincing technicality': Sherwin-White, *op. cit.*, p. 47.

Via Dolorosa, 'defined by faith, not by history': Murphy–O'Connor, *op. cit.*, p. 37.

25 THE PLACE OF THE SKULL

The archaeology of Golgotha: Dan Bahat, 'Does the Holy Sepulchre Church Mark the Burial of Jesus?', *Biblical Archaeological Review*, May/June 1986. Bahat assesses Professor Virgilio Corbo's three-volume report (in Italian) covering twenty years of excavation and research on the traditional sites of Joshua's execution and burial. Bahat is critical but broadly accepts Corbo's findings, with due consideration of some variant opinions expressed by Magen Broshi and Gabriel Barkay. See also: Wilkinson, *op. cit.*, pp. 144–50 (Golgotha) and 153–9 (the tomb); Murphy–O'Connor, *op. cit.*, pp. 49–54; Cornfeld, *op. cit.*, pp. 199–217, including the work of Florentino Dize de Leon on the Rock of Golgotha — The Skull. See also Biddle, *The Tomb of Christ*.

The two *lestai*, 'under the same sentence' or 'on a similar charge': Eisler, *op. cit.*, p. 510.

Talmudists confuse Joshua with Ben Netzer, robber king: Herford, *op. cit.*, pp. 95–6; Edersheim, *The Life and Times of Jesus the Messiah*, Vol. 1, p. 222.

The physiology of crucifixion: For my knowledge of crucifixion I am indebted to the body of research conducted by students of the Shroud of Turin — initially, Group Captain Leonard Cheshire VC, whose exposition of the extraordinary artifact was persuasive and deeply moving. The aberrant and seriously flawed carbon-dating exercise of 1988 created a far greater mystery than it supposedly solved. How could a medieval forger create an anatomically perfect negative that incorporated a mass of clinical and historical detail on death by crucifixion — detail that was only confirmed by almost a century of intensive research? That research on the process of crucifixion has informed this account — from the scourging in Pilate's praetorium to the nailing on the cross, the slow death, the lance thrust, removal from the cross and burial. Only eighteen years ago, neglected research on Jewish burial clinched the last controversial detail portrayed on the shroud — entombment of the *unwashed* corpse of a crucified Jew.

I acknowledge my debt to the following writers whose work is fully credited in the Bibliography: Rodney Hoare, Rex Morgan, Lynn Picknett and Clive Prince, John Reban, Peter M. Rinaldi, Robert K. Wilcox and the remarkable Ian Wilson.

Quotations from Barbet on damage to the median nerve: Morgan, *Perpetual Miracle*, p. 102.

Sabachthani as slaughtering me : Drazin, *op. cit.*, p. 156.

Not history remembered but prophecy historicized : Crossan, q. Witherington, *op. cit.*, p. 76.

Sponge on *javelin* not on *hyssop*: *John* 19:28-9 is correctly translated in Gaus, *The Unvarnished Gospels* and the *Revised English Bible*.

Vinegar, the auxiliaries standard drink : Cottrell, *The Great Invasion*, p. 85.

Joshua s last words: To recognise Joshua's last words as the conclusion of Psalm 22 demands some adjustment of translation. Reading *John* 19:20 as 'It is accomplished' rather than 'It is finished' converges with Psalm 22:31, which speaks of God delivering a people yet unborn and concludes, 'He has done (or 'accomplished') it.'

I am grateful to my friend and former pastor, George Spence, for pointing out that 'Into your hands I commit my spirit' (Psalm 31:5) was a nightly prayer of Jewish children.

Blood and water from the javelin wound: Barbet's experiments are well described in Morgan, *op. cit.*, pp. 92-4. Differing (though not opposing) theories have been advanced, notably by Professor Hermann Moeder (fluid from the pleural sac following asphyxia) and Dr Anthony Sava (separation of haemorrhagic fluid in the pleural cavity following chest injury). American pathologist, Robert Bucklin, opts for a combination of the Barbet and Sava theories, concluding: 'I feel that an actual puncture of the heart must be accepted as factual.' (Morgan, *op. cit.*, pp. 94-7); Ian Wilson, *The Turin Shroud*, pp. 20-1. For the dissenting view of K. J. Schulte (1963) see Wells, *op. cit.* p. 85.

Body in a shallow grave, eaten by dogs: Crossan, *Jesus, a Revolutionary History*, p. 154. The 'survival' theories: raises a family, dictates the Gospel of John, accompanies Paul to Rome and dies there (Thiering); dies in Kashmir (Kersten); at Masada (Joyce).

The place of burial: at Golgotha or 'Gordon's Calvary'? (Wilkinson and Murphy-O'Connor); in the Kidron Valley (Joyce); at Qumran (Thiering).

Theories about Simon of Arimathea: as the historian Josephus (Schonfield, p. 188); as Mary's former husband (Joyce, p. 138); as James and the 'rich man' (Thiering, *Jesus the Man*, p. 543).

Jewish burial custom and crucifixion: The rabbinical sources are carefully examined in the ambiguously titled article, 'The Body of Jesus Was Not Washed According to the Jewish Burial Custom' by B. B. and G. R. Lavoie, D. Klutstein and J. Regan, in *Sindon* (*Journal of the International Centre of Sindonology*, Turin), Dec. 1981.

Eclipse of the Passover moon: Rudolf Smit, *op. cit.*, *F.A.A. Journal*, Sept. 1987; confirmation and additional detail from Tanya Hill, Astronomer of the Melbourne Planetarium. It is hard to explain the Gospel silence on this phenomenon of the crucifixion evening. The Apocryphal *Report of Pilate* — which, according to Montague Rhodes James, may be based on an early document — reports that 'the moon appeared like blood' on the evening of the crucifixion (*op. cit.*, p. 154). Note that, only seven weeks after the crucifixion, *Acts* 2:20 has Peter quoting Joel: 'The sun will be turned into darkness and the moon into blood before the coming of the great and glorious Day of the Lord' (*Joel* 2:31) — as though these phenomena are relevant to this time.In ancient texts, 'moon of blood' was often used as a synonym for a lunar eclipse — as well as describing the specific phenomenon of a red moon, as in the quoted passage from *Sukkah*. See also: *Matthew* 24:29, *Mark* 13:24–7 and *Revelation* 6:12 ff.

26 EMPTY TOMB

'Subjectivity ... the only criterion of Gospel truth': A. N. Wilson, *op. cit.*, pp. 240–1).

'...belongs to the aftermath of his life': Sanders, *op. cit.*, p. 276.

'...things removed from historical scholarship': Bornkamm, *op. cit.*, pp. 180, 183. Visit of the women, 'obviously a legend': *ibid.*, p. 182.

'The whole truth of Christianity': Barnett, *Resurrection – Truth or Reality*, p. 28.

The Archbishop of Canterbury and the resurrection: Melbourne *Age*, 2 Aug. 1999.

'Privileging the resurrection': Funk, *op. cit.*, p. 258.

'Inappropriate' to disentangle 'objective' events from narrative: Wilkinson, *op. cit.*, p. 161.

Ascension discrepancy 'not difficult to explain': Sanders, *op. cit.*, p. 179.

'The Central Event of Universal History': book title used by Joseph Palmer.

Resurrection events, 'sporadic, elusive, evanescent': Dodd, *The Founder of Christianity*, p. 174.

Acts of Pilate *(Gospel of Nicodemus)*: James, *op. cit.*, pp. 97–8, 106–7.

'Most elaborate explorations of the empty tomb': *ibid.*, p. 151.

Stories from Justin and *Toledoth*: q. Cornfeld, *op. cit.*, p. 184.

Bartholomew's *Resurrection*, 'better described as a rhapsody': James, *op. cit.*, p. 186.

Faith kindled by resurrection turns disciples 'from cowards into ... fearless leaders': Peterson, *Resurrection — Truth and Reality*, p. 5.

'Different degrees of impossibility ...': Rod Sangwell, The Resurrection: Resuscitated Corpse or Ghost? (unpublished paper), p. 3.

The Crucifixion by an Eye Witness, extensively quoted: Prajnanananda, *Christ the Saviour and Christ Myth*, pp. 52–76 (for the date, see, p. 24).

Glossary

Antonia	Fortress attached to the Jerusalem Temple (see Temple below); became headquarters of the Roman garrison.
Apocalypse	God's destruction of a flawed world and his creation of a shining new age.
Apocrypha	Books and other scriptural works not accepted within the 'canon' of Christianity.
Apostles	Strictly, 'envoys' or 'messengers', often applied to the Twelve Disciples who accompanied Joshua.
Aramaic	Language closely related to Hebrew spoken by ordinary Jews in Joshua's time.
Archangel	Greatest of the angels, Michael, the warrior guardian of Israel.
Auxiliaries	In the Roman army, recruits from conquered countries who earned Roman citizenship after twenty-five years' service. Roman citizen soldiers were 'legionaries'.
Barjona	(or Baryona) Aramaic for 'outlaw' or 'Zealot'.
bath kol	Hebrew for, literally, 'daughter voice' or 'daughter of a voice'; a divine voice from the sky.
bema	Raised platform in a synagogue where the reading desk was set. Today applied to the desk itself.
centurion	Officer of the Roman army, commanded about eighty men.
chazzan	In Joshua's time, the only full-time employee of the synagogue; Sabbath assistant to the congregation's leader and, during the week, a teacher.
chutzpah	Hebrew for 'impudence' or even 'arrogance'.
codex	Earliest form of leaf-book, made from papyrus (see below) or parchment.
cohort	Roman army unit, usually varying from 500 to 800, even up to 1000, depending on requirements, attachment (archers, cavalry), etc.
cornu	Roman military horn, equivalent of a bugle.
Dead Sea Scrolls	Collection of scriptural texts and other religious writings found in caves near ruins of Qumran (see below). Believed to have been produced by Qumran sect, probably Essenes, but showing close links to the Zealots and Sicarii (see below).
disciple	Based on a Pharisaic term for the students or followers of a teacher.

equites	Roman knight, member of the Equestrian Order.
eschatology	Belief associated with the End Times ushering in the Apocalypse (see above).
Essenes	Sect which was spread throughout Israel and may have had its head-quarters at Qumran (see below).
Exile	As a proper noun, the forced migration of tens of thousands of Jews to Babylon in the fifth century BC, involving a sixty-year absence from Jerusalem and the heart of their religion.
Gentiles	Non-Jews. Jewish scripture usually referred to the Gentile Nations, so 'Nations' (Goyim) came to mean 'Gentiles'.
glacis	Broad, sloping buttresses to protect walls of a city, etc. from siege.
Gnostics	Widespread 'secret wisdom' sect, one branch of which embraced early Christianity, producing its own Gospels and religious writings.
Gospel	Old English for 'Good News'. The Greek equivalent, *Evangelion*, gives 'Evangelists', a term often used for writers of the Gospels. This work opts for 'Gospellers'.
Hasid	(plural Hasidim; also spelt Chasid and Chasidim) Charismatic Jewish holy men, often associated with healing and occasionally with 'nature miracles', like rainmaking.
Hasmoneans	Priestly Jewish family which won Israel back from the Syrian Greeks, creating a dynasty eventually supplanted by Herod the Great.
Israel	Name for Jacob, ancestor of the Jews; by Joshua's time applied to the Jewish people and to their homeland, as 'the land of [the people] Israel' (*Eretz Yisrael*). (See Matthew 2:20–1 and 10:23). 'Palestine' in this period is an anachronism; a name given to the land by the Romans after crushing the Jewish revolts of the first and second centuries AD.
Jubilee	In Joshua's time, the last year in a cycle of seven seven-year periods. Slaves were liberated, debts cancelled and land returned to its traditional owners. See Shemittah.
Kiddush	('Sanctification') Simple meal ceremony which ushered in the Sabbath, also observed on the eve of Festivals.
legion	Major unit of the Roman army; approximately 6000 men.
Levites	Tribal clan descended from Levi, one of Jacob's twelve sons. Traditionally, played a major role in Temple activities. Priests were descended from Aaron, a member of the tribe; i.e. priests were Levites but not all Levites were priests.
Lost Tribes	Members of the Ten Tribes of Israel deported by Assyria in the seventh century BC.
Maccabees	Widely used nickname of the Hasmoneans (see above), probably from the Aramaic for 'hammer'.
Magi	Priestly astronomer/astrologers widely spread through Persia and

Babylonia. Often translated in the New Testament as 'wise men'.

Messiah	Descendant of King David who would establish God's rule over a perfected earth.
meturgeman	Officer of the synagogue who recited an Aramaic paraphrase of Hebrew scriptural readings for the benefit of congregation members who did not speak Hebrew.
Midrash	An interpretation of Hebrew scripture which often finds a deeper meaning behind the literal reading. In rabbinical literature, a major body of writing (Pesiqta, Rabbah, etc.) quoted by chapter and verse.
mikveh	A special bath used for ritual purification.
Mishnah	Massive record of the Pharisees' oral Torah (see below) begun by Judah ha-Nasi ('The Prince') and completed by his disciples after his death in the third century AD. Its books ('Tractates') are quoted by chapter and verse.
papyrus	Earliest form of paper, made from stems of the papyrus reed.
Passover	Springtime festival commemorating the liberation of the Children of Israel from Egypt.
Paulian Christianity	The form of Christianity fostered by the self-styled 'Apostle' Paul and aimed at Gentiles. The fact that he changed his name from the Jewish 'Saul' to the Roman 'Paul' (Paulus) is eloquent of his approach.
pesher	Inspired (or 'oracular') interpretation of the scriptures, closely related to Midrash (see above).
Pharisees	One of Judaism's leading sects, widely respected by the ordinary folk of Israel and generally more liberal in their approach than the aristocratic and literalistic Sadducees (see below). After the destruction of Temple-based Judaism, Pharisees provided the Rabbis who enabled the religion to survive.
prefect	Roman official, usually a knight, appointed to govern minor provinces of the empire such as Judaea.
prosbul	Financial/legal mechanism to avoid the cancellation of debts in the Shemittah (see below).
quaternion	Four-man squad of the Roman army.
Qumran	Fortress-like settlement beside the Dead Sea, housing a religious community which produced and/or collected the Dead Sea Scrolls (see above).
Rabbi	Hebrew for 'my master'; in Joshua's time an honorific form of address to a teacher, but within a century, the title of a congregation's leader.
Royal Stoa	(also called the Royal Portico) A magnificent, roofed colonnade along the south side of the Jerusalem Temple's terrace.
Sabbatical	See Shemittah.
Sadducees	In Joshua's day, the second influential religious group — highly conservative, wealthy and closely allied to the priestly Temple hierarchy.
Samaritans	People of Samaria, located between Judaea and Galilee; politically

part of Judaea but home to a rival form of Judaism not recognising Jerusalem's Temple.

Sanhedrin	Council of elders. The Great Sanhedrin in Jerusalem was a supreme court and governing body of Temple Judaism. It comprised seventy or seventy-one Sadducees and Pharisees (see above).
Septuagint	Famous Greek translation of the Jewish scriptures made in the third century BC.
Shekinah	The presence of God as experienced by humankind.
Shema	Brief morning and evening prayer which opened every synagogue service, named from its first word, 'Hear (*Shema*) O Israel ...'
Shemittah	Last year of a seven-year cycle when farmers rested their land and debts were cancelled.
Sicarii	('Dagger men') Most extreme branch of the Zealot movement (see below).
Synoptic	Applied to the first three Gospels, from the Greek, meaning that they can be read side-by-side.
Talmud	('Study') Massive collection of commentaries on the earlier Mishnah (see above), in the form of discussions and debates among Rabbis. The 'Jerusalem' Talmud dates from the fifth century AD, and Babylonian from the sixth. Its 'Tractates' (Sanhedrin, Shabbath, etc.) are quoted by page number with 'a' or 'b' to mark the side of the page in the Hebrew text. Quotations from the 'Jerusalem' Talmud are prefixed by 'j'.
Tanakh	Hebrew Bible, an acronym of its contents.
Targum	('Translation') Aramaic paraphrase of the Hebrew scriptures recited by the synagogue's meturgeman (see above).
Temple	Complex of religious buildings that made Jerusalem central to Jewish religious life; especially a focus of the pilgrim festivals. The Jerusalem Temple was the only place where sacrifices could be offered.
Testimonium	Account of the ministry and execution of Jesus found in *Antiquities of the Jews* by the Roman/Jewish historian Flavius Josephus. Often regarded as a Christian interpolation, it probably retains some authentic material — though 'inconvenient' details appear to have been deleted.
tetrarch	'Ruler of a fourth part', the title granted to Herod Antipas and his brothers.
Torah	('Teaching') First five books of the Hebrew Bible, including the Mosaic Law. The core of Jewish faith.
triclinium	Graeco-Roman arrangement of three couches and a central table, adopted for formal Jewish feasts and banquets; used at The Last Supper.
Zealots	Fanatical religio-patriotic sect founded by Judas of Galilee in the rebellion that followed Herod the Great's death in 4 BC.

Index

KEY
1. The Temple; 2. The Antonia; 3. 'Pinnacle' of the Temple;
4. House of the Last Supper; 5. Herod the Great's Palace
(Pilate's Praetorium); 6. Golgotha; 7. Kidron Valley;
8. Gethsemane.